I0763116

Shadow
OXYRHYNC
MAP

painting
like innards of a painting

(2.) Wipe
sweeps
over dark
areas

the nymph &
the shepard

Think of
the SOUND
you want

art documentary
FRANCIS
BACON
DVD

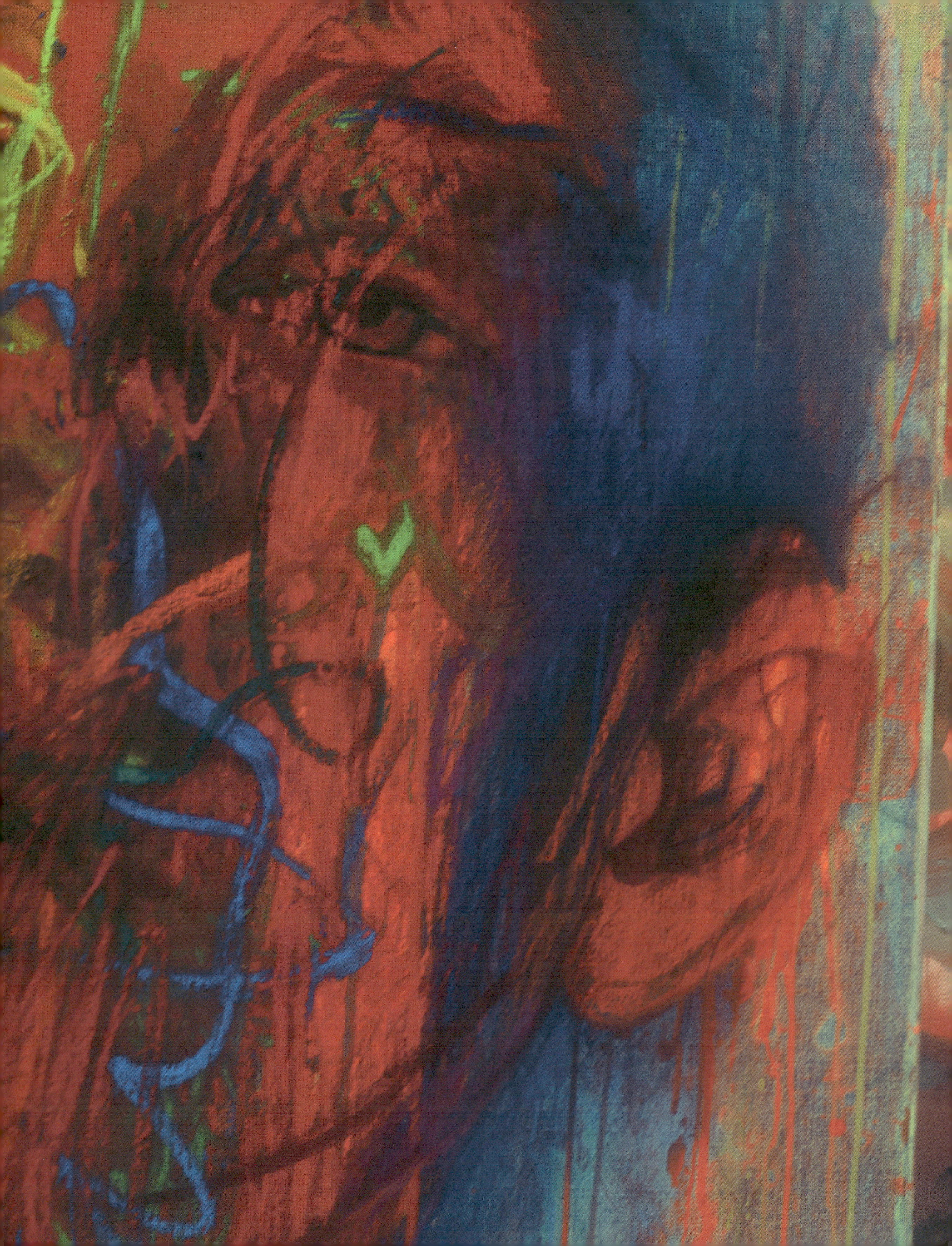

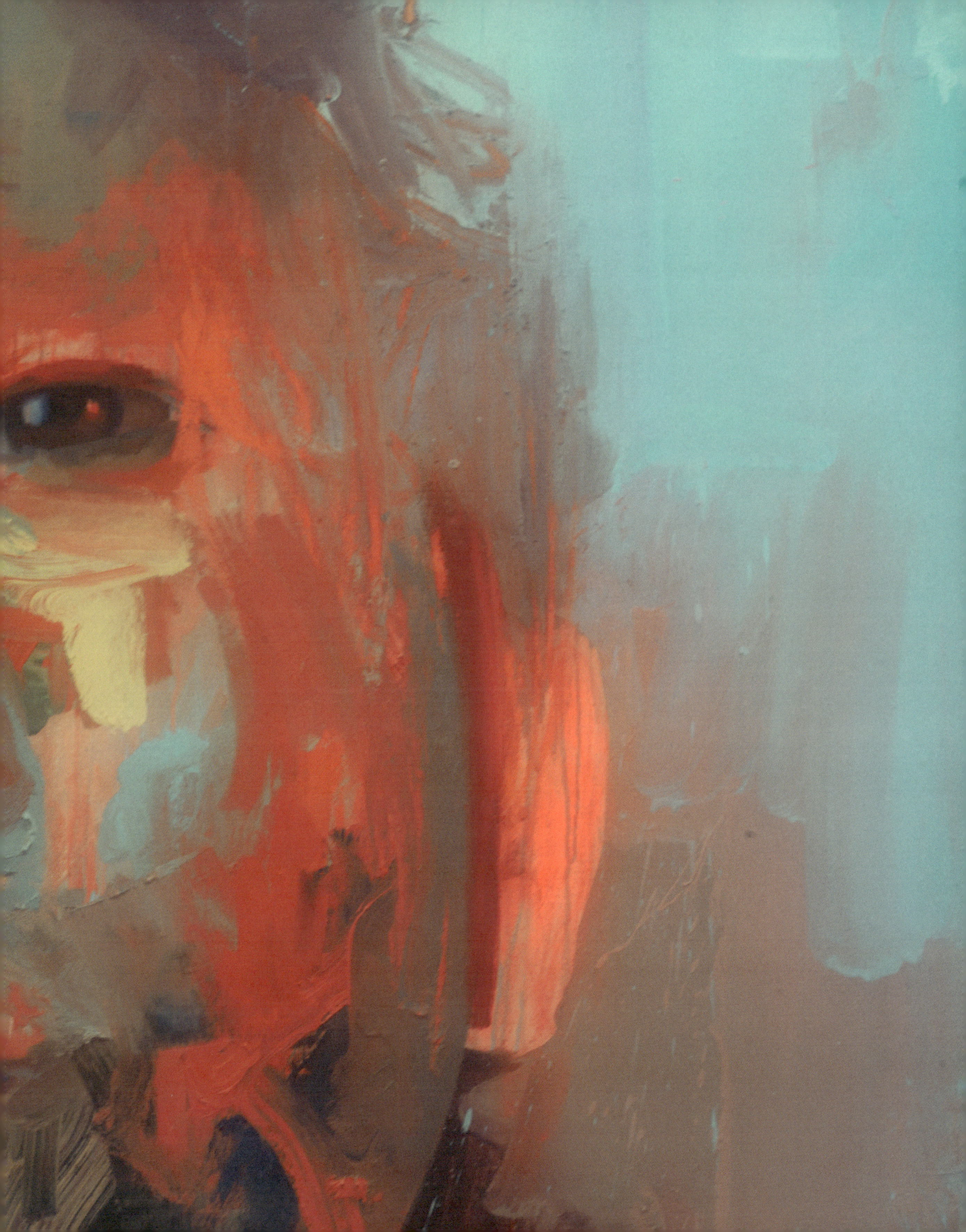

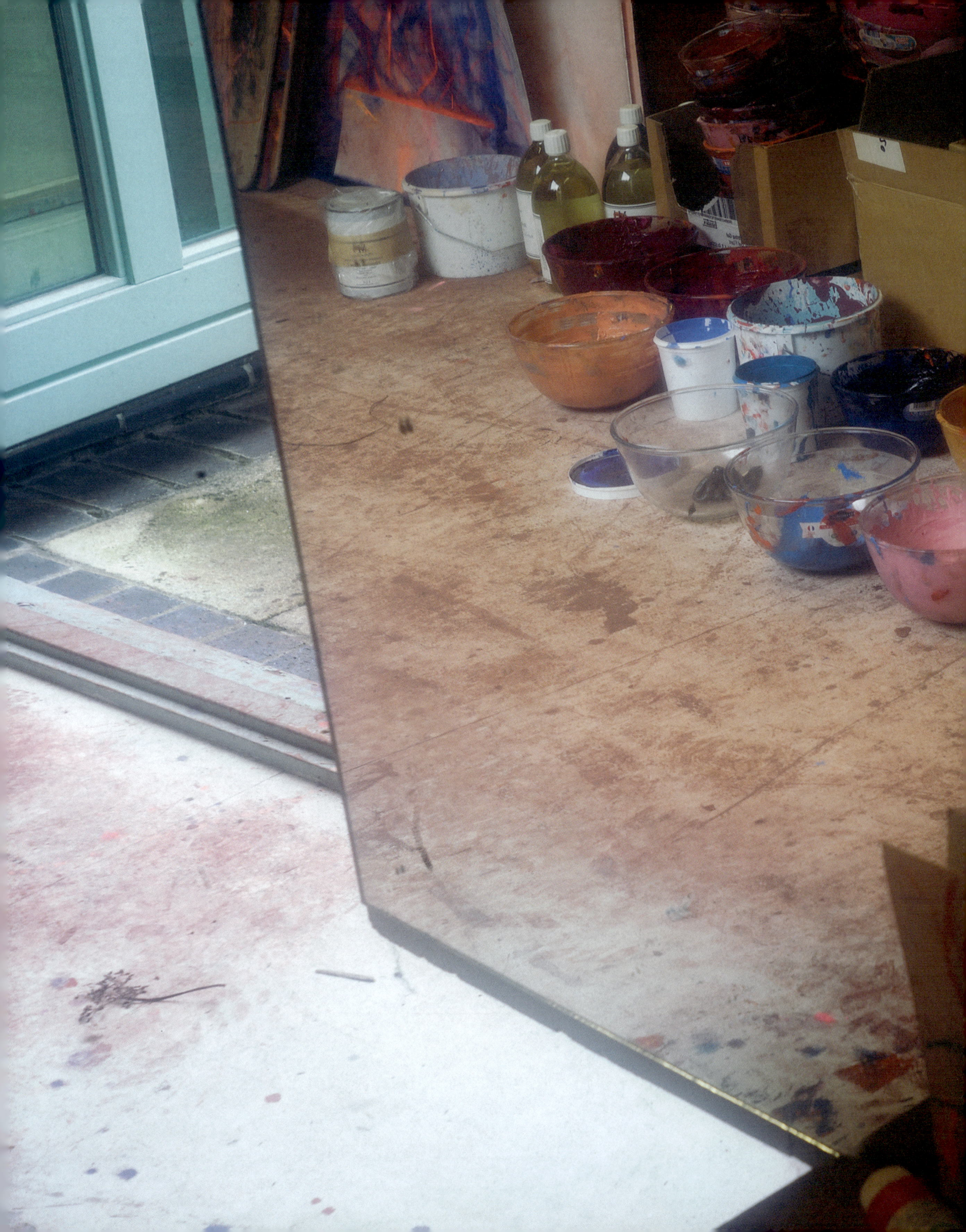

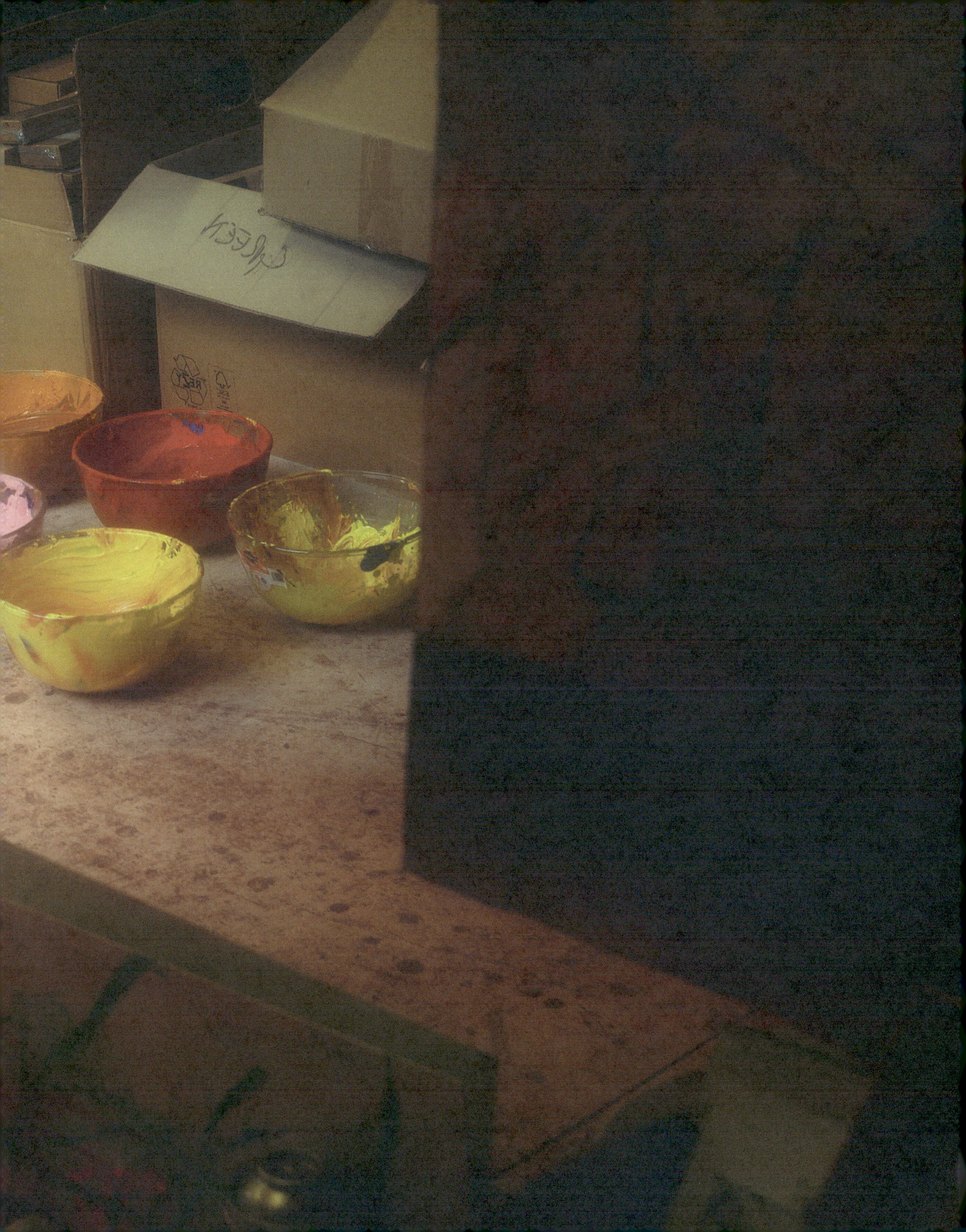

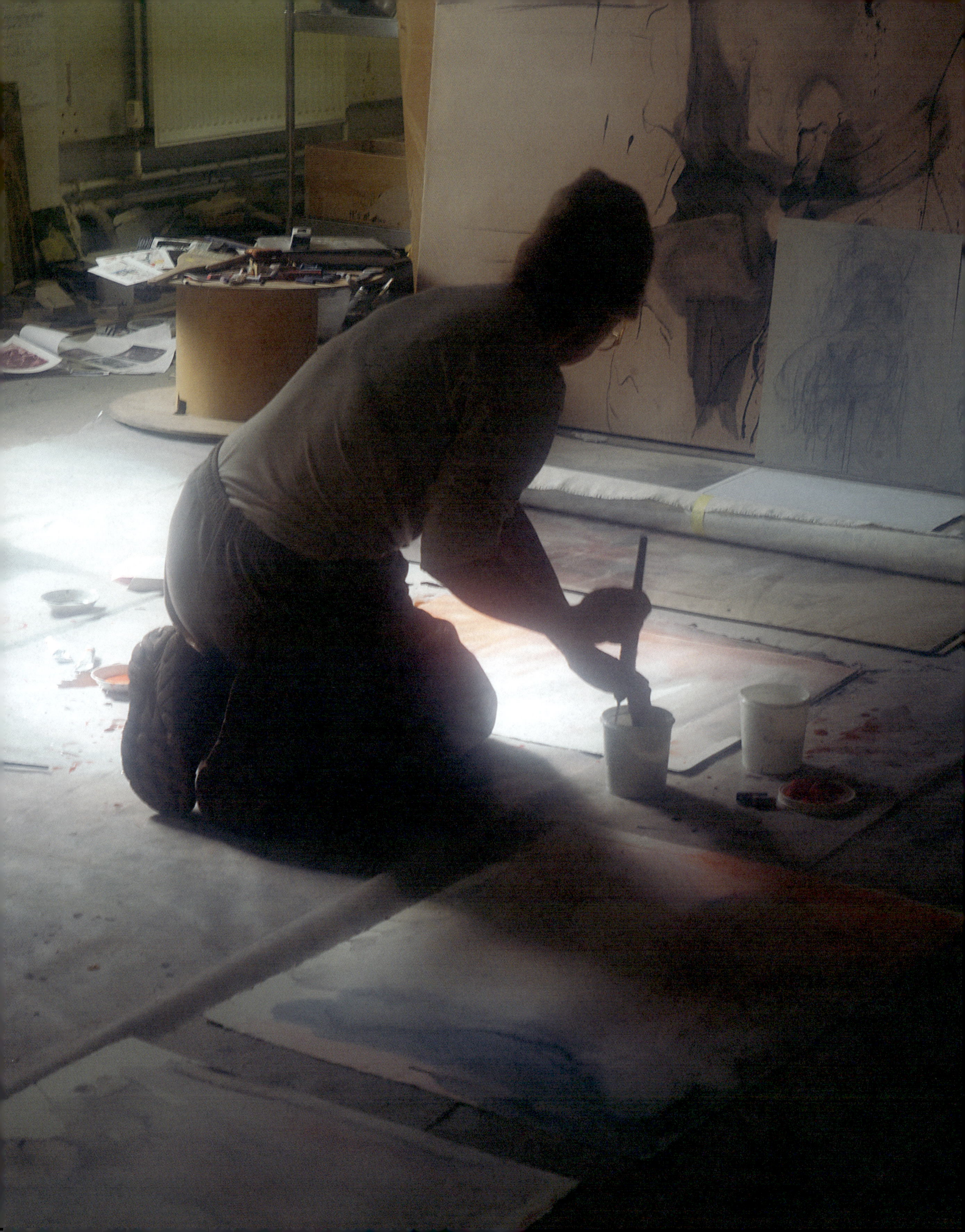

Jenny Saville

The Anatomy of Painting

National Portrait Gallery, London

RIZZOLI Electa

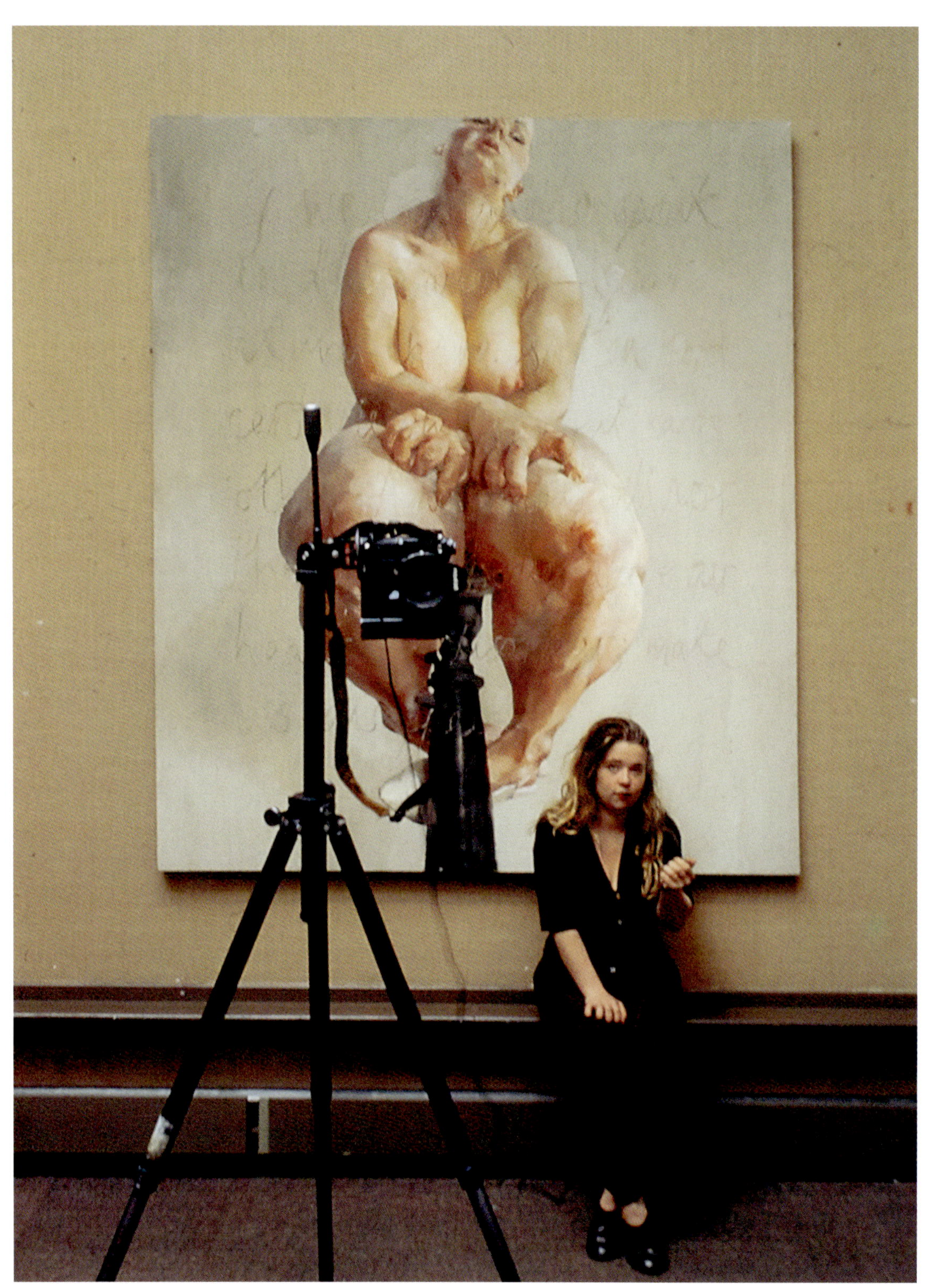

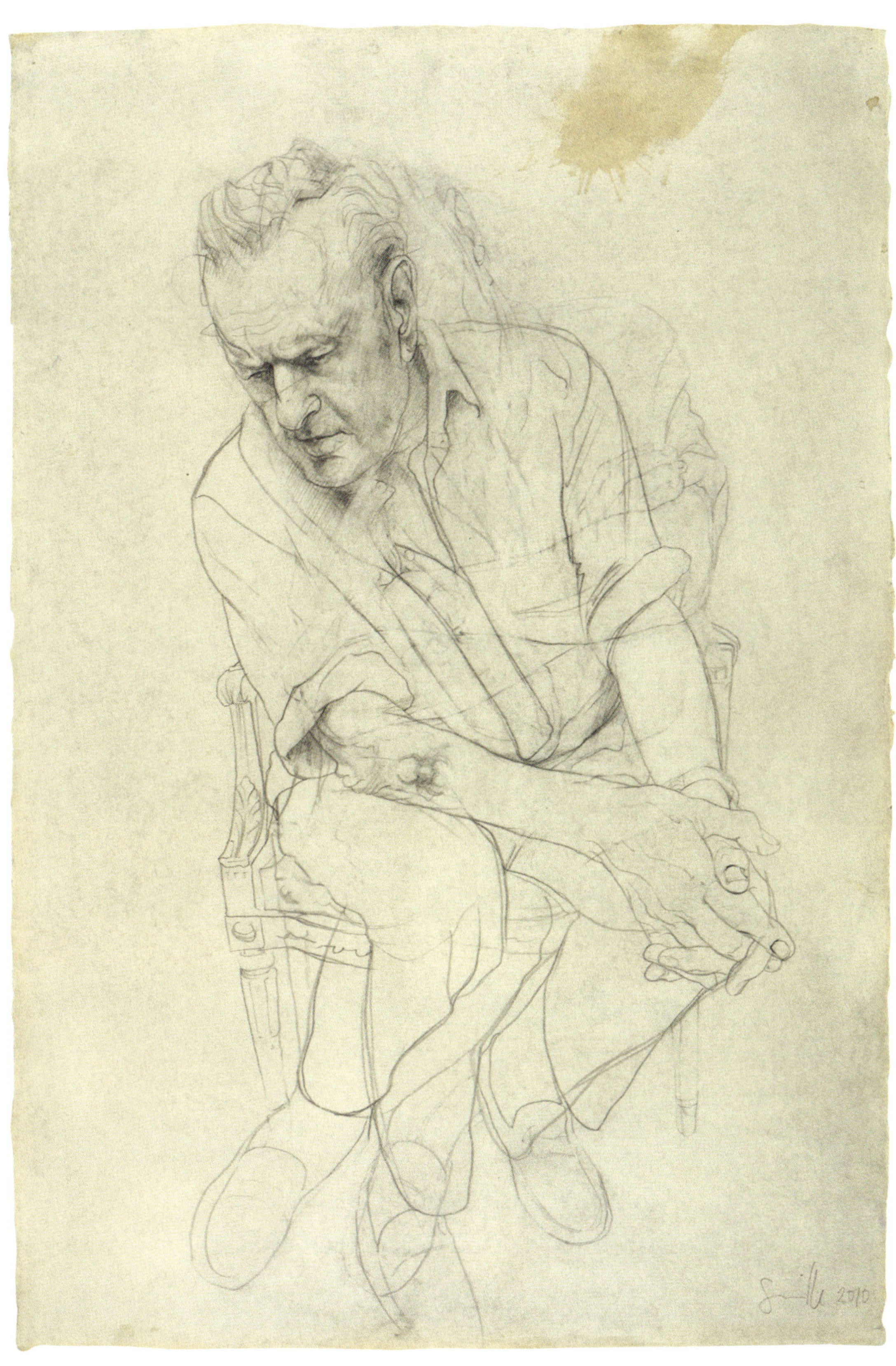

Jenny Saville
Study of John, 2010
Pencil on paper
976 × 642 mm
National Portrait Gallery, London

Contents

Foreword

Bringing together paintings and drawings made throughout Jenny Saville's extraordinary career, *The Anatomy of Painting* traces her practice from the 1990s to today. It explores Saville's lasting connection to art history and highlights her unique ability to create visceral works from thick layers of paint, revealing her to be an artist with a deep passion for the painting process. The title, *The Anatomy of Painting*, originates with the artist, whose work celebrates both the figures she depicts and the nature of paint itself.

I speak on behalf of everyone at the National Portrait Gallery when I say how honoured we are to present the first major institutional exhibition of Jenny Saville's work and to have collaborated with her to produce this book. We are all immensely grateful to Saville for her unstinting generosity and enthusiasm.

My congratulations and thanks go to Sarah Howgate, Senior Curator of Contemporary Collections, for the vision and energy she has brought to realising this project, and to my predecessor Dr Nicholas Cullinan OBE for his foresight in offering Saville this exhibition.

We are delighted that the exhibition will tour to The Modern Art Museum of Fort Worth, Texas; it is a pleasure to be working with the Museum, and I am particularly grateful to Chief Curator Andrea Karnes, as well as to the wider team there. I extend my heartfelt thanks, too, to the wonderful authors who have contributed to this publication, and to Sally Mann, for her beautiful photographs documenting Saville's studio practice, a selection of which can be seen for the first time in the pages at the beginning and end of this book.

The generosity of our supporters and lenders is vital in staging a project of this scale and ambition and I would particularly like to thank Gagosian for their invaluable contribution. My thanks also go to major supporters AMA Collection, Nicholas Leonidas Goulandris, Christie's, and supporters Cockayne Grants for the Arts, The George Economou Collection, Batia and Idan Ofer, Veronica and Lars Bane Foundation, Cingilli Collection, Firebird Collection and Ryan Taylor Collection.

Finally, on behalf of Jenny Saville and all those at the National Portrait Gallery and Gagosian who worked with him, I wish to dedicate this book to its wonderful designer, Peter Willberg. His expertise, dedication and good humour will be greatly missed.

Victoria Siddall

Director, National Portrait Gallery, London

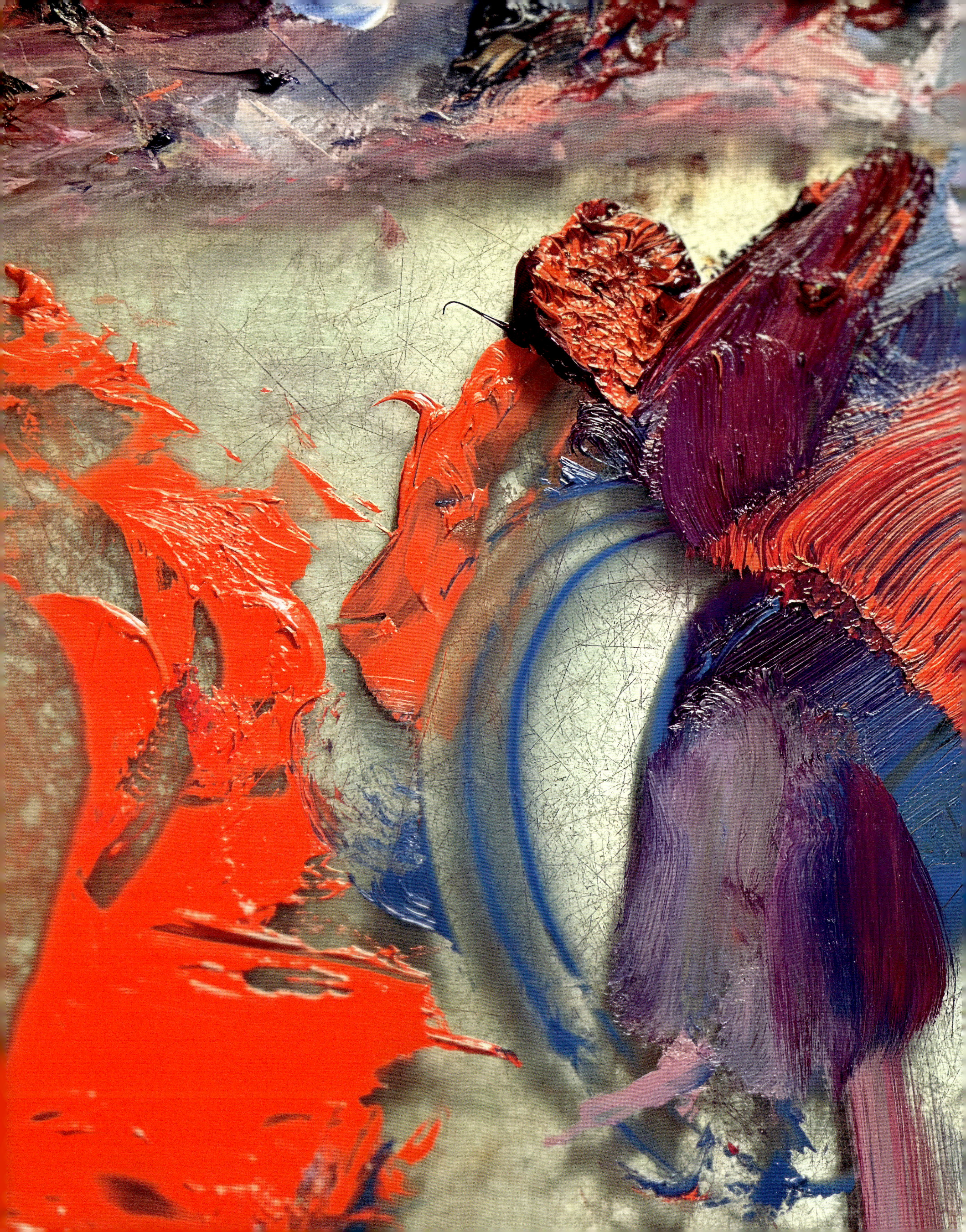

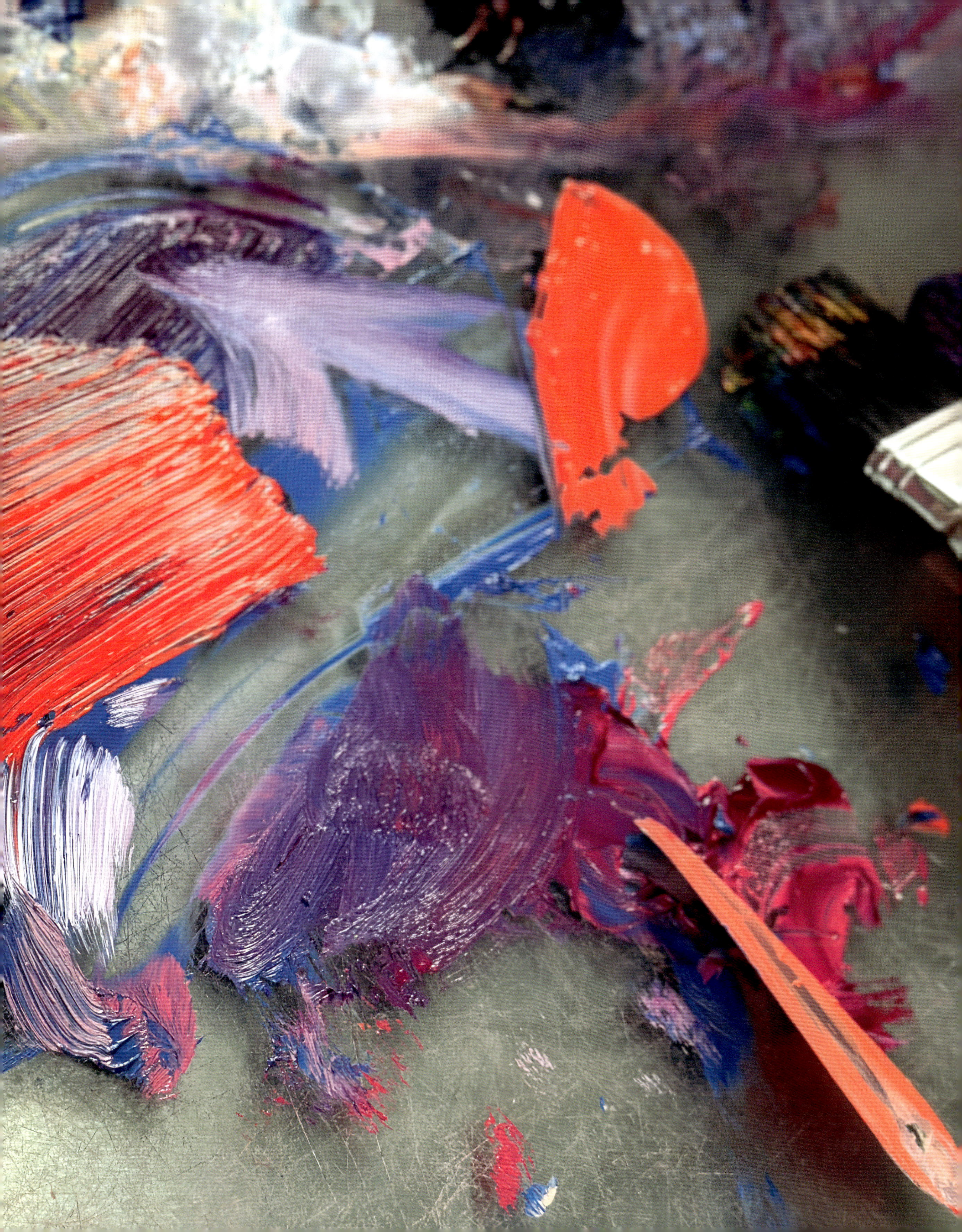

‘I started to think about not just the anatomy of the body, but about the anatomy of a painting.’

Jenny Saville in conversation with John Richardson, 2012

The Anatomy of a Painting

John Elderfield

This introduction is an appreciation of Jenny Saville's art in the form of a study of contexts in which it emerged and has developed. It is not a survey of all such contexts, such as the place of her body images in contemporary culture, the importance of her pictorial sources, or the relationship of her work to that of Willem de Kooning, topics that are the subjects of subsequent essays. They will be mentioned briefly here, but the present text mainly addresses a selective range of affinities and associations, recent and historical, that may or may not be actual sources for her art but aid our appreciation of it. Such at least is the premise of what follows.

Saville has acknowledged some but not all of these contexts.[1] However, as critic Christopher Ricks remarks of the multiple associations of Bob Dylan's work, an artist is 'more than usually able to effect things with the help of instincts and intuitions of which he or she is not necessarily conscious'. What matters is that Saville, like Dylan, 'is doing the imagining, not that [she] is fully, deliberately conscious of the countless intimations that are in [her] art'.[2] Such is the nature of an open and vigorous artistic imagination.

Un tableau dégoûtant

When Saville's earliest works were first exhibited, the seven-foot-tall *Propped* (fig.1) – painted in 1992, when she was barely into her twenties – was the painting that attracted the most attention, not only for the gigantic size of the body it showed but also because, as one writer put it, 'the woman on the pedestal gouges her gargantuan thighs in self-castigation'.[3] A body displayed thus harmed, and staged to face the viewer, seemed to animalise it in a truly disturbing way. This may have suggested to some viewers that Saville was responding to Francis Bacon's work, and her practice continues to be likened in spirit to his. But *Propped* also invites a much earlier comparison.

This is to one of the most famous of such disturbing canvases, exhibited in 1728 by almost as young an artist: the twenty-eight-year-old unknown Jean-Siméon Chardin. For the esteemed critic Denis Diderot, *La Raie* (The Skate; fig.2) was '*un tableau dégoûtant*' (a disgusting, repugnant picture), yet demonstrated how it is possible to 'salvage objects of disgust through sheer talent'.[4] He was following Aristotle, who had written in his *Poetics*

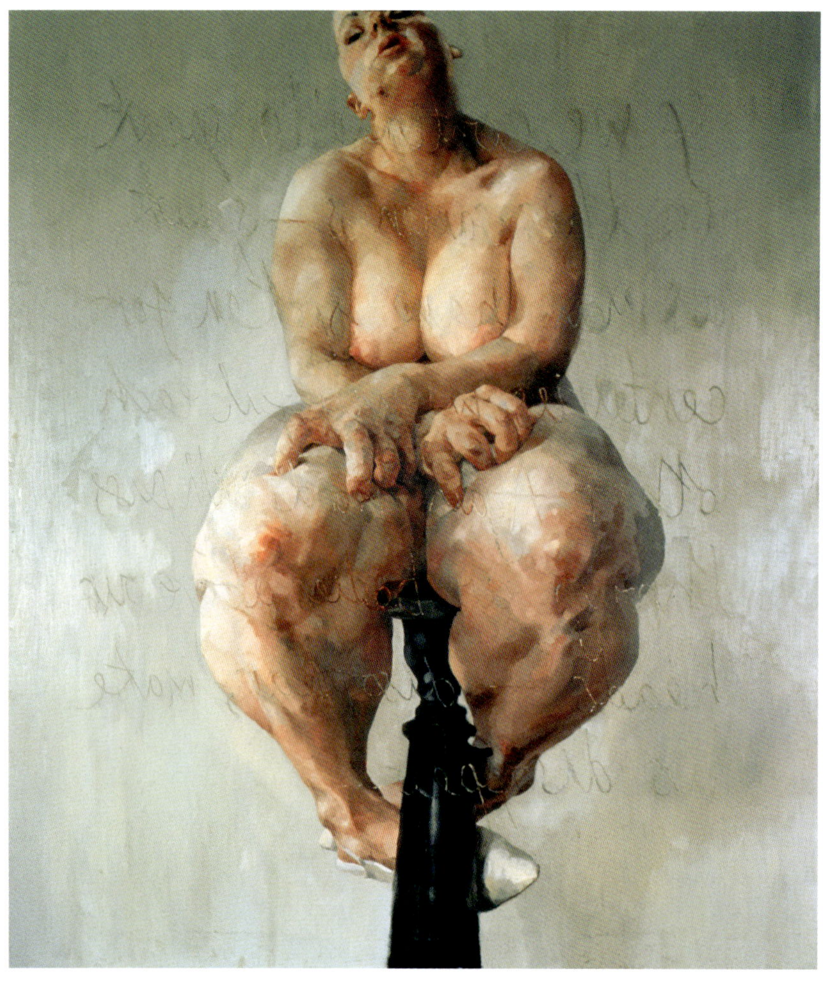

Fig.1
Jenny Saville
Propped, 1992
Oil on canvas
2134 × 1829 mm
Private Collection

Fig.2
Jean-Siméon Chardin
La Raie, 1725–6
Oil on canvas
1145 × 1460 mm
Musée du Louvre, Paris

that it is 'natural for all to delight in works of imitation', even 'though the objects themselves may be painful to see'. However, 'one's pleasure will not be in the picture as an imitation… but will be due to the execution or colouring or some similar cause'.[5] Saville places her viewers in a comparable position, where the *picture*, as an imitation, may be painful to see, while the *painting* of it, if not quite pleasurable to see, is so extremely compelling of our attention that we do not want to look away – a conflictedness to which I will return.

Saville's woman's body set upright on a stake in *Propped* reprises the frightening anthropomorphism of Chardin's giant fish, which, although suspended, appears to be standing to attention at the back of his composition. In Chardin's painting, art historian and curator Philip Conisbee observes, 'the young cat arching its bristling back seems to echo the *frisson* of horror felt by the spectator at the frightful sight of the grimacing fish, its bloody entrails on full display'.[6] Saville did not need to represent a spectator; *Propped* was made with the spectator in mind, to be seen in the mirror that it invites us to face it in order to read, scratched backwards in the paint, a defiant text by the feminist author Luce Irigaray, calling for the time 'When Our Lips Speak Together'.[7]

This was the title of chapter 11 in Irigaray's book *This Sex Which Is Not One*, published in English in 1985, in which she wrote: 'If we keep on speaking sameness, if we speak to each other as men have been doing for centuries, as we have been taught to speak, we'll miss

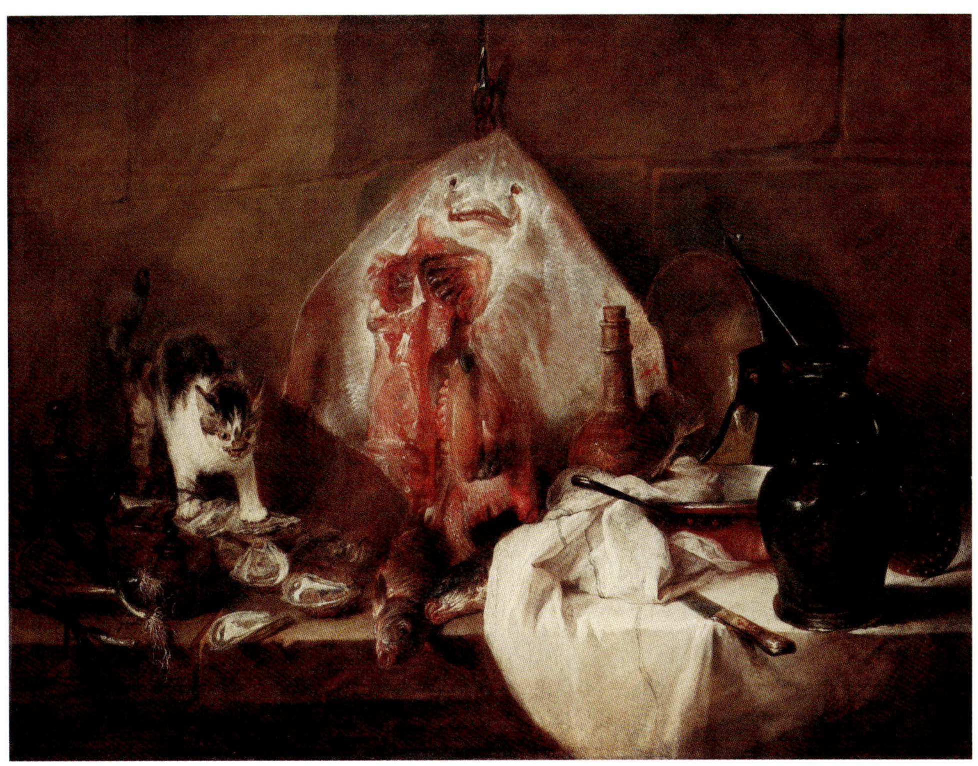

each other, fail ourselves'.[8] Reading the chapter title indirectly in the mirror, then seeing it in the paint, is also to see it as a text scratched into the wall behind the propped-up body. *Branded* (p.33), painted the same year as *Propped,* has a barely visible, ironically condescending text marked on the body of a woman grasping a generous handful of stomach flesh: 'SUPPORTIVE, DECORATIVE, IRRATIONAL, DELICATE.'

Epidermal Episodes

The year before Saville painted *Propped,* she had seen de Kooning's *Easter Monday* (p.36) at The Metropolitan Museum of Art, New York, a work 'as powerful and full of tension as works by the great old-master painters in Europe, except that it was abstract. It was just paint and human movement, but it was so much more of a painting in the flesh than I could have expected. The paint was right on the surface'.[9]

In the short lecture 'The Renaissance and Order', delivered in 1949, de Kooning said that 'flesh was the reason why oil painting was invented'.[10] This was to become one of his most famous statements – famous but fallacious: oil paint had first been used in the fifteenth century by early Netherlandish masters such as Jan van Eyck, as a way of creating luminous, translucent glazes of colour over the light-gesso grounds of their wood-panel paintings. What de Kooning was referring to was actually the *reinvention* of oil painting by the Venetian painter Giorgione in the years after 1500, and the fulfilment of the opaque, rather than translucent, possibilities of the medium – and on stretched canvas rather than on wood – by his disciple Titian, and by Titian's fellow Venetian, Veronese; also by their northern disciples Rembrandt and Rubens. The latter seems to have been de Kooning's favourite historical painter, and his work indubitably speaks to Saville's. She had read de Kooning's remark on how contemporary painting was connected to the art of the Renaissance: 'It is the vulgar and fleshy part of it which seems to make it particularly Western'.[11] And she would speak later of her own paint as 'tins of liquid flesh' that she spreads on a canvas.[12]

In January 1857, the French painter Eugène Delacroix had written in his journal that 'the greatest masters' of all painting were the Venetians and their disciples; and that the great failure of the popular early nineteenth-century neoclassical artist Jacques-Louis David was his 'contempt for the material means' of painting.[13] In David's painting, he added, 'the epidermis is everywhere lacking'.[14] Delacroix's analogy between the marked surface of painting and the surface of flesh meant, in the case of figure paintings, effectively thinking of a painting as a body.

Of course nobody, not even Delacroix, can reasonably pretend that only oil paint freely applied will do a good job of vividly representing either the epidermis or the flesh: drawings, engravings, and watercolours by precisionist portraitists on the one hand, and students of anatomical dissection on the other, have demonstrated otherwise, at times with stunning results. However, while the work of a great anatomical illustrator may produce an unsettling shudder of emotion, it will be to the extent of its efficacy as an illustration, not in the actual material of the execution. Conversely, if the shudder is delivered in the paint itself, the illustration may be anatomically less accurate and may produce just as unsettling a reaction – or a more unsettling one, as de Kooning's paintings of women famously did in the early 1950s, especially his *Woman I* (p.101). In these works, the painterly execution so dominates the illustration that Clement Greenberg was but one of many critics who spoke of de Kooning's brushstrokes in such terms as constituting 'savage dissections'.[15]

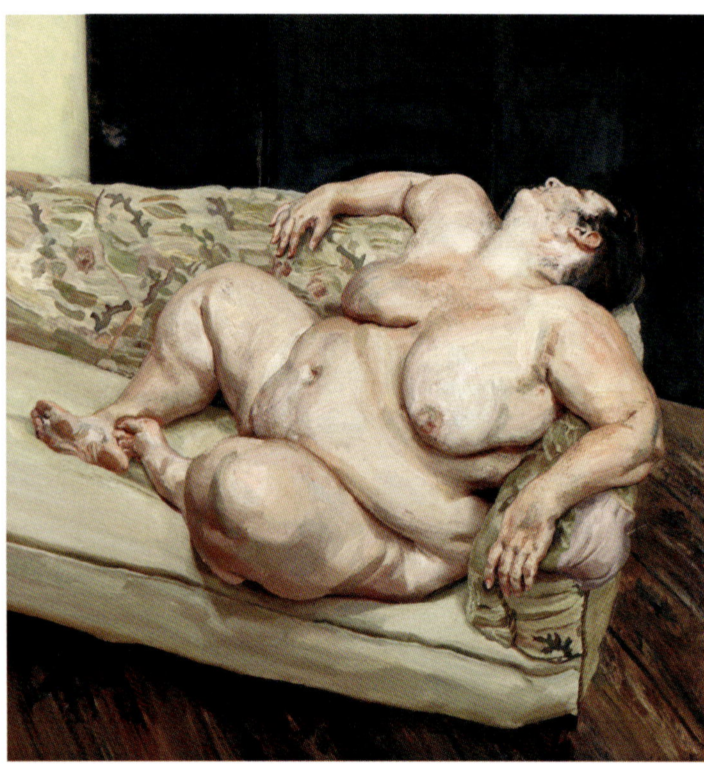

Fig.3
Lucian Freud
Benefits Supervisor Resting, 1994
Oil on canvas
1505 × 1612 mm
Private Collection

Fig.4
Diego Velázquez
The Toilet of Venus
('The Rokeby Venus'), 1647–51
Oil on canvas
1225 × 1770 mm
The National Gallery, London

Image from *Illustrated London News*, 14 March 1914, showing the damage done to the painting by 'the suffragette with a chopper', stating that 'the first blow was struck at the point marked by a star in the reproduction of the picture'.

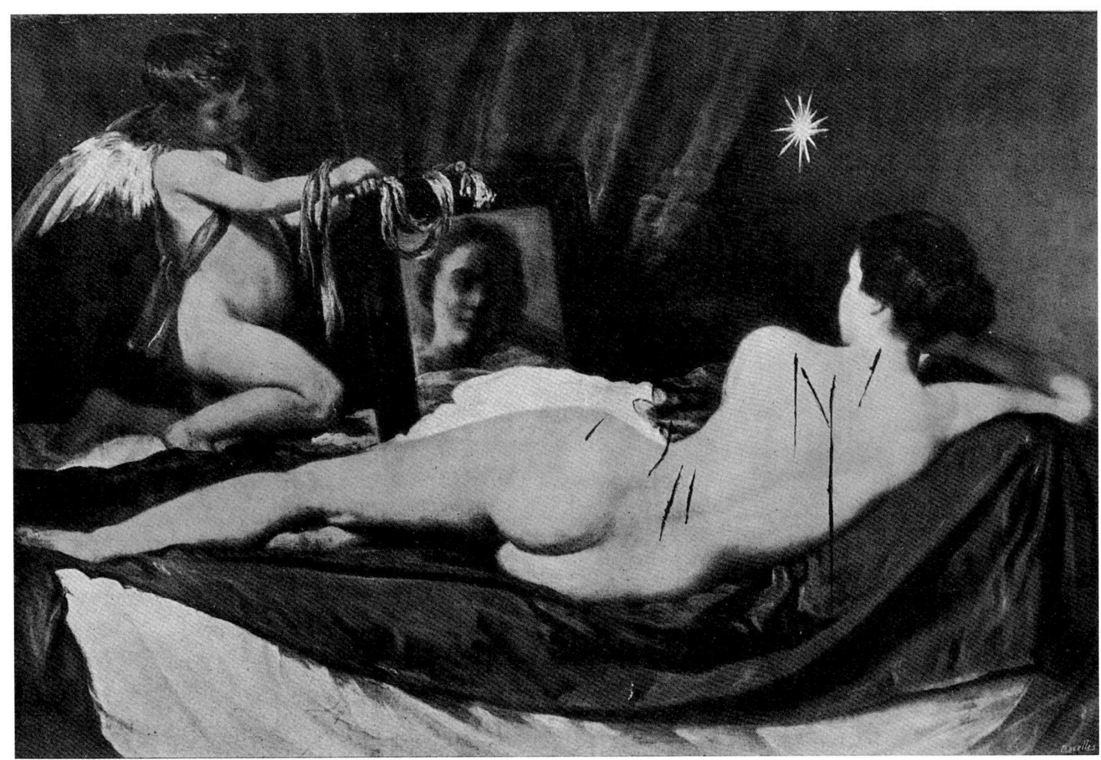

This is to say, fragmented or distorted images of women – by men, of course – allowed interpretation of them as literally having been damaged.[16] The implication was that representation of women's bodies should show them as beautiful and perfected; it was alarming to imagine them not.

When Saville's canvases were first shown, it was immediately clear that their execution did not disguise their illustration but patently realised it; and therefore that her aim was to show women's bodies that were in reality far from conventionally beautiful and perfected. As such, they adopted the negative responses to a man's famous paintings of women to rebut it directly in a woman's, feminist terms. The art historian Leo Steinberg defended de Kooning's paintings of women by asserting that, like Rubens, he 'had the stomach to love real things, to accept men and women without idealising, Platonising, and Italianising them'.[17] We may think of Saville's early – and later – canvases as using a Rubenesque template onto which to graft a degree of imperfection far greater than Rubens allowed.

Steinberg also likened de Kooning's 'fierce generosity' to that of Rubens, who loved his wife, Helena Fourment, 'for all her puckered, sag-flesh knees'.[18] Forty years later, when Saville gave her figures 'gargantuan, aggressive shoulders and breasts defying society's demands for slim feminine allure', they early on won her such descriptions as 'fiercely feminist'.[19] She herself accepts the interpretation, while referring in this respect not to de Kooning but to painters nearer to hand, saying in 2005, 'I grew up looking at [Lucian] Freud, [Francis] Bacon, and [Frank] Auerbach'. Her then speaking of wanting her images 'to be kind of obese' makes us think of certain famous works by Freud (fig.3).[20] But Saville rarely simply represents obese figures; rather, she shows us figural volumes marked into imperfection, or unlimited by their epidermal containers.

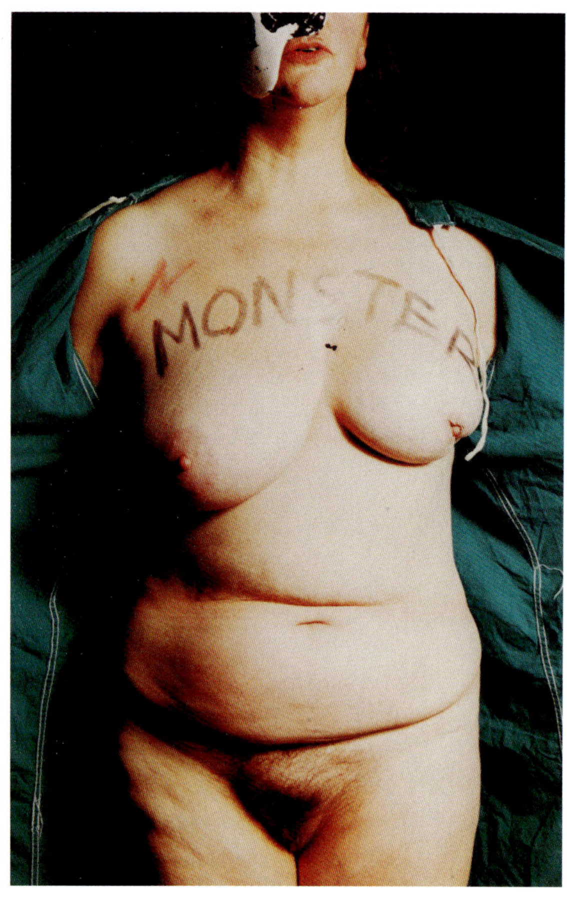

Fig.5
Jo Spence, in collaboration with Dr Tim Sheard
Exiled, from the series *Narratives of Dis-ease*, 1989
Chromogenic print
646 × 406 mm
Victoria and Albert Museum, London

Given the implication of damage thus done to the female body in Saville's early paintings, it is surprising that no mention appears to have been made at the time of the most celebrated 'fiercely feminist' response in Britain against the ideal of feminine allure – especially since it cut into the painted skin of 'the most beautiful woman in mythological history'.[21] This was suffragette Mary Richardson's description of Velázquez's *Rokeby Venus*, which she slashed with a meat chopper at London's National Gallery on 10 March 1914 (fig.4). 'I didn't like the way men gazed at it all day long', she explained long afterwards, perhaps thinking of how Velázquez had objectified the reclining nude by obscuring her face, only visible as a reflection in her mirror.[22] A fiercely destructive response lies buried behind Saville's fiercely creative response to the same issue.

So did a different kind of feminist response: the images that the English photographer Jo Spence made of her own body after her diagnosis with cancer in 1982.[23] Most striking is one in her 1988–9 series *Narratives of Dis-ease* that shows only a fragment of her face above a naked body inscribed with the word 'MONSTER' (fig.5). Spence died of leukaemia in June 1992, and Saville may be thought to be her immediate successor.

Making and Unmaking

Another, very different, and frightening work on the theme of the woman's body appeared when Saville was working on her first paintings, in 1991. The most famous welcoming sentence spoken that year was 'Hello Clarice, it's good to see you again.'

Saville saw Jonathan Demme's film *The Silence of the Lambs* (1991), based on Thomas Harris's novel (1988) of the same title, but for those who have not, these words are delivered by the imprisoned, cannibalistic serial killer Hannibal Lecter (Anthony Hopkins) to Clarice Starling (Jodie Foster), the FBI trainee sent to seek his help in order to find another serial killer, known as Buffalo Bill (Ted Levine), who flays women to make a coat from their skins.[24] The film is not only a dark, suspenseful, at times extremely unpleasant *tableau dégoûtant* to watch, it is also fascinating in the way Lecter taunts Starling as she tries to have him help solve her case. The most extraordinary exchange follows the welcoming sentence quoted above:

> LECTER: First principles, Clarice. Simplicity. Read Marcus Aurelius. Of each particular thing ask: What is it in itself? What is its nature? What does he do, this man you seek?
>
> STARLING: He kills women…
>
> LECTER: No. We begin by coveting what we see every day. Don't you feel eyes moving over your body, Clarice? And don't your eyes seek out the things you want?

This is an unexpected, chilling exchange. Coveting is served by killing; and coveting is ubiquitous. Our eyes are covetous organs as they scan the surface of bodies.[25] The irony of the exchange is Lecter's reference to the second-century Roman emperor and Stoic philosopher Marcus Aurelius, who disparaged interest in the body and its functions. For him, the flesh was to be disdained: 'nothing but blood and bones, and a network of nerves, veins, and arteries'.[26] The perversion of Buffalo Bill is that he takes pleasure in uncovering the blood and the bones and the rest. And when Lecter bullies Starling – 'Don't you feel eyes moving over your body, Clarice?' – we are meant, given the context, to catch the association of 'moving' and 'removing'. Lecter is not only challenging Starling to think of his eyes moving over the surface of her body as he speaks, he is also inviting her – and us, watching the film – to think of Buffalo Bill's eyes moving over the surface of a victim's body as his knife is removing it.

The film follows Harris's novel in making the victims 'Rubenesque' women (like those Saville would paint), the better to harvest their skin. It is quite possible that Harris and/or Demme knew of Titian's *The Flaying of Marsyas* (fig.6). This painting, which now resides in the archbishop's palace in Kroměříž, in the Czech Republic, was seen in an exhibition in London in 1983, receiving a sensational, highly publicised response and a reimagining by the painter Leon Kossoff.[27] Saville did not see it in person until 2016, when it was shown in New York, but it inspired her 2009 painting *Witness* (cat.14), showing what she called 'a half-alive/half-dead head' with a bloodied, screaming mouth.[28]

Harris and/or Demme may also have known an extraordinary book on the vulnerability of the human body, published in 1985: Elaine Scarry's *The Body in Pain: The Making and Unmaking of the World*, on the 'unmaking' of an individual's world by deliberately inflicted pain and its 'making' in acts of creativity.[29] Anne Hollander wrote, in *Seeing through Clothes* (1975), of how the nude in the Western tradition of painting carries the impression of the shapes and materials of the body's normal covering.[30] Scarry reminds us of the reciprocal reverse, the translation of skin into clothing: but one example, although an important one, of how a made object is a projection of the human body, extending its powers and acuity.[31] Buffalo Bill performs this projection by repurposing human tissue, but as Scarry points out, such a projection is meaningless without the artifact's consequent act of reciprocation.[32] As Lecter puts it: 'What needs does it serve?' The usual motive for making a coat is to make someone warm; but Buffalo Bill did not remake human tissue to be free of being cold. He was by profession a tailor who wanted to make for himself 'a woman suit', because he had been turned down for what was then called a sex-change operation.[33]

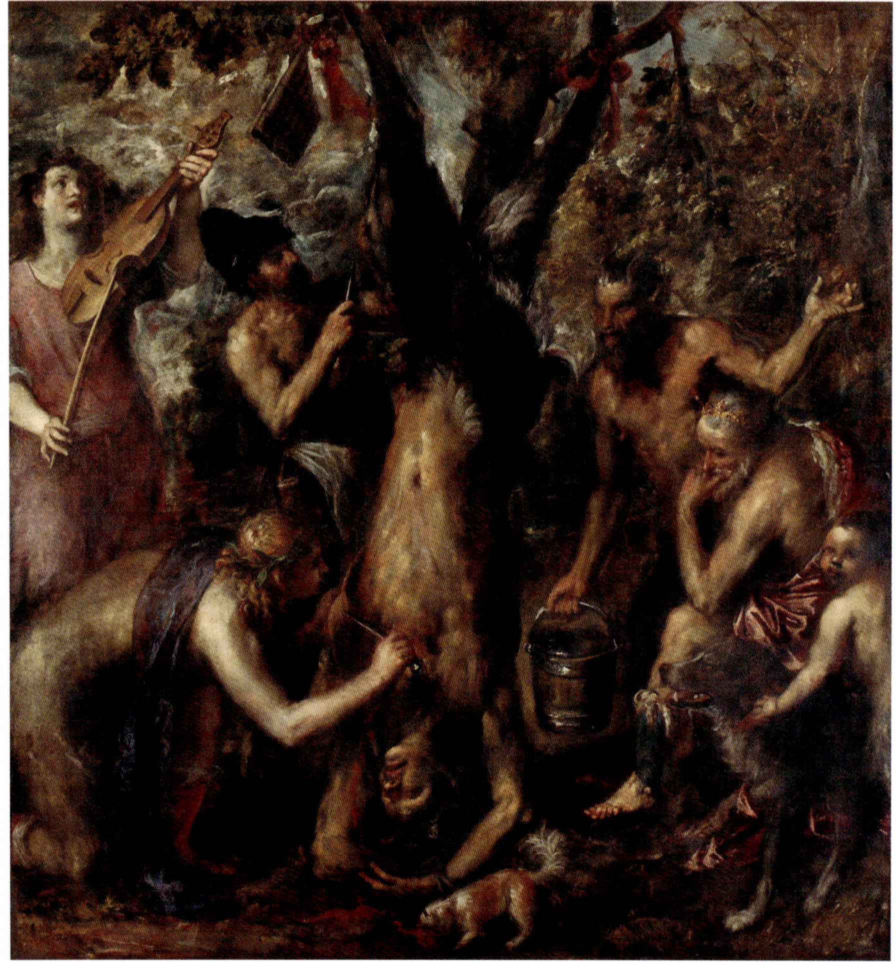

Fig.6
Titian (Tiziano Vecellio)
The Flaying of Marsyas,
probably 1570s
Oil on canvas
2200 × 2040 mm
Archdiocesan Museum
Kroměříž

Boundaries and Layers

Speaking of *Plan* (cat.3), Saville has compared skin marked for surgery to cloth marked for making clothes: 'Looking at photographs of plastic and cosmetic surgery, I found these target marks, which are how the bodies are marked out for an operation. I had looked at patterns for dressmaking, and I looked at contour maps. … And I found this system of drawing targets on the body … targeting areas of flesh that people want to get rid of, getting rid of this pollutant of flesh. I wanted a feeling of alteration'.[34] Her interest in 'a feeling of alteration' led her further: 'I'm drawn to bodies', she explained on another occasion, 'that emanate a sort of state of in-betweenness'.[35] And, watching plastic surgery, she re-experienced for herself de Kooning's statement that 'flesh is the reason why oil painting was invented', saying, 'Witnessing a surgeon cutting into flesh makes you see how layered flesh is, how vulnerable and easy it is to penetrate … I started to think about not just the anatomy of the body, but about the anatomy of a painting: the layering, the pace and tempo of the painted surface, the viscosity of paint'.[36] Saville is effectively comparing the layering of the body around its skeletal structure to the layered structure of an impasto painting on the support of a stretched canvas.

When the film of *The Silence of the Lambs* was released, in January 1991, Saville was at the University of Cincinnati for a term, taking courses in the Department of Women's, Gender, and Sexuality Studies, and reading feminist literature by Irigaray, Hélène Cixous and Julia Kristeva, whose *Powers of Horror: An Essay on Abjection* (1980) was the subject of her college dissertation. 'This attempt to write the female became a way for me to look', she explains.[37] And on page 4 of Kristeva's book, she would have read that 'abjection' was 'what disturbs identity, system, order. What does not respect borders, positions, rules. The in-between, the ambiguous, the composite'.[38] Such terms would be used to describe bodies like those that Saville would paint.

Irigaray's chapter 'The Mechanism of Fluids' in *This Sex Which Is Not One* is explicit on the subject of the porosity of the bodily subject.[39] Insofar as representation is concerned, the author's conclusion was, effectively, that the convention of the nude, being the creation of male artists, shaped the female body as a solid, impervious vessel, rather than the leaky, erupting one it actually is.[40]

What the sculptor Robert Morris in 1968 called 'Anti-Form' had been a theme of contemporary art and its discussion since that decade, fuelled by increasing interest in the writings on '*l'informe*' (the formless) by the French philosopher Georges Bataille.[41] Saville has said that the book of Bataille's she liked most was *The Tears of Eros*, published in Paris in 1961, as *Les larmes d'Éros*, but not translated into English until 1986. The book includes a famous photograph of a person hacked to pieces alive, given to Bataille by his psychoanalyst, which needless to say caught Saville's attention. Through this book, she became aware of the Surrealist journal *Documents* of 1929–31, with which Bataille was strongly associated and which was reprinted in 1991, at the beginning of her painting career.[42] She especially remembers 'interesting images of slaughterhouses'.[43] Such publications continued to interest Saville: she would later obtain a copy of a book called *Death Scenes: A Homicide Detective's Scrapbook*, a particularly horrific compendium of mid-twentieth-century photographs of death, depravity and degradations of the human form assembled by a Los Angeles policeman.[44]

Such interests very much remained in the discussions around art in the early 1990s, along with increasing attention to the female body. Even the quickest survey reveals that, in addition to theoretical texts by feminist authors, an average of one book a year on the visual arts published in English between 1988 and 1994 has the word 'body' or 'nude' in its title, two of them anthologies with eleven or twelve authors.[45]

Many of these publications discuss bodily boundaries, and were this a different, broader essay, two of the sources they cite most would require elaboration here: anthropologist Mary Douglas's *Purity and Danger* (1966), in which she writes, 'The mistake is to treat bodily margins in isolation from other margins', since they mirror cultural and social boundaries as places vulnerable, dangerous, and broken only with impunity;[46] and the development of this proposal in Kristeva's *Powers of Horror*, speaking of how objects that cross the boundaries between the inside and outside of the body generate both attraction and repulsion.[47] Both clearly have relevance to Saville's early work, especially; while mention of the porosity of boundaries between male and female in some of the early 1990s books bears on Saville's interest in 'a sort of state of in-betweenness', evident in later paintings.

Oxyrhynchus and Ekkyklema

In a number of Saville's earliest canvases, the shape of the depicted body and of the canvas on which it is painted are almost coterminous. The most striking instance of this is *Juncture* of 1994 (fig.7), a painting kin to a bas-relief sculpture of a back, such as Matisse's 1908–9 *Back I* (fig.8): the head is turned and flattened to the plane, the nose is squished by the upper-left edge, and the fingers of the right hand are folded up to fit into the bottom-right corner. Even in paintings from this period that show more background, we are not invited to infer what is behind the modelled front surface of a figure or a face presented to us; it is a neutral flat substratum. *Hybrid* of 1997 (p.35), clearly painted from an assemblage of photographs as if pasted onto the surface, suggests that her use of a camera may account for this quality.[48]

After around the first decade of her work, Saville began painting multiple figures, overlapping and entwining in space rather than abutting in plane, which meant that a continuous bas-relief effect of a figure or figures set against a neutral flat ground was no longer possible. Or, we might say, it was no longer wanted, since what was now desired was the greater animation of entwined figures, and, just as important, space had to be opened for – and by – layering bodies.[49]

Saville had previously been using two kinds of lines in her bodily images: she had used *written* lines to form the words of a feminist text adjacent to a body, and, more often, she had used *borderlines,* that is to say, lines to describe divisions between things or parts of things. Now, to engage a layering effect, she began to use purely *drawn* lines; thin, usually black charcoal lines that seem at once loosely woven around the figures – like borderlines without bodily shapes to border – and independent graphic strokes written on the surface of the painting without forming words. The result of drawing pulled away from the body in this way is that the graphic may be read independently of the painted illustration.

Fig.7
Jenny Saville
Juncture, 1994
Oil on canvas
3051 × 1683 mm
Private Collection

Fig.8
Henri Matisse
Back I, 1908–9
Bronze
1889 × 1130 × 1650 mm
The Museum of Modern Art, New York

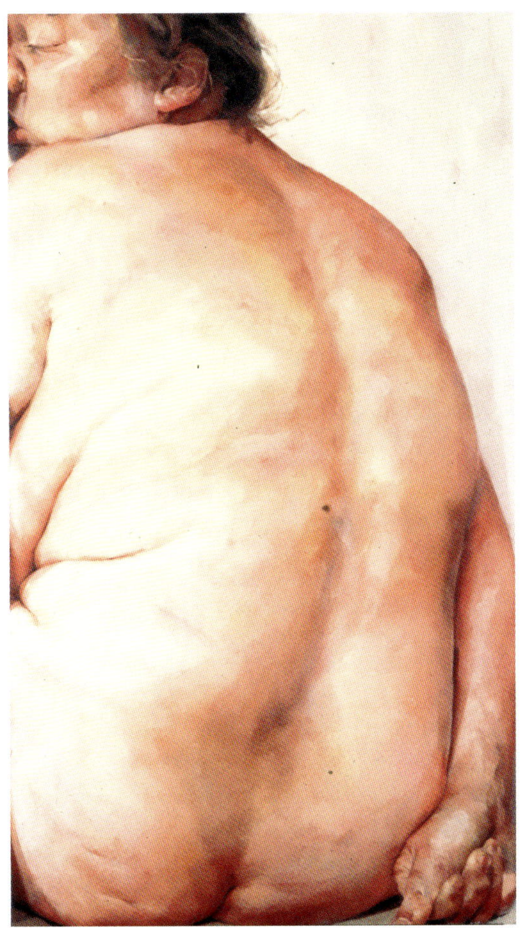

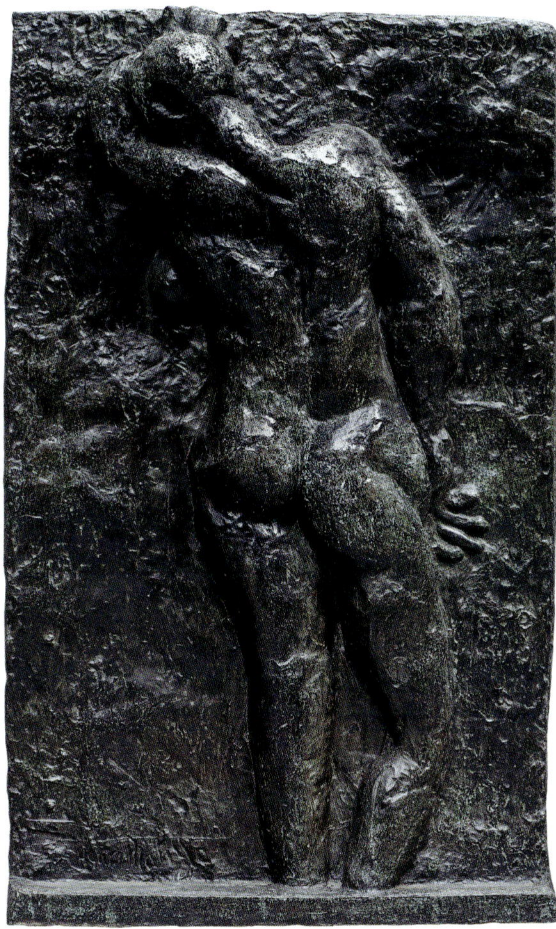

Pitting the arts of drawing and painting within one canvas invokes the so-called *disegno-colore paragone* debate over the relative merits of central-Italian and Venetian schools of painting in Renaissance Italy: the concentration in the former on linear design, and in the latter on colour.[50] In 2024, Saville spoke of a dual interest in her works of this period. First, she was working 'in sections, building up layers and fragments of intimate body parts and images from art history'. With this in mind she named a series of paintings *Oxyrhynchus* after an Egyptian archaeological site that was effectively an ancient rubbish dump, with 'fragments captured in layers of time'. Second was her 'pervasive interest in sketches and unfinished "open" works that are typically not as celebrated as the grand masterpieces'.[51] She did not specifically relate the first interest to painting and the second to drawing, but the works themselves give a permit to that interpretation.

In any event, these paired concerns offered a means of working that afforded great flexibility, as she explained: 'Often I will draw lines and forms of the body so that they float over the top of other bodies, in contradiction to the forms below'. Also, 'being able to perceive a breast or a hand buried in the distant innards of the painting while simultaneously seeing a leg forming on the surface visually excites me – it feels very real. … As though you could perceive several realities collectively at once. What I want is a solid, embodied image that feels real and intrinsic to nature, but does not necessarily form a "singular scene" as such'.[52] A singularity, rather, could be produced by 'making sure the right combination of marks

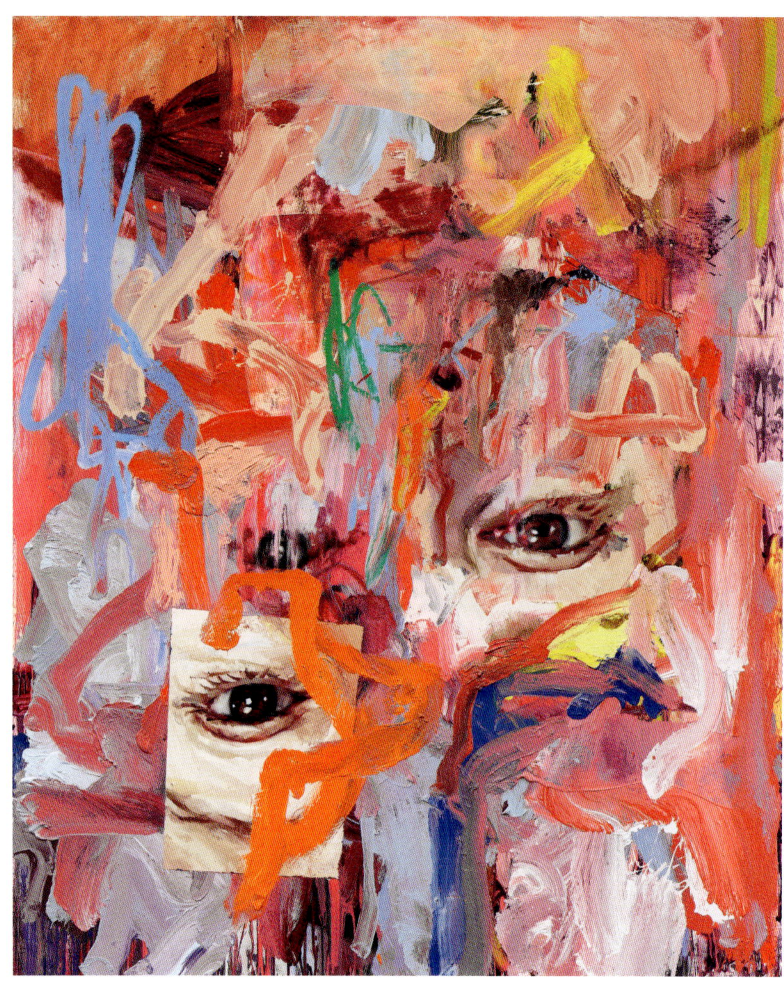

Fig.9
Jenny Saville
Cascade, 2020
Oil on linen
2000 × 1600 mm
Private Collection

Fig.10
Willem de Kooning
Woman VI, 1953
Oil on canvas
1740 × 1486 mm
Carnegie Museum of Art, Pittsburgh

and bodies are in there, and then I have to keep working to allow them to emerge to bring them up to the surface'. This issue for Saville placed her figurative art firmly in the orbit of the most ambitious modernist painting, from de Kooning and Jackson Pollock to Jasper Johns and Brice Marden, the latter of whom famously maintained, 'The whole evolution of modernism is about getting up, up, up to the surface, tightening the surface to the plane'.[53]

We may remember that Saville said of her first sight of de Kooning's work in 1991, 'The paint was right on the surface'. She said this in 2013. By the end of that decade, she was giving greater emphasis to the surface in her own work, making figure compositions and portrait heads from coloured paint or pastel without contrasting dark lines but with linear tracks, also of paint or pastel. In addition, in a group of richly coloured pastels, she made explicit the appearance of an assemblage of images pasted onto the surface that had been implicit in the 1992 *Hybrid*. She named this series *Ekkyklema*, after the Greek for 'roll-out machine', a platform rolled out onto the stage in ancient Greek theatre to bring interior scenes into the view of the audience. (Also, since the depiction of violence was prohibited in those theatres, it was used to bring the bodies of dead characters onto the stage.) Saville's works comprise parts of bodies below and within geometric shards and rectangles, whether frontal or in perspective, that seem as if collaged on the surface, with a profusion of drawn lines above, below and between.

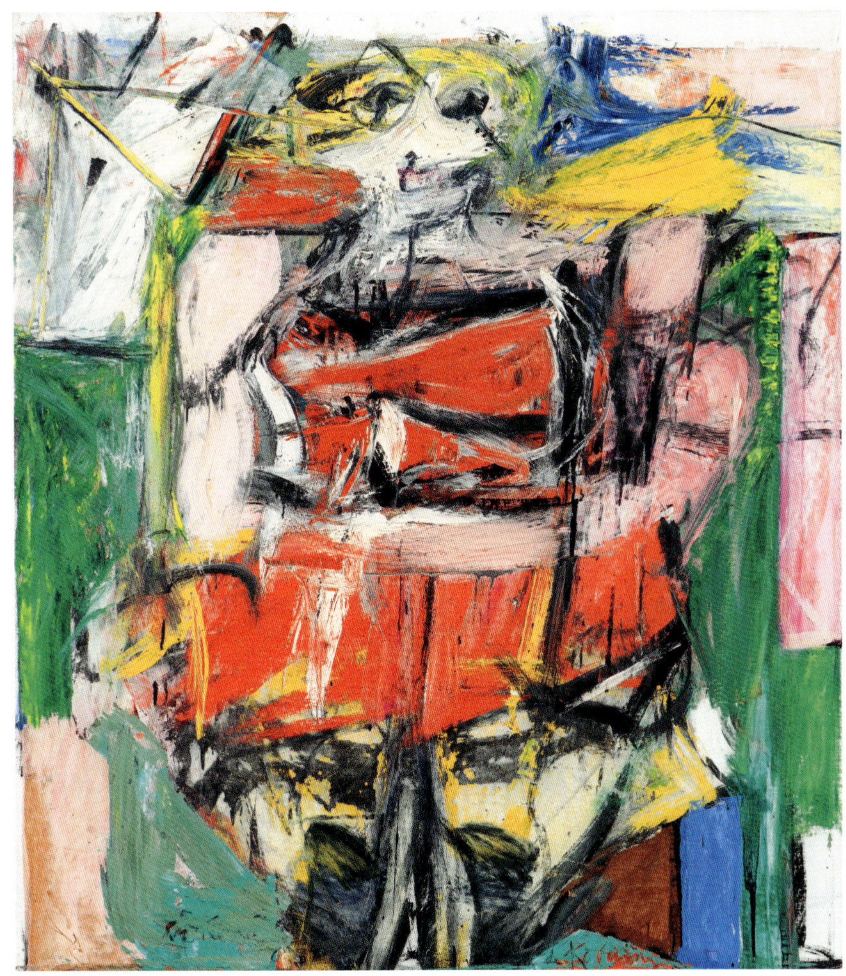

Complementing these were studies of heads, whose methodology had remained more or less constant in Saville's work since around 2006. The new heads, such as *Cascade* of 2020 (fig.9), have faux-collaged eyes apparently on top of paint or overlapped by highly coloured paint, applied in abstract patches, broadly drawn strokes, and allowed to run down the surface. These comprise what Greenberg had called, in reference to the work of de Kooning (fig.10) and Johns (fig.11), an 'exhibitedly and poignantly superfluous' painterliness, to which he had added of Johns's work, 'When the image is too obscured the paint surface is liable to become less pointedly superfluous; conversely, when the image is left too prominent, it is liable to reduce the whole picture to a mere image'.[54] Saville also works between these two poles.

The Sublime and the Grotesque

Previously in this essay, I wrote of Saville's early paintings as works that may not always be quite pleasurable to see but are so compelling of our attention that we do not want to look away from them. In conclusion, I want to sketch two broad associations of her art that speak to a viewer's confrontation with the less than pleasurable.

The first is 'the sublime', a term that has long passed into the vernacular to mean the

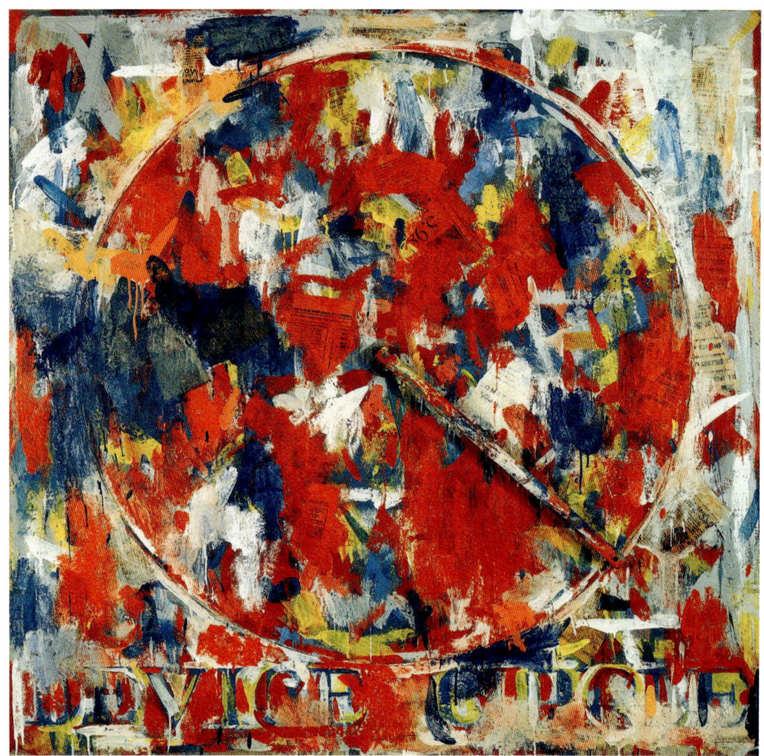

Fig.11
Jasper Johns
Device Circle I, 1959
Encaustic, oil, newspaper, wooden arm and metal screw
1017 × 1017 mm
Private Collection

affectingly spectacular. In the eighteenth century, however, it became fundamental to the emerging Romantic movement through the treatises of Edmund Burke and Immanuel Kant, of 1747 and 1790 respectively, to describe a 'vastness' or 'magnitude' whose extent was impossible to grasp, and that was 'fearful' in its effect, as opposed to the calming influence of the 'beautiful'.[55] Insofar as both were speaking of landscape, the former association is not relevant to the present discussion. But the 'fearful' is, in that, as Burke wrote, 'Whatever is fitted in any sort to excite the idea of pain and danger ... is a source of the sublime'.[56] Also, while the sublime was unquestionably, aggressively masculine, he wrote, the beautiful was associated with the 'beauty of women [which] is considerably owing to their weakness, or delicacy ... their timidity'.[57] Faced with Saville's hardly weak, delicate or timid paintings, two questions present themselves.

The critic Jon Cook observed in 1991 of the sublime within Romanticism, 'From a historical distance the sublime can seem the invention of a culture which wanted to feel more secure by frightening itself'.[58] One question for the viewer of Saville's paintings then is: does our culture want that too? A few years earlier, the critic Michael Fried had drawn attention to the way, in art, the fearfulness of the sublime has been thought of in relationship to the threatening paternal power of major predecessors, and hence to issues of 'artistic belatedness and the struggle for originality'.[59] Another question for viewers of Saville's paintings then is, do they adopt qualities of the sublime in order to fight on equal terms against that paternal power and its ideal of regulation and mastery? Or, more to the present point, do they comprise a 'feminine sublime', composed of an iconography of abjection?[60]

A second association of Saville's art, with 'the grotesque', is more complicated. Like 'the sublime', the term has passed into the vernacular with a judgmental meaning; in this case, the nastily unpleasant, ugly, or unnatural. Its pedigree, however, is longer than that of 'the sublime', and has so many mutations that many books have been devoted to them. What deserves notice here, as with 'the sublime', are early-modern interpretations that speak to Saville's paintings. A fine guide to them by critic Geoffrey Galt Harpham, to which I am indebted in what follows, explains that 'broadly and basically speaking, we apprehend the grotesque in the presence of an entity – an image, object, or experience – simultaneously justifying multiple and mutually exclusive interpretations … with the unifying principle sensed but occluded and imperfectly perceived'.[61]

Harpham does not mention 'abjection', Kristeva's book on that subject does not mention the grotesque (their books appeared in English in the same year, 1982), but the two concepts overlap. For Kristeva, as noted earlier, the abject is 'what disturbs identity, system, order. What does not respect orders, positions, rules'.[62] A circle is not only a shape, says Harpham, but effectively an ideology, speaking of total coherence and unity.[63] What we perceive as grotesque is 'an energy that aborts, as if to express its dissatisfaction with available boundaries', a 'trammelling of energy' that separates what we expect to be joined and joins what we expect to be separated.[64]

When speaking of how the boundaries between the inside and outside of the body can generate both attraction and repulsion, Kristeva, like Scarry and others, was referring to adult experience of the adult body. Saville, the mother and painter of children, knows that children are different: as Harpham nicely puts it, 'children are intensely interested in the sensory, and especially intent on the alimentary and reproductive systems; they are indifferent to such concepts as tragedy, nobility, and sanitation'.[65] The poet Charles Baudelaire, in his essay 'The Essence of Laughter', wrote of the 'absolute comic' quality of the grotesque, which 'has about it something profound, primitive, and axiomatic, which is much closer to the innocent life and absolute joy than is caused by the laughter caused by the comic in man's behaviour'.[66] By 'innocent life and absolute joy' he was referring to the laughter of children, who have not yet learned the discriminatory grid between laughing at someone slipping on a banana peel and laughing at something grotesque that an adult may find disturbing. 'For the laughter of children', he wrote, 'is like the blossoming of a flower. It is the joy of receiving, the joy of breathing, the joy of contemplating, of living, of growing. It is a vegetable joy. And so, in general, it is more like a smile'.[67]

A final question, then, for viewers of Saville's paintings: may we too find in them a vegetable joy? Another great nineteenth-century critic, John Ruskin, would have answered, It depends upon the viewer: 'Wherever the human mind is healthy and vigorous in all its proportions, great in imagination and emotion no less than in intellect, and nor overborne by an undue or hardened pre-eminence of the mere reasoning faculties, here the grotesque will exist in full energy'.[68]

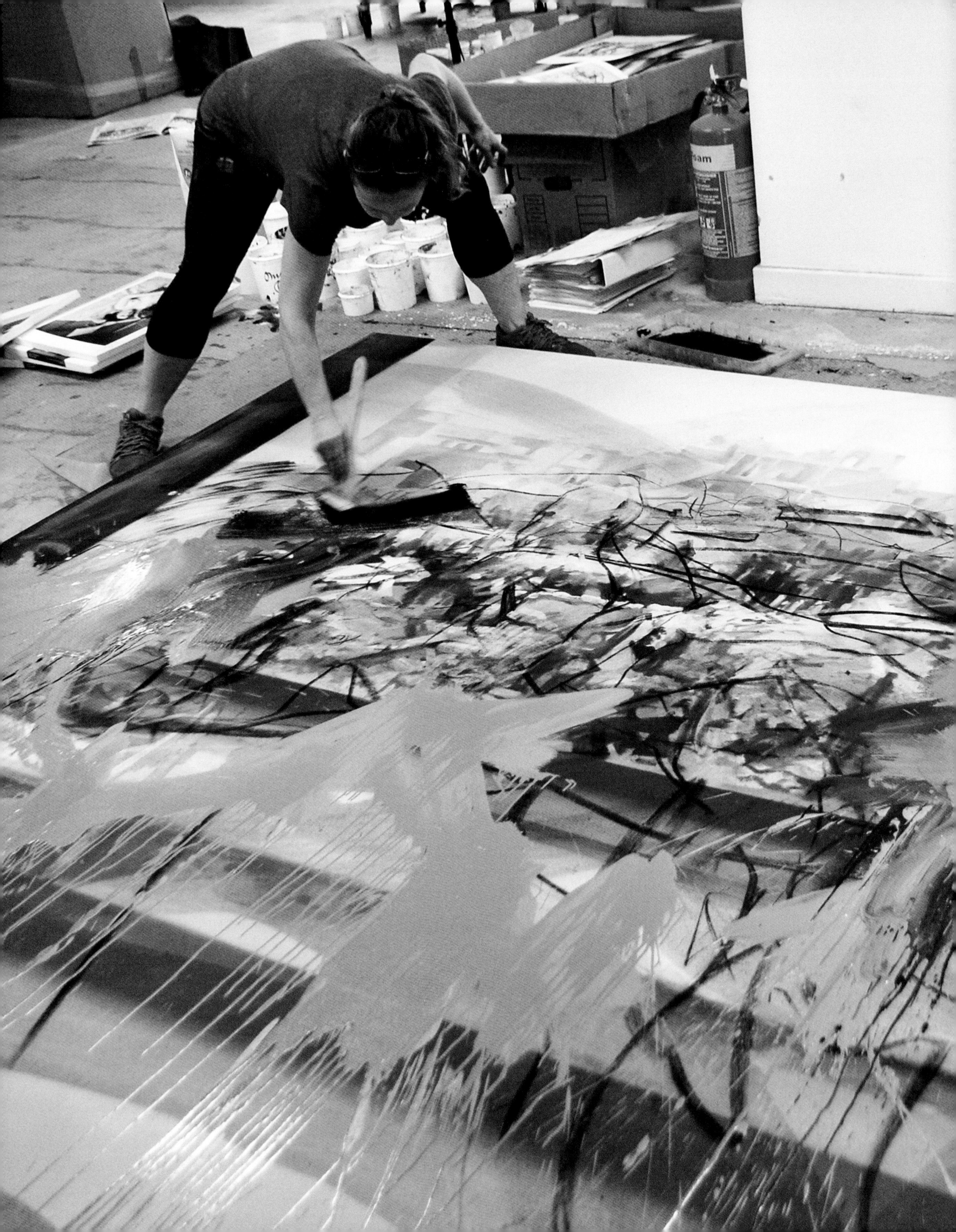

The Hard-Won Image

Jenny Saville and Sarah Howgate in conversation

SARAH: Could you talk about your experience as a student at the Glasgow School of Art and your early career trajectory?

JENNY: One of the aspects I really liked about the Glasgow School of Art was that it had an independent painting department, which used to be housed in the Mackintosh Building. The school has a strong figurative tradition, and painters like Frank Auerbach, Francis Bacon, Lucian Freud and Rembrandt were big influences for me. Just before going to art school, I saw the exhibition *Lucian Freud: Paintings* at the Hayward Gallery in London in 1988, which had an enormous impact on my work, and copies of the exhibition catalogue were everywhere in the painting department at Glasgow.

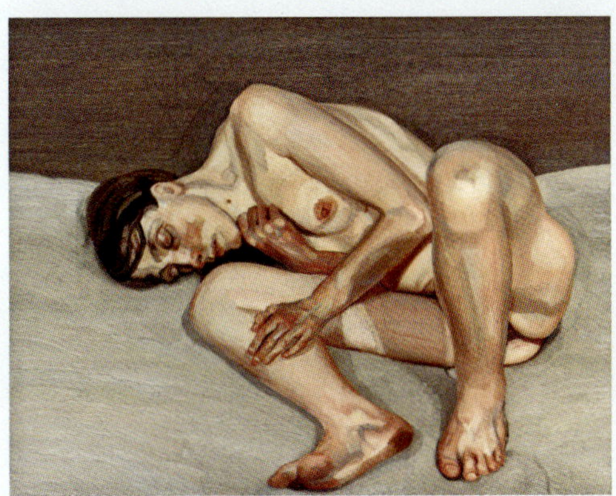

Lucian Freud, *Small Naked Portrait*, 1973–4

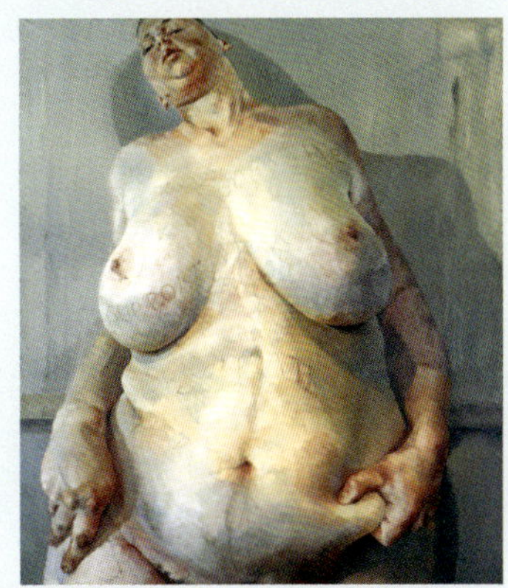

Jenny Saville, *Branded*, 1992

By the time of my degree show, which included my paintings *Propped* (cat.1) and *Branded* (above), I felt I'd found a language to combine the way I painted with the theory I had been reading. It was an exciting time because, at graduation, I was awarded the Newbery Medal[1] and *The Times* newspaper's Saturday supplement, which was running a feature on UK graduation exhibitions, put *Propped* on the front cover. [British art collector and gallerist] Charles Saatchi saw it and, after also seeing a couple of my paintings in an exhibition at Cooling Gallery on Cork Street, London, in 1993, he purchased the works and commissioned a body of new paintings for his phenomenal gallery space on Boundary

Road in St John's Wood. When I look back, it was an incredible opportunity for a 22-year-old graduate.

SARAH: Despite your formal training, you made the decision, while still at college, to work from photographs rather than life models. This seems to have freed you up to be more playful and to walk the tightrope between figuration and abstraction.

JENNY: I worked in the life room at college, but I found the academicism of it – particularly the 'life room' poses the models often held – much less appealing than working with models I asked to pose privately.

Looking at how Bacon worked from photographs to paint bodies gave me the confidence to do that. With photography, I can get a close-up of teeth or an eyeball or even a hand momentarily posed in a way a life model wouldn't be able to hold for a long time. I could try more extreme poses, so I could bring a better dynamic into the work. The *Prop* series (1992–3) was based on poses that I couldn't hold for long as I was pushing my knees out as far as I could. Having photos of that pose to work from offered me the possibility to create those kinds of paintings.

Generally, I like creating paintings of bodies and heads from a low-to-high perspective so that it creates a sense of grandeur and helps give the model a powerful presence. When I made paintings like *Propped*, *Prop* (p.67), *Plan* (cat.3) and *Strategy* (below), I wanted to create these mountains of flesh, so your eye traversed up and over the model's body.

Using photographs to paint from meant I could not only freeze these difficult poses but I could paint at any time – I wasn't bound to work only when there was a model available.

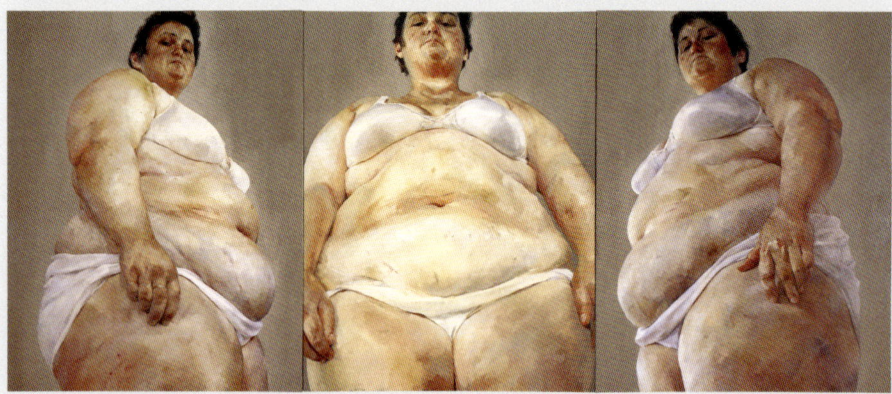

Jenny Saville, *Strategy*, 1994

I wanted to paint on a larger scale, and photography helped with that possibility, but it also opened up my work to ways of reconstructing reality. To start paintings, I'd often begin by making collages from photos, playing with images taken using flash photography and mixing them with ones taken in daylight to change the flesh temperatures. I used this technique in paintings like *Ruben's Flap* (cat.5) and *Fulcrum* (cat.6). In *Fulcrum*, I made a collage using different temperatures of photographic images and painted the bodies in a naturalistic way, mixing the artifice of photographic panels with naturalistic flesh. Around that time, I was making paintings where bodies and flesh were the only story. I didn't want to place the figures in a narrative setting, so I tried to limit back-grounds or objects around the figures. I like the dynamic of a tabletop as it creates a strong horizon line, which I went on to use in *Fulcrum* and a couple of paintings of pigs, *Host* (2000) and *Suspension* (cat.13). I thought of these works as being landscapes of bodies, which is why I called my first New York show *Territories* [Gagosian Gallery, 1999].

For *Sensation: Young British Artists from the Saatchi Collection* [Royal Academy of Arts, London, 1997], I made the painting *Shift* (below), which was an attempt to create a curtain of flesh. I worked from a hopelessly small polaroid, so when I started *Fulcrum* I made a larger collage as a source. I enjoy working on a large scale so that, when you're up close, the painting goes beyond your body and it's all about the paint.

You do lose some aspects painting from photographs compared to working directly from the model, especially in shadows. When I taught a life class in New York, I remember looking at the colour of the shadows in and around the model: they were much more nuanced and with greater depth. When I paint, I take the two dimensions of a photograph and think back into three dimensions to build the structure of a body or paint an eyeball, for example.

If I'd only painted from the life model, I might never have looked at so much abstract painting – the works of Cy Twombly and Willem de Kooning, for instance – and brought certain aspects of abstraction into my figuration. Painting from photographs frees up time to think about the way I'm applying paint – the mark-making, paint consistency and colour. It enables me to play with the fundamentals of painting.

I can begin a painting in a completely abstract way, laying down a kind of painting

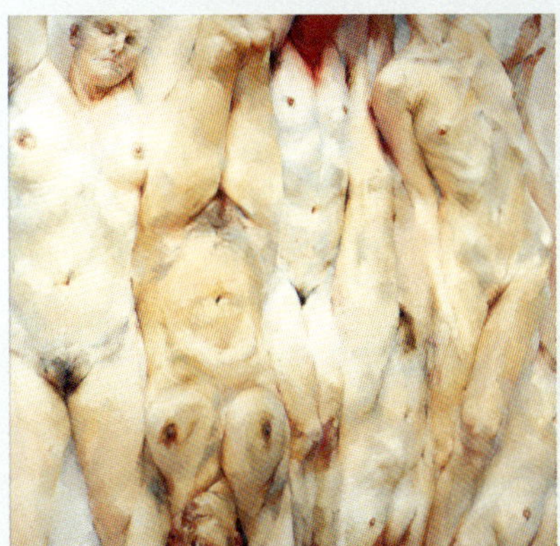
Jenny Saville, *Shift*, 1996–7

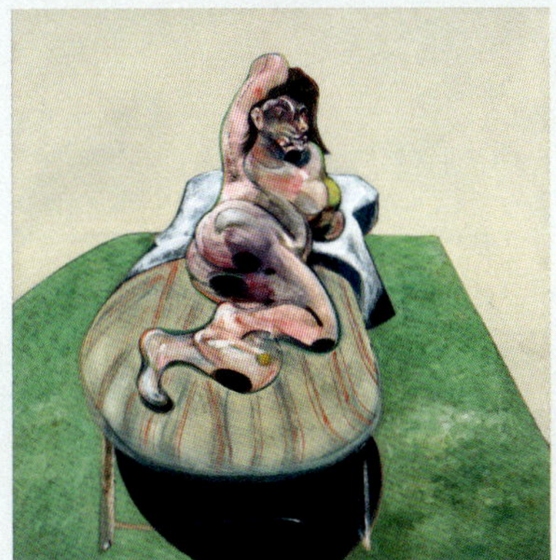
Francis Bacon, *Henrietta Moraes*, 1966

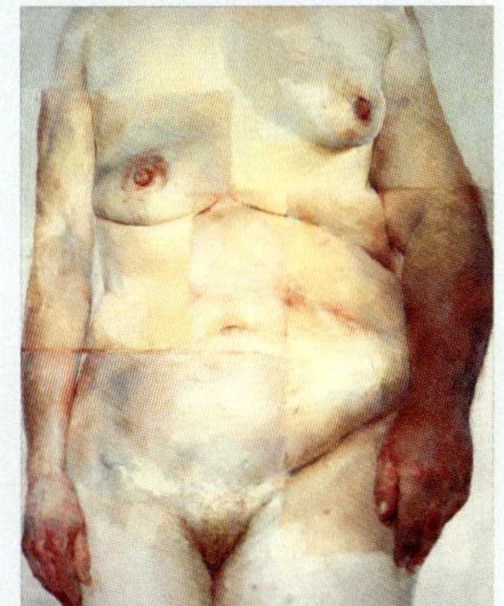
Jenny Saville, *Hybrid*, 1997

'nature', and then build out a head or a body from that. This technique offers a way to construct reality that I couldn't get if I'd started from the image first. Once you have the body or the head drawn up, there's a reluctance to destroy it through abstraction. I found my instinct often protects the image. So, if I begin completely abstract, it throws up interesting tonal passages and I build the painting around those. Sometimes, I like to start with the drawn-out structure; sometimes, I lay down abstract paint first. Both ways can work. Recently, I've been working with pastels first, then laying down oil paint on top. This creates an oil stain on the pastels that acts as a shadow which I can then build on.

SARAH: How did discovering de Kooning's work elevate your practice?

JENNY: I encountered his work for the first time when I spent a semester in Cincinnati in 1991. I found it visually thrilling. Then, looking at the exhibition David Sylvester curated at Tate [*Willem de Kooning: Paintings*, 1995] and another exhibition in New York [*A Centennial Exhibition*, Gagosian, 2004], I saw how he painted fleshiness – whether he was painting an actual body or a more abstract landscape. I liked his dexterity: it was an extensive vocabulary with scraping, dripping and running different colours together.

I knew I wanted the visual presence in my painting that I saw in de Kooning and Twombly, so I started to break down the elements of my process, similar to the way a musician composes by building up sounds. I began to consider every element – from the first stain through to impasto – and to consider the various possibilities of painting while still building a body or head.

SARAH: How have you gone about developing this language?

JENNY: Over so many years of painting, I've developed a bag of techniques, and my vocabulary of what's possible to do with paint has grown. These techniques create a freedom in the moment of painting to think about the way I'm applying the paint, the consistency and movement of my mark-making in building the form. I'm able to charge the paint with sculptural force. For example, I've found I can drive bright green or yellow oil bar right through the structure of a head, and then build the flesh around that. This way of working hopefully embeds an inner tension and life force to the painting, which I find exciting.

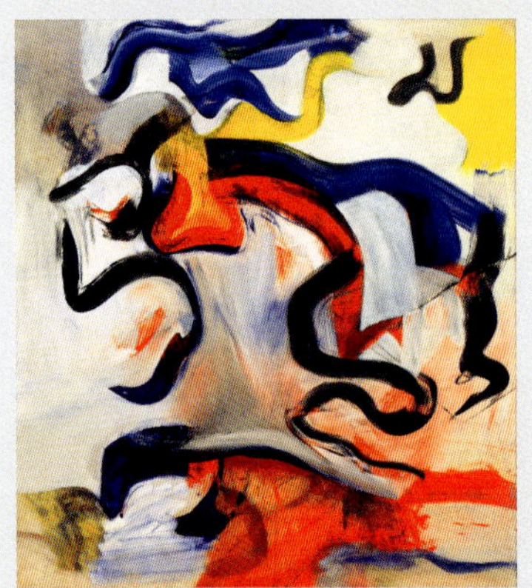

Willem de Kooning, *Untitled V*, 1982

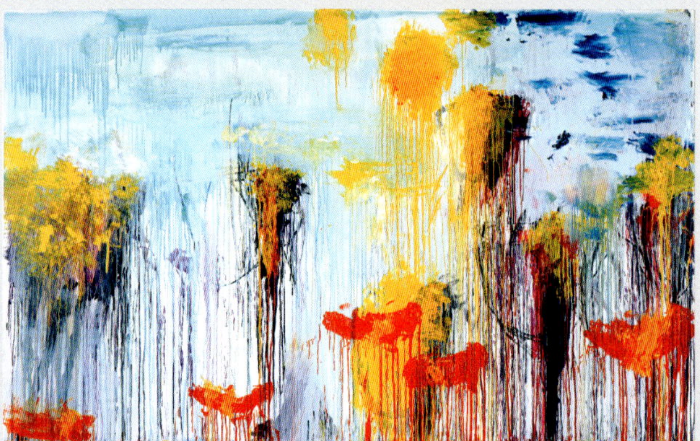

Cy Twombly, *Lepanto (Part VII)*, 2001

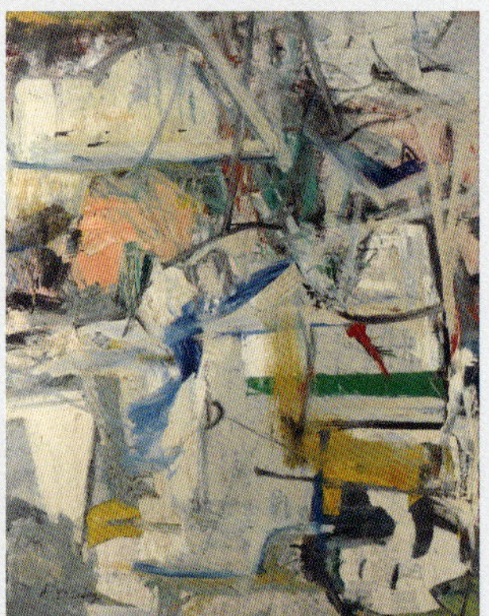

Willem de Kooning, *Easter Monday*, 1955–6

SARAH: When did you start working on the floor?

JENNY: Looking back, I've worked on the floor intermittently for years. In *Hyphen* (cat.4), I put a dark red stain down while the canvas was laid on the floor, and I also worked on the floor at the beginning of *Suspension*. Frequently, I've started backgrounds on the floor.

When you put the canvas on the floor, you take away your control over the paint and make different kinds of marks. I often start with quite fluid paint in bowls and use large household brushes so the bristles separate and produce an interesting splash technique to create light and movement. If you use Cadmium Red Light and Kings Blue Light or

Kings Blue Deep on top, the combination of colour gives a vibrant visual hit. I often use a plastic, bendy scraper to pull light back into the work, which creates good mid-tones and an airiness at the beginning of the painting. Then, when I'm building the form, some of this underneath paint remains, and some gets embedded within the painting as I end up adding new layers on top because I need that tonal structure.

The de Kooning show at Gagosian in 2004, where I was fortunate to spend time with the paintings while the technicians were installing his work, was important for me in this regard. De Kooning often worked on the floor, and I remember seeing this blue handle mark at the bottom right of one of the paintings that you could almost lift off; I saw this movement in and out of the painting.

In the head series *Stare* (2004–11, see cats 15–19), I made a lot of marks on the floor. When starting backgrounds on the floor, I can run paint in long sweeping marks to create a dynamism. In *Rosetta II* (cat.22), I threw tinted primer to make a splash up the right side of her cheek, so when I built the ear to the right of that there was a combination of painting techniques with different dynamics of movement.

I like the way Rembrandt painted the white cloth caps that he wore by swinging an impasto mark around the head. I often think about that when I build marks around the structure of a jaw or an ear.

SARAH: Could you talk about the importance of copying works by other artists to inform your own – for example, the drawing you made based on a study for Georges Seurat's *Bathers at Asnières* (1884).

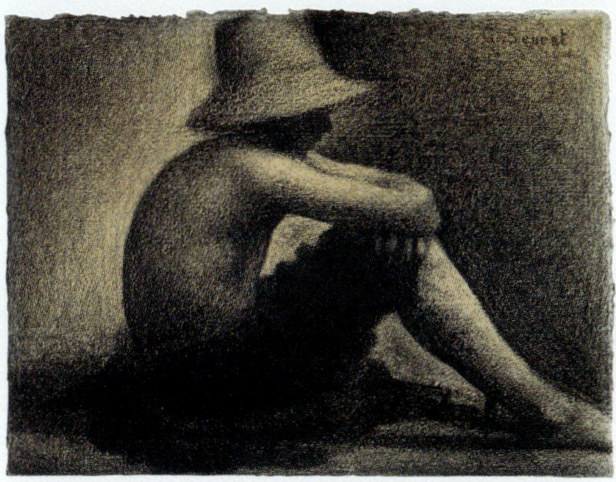

Georges Seurat, *Seated Boy with Straw Hat*, 1883–4

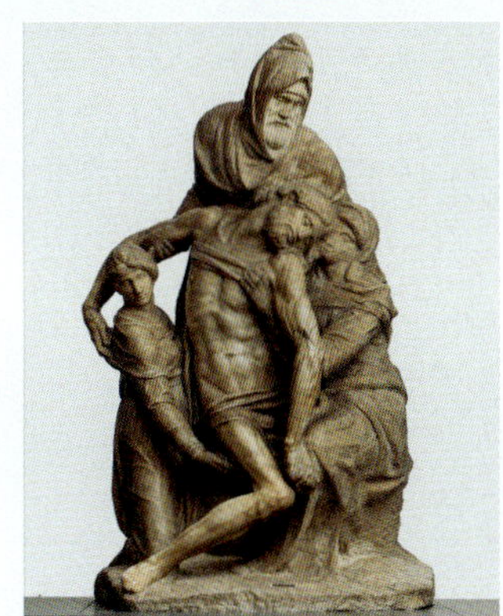

Michelangelo Buonarroti, *Pietà Bandini*, c.1547–55

JENNY: Once, on a 12-hour flight, I had a book of Seurat's conté drawings with me. I thought: What do I want to know about Seurat's process? How do you get that kind of vibration? So, I made a small study in a sketchbook and worked out it was by slowly building up form and developing these pockets of light called irradiation.

SARAH: And how has Michelangelo influenced your work?

JENNY: What's so poignant about Michelangelo is the way he combines different moments of reality to create a human mass, such as in his *Pietà* sculpture in the

Museo dell'Opera del Duomo in Florence. This grouping of bodies couldn't physically exist like this in real life, but he works the figures – the twists of the bodies, the placement of the hands – in such a way that it creates a heightened sense of humanity and pathos. Being aware of the materiality of marble – the rough, course areas combined with the polished realism – gives a tension of nature.

When I've made works like the big *pietà* drawings *One Out of Two Symposium* (cat.41) and *Aleppo* (cat.44), for example, I built the figures thinking about sculptural form. It's an organic process, developing one figure after another until the mass of humans have a solidity. It's one of my favourite ways of working, because you visually build something trying to embody a strong armature. Although this particular grouping of figures couldn't exist in real life, it hopefully has a believable feeling of a sculptural, human mass.

SARAH: Could you talk about the importance of drawing in your practice and the way you separate it from painting, even down to having different studios for each activity? *Neck Study II* (cat.33), for instance, is a beautiful, almost sculptural drawing of a woman's head and neck.

JENNY: It was fortunate that I ended up with two studios, one of which morphed into a drawing studio. I try to be experimental in there. I make abstract and figurative drawings and try out different types of materials and surfaces. In terms of the drawing you're referring to, it's a challenge to get a long neck to dip in then back out and hold muscular tension. Michelangelo's drawings taught me to think more in three dimensions, to work at the paper and to carve out form. In his famous *cartonetto* for the *Pietà*, the area of

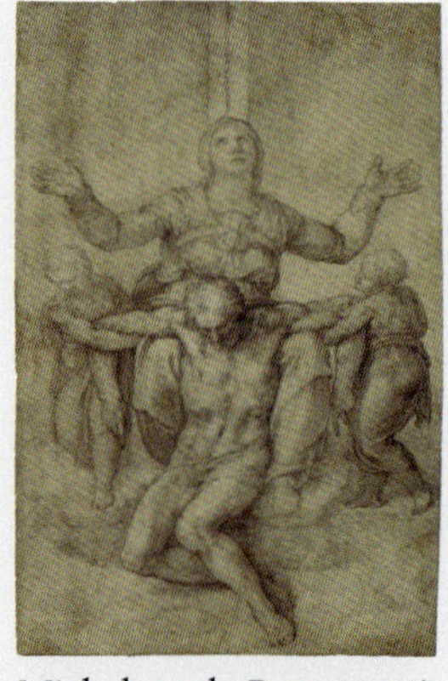

Michelangelo Buonarroti, *Pietà for Vittoria Colonna*, 1538–44

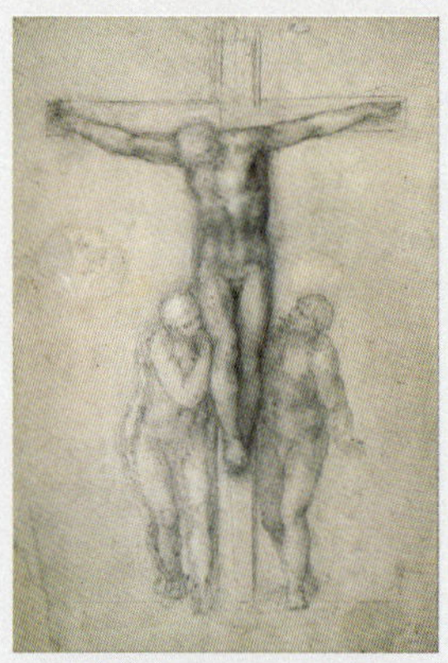

Michelangelo Buonarroti, *Christ on the Cross with the Virgin and St John*, 1555–64

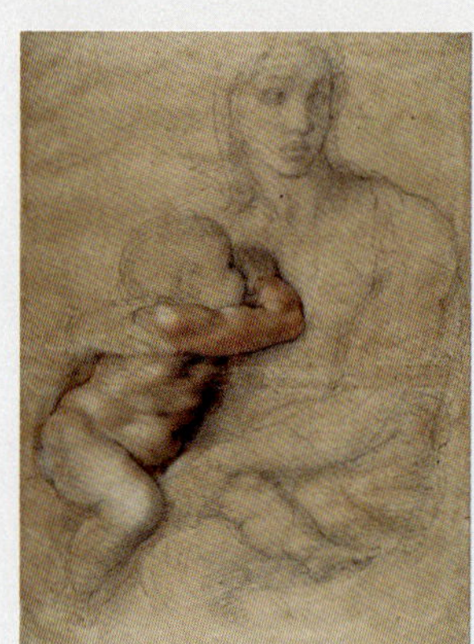

Michelangelo Buonarroti, *Madonna and Child*, 1525

Christ's body touching the Madonna is worked again and again, the paper and material are really embedded.

SARAH: Your survey at the National Portrait Gallery isn't a portrait exhibition in the traditional sense; it demonstrates how you have re-invented figure painting for the twenty-first century. You've talked in the past about how your work could be seen as a portrait of painting rather than as conventional portraiture.

JENNY: When you see a show of Pablo Picasso's portraits, you don't necessarily think of him as a traditional portrait painter. Some of his portraits are wild and use unexpected distortions and colour combinations. Like Bacon, his inventiveness pushed portraiture and painting. I've made more traditional portraits and, in paintings like *Rosetta II*, *Witness* (cat.14) and *Entry* (below), tried to approach unusual subjects. In *Rosetta II*, I hope the painting calls to mind the classical idea of the mysticism of a blind person's stare.

Freud once said that he was trying to get to the particular in his painting because, through the particular, you reach the universal, which has a long tradition. But, there are also other ways to reach a sense of the universal, which I've learnt from looking at abstract painting. In a work like *Stanza* (cat.50), I wanted to see if I could make an almost abstract portrait, pivoting between a portrait of painting and a painting of a head.

SARAH: What drew you to working from medical imagery?

JENNY: Probably looking at Bacon's work. Also, I think I have quite a scientific eye. I used to go to the Hunterian Museum in London, and I was fortunate enough to be able to observe plastic surgery in New York. Watching a surgeon with his hand inside a woman's face pulling upwards, I could see flesh as a moveable mass. Through research into reconstructive surgery, I discovered the ways in which surgeons would move flesh around the body to rebuild it. I used this as a reference when I painted *Ruben's Flap*. The title refers to a plastic surgery technique that takes flesh from a woman's thigh to use in breast reconstruction, so I started to make paintings with parts of the body, playing with scale changes, angles of bodies and heads, mixing types of bodies together. Sometimes, I would pull photographs

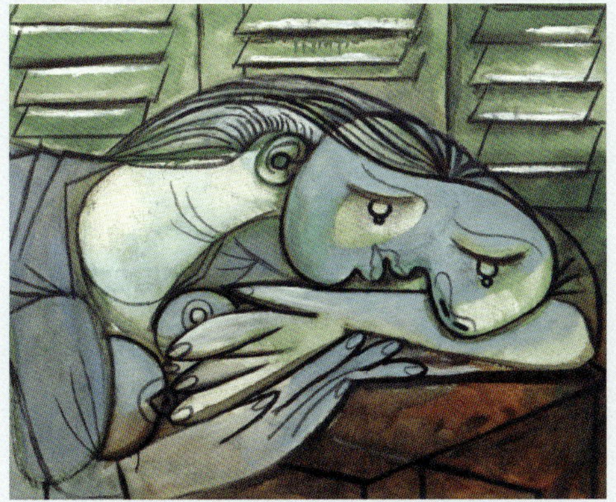

Pablo Picasso, *Dormeuse Aux Persiennes*, 1936

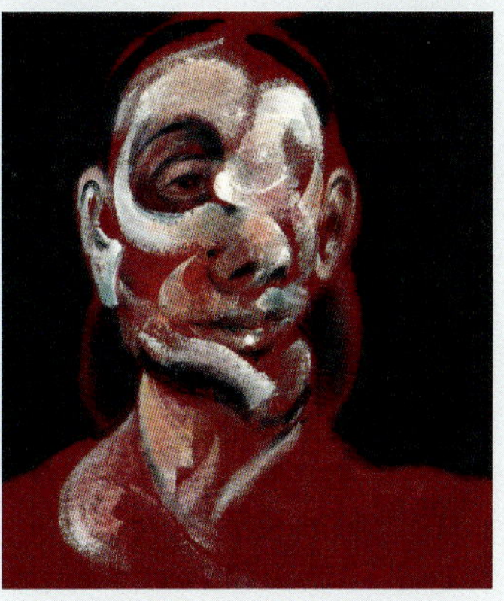

Francis Bacon, *Three Studies of Muriel Belcher*, 1966. Central panel of triptych

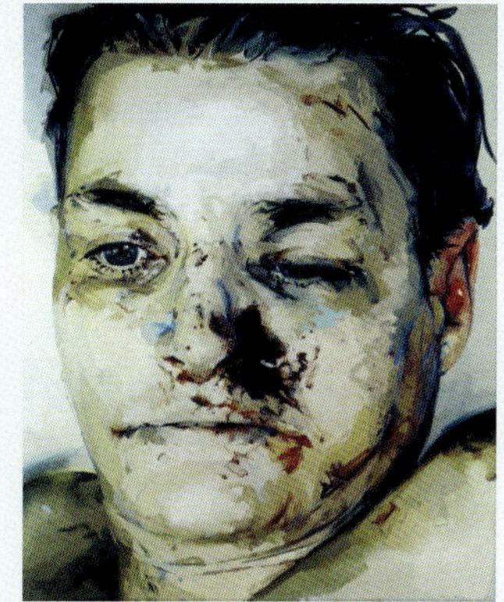

Jenny Saville, *Entry*, 2004–5

in an old fax machine to elongate the image – a technique I used in *Hyphen*.

When I've worked from images in medical books, despite not knowing the person in the photo, a familiarity develops through the journey of making the painting because you spend time looking at them and constructing their head.

The birthmark in the *Stare* series was taken from a book on dermatology. I made several versions in different colours and the birthmark went from a physical mapping of the stain to just being about painterly possibilities. When making a figurative painting, you spend most of the journey learning about that person's anatomy and how their body sits in space. How does the twist of this arm or leg go? What shape is the bridge of the nose in a portrait? That particular image is an uncharted journey, so most of my time is spent considering this. By creating multiple versions in the *Stare* series, it gave me the possibility to experiment and develop a stronger painterliness. Because I'd walked one particular path in the first few *Stares*, I could get looser as I went on, experimenting with colour or working in a shorthand way to give the image greater charge.

I usually work in sections on a large-scale head. With the *Stare* heads, I developed ways to swing the white paint to create the neckline of the sitter's shirt at the bottom of the canvas, or travel my brush or scraper up the side of her nose. I like the structure at the sides of noses and often find ways to swing paint around it towards the eyeball, which hopefully gives a dynamism and internal movement right in the middle of the head. Side panels – whether sides of noses, or the cheek section next to an ear – often catch the light, so I can play with colour combinations and movement in those parts of the painting.

Because of my familiarity with the head in the *Stare* series, I was able to concentrate on ways to move paint more freely in the other canvases. Even though it's less worked than many in the series, *Red Stare Collage* (cat.16) became one of my favourites. It started with just red and white abstraction at the hair area with a white primer, and I built her head up from there. What's good about using primer is that it has a different flow, a bit like regular household gloss paint. At the time, I was painting a lot on large sheets of paper that were stapled to wooden boards and the boards became part of the paintings. The series started with cyan tones, then moved to pinks and reds.

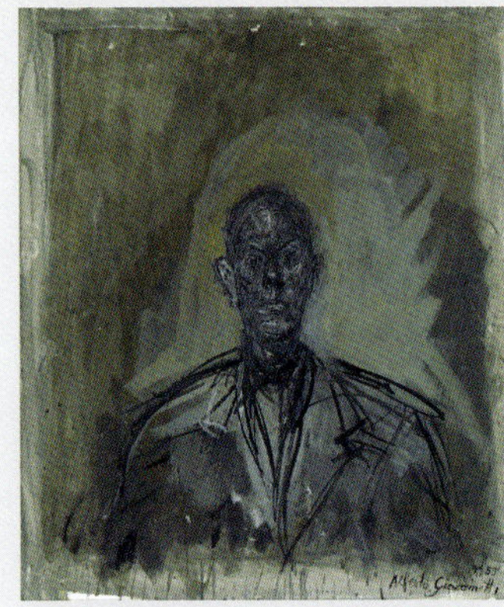

Alberto Giacometti, *Diego*, 1959

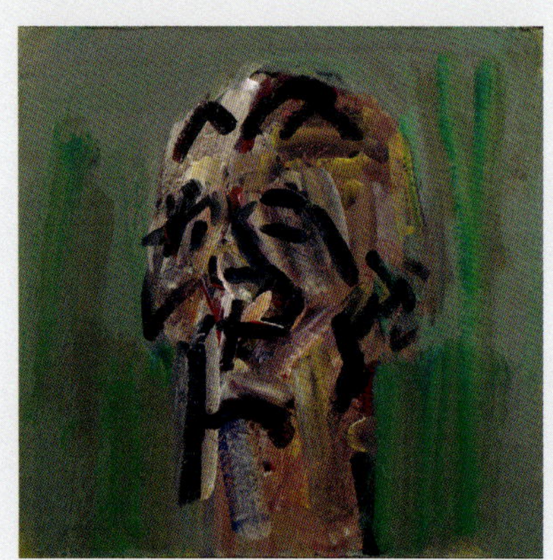

Frank Auerbach, *Self-portrait VI*, 2022

Sometimes, I'll start by putting a black stain underneath my painting, which was an influence that came from Gerhard Richter's black and white works and from Alberto Giacometti. In a lot of Giacometti's portraits, there are these terrific drips that fall beyond the square which he draws around the edge of his pictures, so the image of the portrait falls away at the bottom. I used a similar technique in *Rosetta II* and have often started building portraits with this drip technique first as it gives a gentle gravity that I can then overlay with thicker paint.

SARAH: It seems you transitioned from working with found medical imagery into drawing on your own experiences of childbirth and motherhood. How did having children affect your creative development?

JENNY: Spending most of my life painting flesh and then growing a body inside my body was a profound experience. Giving birth was beautiful and primal. I continued painting after my children were born at the times they were sleeping, and then drawing became increasingly important because you can start and stop with ease, whereas with painting there's a lot of preparation and clearing up. With drawing, I was able to spend time with my children and still be creative.

I wanted to get the rapid movement of children's bodies and pregnancy into pictorial form, so I found it interesting to look at Renaissance drawings of the Madonna and child, as well as Rembrandt's pen-and-ink drawings of mothers and children.

SARAH: Do you find it difficult to finish paintings? I know you like working down to the wire.

JENNY: I've made paintings for exhibitions that have taken several years to finish, but I've also made paintings fast. Sometimes, paintings I've made quickly have a sense of urgency to them that I like because I was forced to be decisive. The portraits I showed in *Elpis*, my 2020 exhibition at Gagosian, have passages of paint that have the fluidity and movement I was interested in – especially a painting called *Rupture* (cat.57), where I put yellow right up through the right eyeball. Painting is a constant game of problem-solving and flexible thinking – that's what I enjoy about it so much. Every painting is a journey to get sections

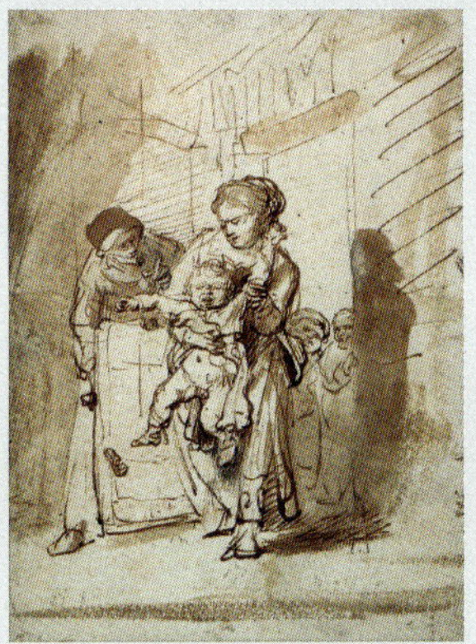

Rembrandt van Rijn, *The Unruly Child*, c.1635

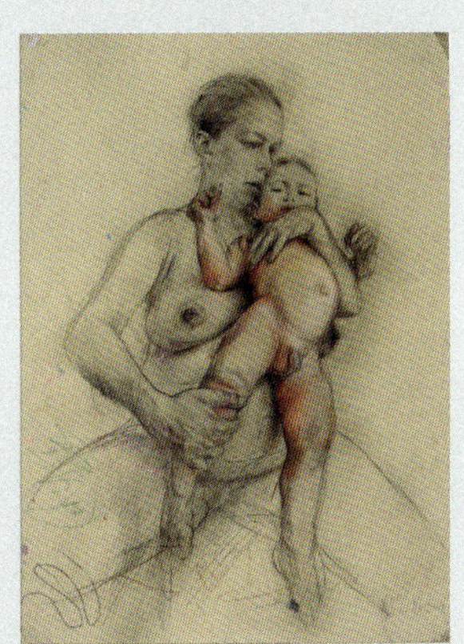

Jenny Saville, *Mother and Child Study V*, 2009

of it to work until all those sections come together with balance and gravity. Sometimes, I make decisions well when I'm at the latter part of producing a body of work. There are usually months of work building up to that point, but I can make quite radical decisions at the end of a painting. In *Drift* (cat.47), for instance, I put a rust and green section up the side of the curvature of her cheek that's probably one of the best parts of the painting. If I had pondered for too long, I might not have been that decisive.

SARAH: Do you destroy works? I'm thinking of de Kooning's words, which remind me of your own philosophy of painting: 'I never was interested in how to make a good painting. I didn't work on it with the idea of perfection, but to see how far one could go…'[2]

JENNY: Over the last decade or so, I've started a lot of paintings and played around with materials. I got into a rhythm of working on a few paintings on the same subject, so I could experiment with ways to approach sections of the painting and to be more open. I've even spent weeks making completely abstract pastel drawings, just making marks without an image. And I've learnt that this freedom makes its way back into my main body of paintings, so it's never wasted time. It's a way of being more radical and bringing new techniques into my work. Keeping paintings at open stages for a time has been helpful over the years, as I sometimes return to them with a whole new approach. Recently, I had a large pastel head drawing that I hadn't worked on for some time. I went into the studio, saw a possibility of what I could do by making these rectangular, stencilled sections and painted an abstract, fluid layer on the top in about half an hour. It's got a dynamic that I'd never have found had I stuck to working continuously on it. But, because I'd left it for a period of time, I didn't care about it in the same way as you do when you work continually on one piece. Now, I'm going to start building the form of this head on top of this fluid paint and see if I can create some new spaces within the painting. It's an exciting way to work.

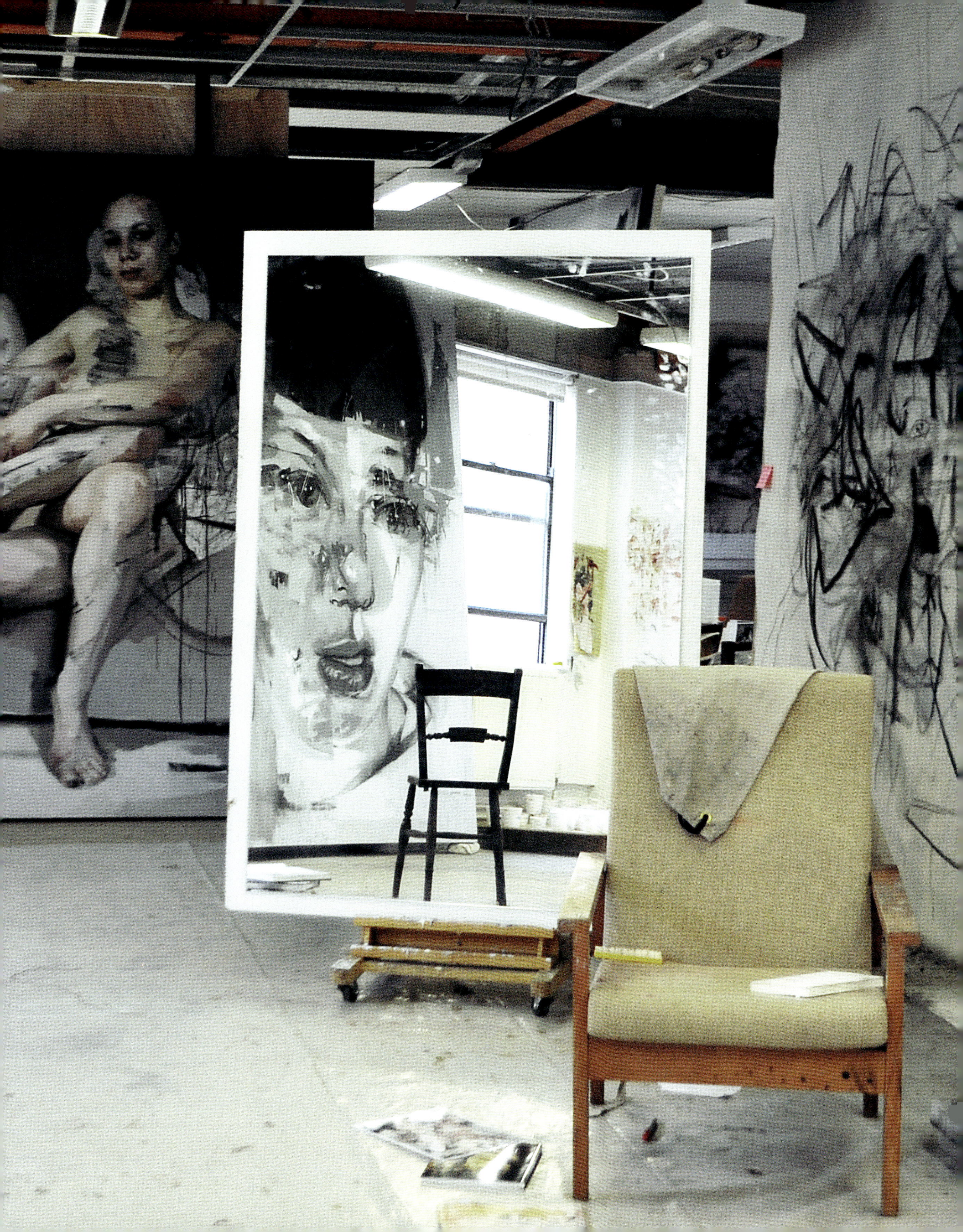

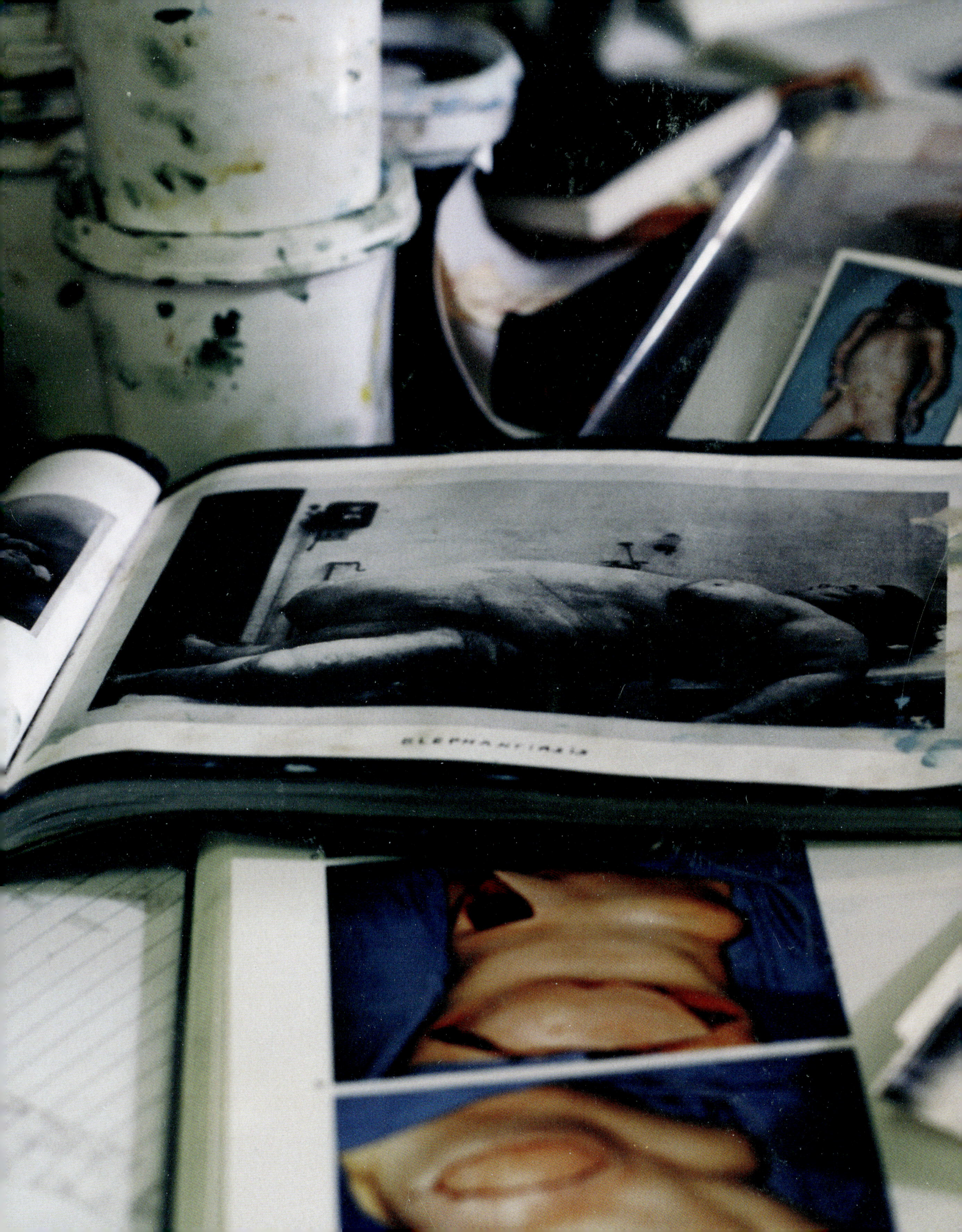
ELEPHANTIASIS

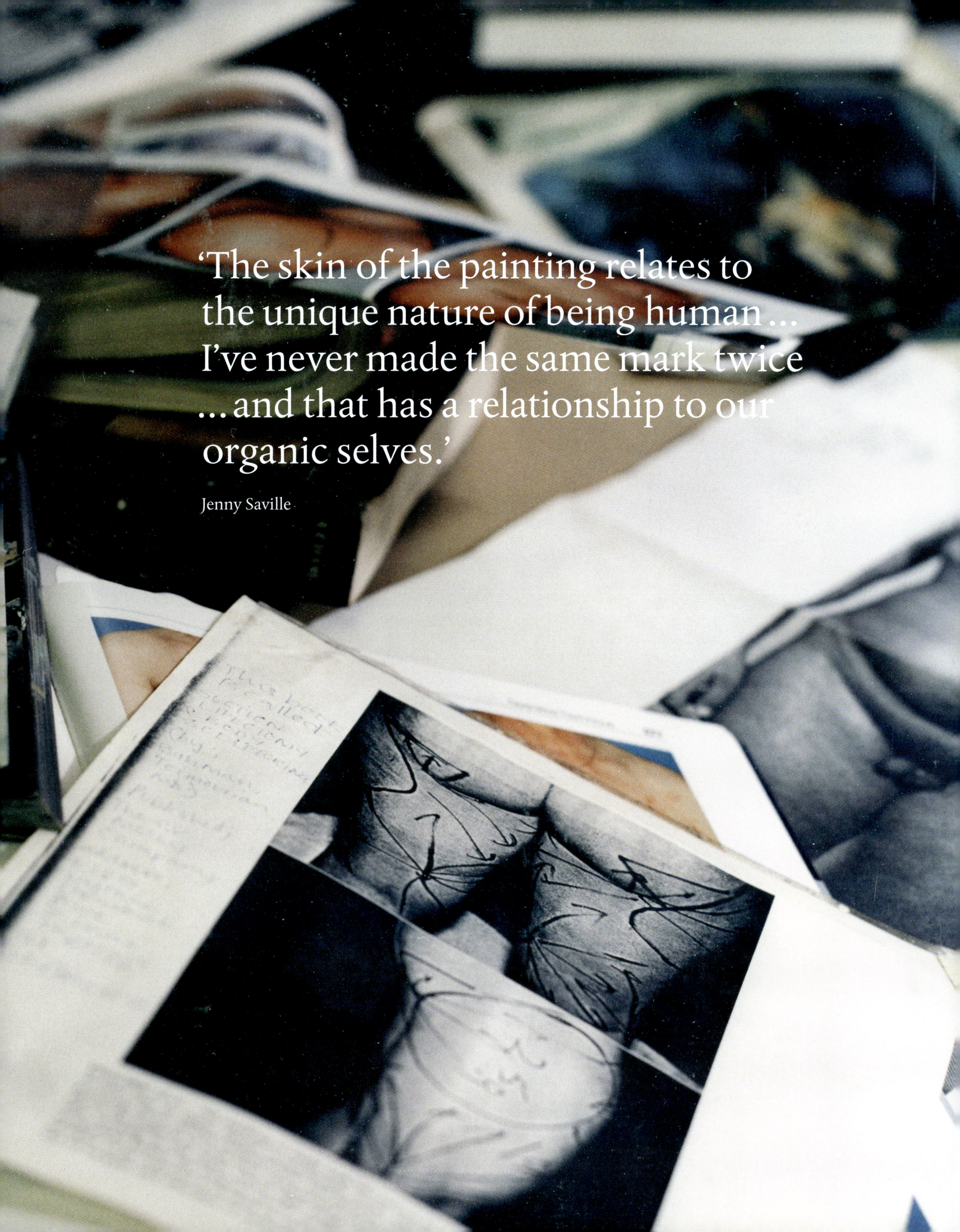

'The skin of the painting relates to the unique nature of being human ... I've never made the same mark twice ... and that has a relationship to our organic selves.'

Jenny Saville

1 *Propped* 1992

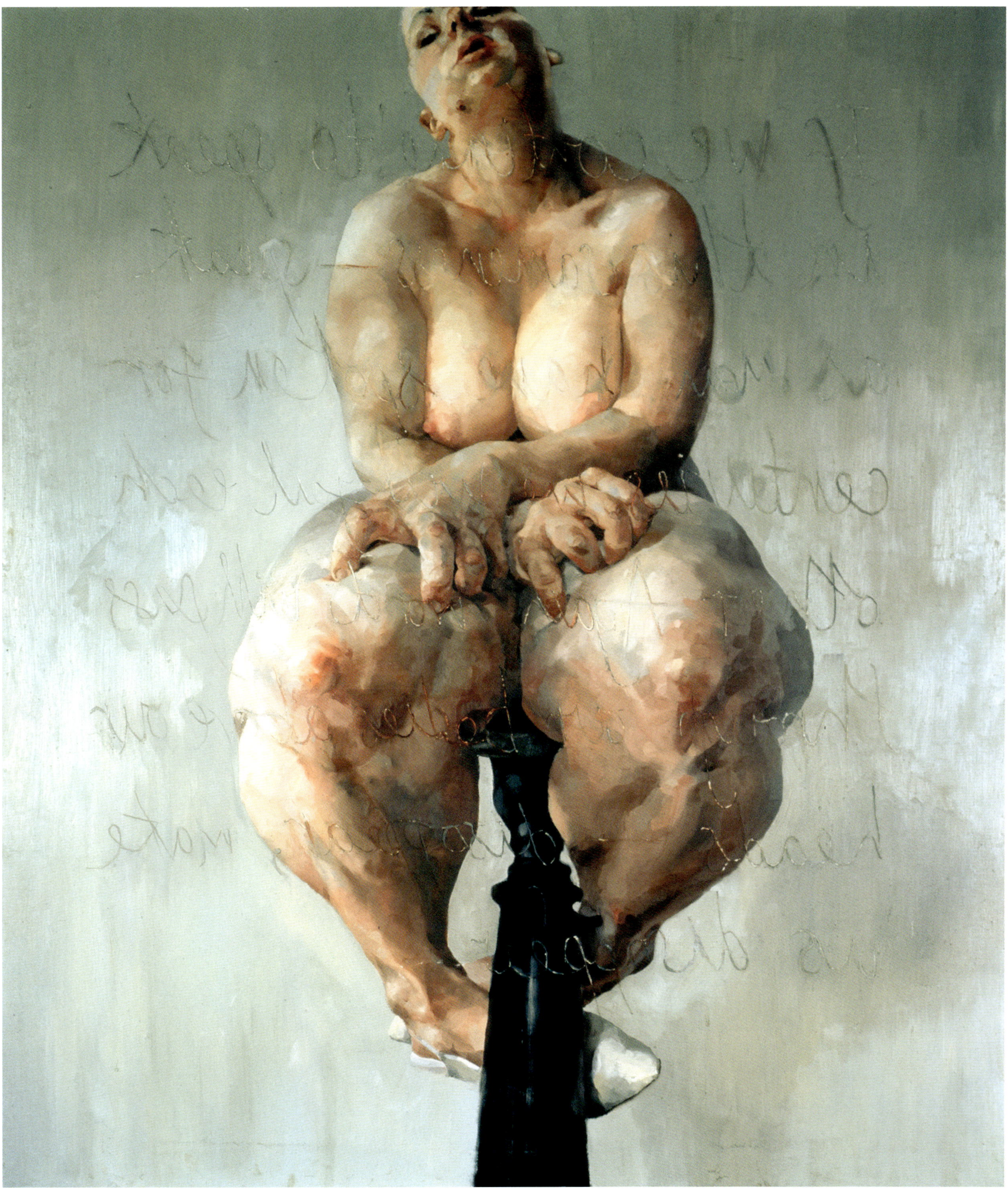

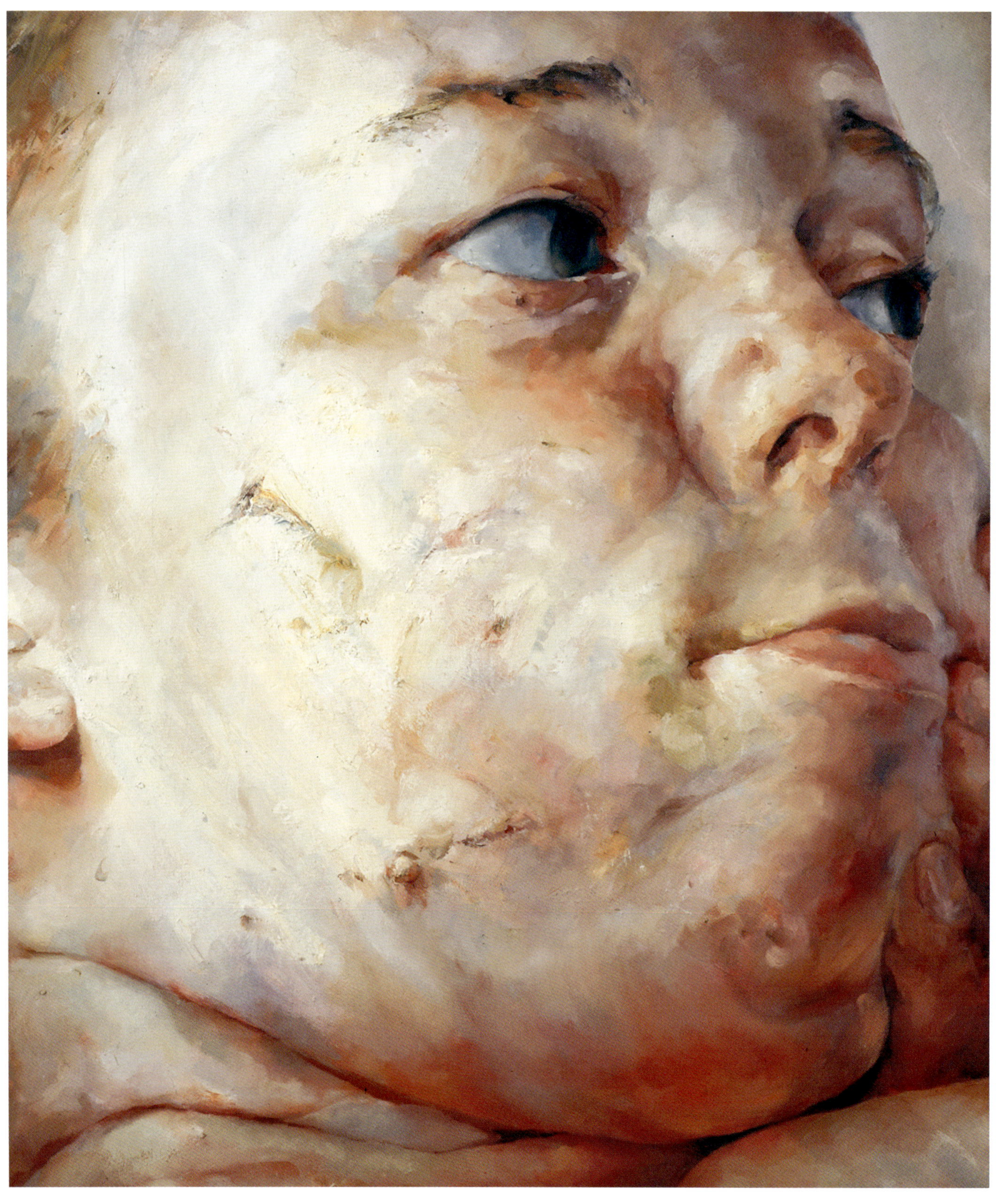

3 *Plan* 1993

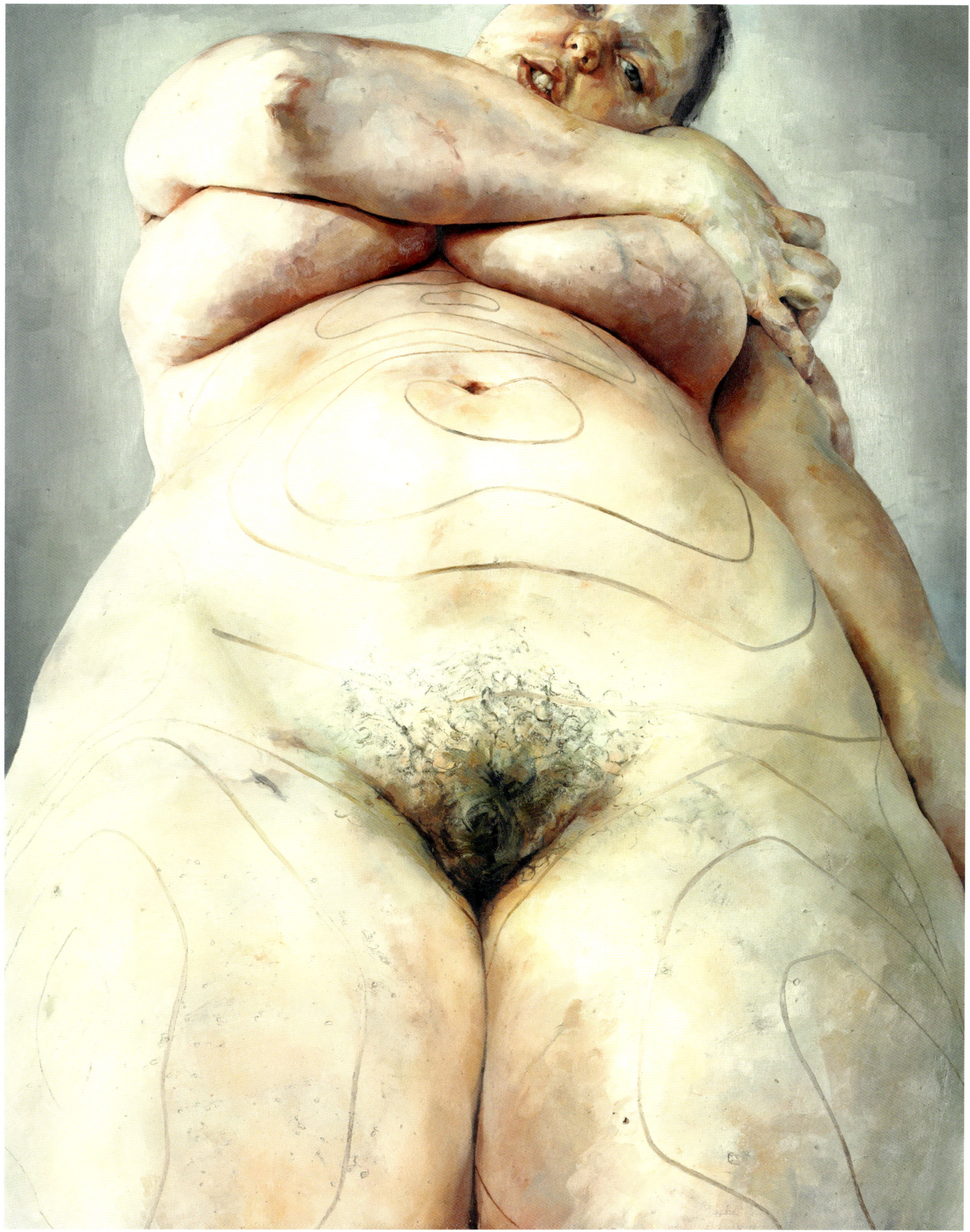

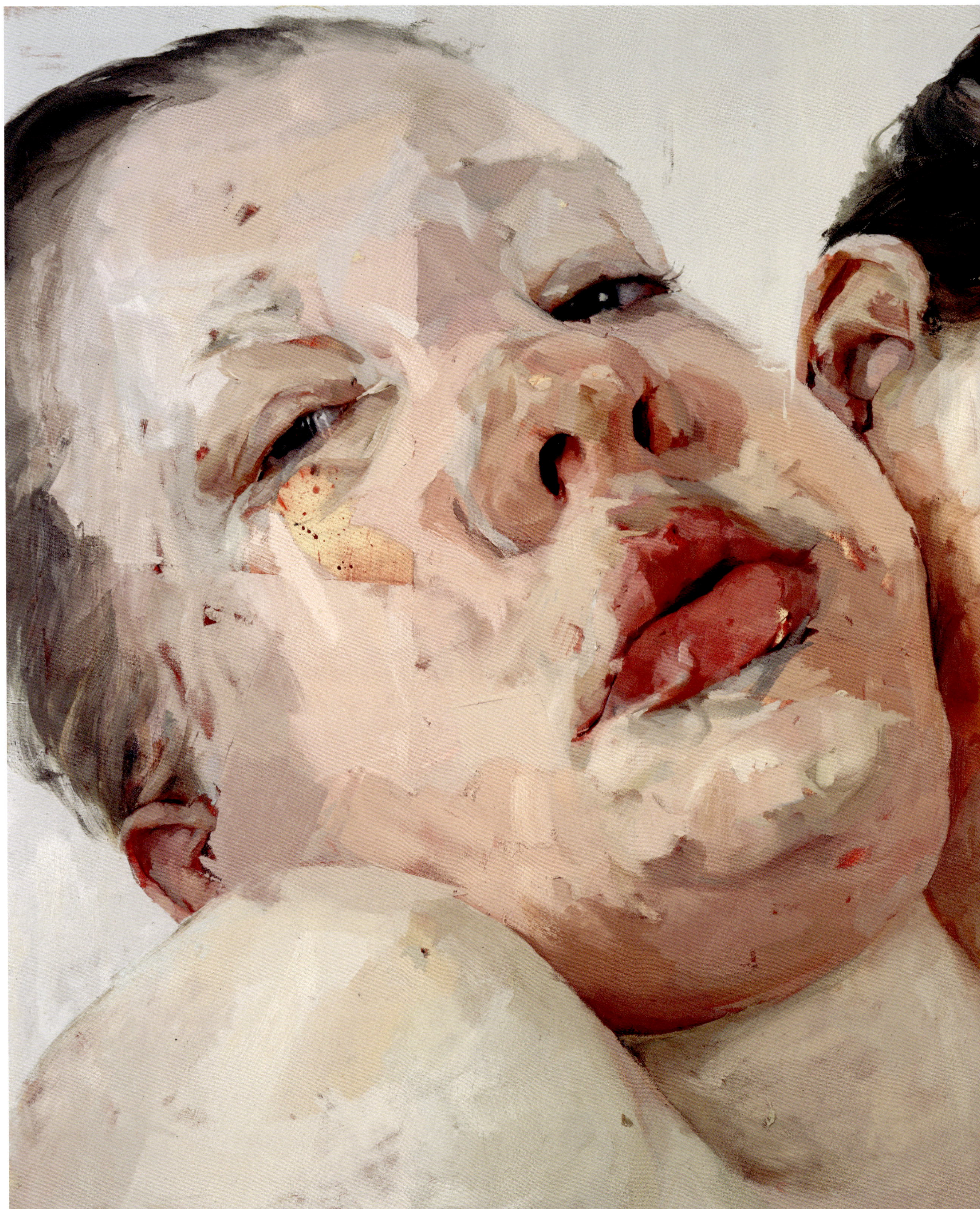

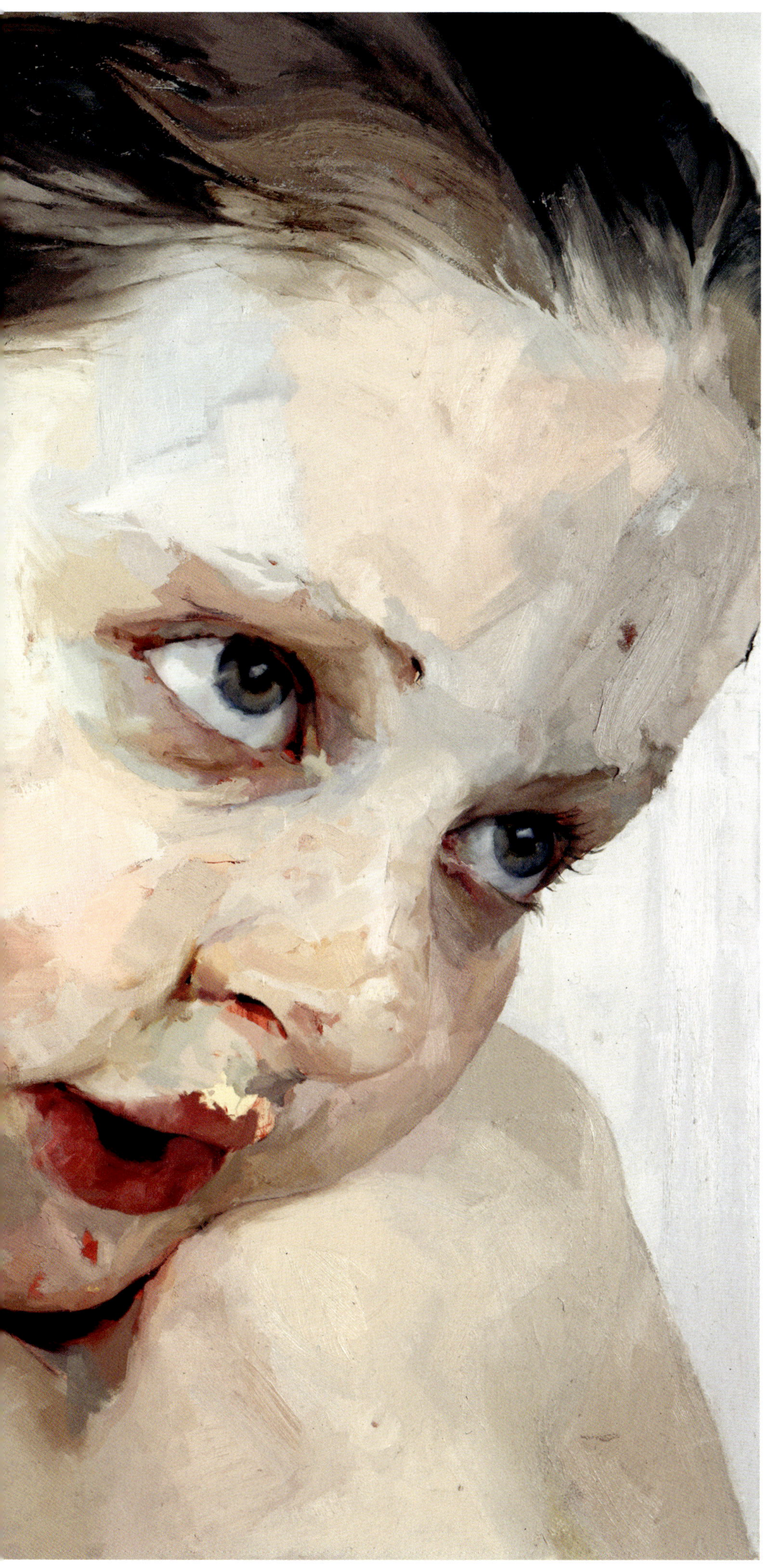

4 *Hyphen* 1999

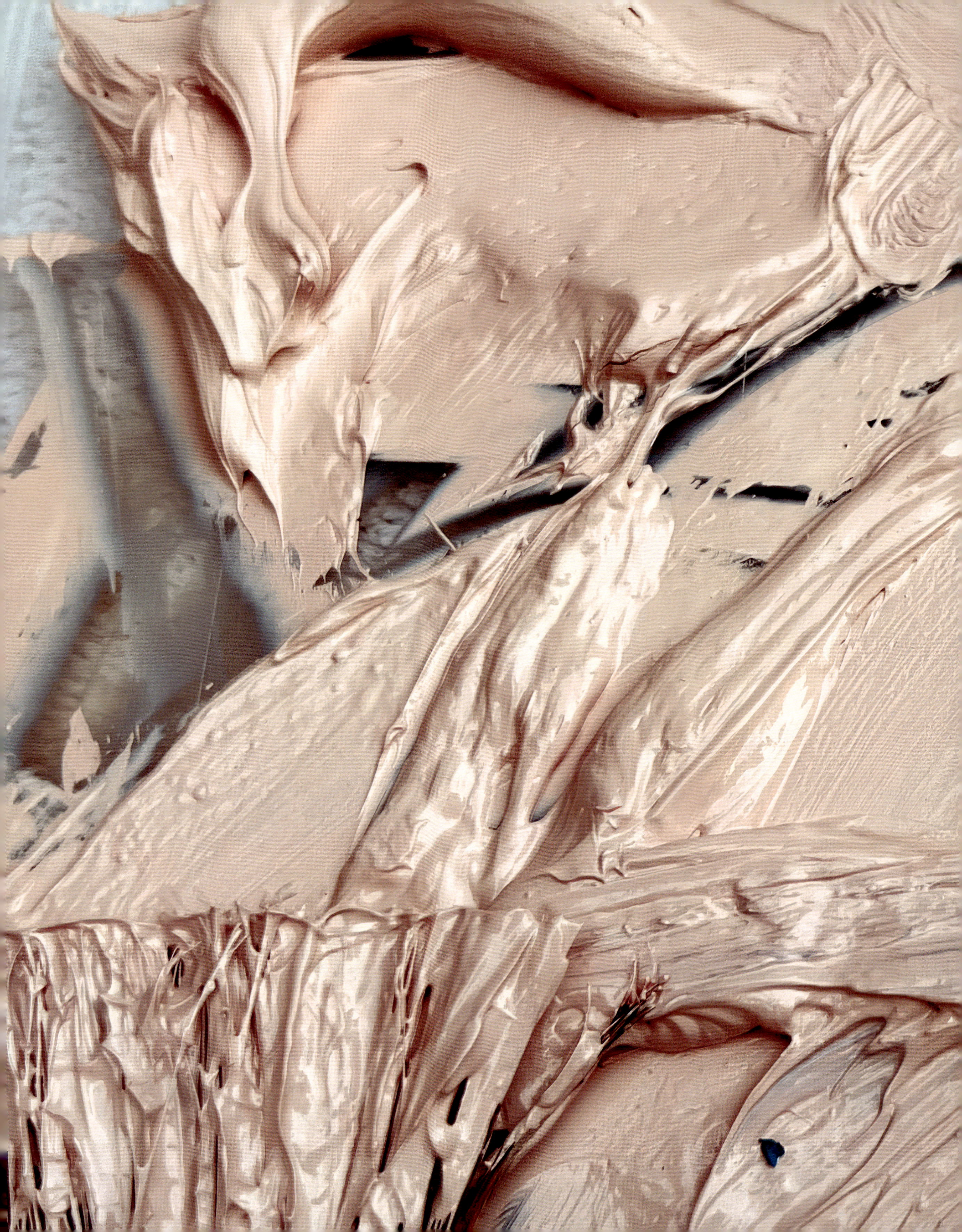

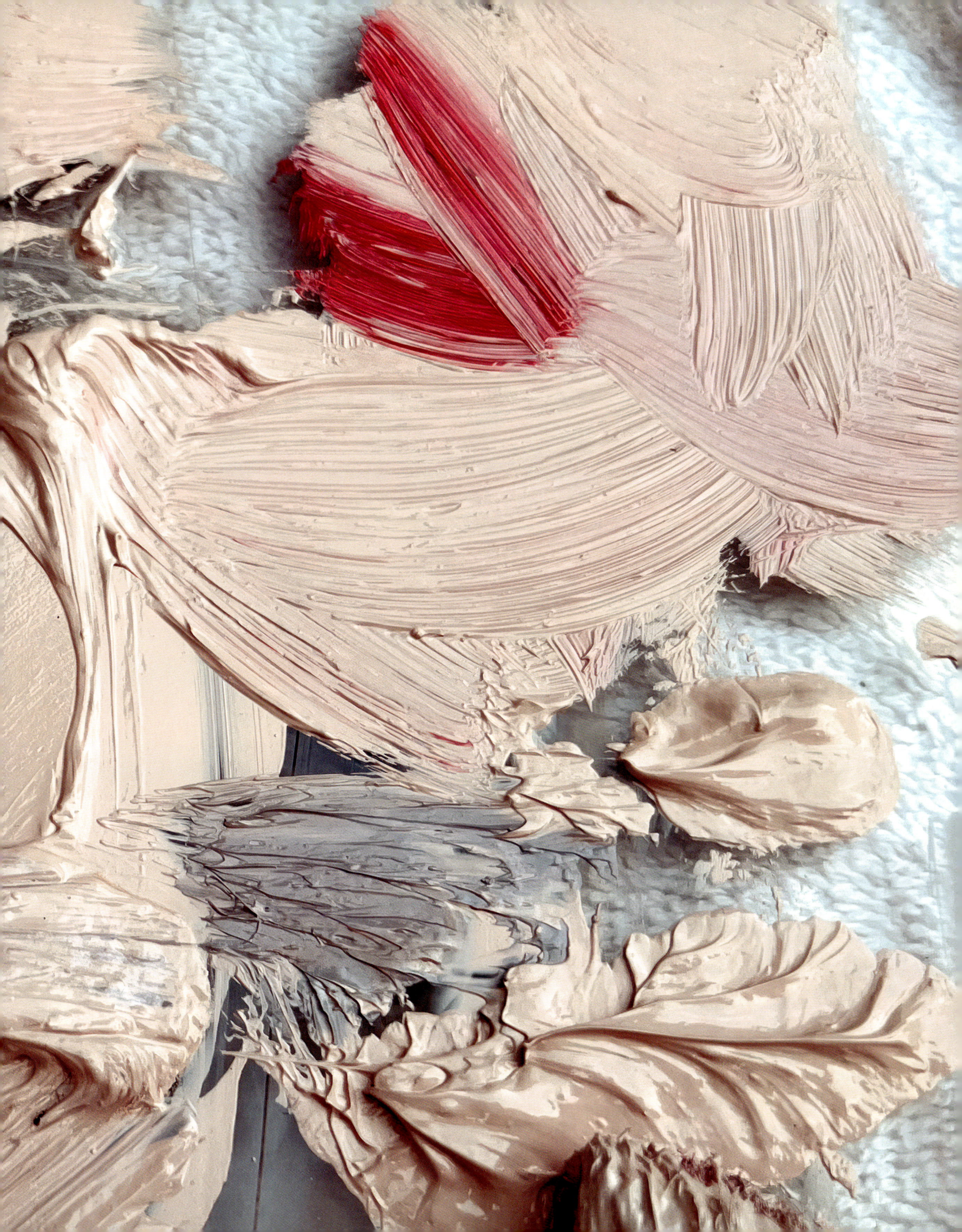

5 *Ruben's Flap* 1998–9

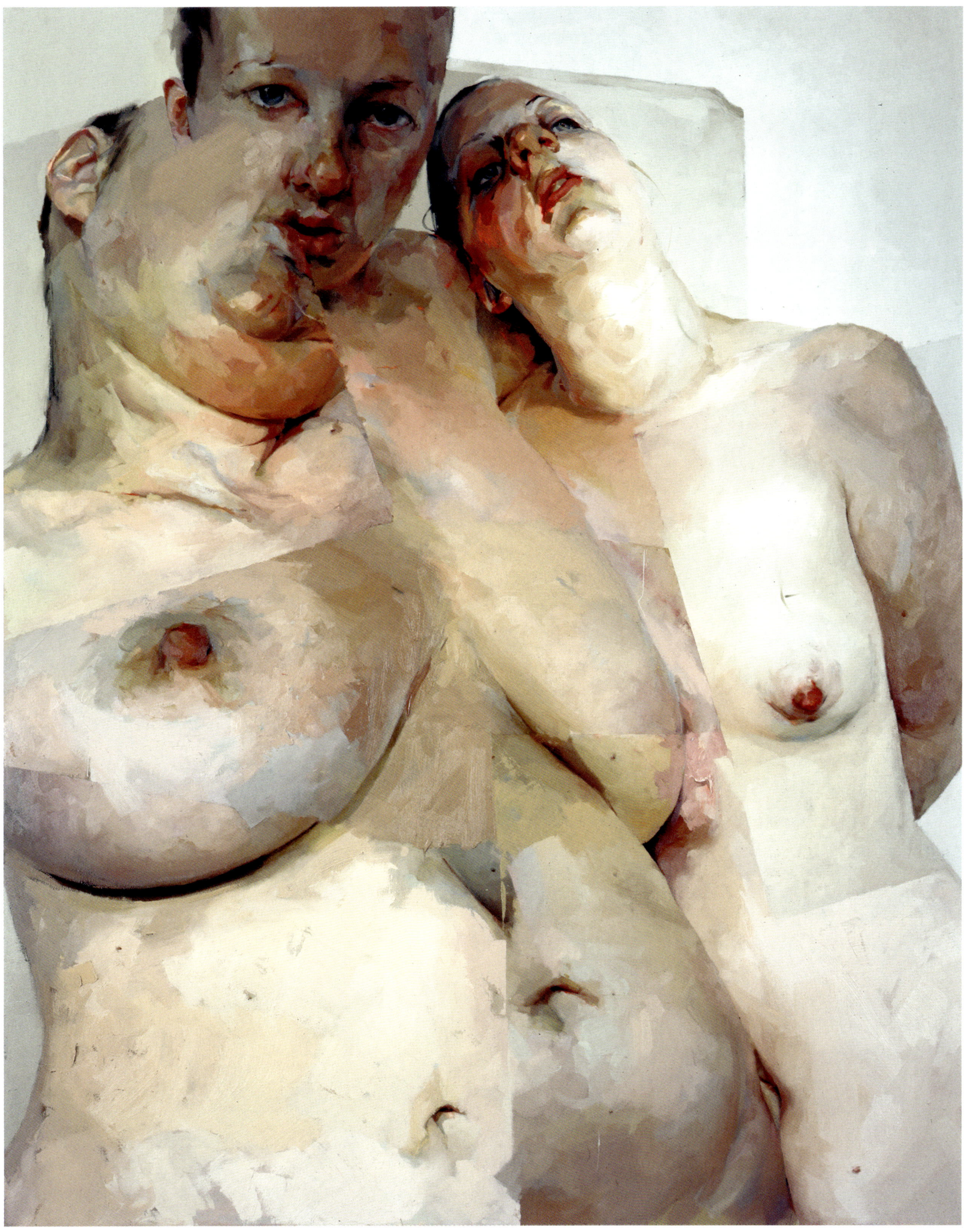

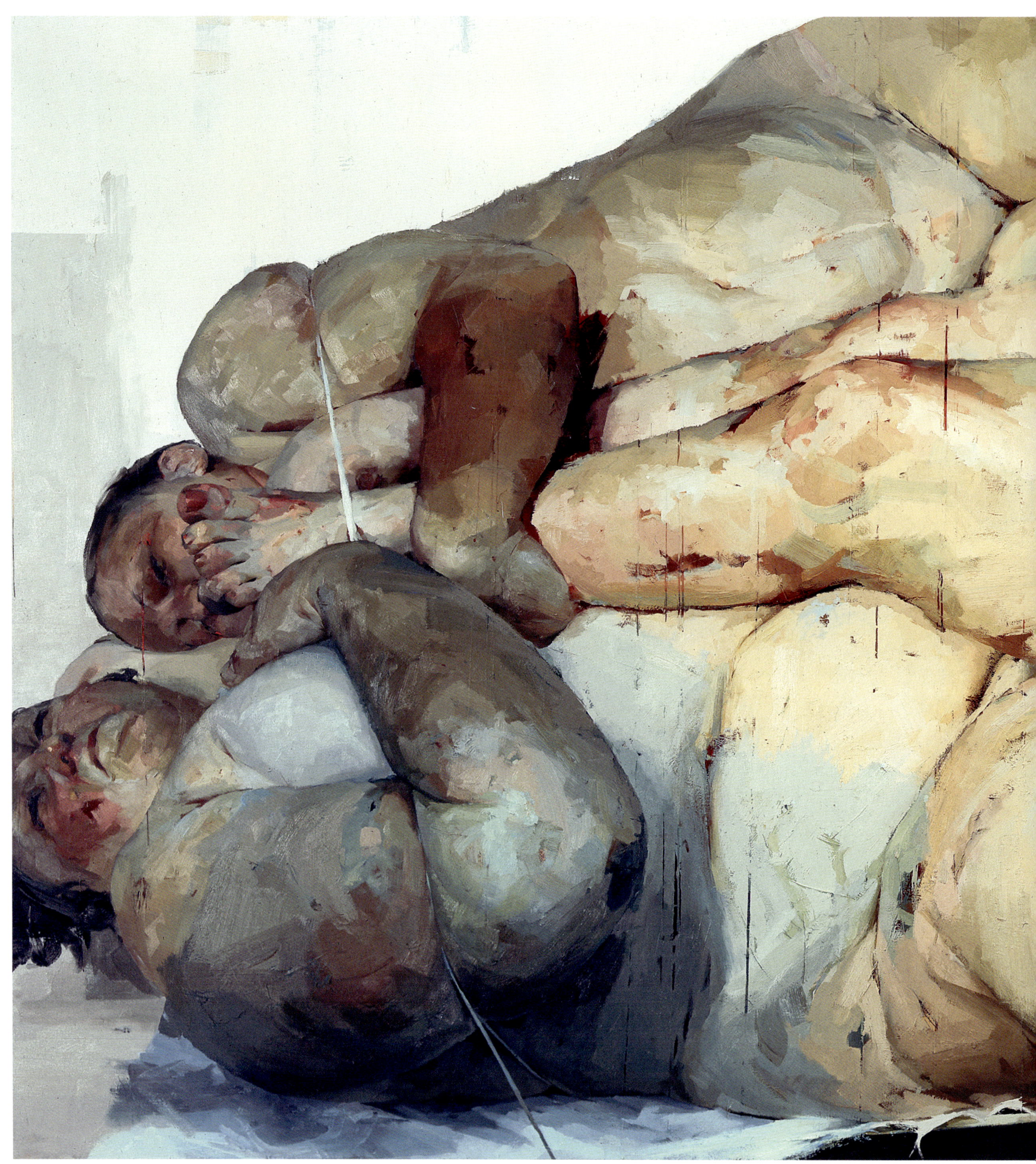

6 *Fulcrum* 1998–9

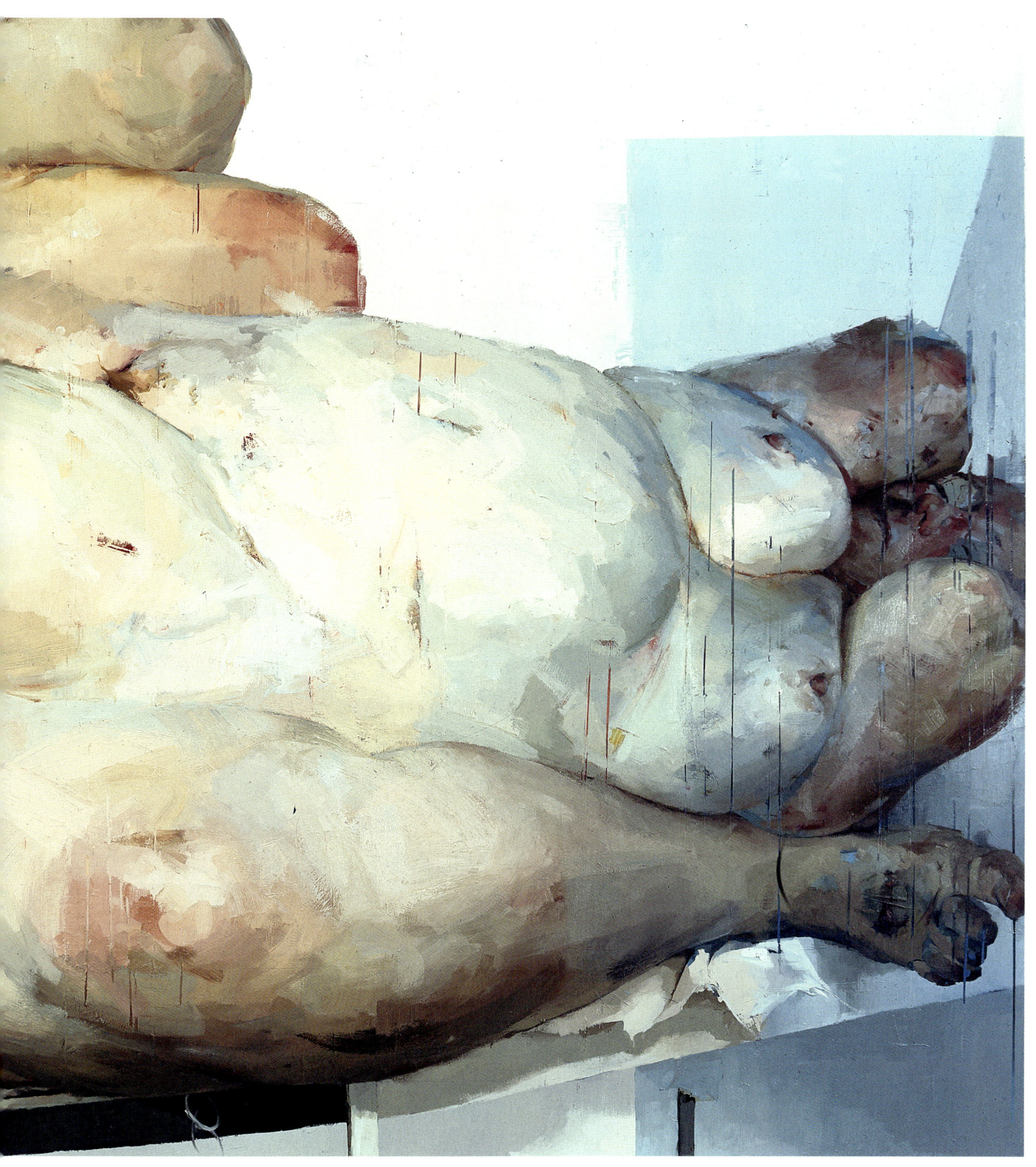

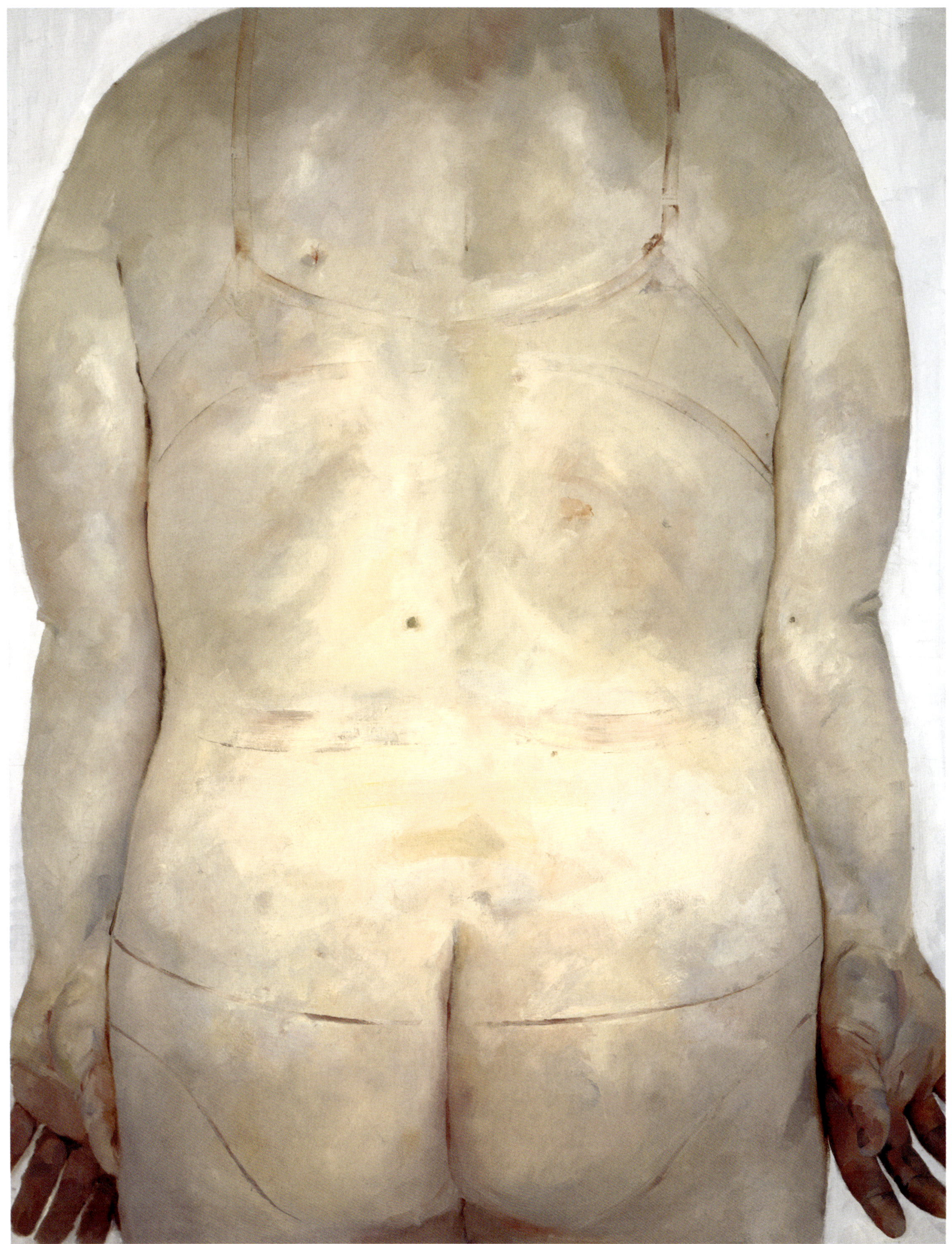

7 *Trace* 1993

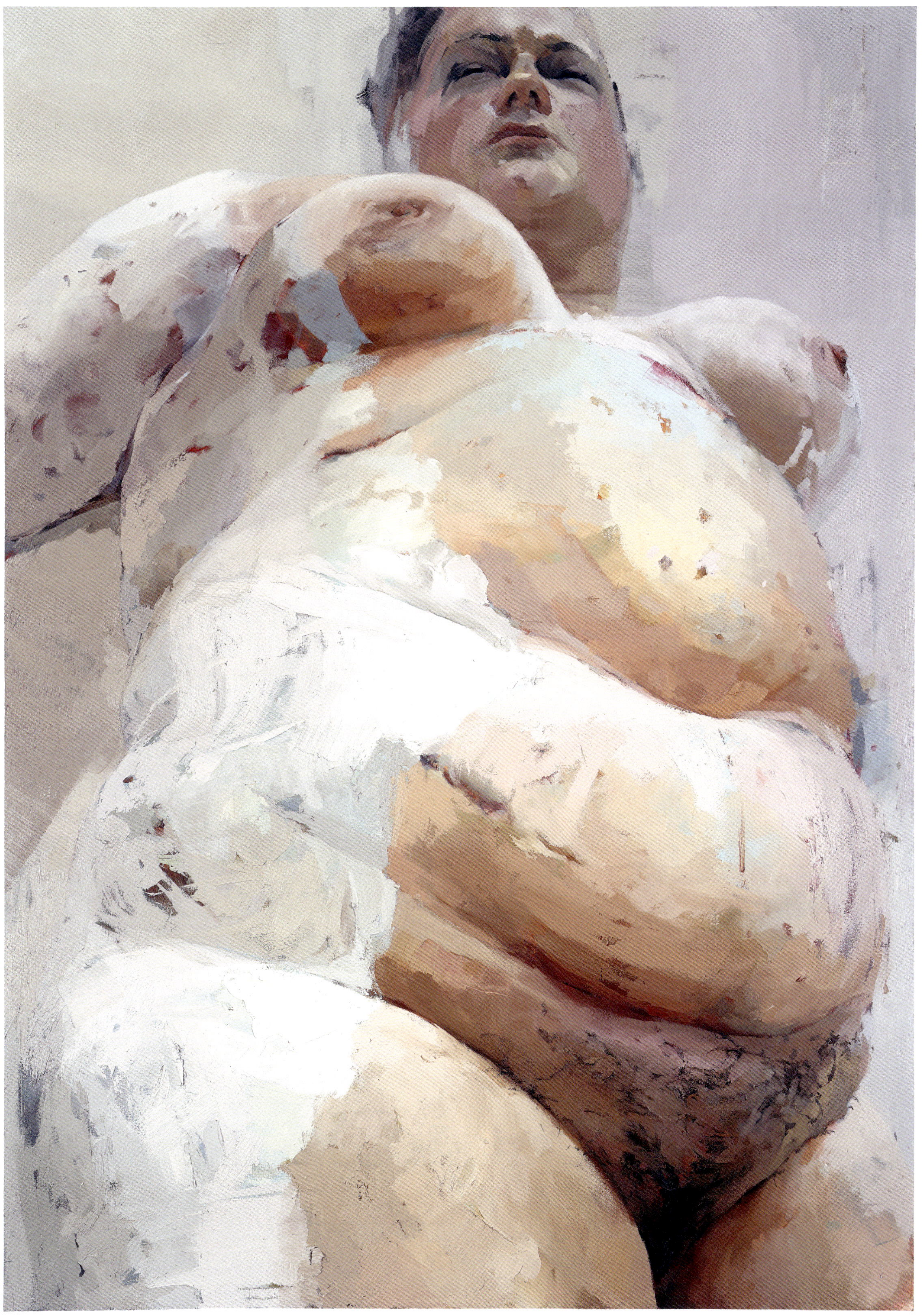

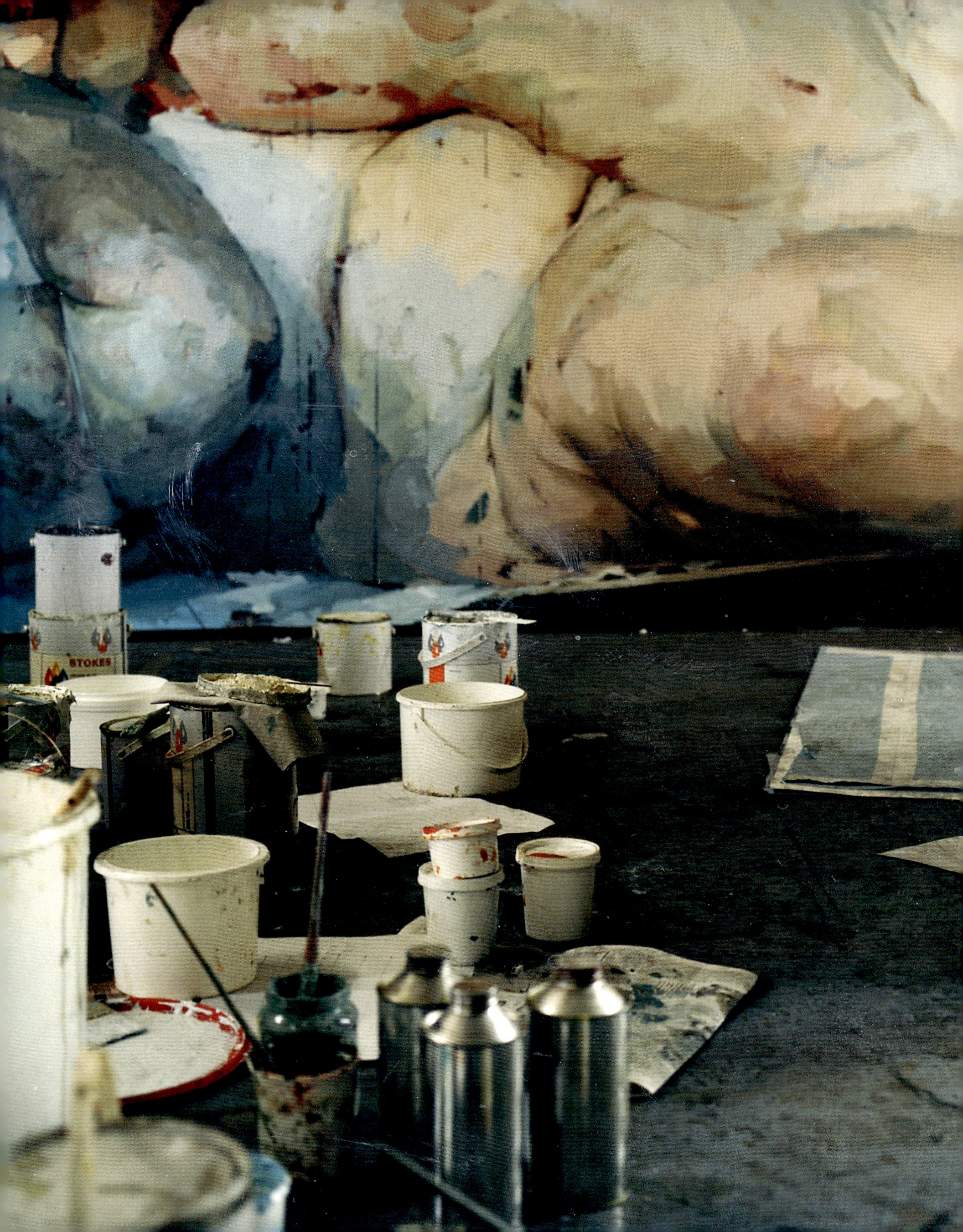
STOKES

Unabashed, Abundant Bodies

Roxane Gay

When I first saw Jenny Saville's large-scale paintings of naked women, often fat, I was suspicious. I live in a fat body. I know how this body is viewed and treated and judged by most people. It has taken most of my adult life to make peace with my body and to recognise that I have as much right to take up space as anyone else. And still, some days are more difficult than others. Some days, there is no peace to be found. It is hard to admit this because I believe, at least in theory, in body positivity or… fat positivity or… body neutrality. The terms evolve but the overall idea is the same – we should feel at home in our bodies. We have the right to feel at home in our bodies. And, if we dare, we have the right to celebrate our bodies, exactly as they are.

We do not live in a world that is generous toward fat women. We are often the subjects of mockery and derision. We live in unruly bodies and are punished for it. Fat women are rarely portrayed or seen as anything but lacking – lacking desirability beneath the harsh scrutiny of the male gaze, and lacking discipline to conform to societal beauty standards. And as we live in our fat bodies and do the work of embracing our fat bodies, we must also contend with our culture's profound lack of generosity toward our bodies.

I am fifty years old. By any measure, I am in the middle of my life. While I plan on living for a long while, I do know that the time I have left is not something I can take for granted. And I don't want to waste my energy on much of the nonsense that preoccupied me during the first fifty years. I don't know that I am getting wiser as I get older, but I do know I have less patience for self-loathing. It is tedious. It takes up so much energy. And it serves nothing. When you are reviled, nothing will change the minds of the people who harbour such profound animosity toward you. They will not hate you less if you hate yourself more. I try to hold onto this truth as I live each day in my unruly body.

There I was in The Broad in Los Angeles, transfixed by *Strategy* (fig.1), a massive triptych in oil of a fat woman wearing only a bra and panties, presented from three different angles. The paintings stretch across twenty-one feet and stretch up nine feet. Here, is an incredible body taking up an incredible amount of space. The painting's subject is staring down, her expression inscrutable. Her body is a glorious bounty – beautiful expanses of flesh curving around her frame. There is a defiance in the woman's face and strength, in this painting and in all Saville's paintings of bodies. The layers of paint create added dimension as does the use of light and shadow. The canvas practically pulsates. I stood in front of that painting and, I was certainly wary. I wanted to understand why Saville had chosen a woman in this kind of body as the subject of her art. And then I had to ask myself, why shouldn't she make a painting like this? Why was I so distrustful? Why was I so uncomfortable? I did not mind these questions. Good art should make us uncomfortable. It should make us rethink how we see ourselves, how we see others, how we see the world around us.

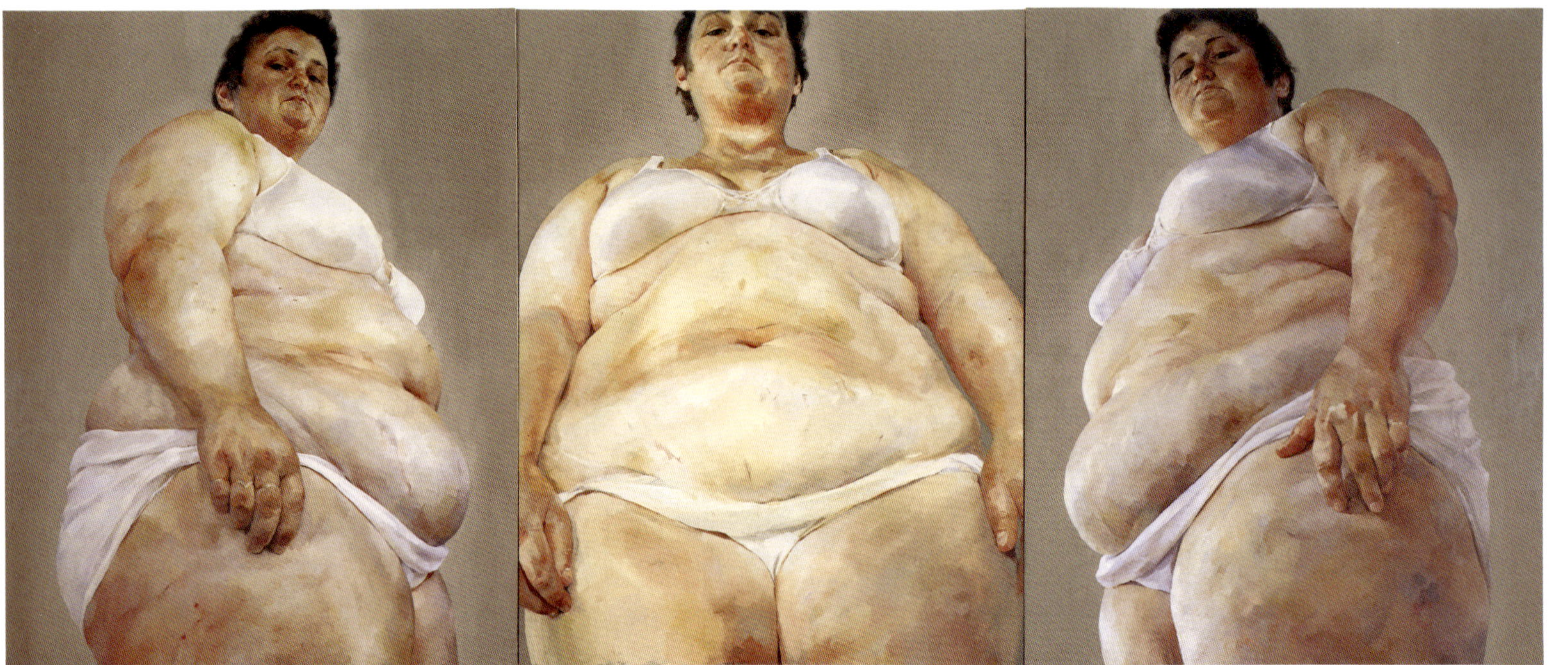

I must have stood in front of *Strategy* for at least a half hour as I contemplated the painting and the questions it asked. I was… transfixed, because I had never really seen a body like mine displayed without judgment. I quickly came to realise that the only judgment in that space, on that day, was the judgment I carried. As I've gotten to know Saville's work since, I have been absolutely obsessed with how she paints the fat body. In looking at her work, I am able to set aside what our culture tells me I should think and feel about fat bodies. Instead, I see an artist's curiosity. I see frankness and honesty. Women's bodies are rendered lushly – voluptuous breasts and ample bellies and thick thighs. We see the hairy triangles between those thick thighs, and languorous expressions as woman stare into the distance or look down at something we cannot see or look out from the canvas and into the beholder.

On Saville's canvasses, these are the bodies we live in, as they are, unadorned because no adornment is necessary. What she offers, for those willing to receive, is unabashed abundance. In *Propped* (cat.1), a bountiful, naked woman perched on a stool, as she looks up, eyes closed. Or in *Prop* (fig.2) another bountiful, naked woman perched on a stool, this time her eyes open as she looks into the distance, one leg crossed, her foot tucked under her thigh, arms crossed over her breasts. Or in *Fulcrum* (cat.6), three abundant women's naked bodies in a tangle of flesh, no borders between them so that we do not know where one

Fig.1
Jenny Saville
Strategy, 1994
Oil on canvas
2743 × 6388 mm overall
The Broad Art Foundation,
Los Angeles

Fig.2
Jenny Saville
Prop, 1993
Oil on canvas
2130 × 1830 mm
Private Collection

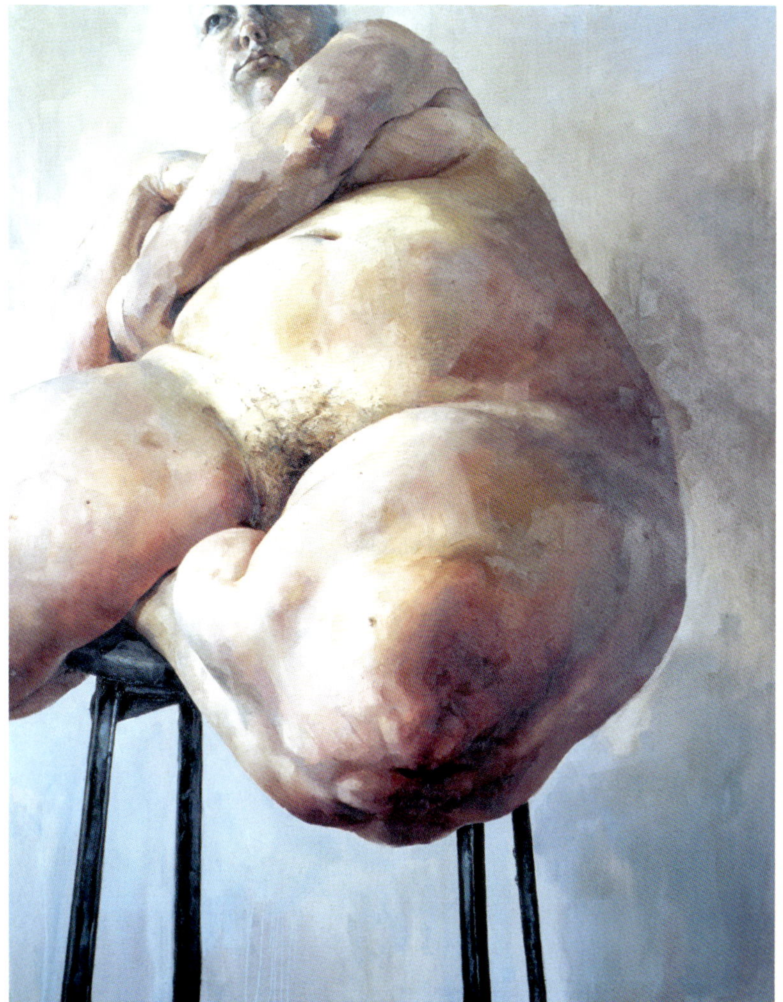

woman ends and another begins and we do not know why they have conjoined in this way, nor do we need to.

Standing in front of *Strategy*, I felt something I am not at all accustomed to feeling. I felt small. I felt seen. It was disconcerting and then it was exhilarating but it forced me to open my eyes. It forced me to see the woman before me. It forced me to see myself without looking away, or walking away. It forced me to set down my suspicions and the frisson of shame I was carrying as I thought about other museumgoers looking at me in my unruly body, looking at her in her unruly body.

Behold this big, beautiful body, the canvas commanded. Leave what you know of the world behind. Behold what all this intimate terrain offers you.

Behold.

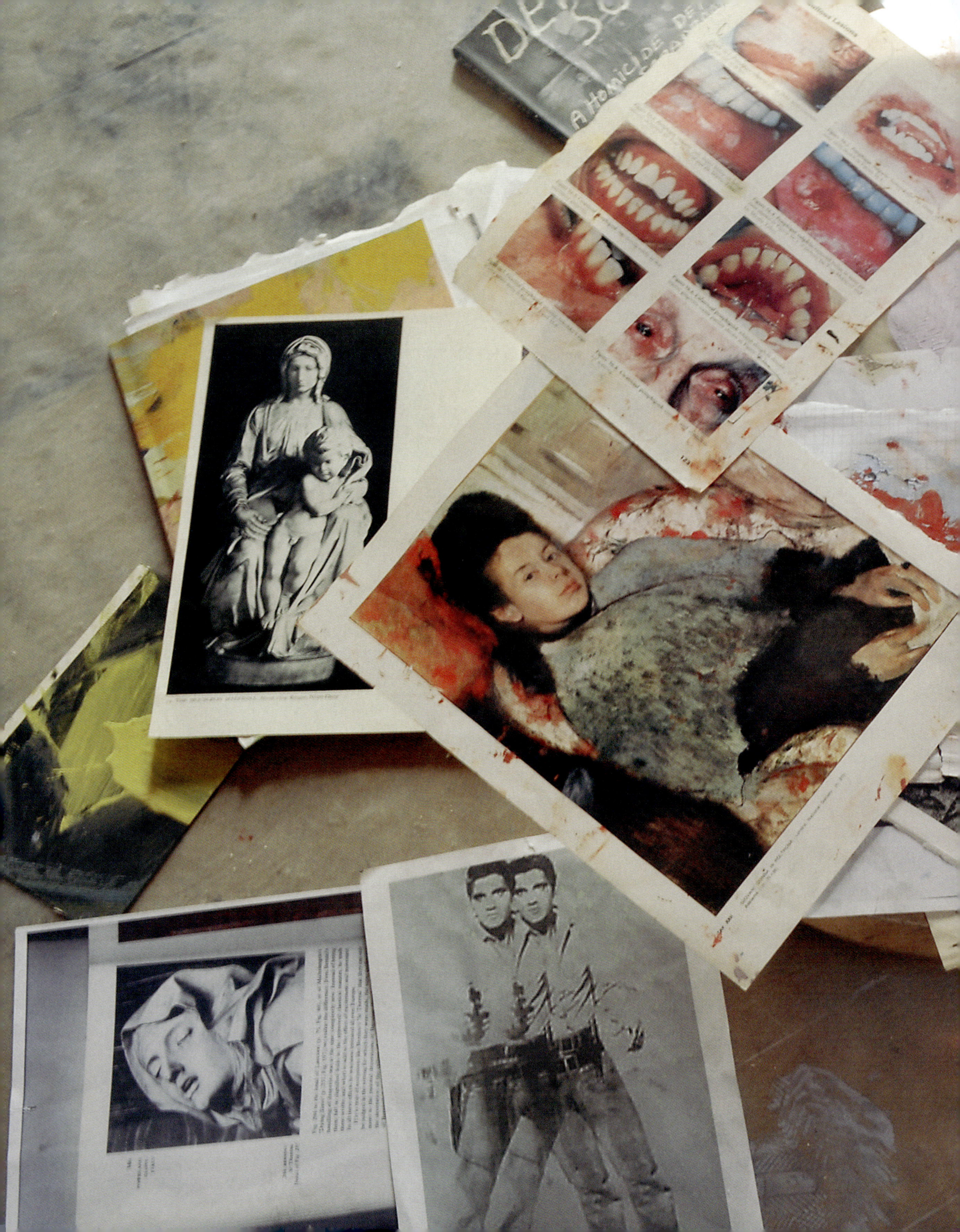

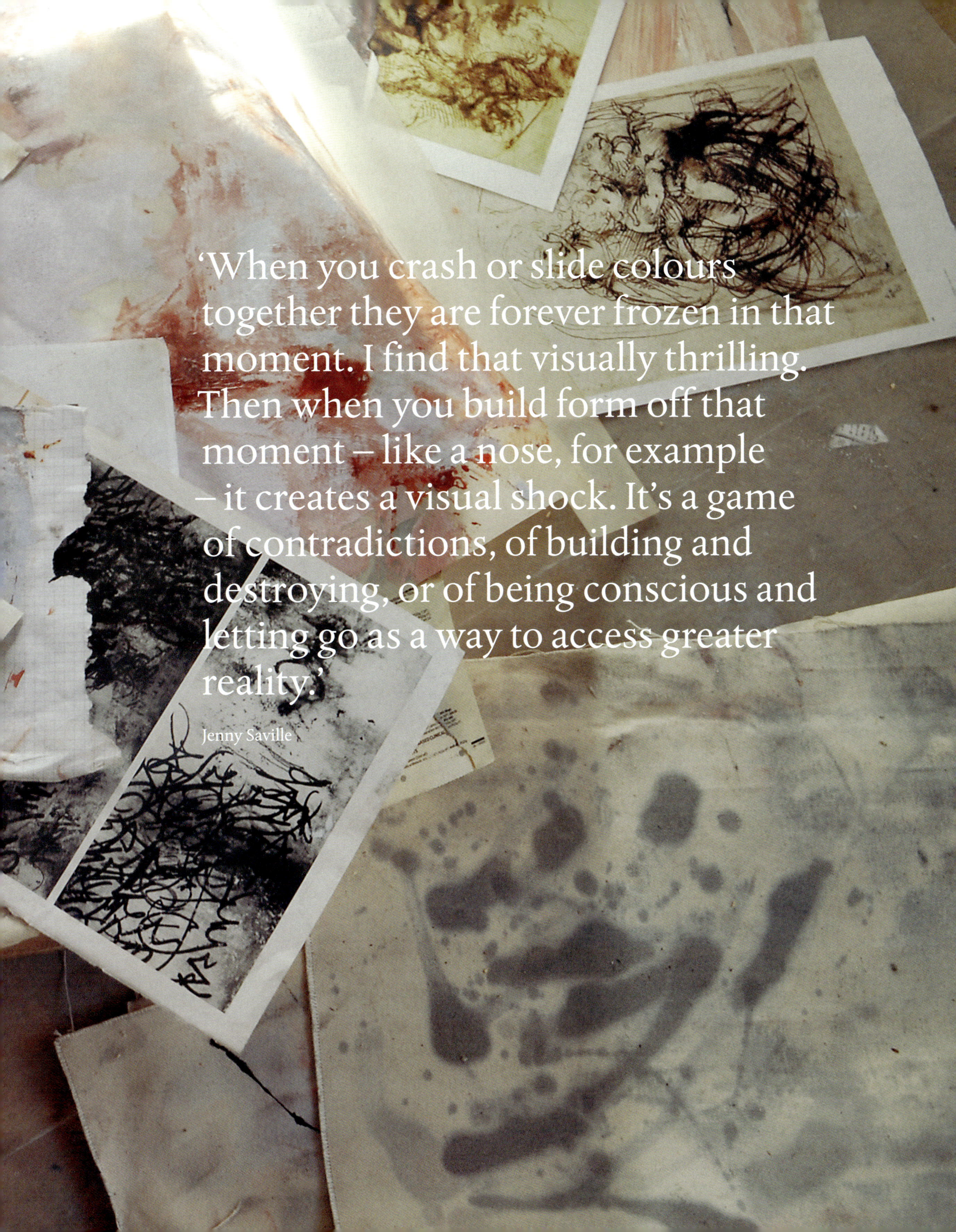

'When you crash or slide colours together they are forever frozen in that moment. I find that visually thrilling. Then when you build form off that moment – like a nose, for example – it creates a visual shock. It's a game of contradictions, of building and destroying, or of being conscious and letting go as a way to access greater reality.'

Jenny Saville

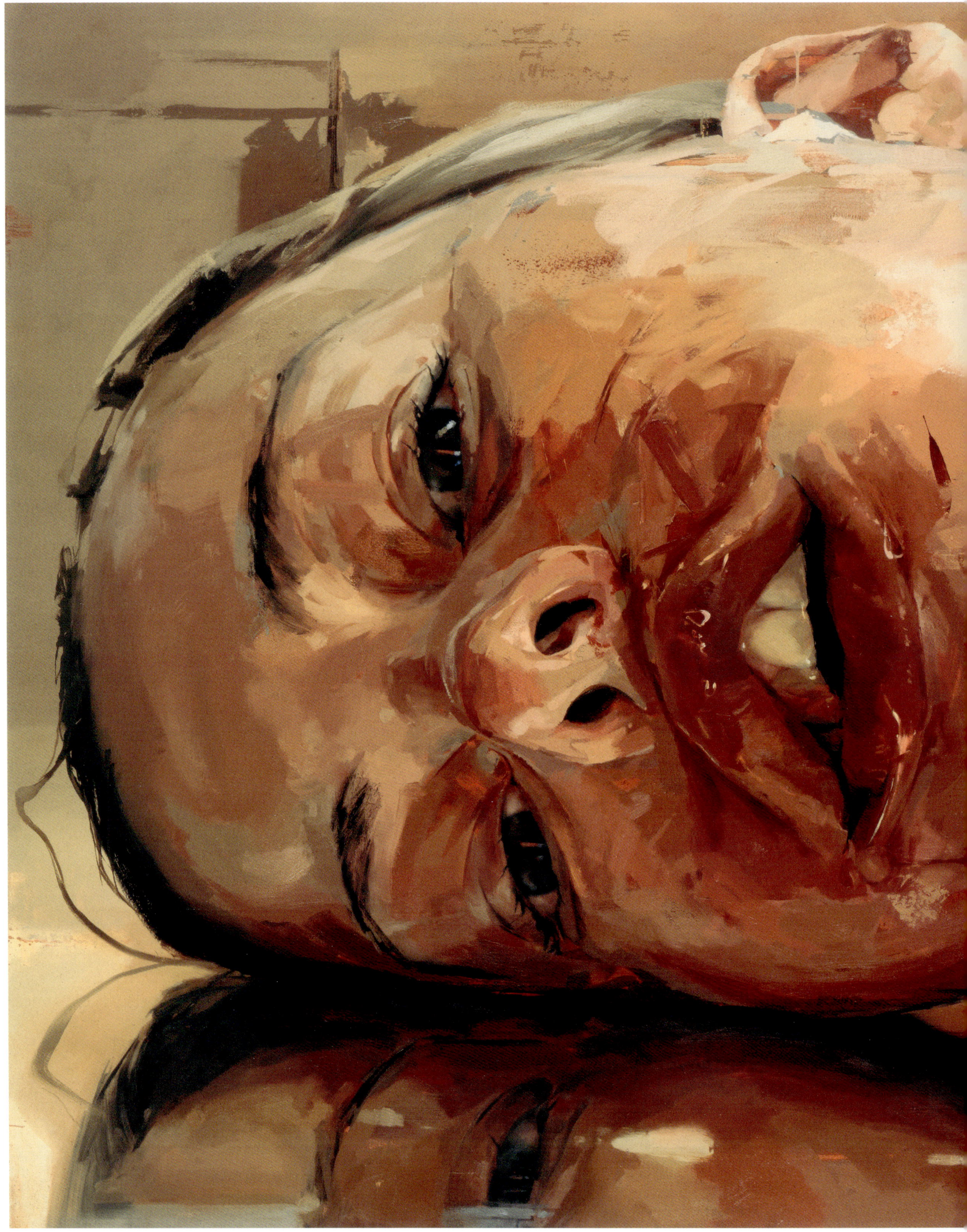

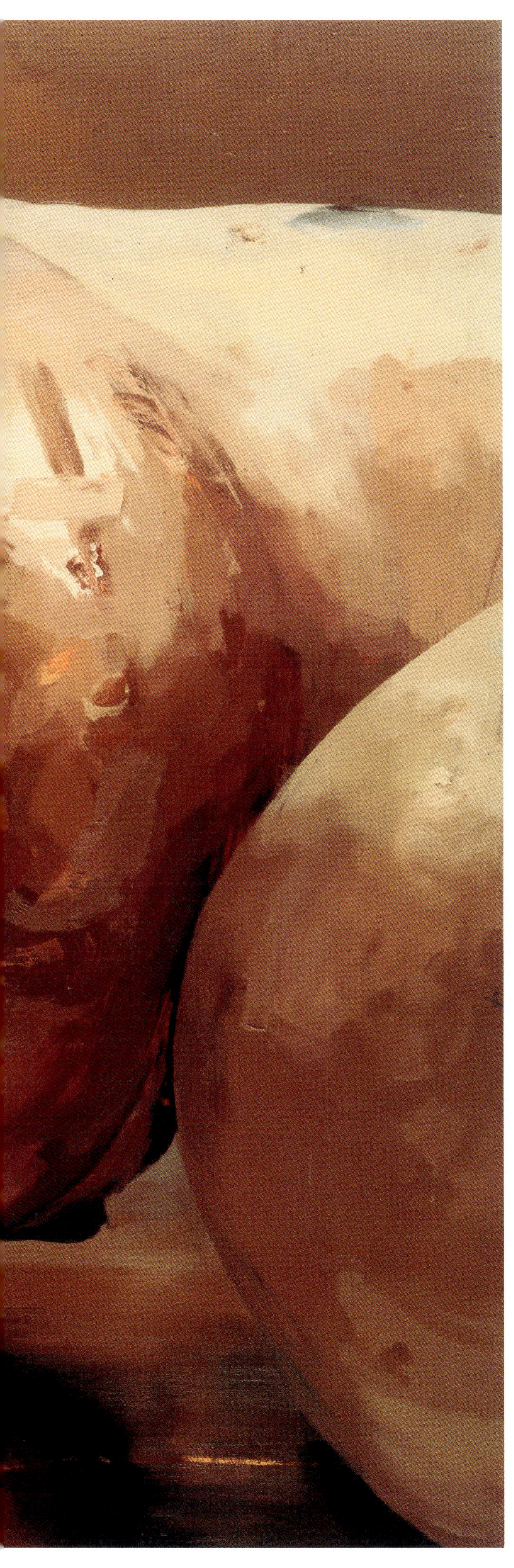

9 *Reverse* 2002–3

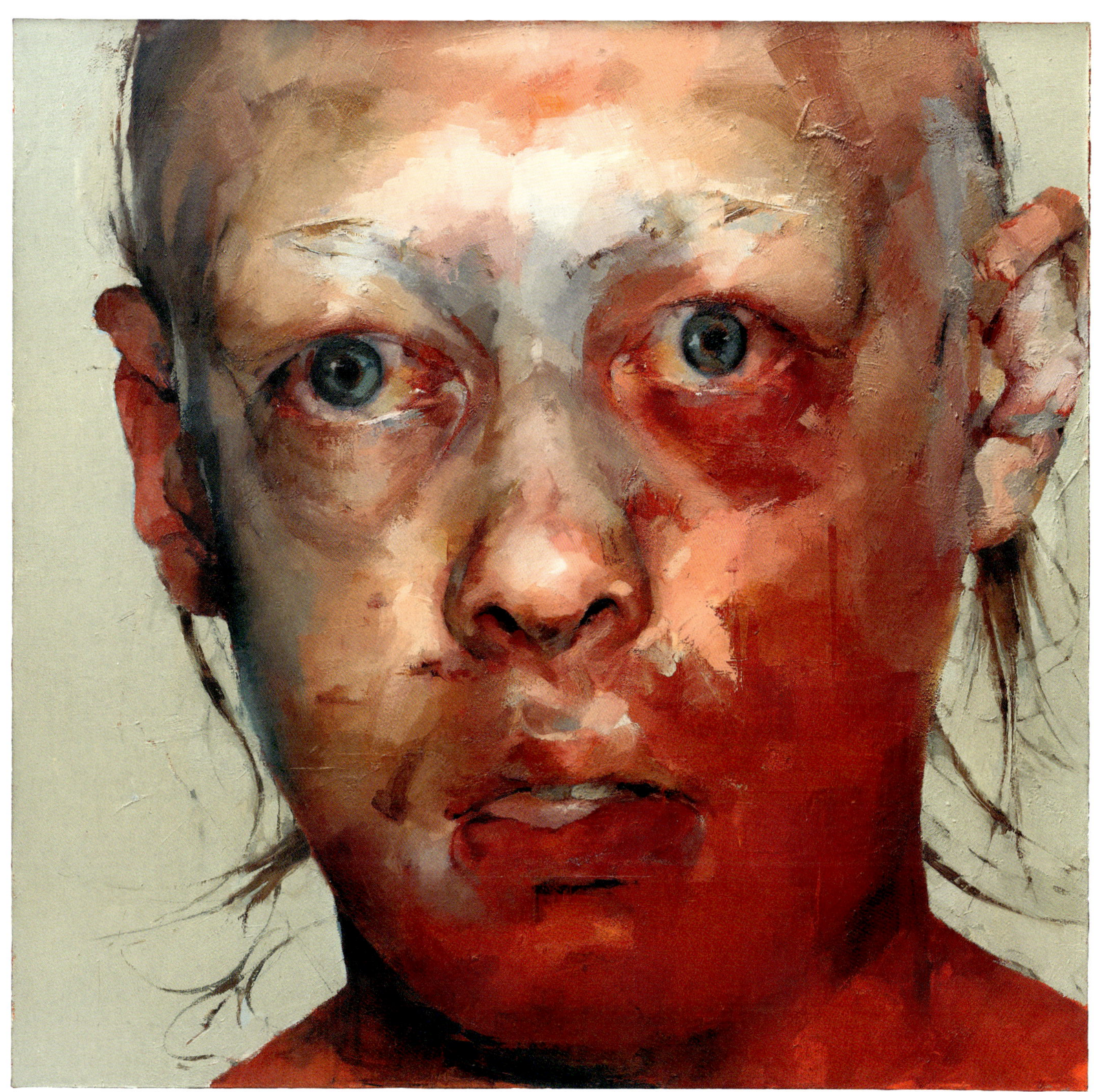

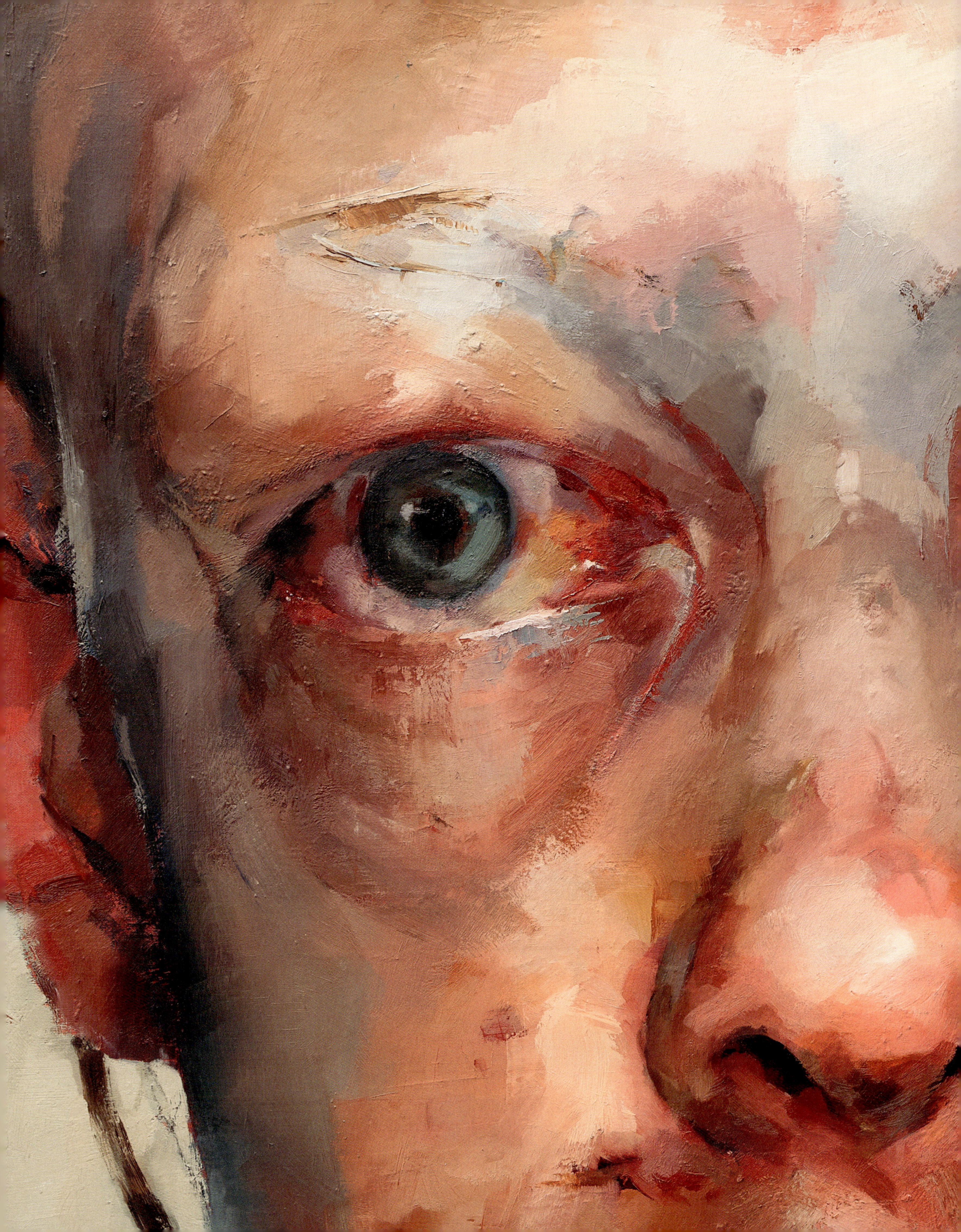

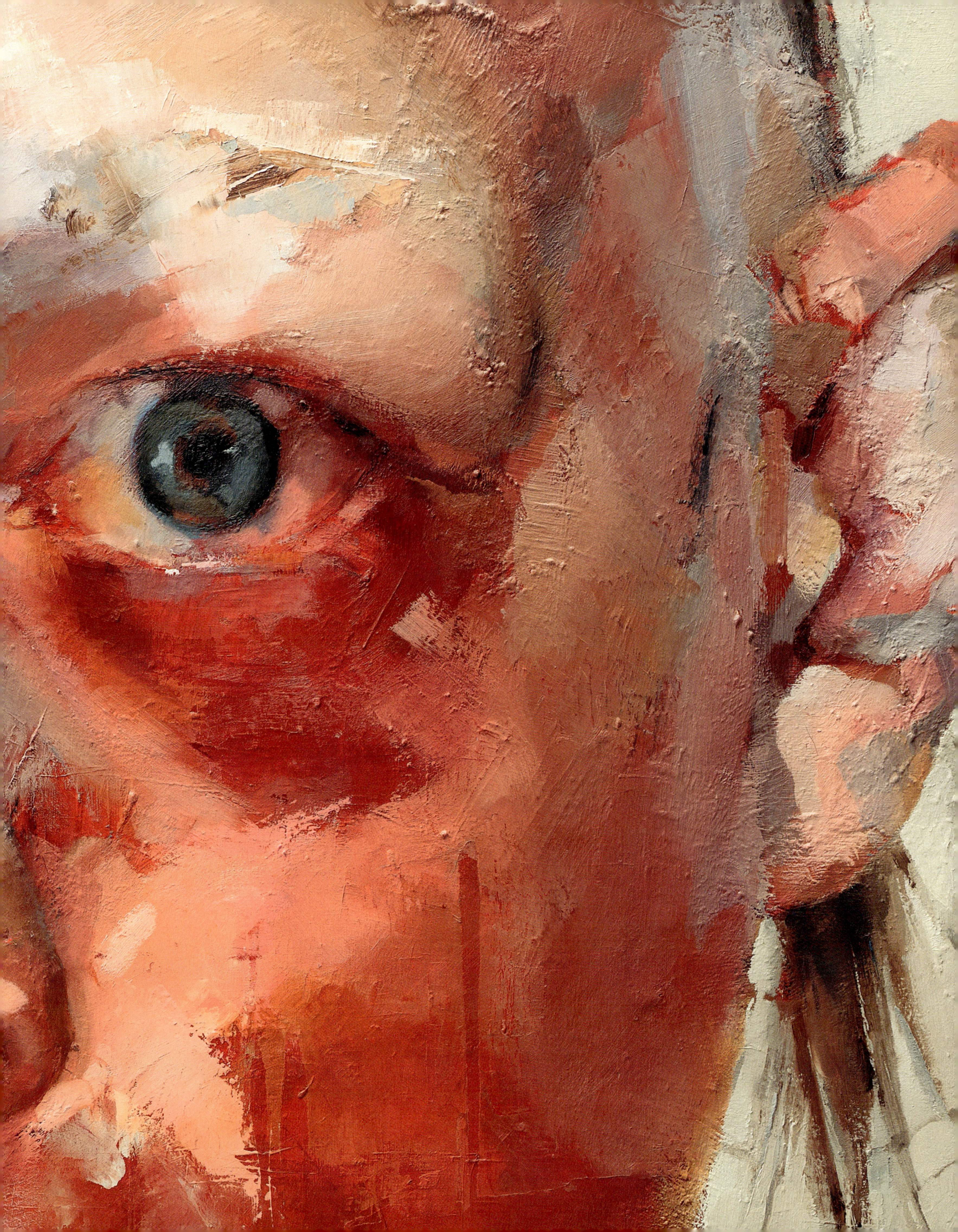

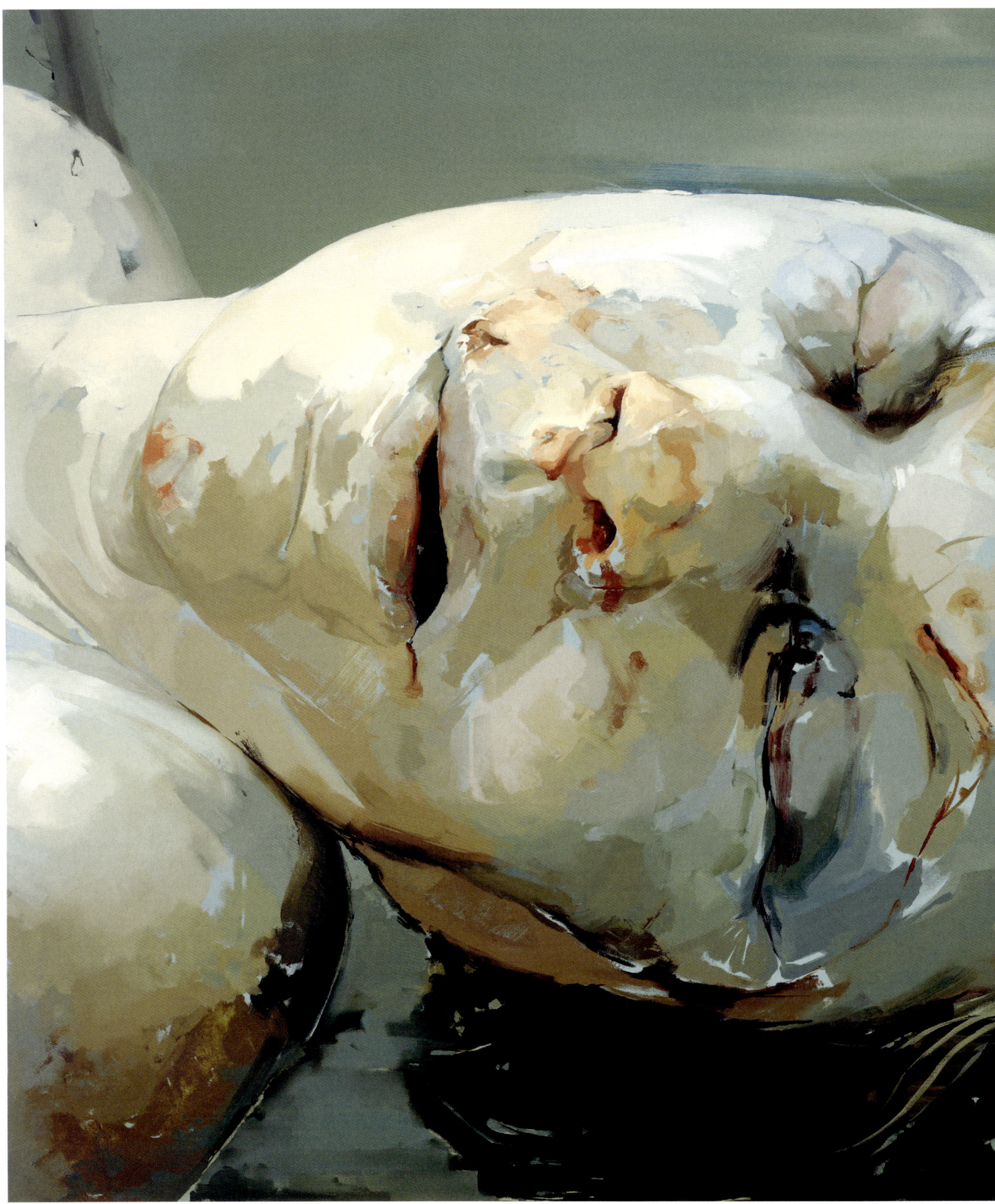

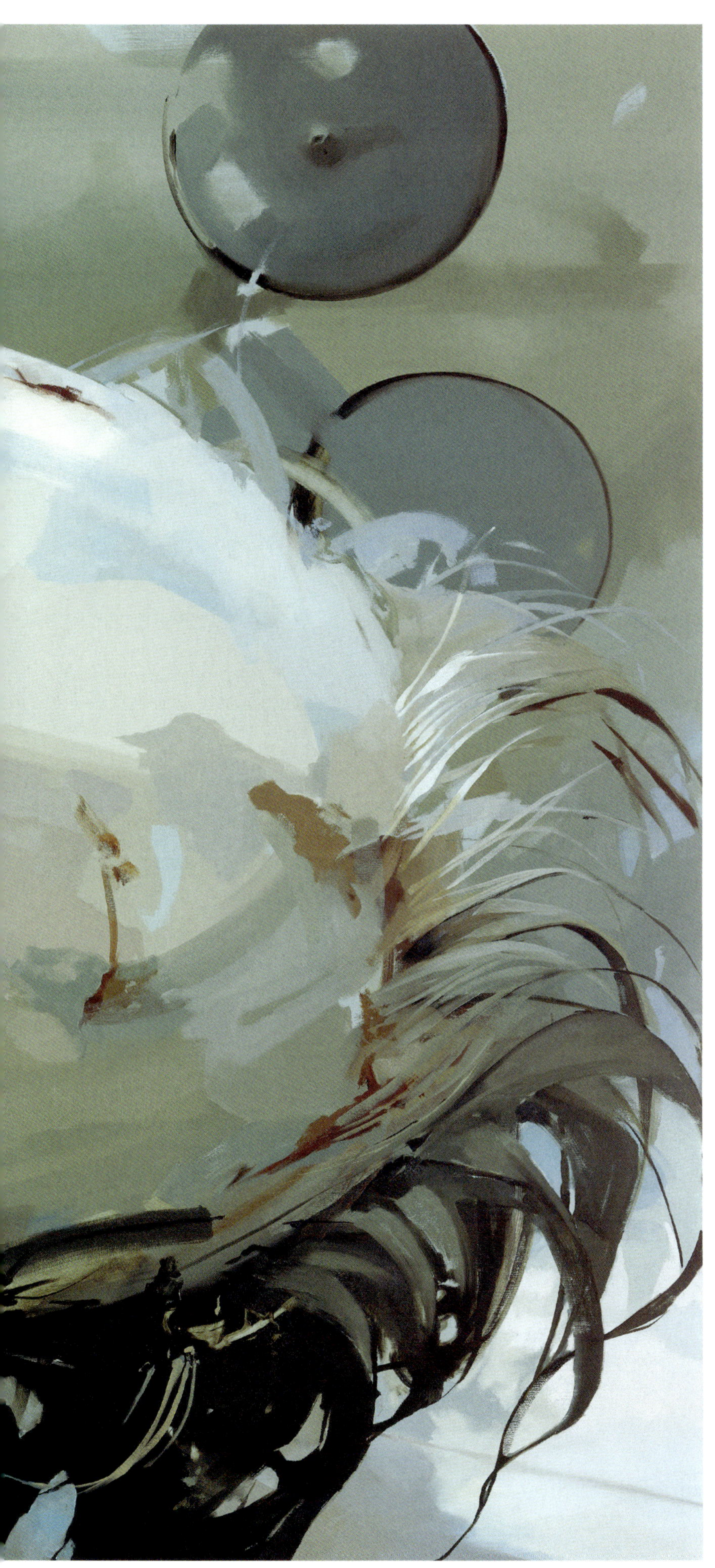

11 *Still* 2003

12 *Torso II* 2004–5

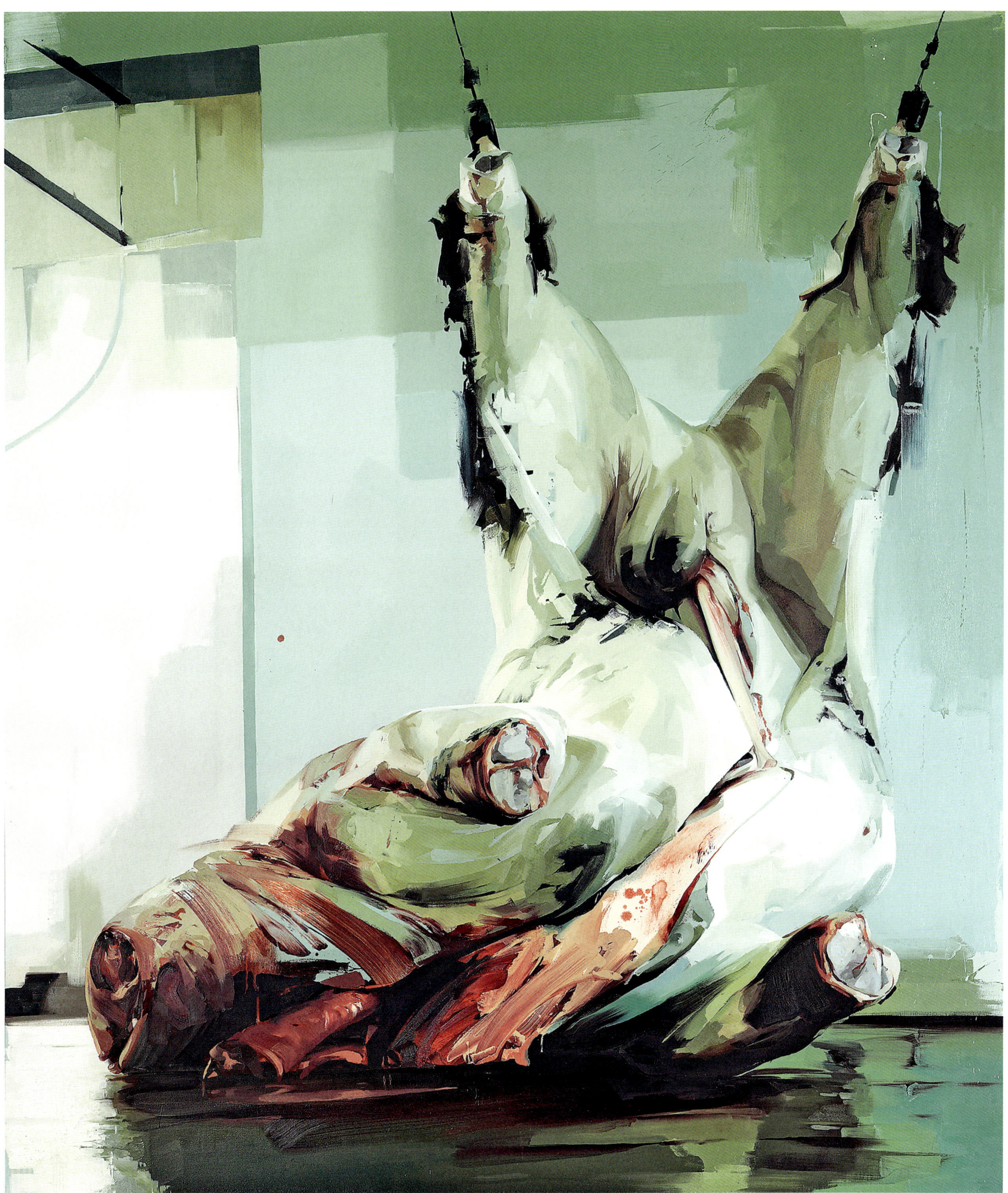

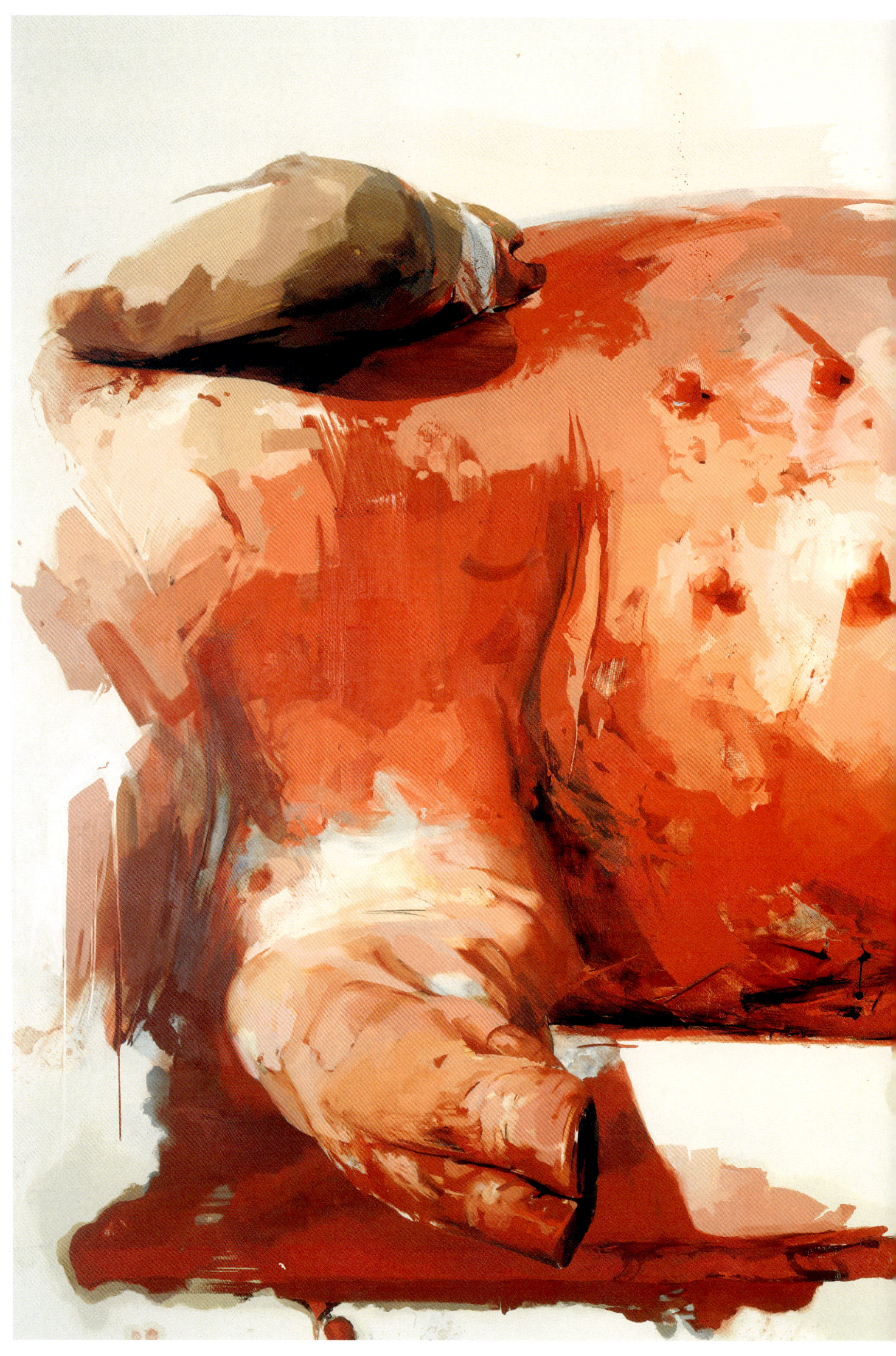

13 *Suspension* 2002–3

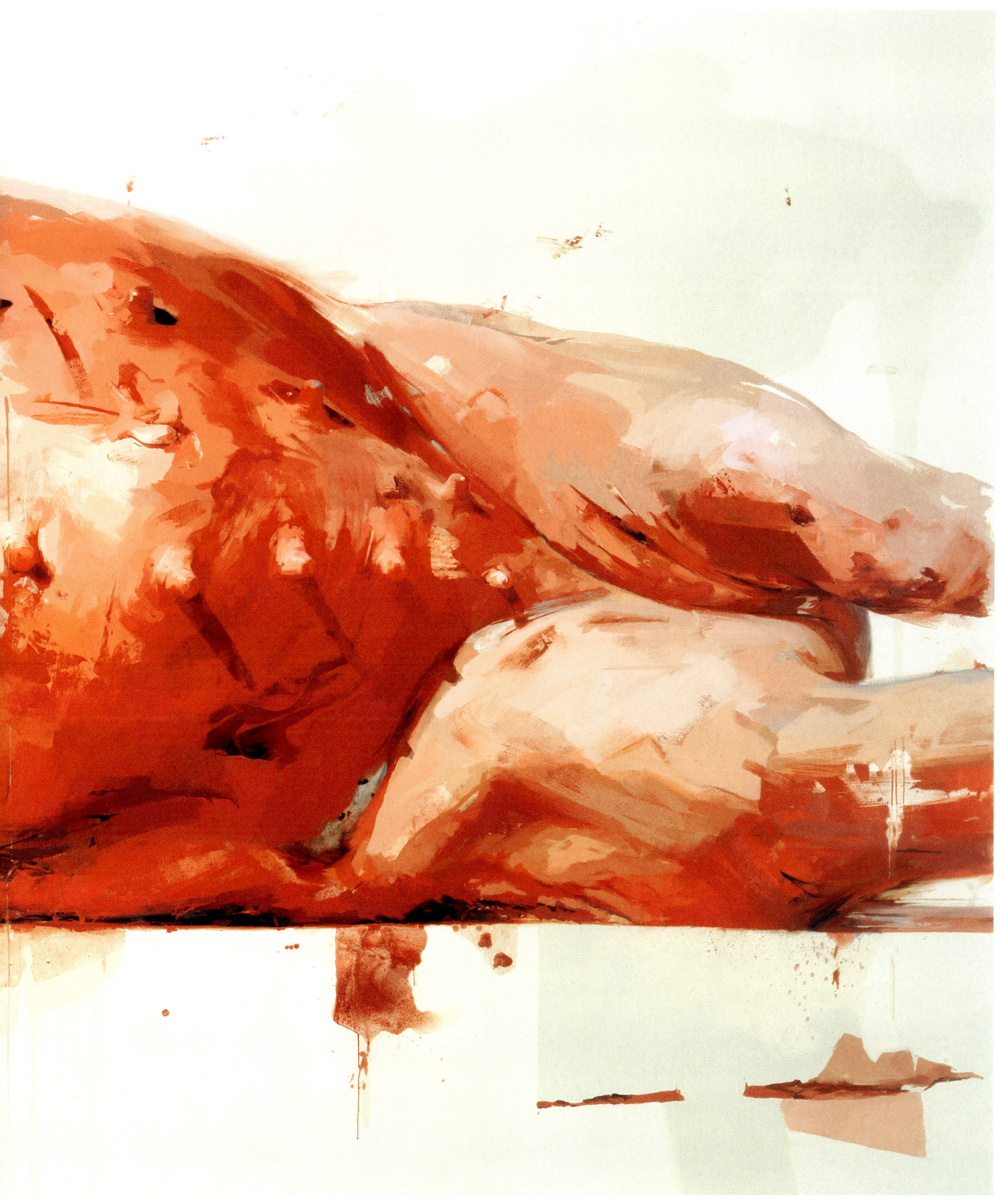

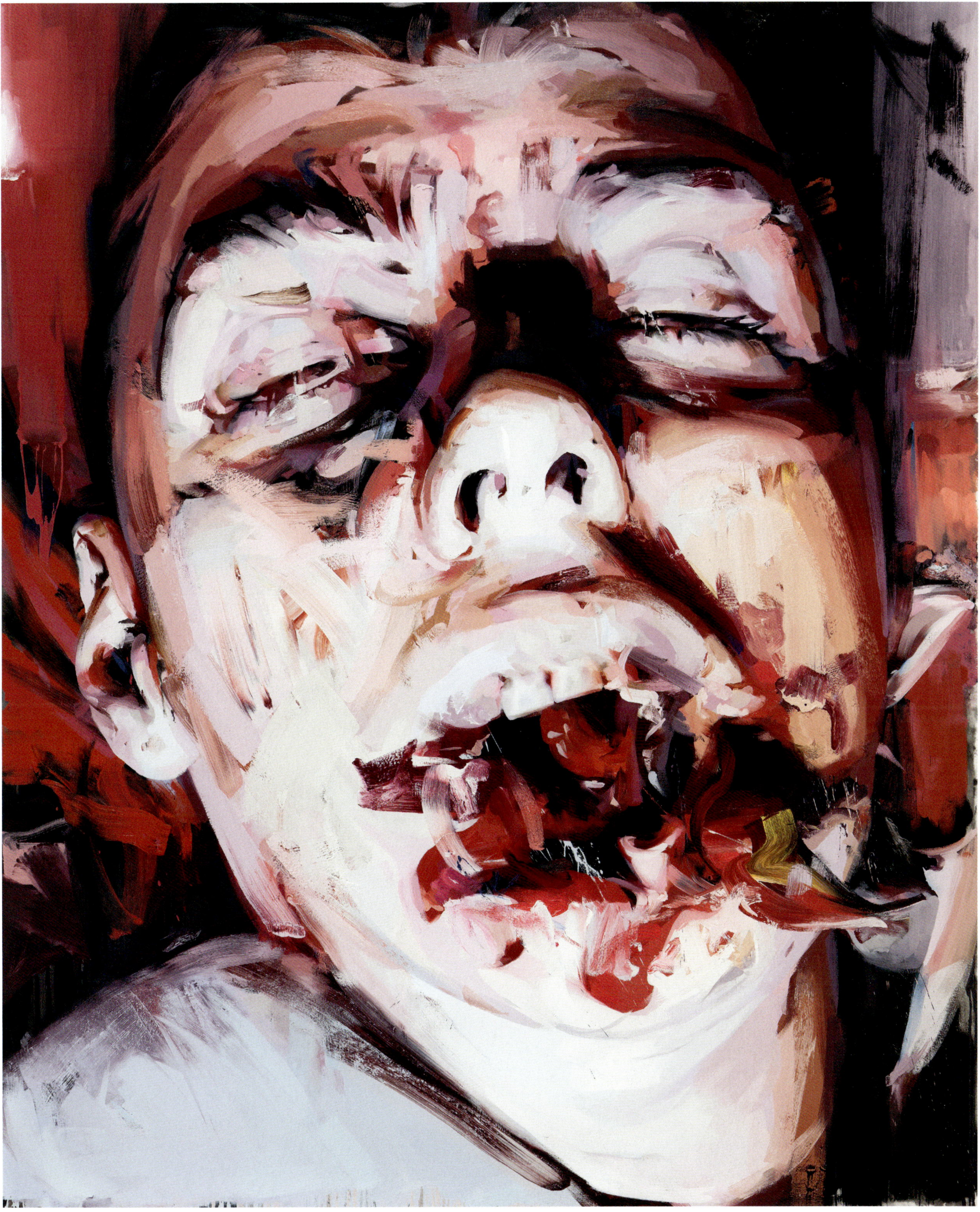

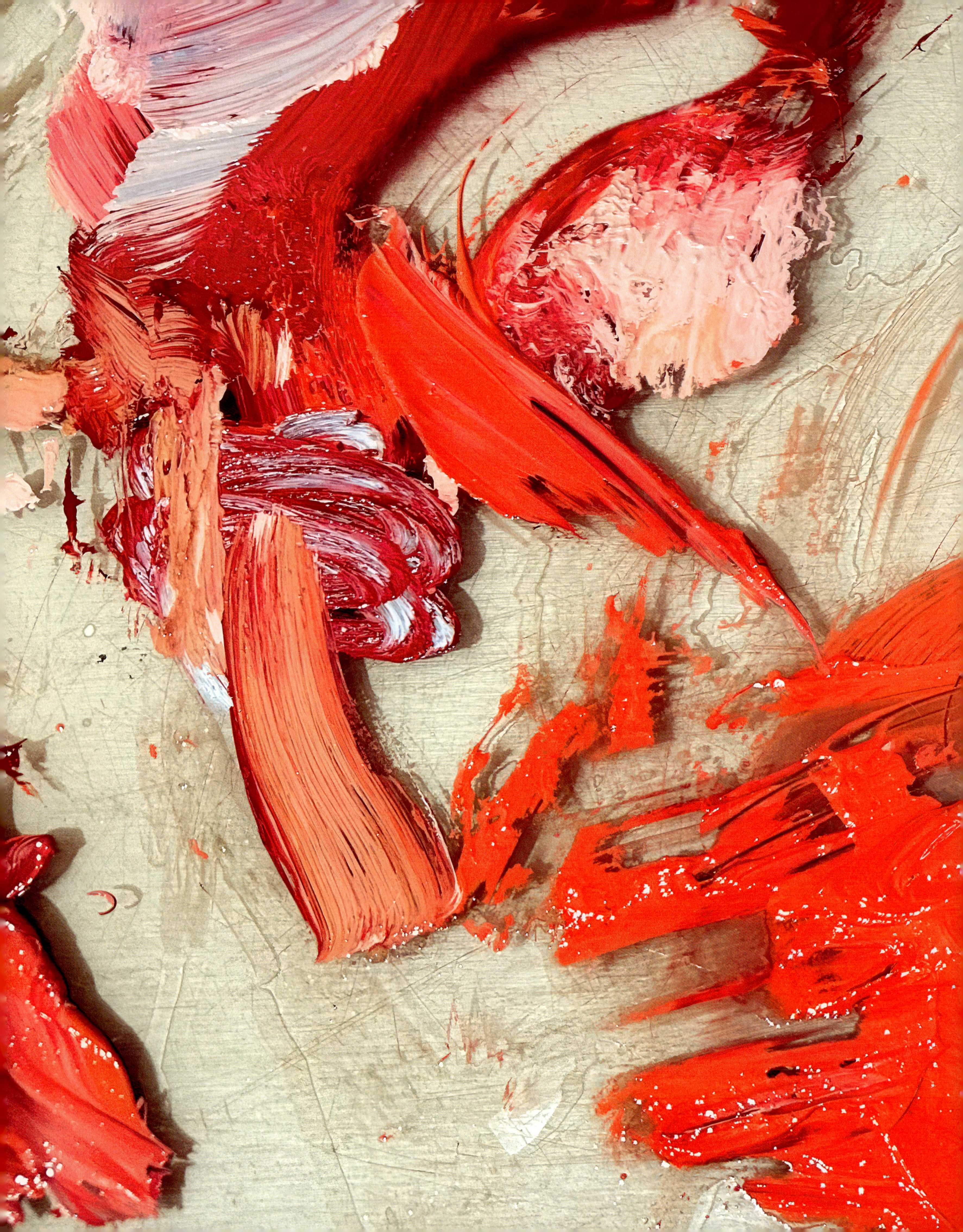

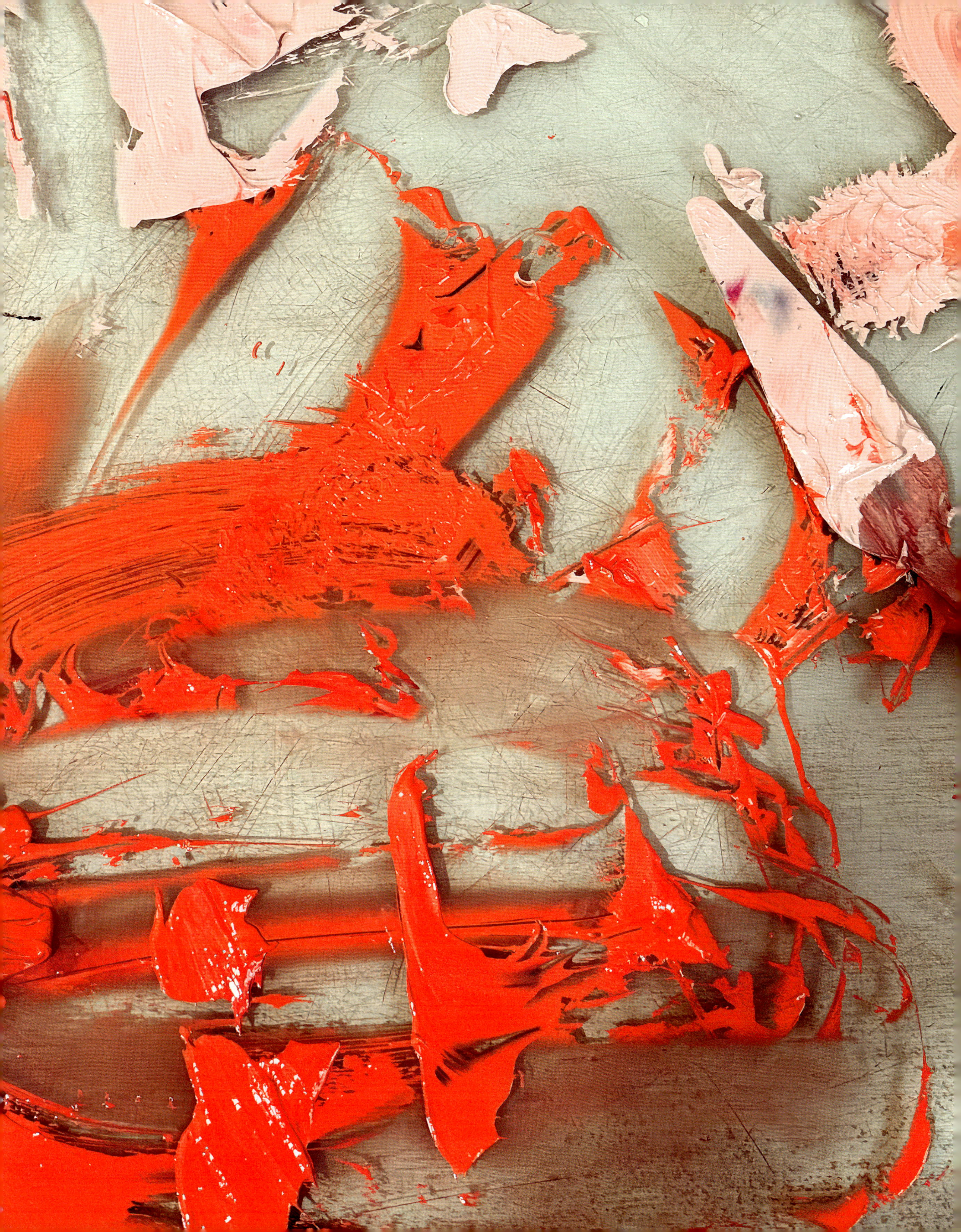

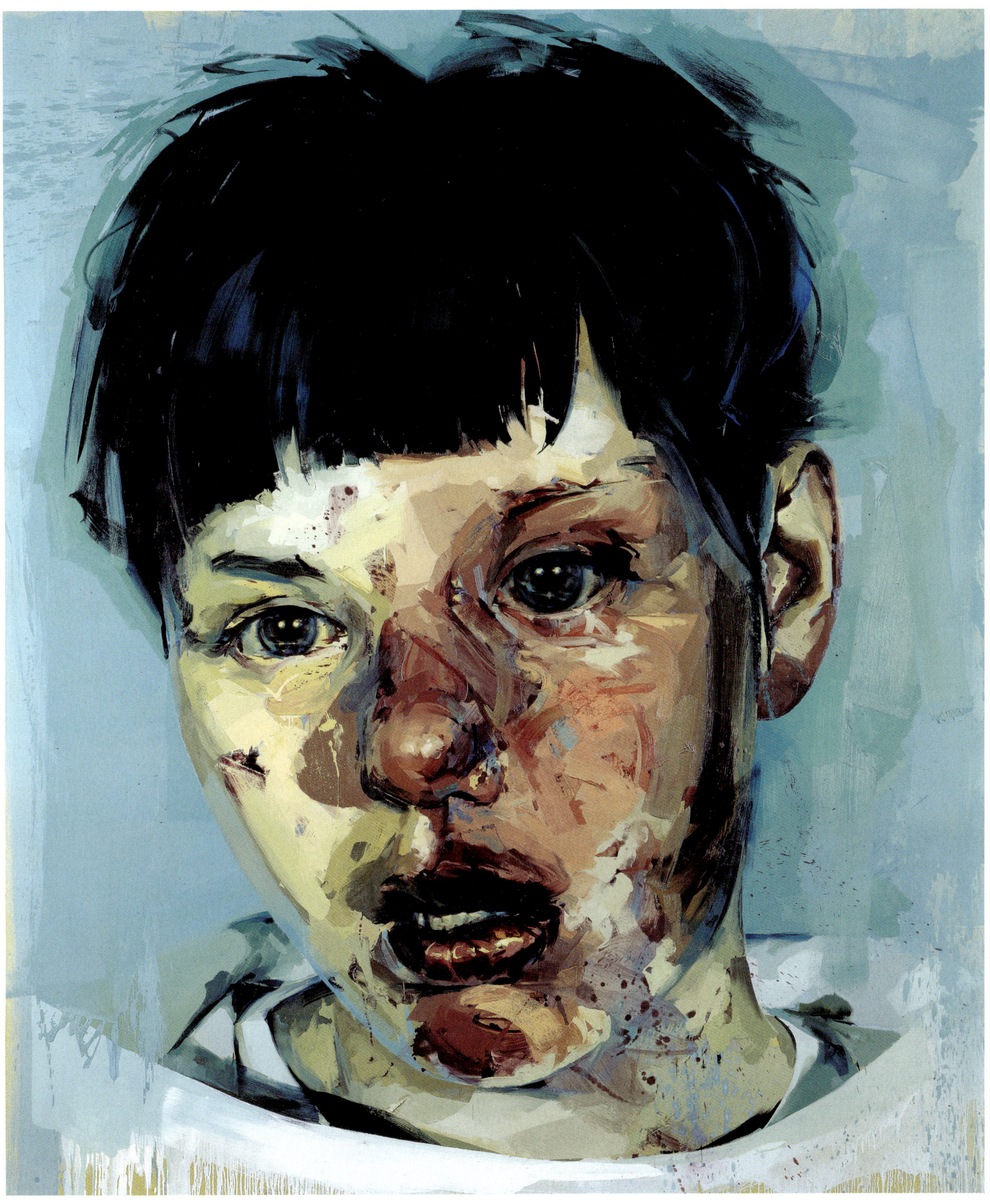

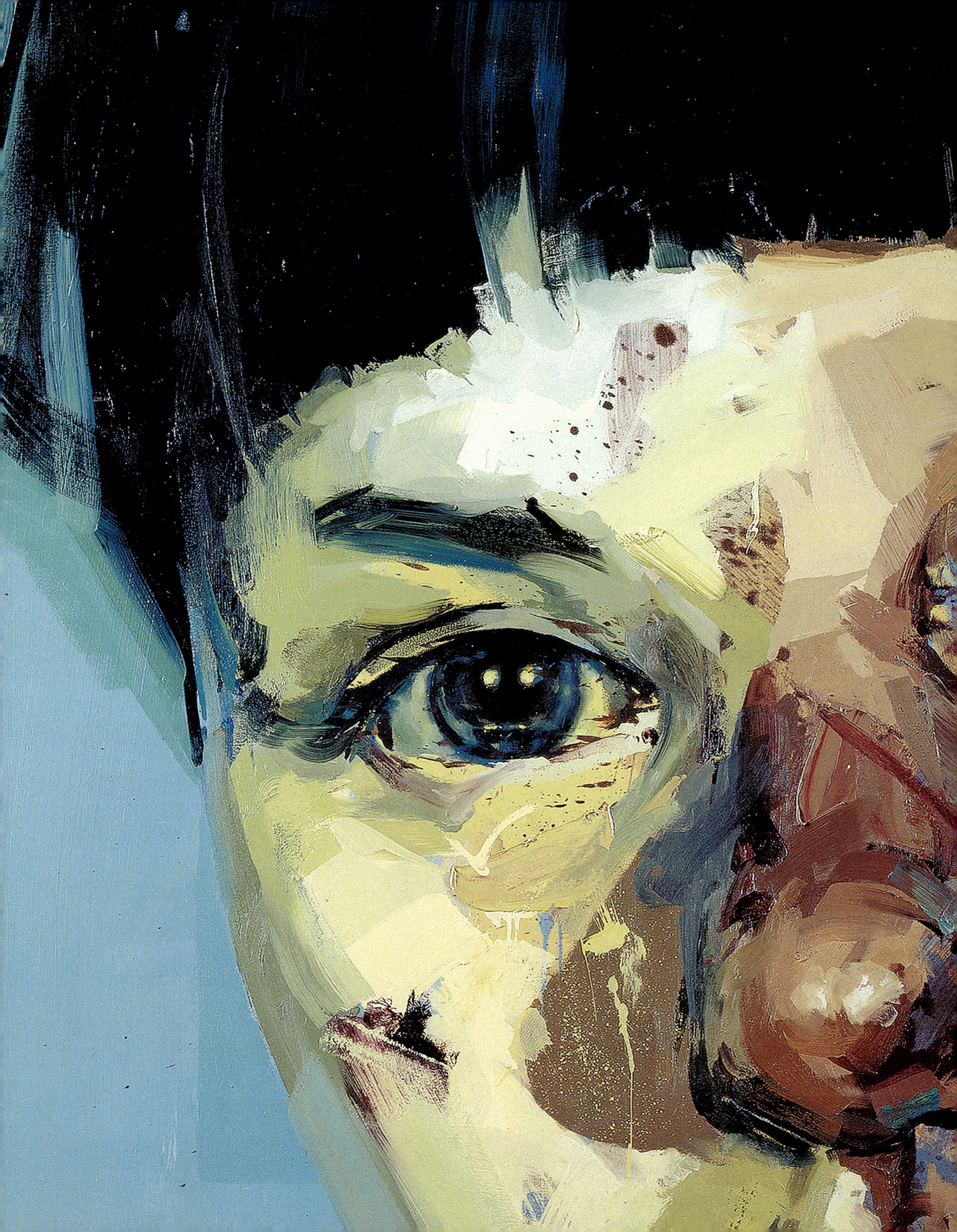

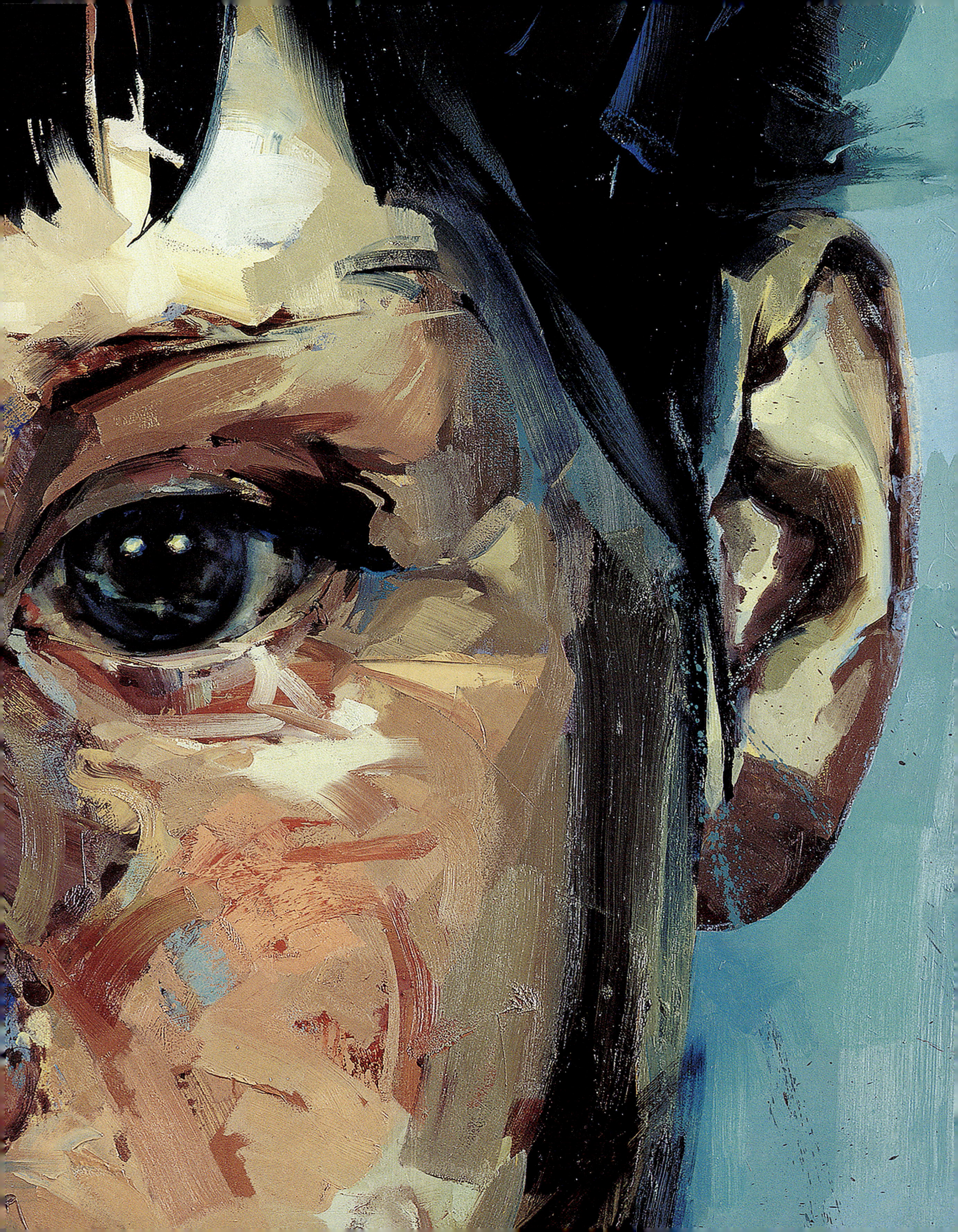

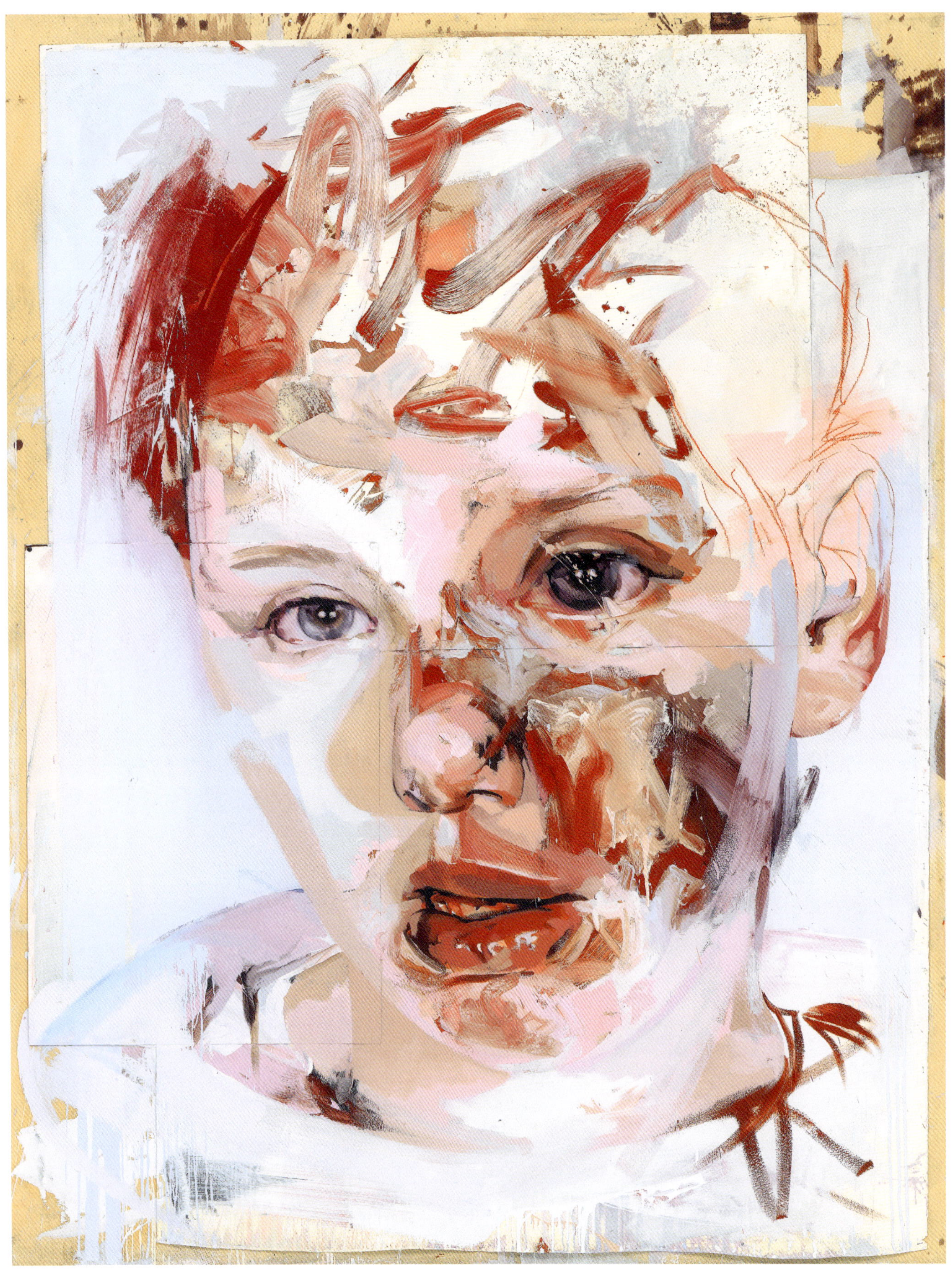

 Red Stare Collage 2007–9

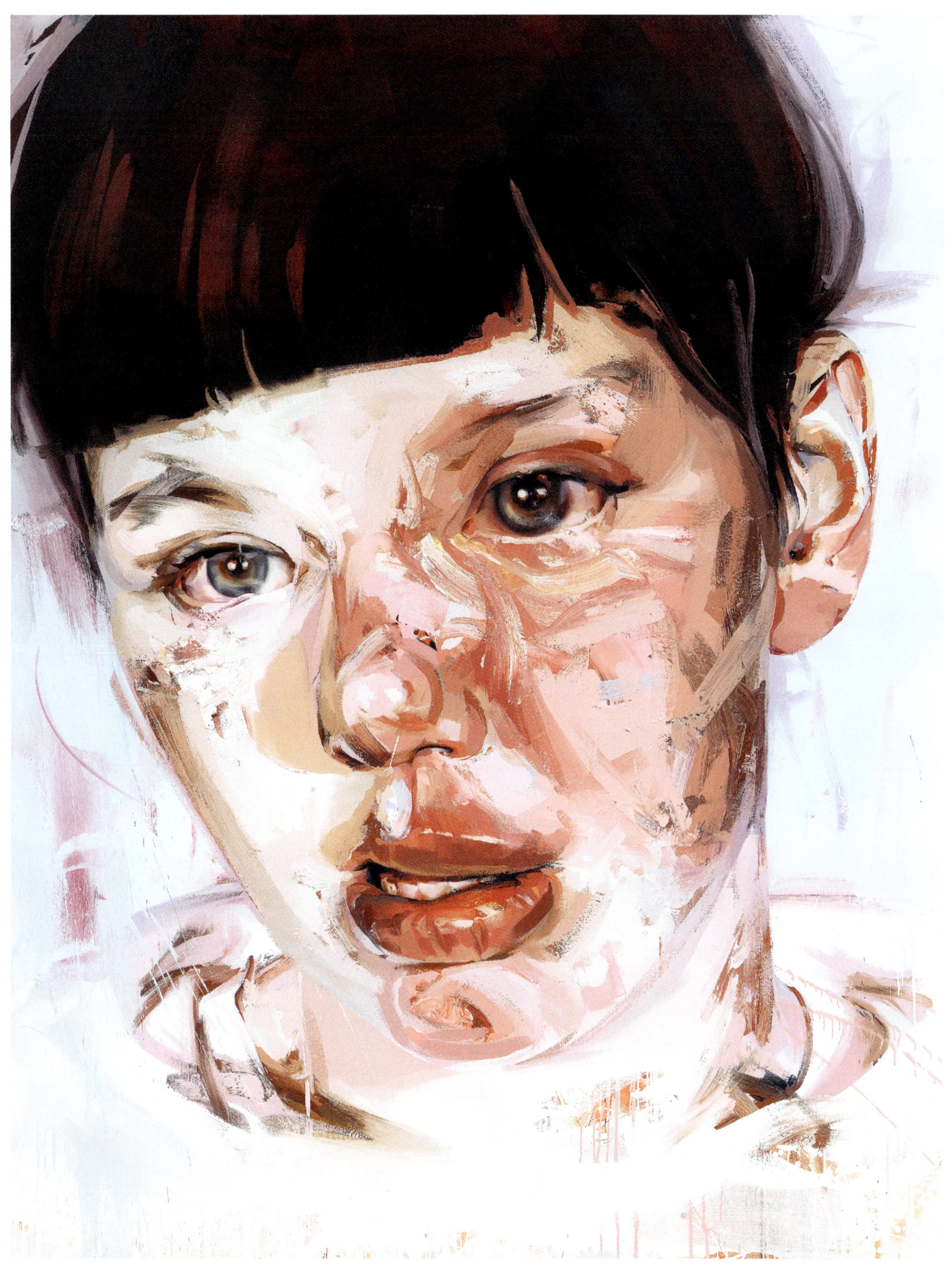

17 *Red Stare Head IV* 2006–11

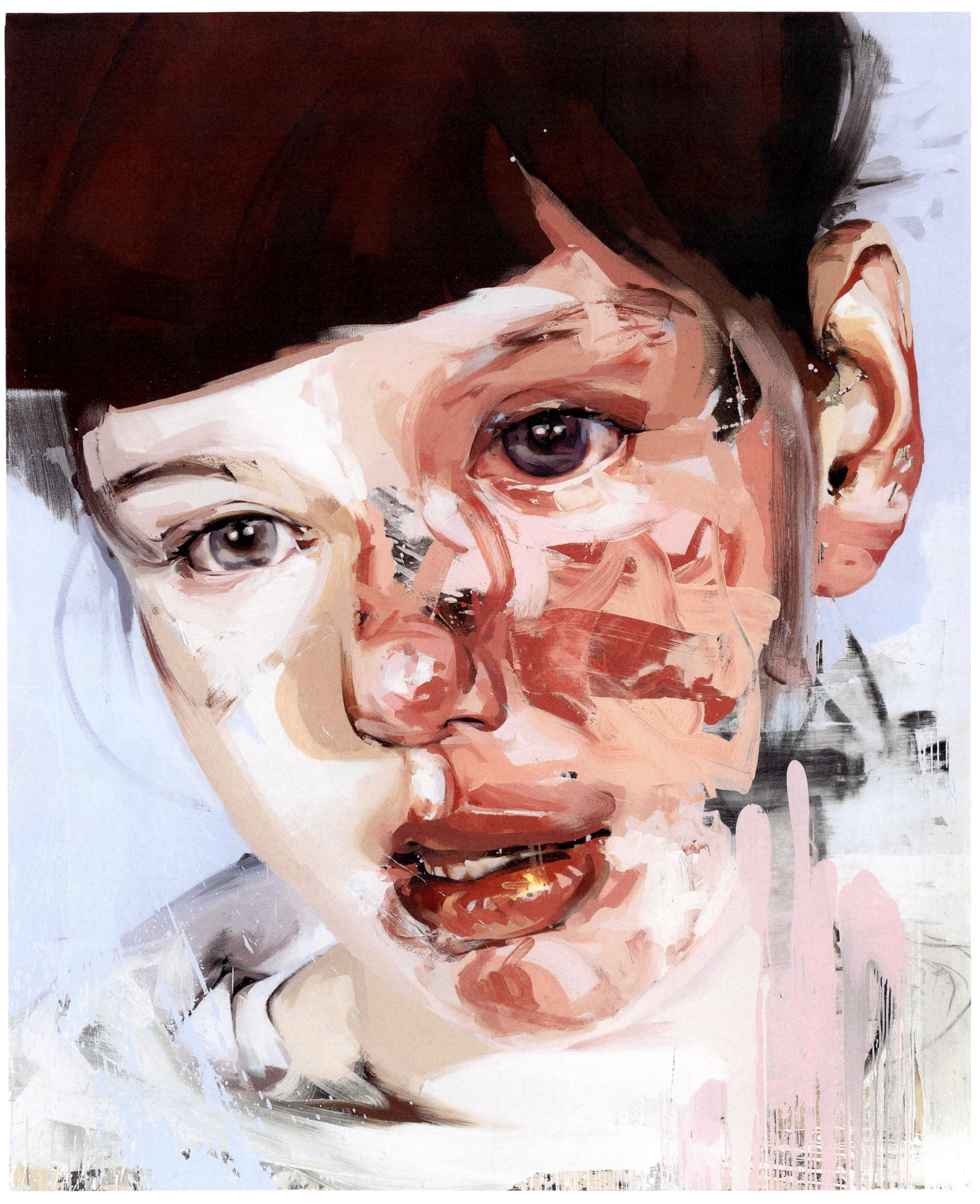

 Red Stare Head I 2007–11

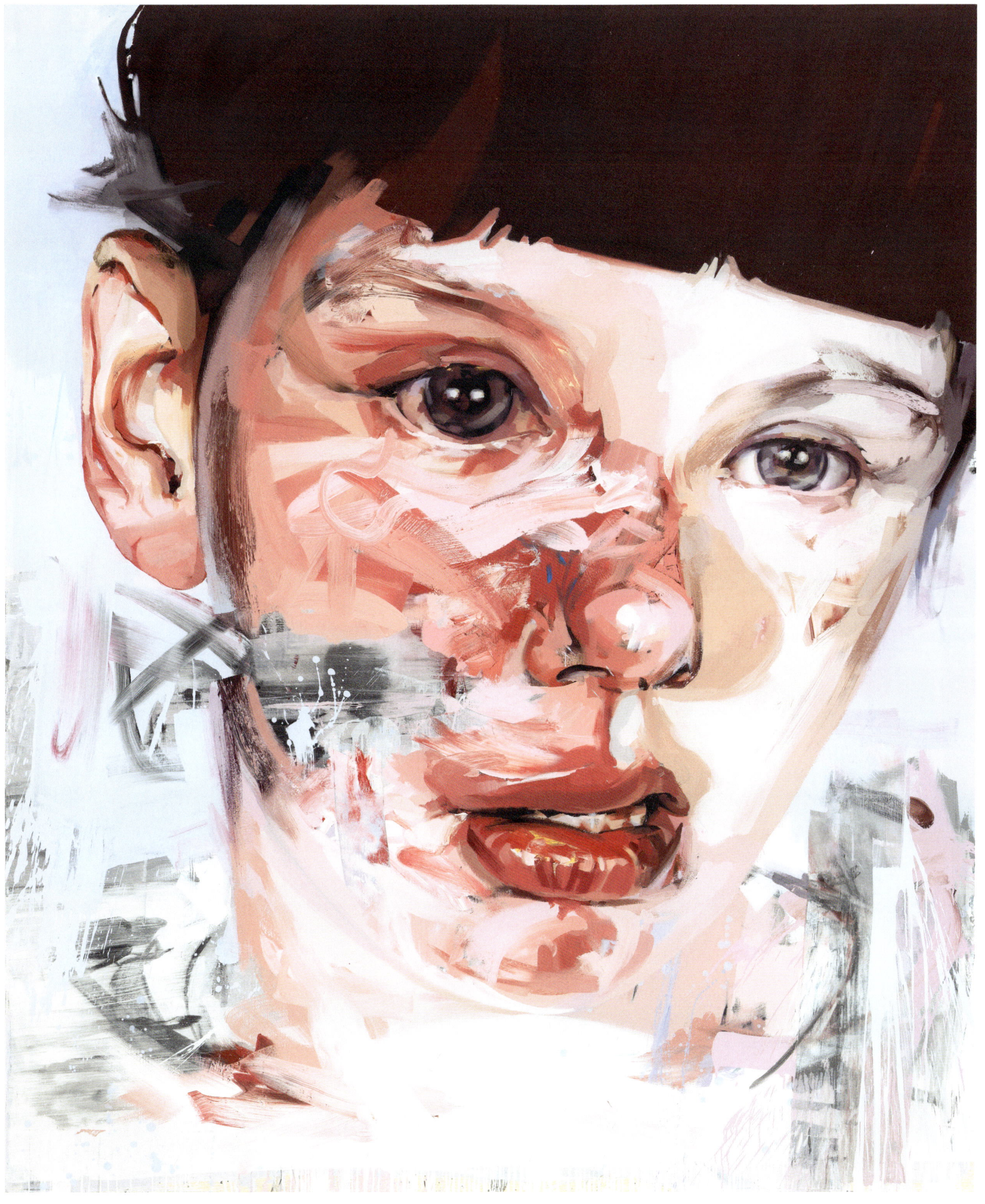

19 *Red Stare Head II* 2007–11

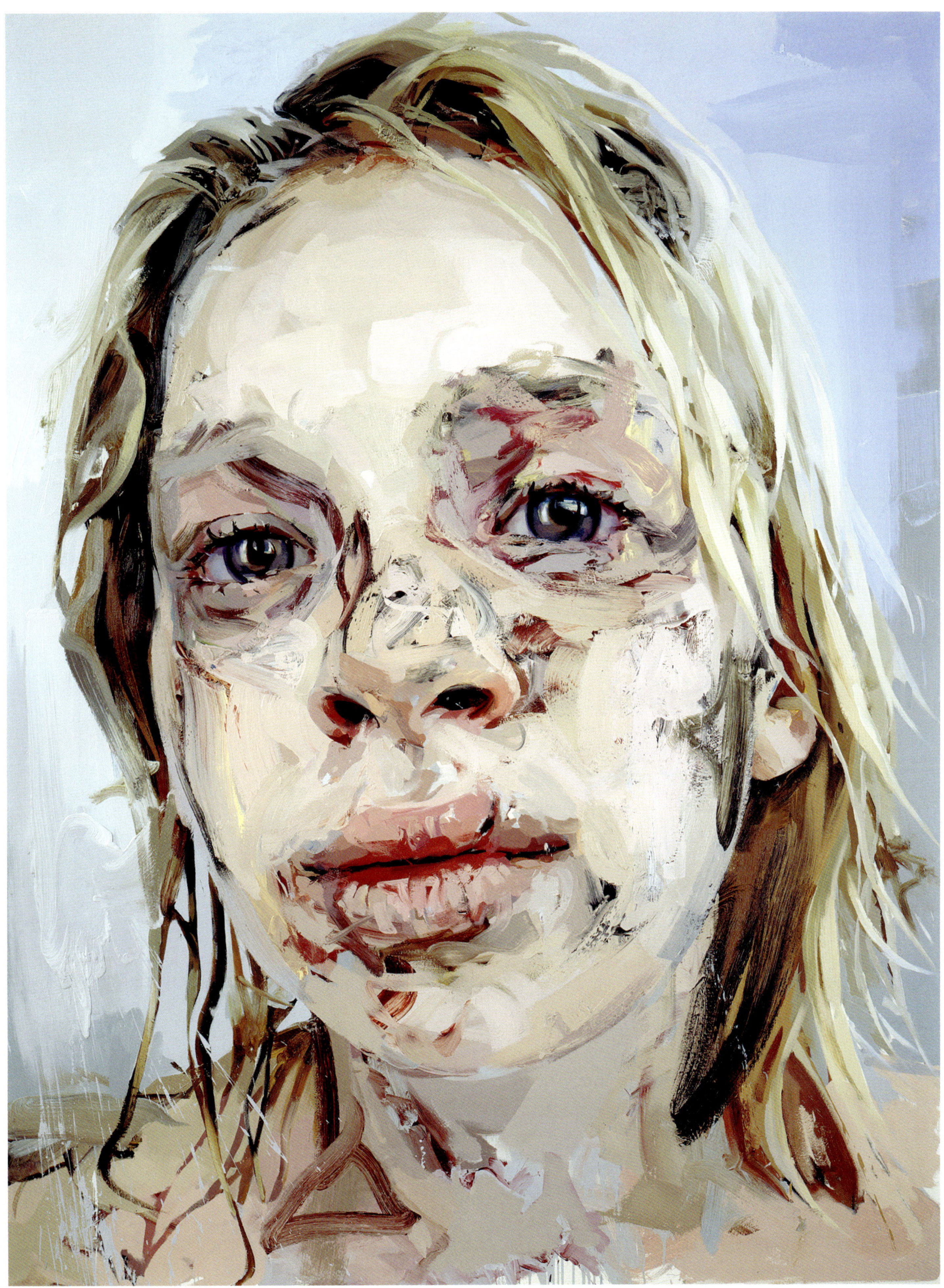

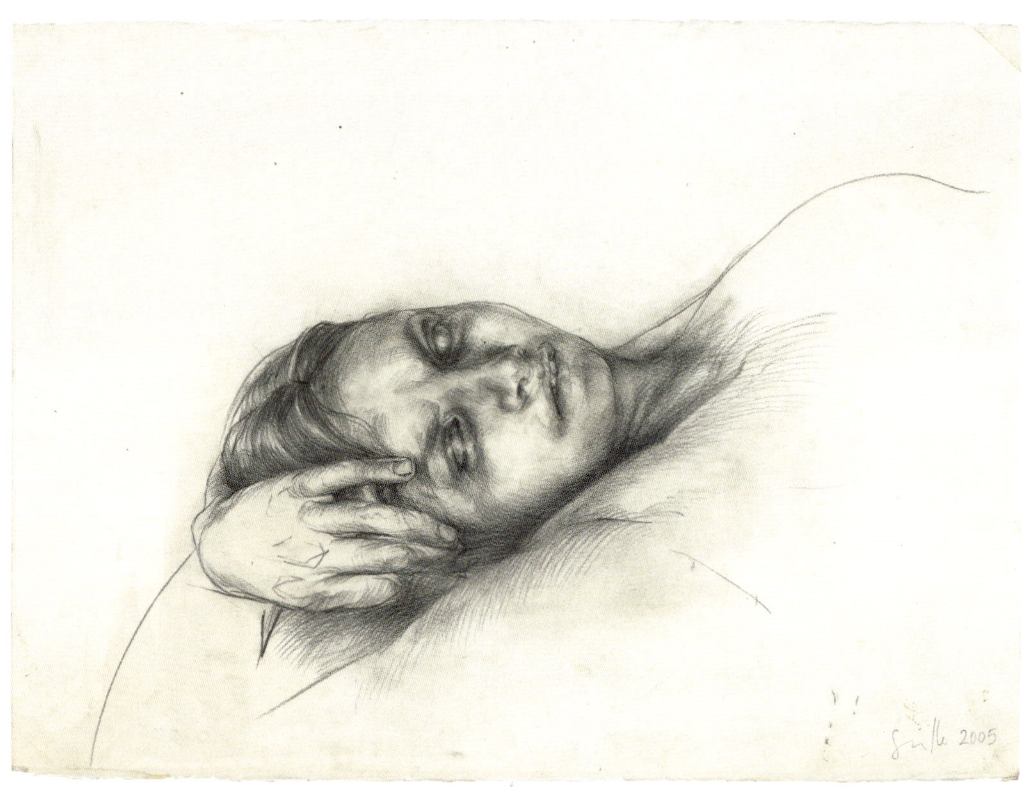

21 *Rosetta Study* 2005

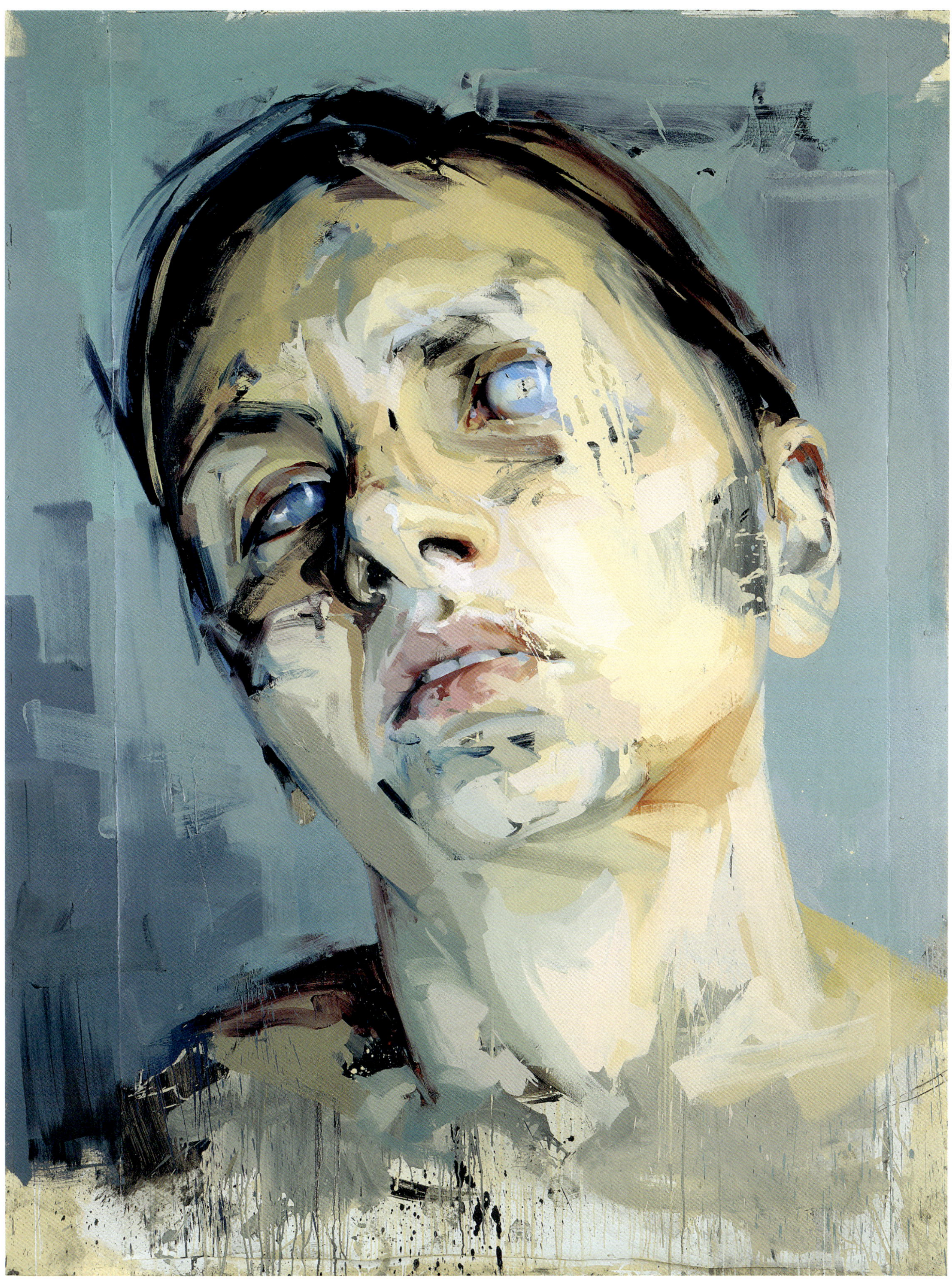

22 *Rosetta II* 2005–6

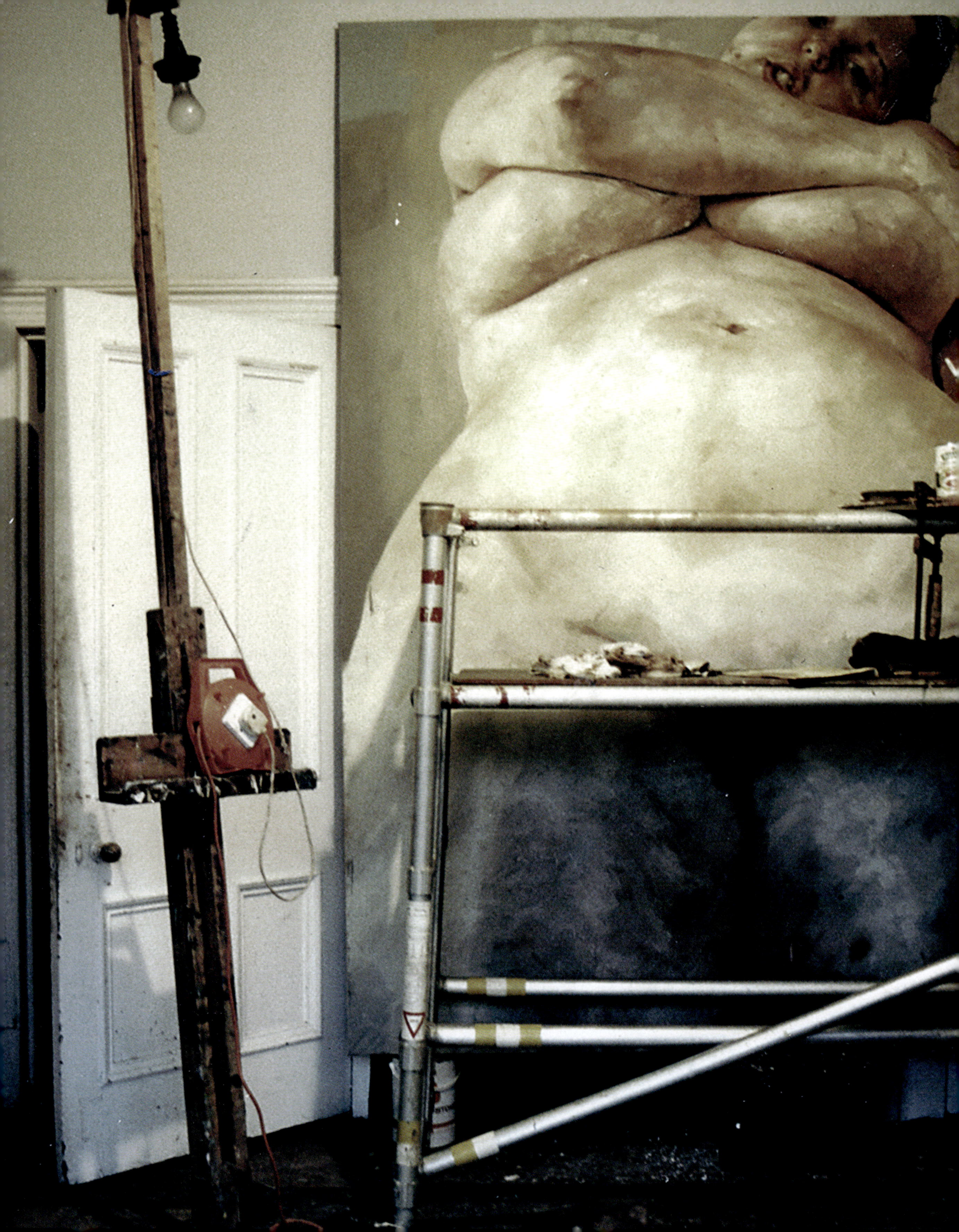

On Jenny Saville and Willem de Kooning

Andrea Karnes

In the spring of 2001 Jenny Saville visited the studio of Willem de Kooning, at the invitation of the painter's daughter, Lisa de Kooning.[1] Saville was by this time several years into a career as a painter of female figures – large-scale, confrontational portraits of women. *Plan* (cat.3), an early painting depicting a naked woman with preoperative maps drawn on her body before liposuction surgery, appeared in the landmark exhibition *Young British Artists III*, at the Saatchi Gallery, London, in 1994. Saville's technique at the time was shaped by the School of London – by painters such as Lucian Freud and Frank Auerbach. But the turn of the century found this still-young artist searching out different models.

Saville's fascination with de Kooning's work ran deep. As a teen she had been so captivated by the potency of his signature painting *Woman I* (fig.1) that she had pinned a reproduction of it to the wall of her bedroom.[2] And during a semester-long scholarship to the University of Cincinnati, she had taken a long bus trip from Ohio to New York to visit the city's museums and had seen de Kooning's paintings there 'in the flesh'.[3] The experience left her thunderstruck. 'I remember this sort of shudder – my neck going back – and it felt like the grand altarpieces I'd seen in Italy when I was younger … It shocked me, and I knew in that moment that that person was going to be very important in my life.'[4]

De Kooning might be seen as a counterintuitive hero for a young woman artist in the late twentieth century. His best-known body of work, a series of abstract/figurative paintings of women, was controversial among modernist critics for its use of discernible imagery. Over time, feminist critics including Dore Ashton and Lucy Lippard contested the series' visceral depiction of women's bodies. This group of paintings had solved one problem for de Kooning, by 'eliminat[ing] composition, arrangement, relationships, light', and 'all this silly talk about light, colour, and form'.[5] But it opened another – that of gender. 'I *like* beautiful women', de Kooning said. 'In the flesh; even models in magazines. Women irritate me sometimes. I painted that irritation in the *Woman* series'.[6] Some critics described the paintings as violent.[7] Saville, however, disagrees: 'My instinct when I saw *Woman I* was not anything to do with de Kooning attacking a woman. For me, de Kooning's women are not passive'.[8] She formed her own relationship to his work.

Saville's visit to de Kooning's studio in 2001 was, therefore, a crucial event, one that allowed her to delve into his methodology, as demonstrated by his fine-tuned workroom.

There she studied his every move, noting the Pyrex bowls he used to mix pigments and encountering approaches to painting she had not considered before, such as using long-handled brushes to achieve full-body gestures rather than relying on hand-and-wrist movements. Likewise, she discovered his technique of putting canvases on the floor to work around them and control the motion of paint, manipulating the artwork with and against gravity – a force she describes as a painter's 'third arm'.[9] The experience changed the way she painted, Saville says, and allowed her to 'shortcut decades of development'.[10]

An occasion to study de Kooning's work in 2004 proved even more pivotal. Saville was invited by her gallerist, Larry Gagosian, to see *Willem de Kooning: A Centennial Exhibition* being installed at his gallery in Chelsea, Manhattan. This commemorative exhibition presented paintings from the 1940s through the 1980s and illustrated the trajectory of the artist's innovations in abstraction. Saville spent four days prior to the opening virtually alone with his works.[11] There she absorbed from de Kooning what she describes as his 'freedom, movement, and an extended painting vocabulary'.[12] The studio visit in 2001 had afforded her an expanded approach to painterly technique; now she felt energised to apply de Kooning's rich lessons in modernist abstraction.

Saville's series *Stare* (2004–11, see cats 15–19 and fig.3) was born from the challenge presented by the 2004 encounter. She set out, in these works, to integrate into her figurative painting the full range of modernist abstraction as de Kooning and others had elaborated it. The problem was how to do so. Usual approaches to modernism had seen figuration and abstraction as divergent options. To be modern, to avail oneself of painting's materiality and expressive truth, meant leaving imagery behind. De Kooning, of course, had fiercely disregarded this false dichotomy, startling modernist critics with his 1952 exhibition at the Sidney Janis Gallery, New York, *Paintings on the Theme of the Woman*, which presented a series of female figures described with aggressive brushstrokes and violent slashes of black outline, while also flaunting his adept paint-handling with abstract loops and sweeping shapes. Saville aimed to breach this divide anew.

Her solution to this problem, distinct from de Kooning's, was to use figuration as an 'armature' for a direct engagement with painting's formal possibilities.[13] She found that armature in a thumbnail photograph, discovered in a medical dermatology book, that depicted a youthful, androgynous head. By repeating this visage across multiple variations,[14] Saville could internalise, and therefore obviate, many of the fundamental problems of portraiture – the difficult task of describing anatomy – and set loose the full repertoire of abstraction.[15] This approach allowed her to be both in and out of control of the form. Departing from anatomical accuracy by already knowing it, she could enter an intuitive zone. As she progressed through the series, Saville began to pressure the boundaries of the figure's expressive potential. When de Kooning initiated *Woman I*, he had arguably done something similar but in reverse, by working human figures back into his abstract canvases.

The painting *Red Stare Head IV* (cat.17) presents a particularly intense puzzling-out of de Kooning's influence. Flesh comes to life in the image through exaggerated facial expression composed of abstraction and through painterly brushwork that is full of gesture. Saville's choice to magnify just a head becomes as evocative as depicting an entire figure would be. By now she was incorporating de Kooning's methods – long-handled brushes, using

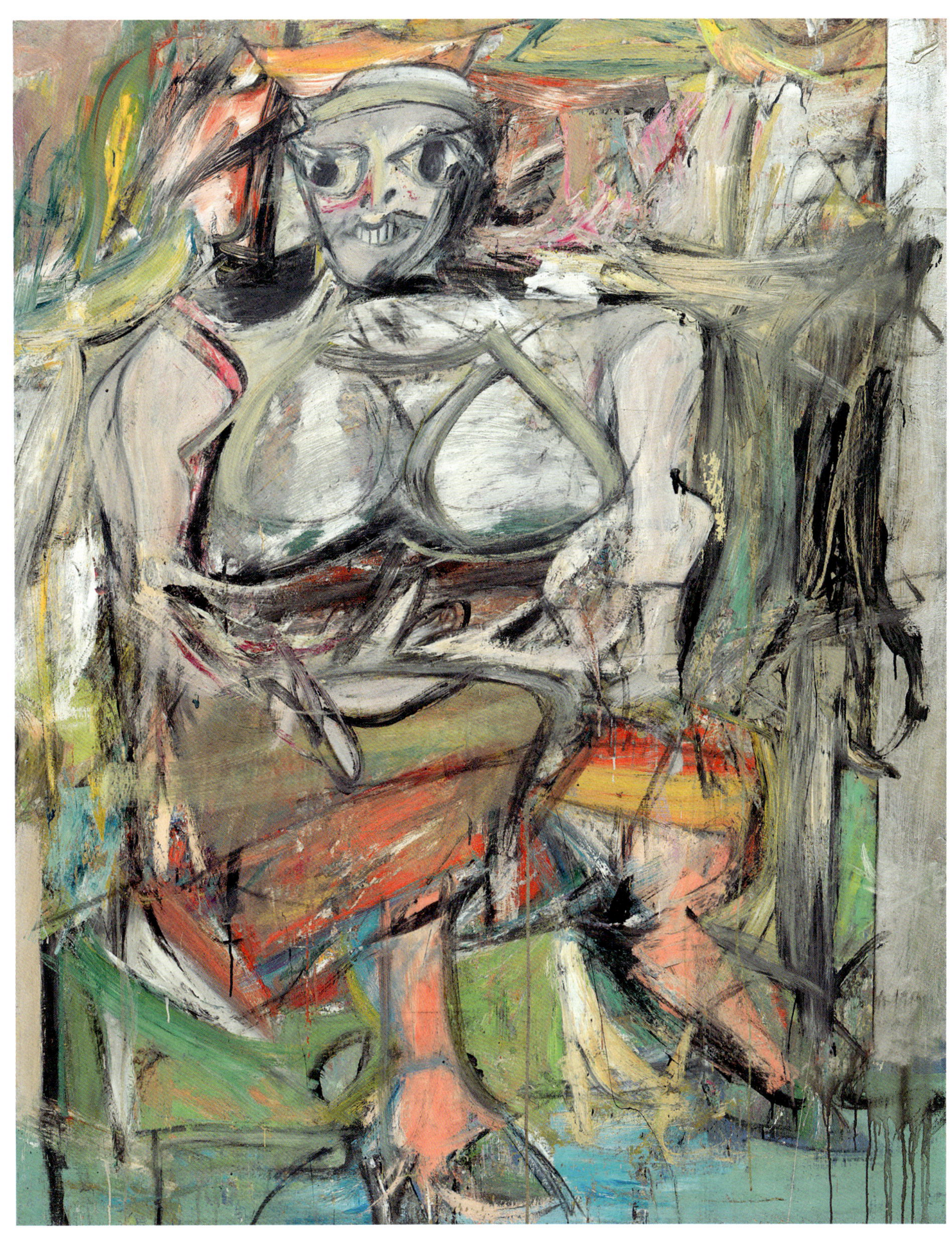

Fig.1
Willem de Kooning
Woman I, 1950–2
Oil and metallic paint on canvas
1927 × 1473 mm
The Museum of Modern Art, New York

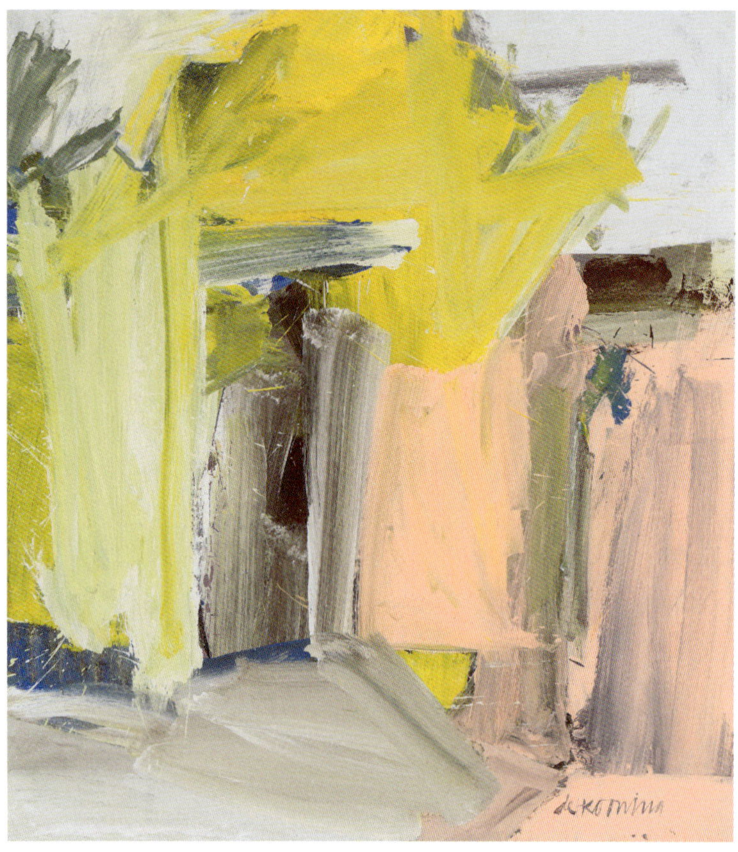

Fig.2
Willem de Kooning
Door to the River, 1960
Oil on linen
2035 × 1781 mm
Whitney Museum of
American Art, New York

Fig.3
Jenny Saville
In-progress *Red Stares*, 2006–11
Palermo, Italy, *c.*2007

the floor to manipulate paint and gravity, and growing space out of areas of abstraction. Likewise, her handling of tonality in the work draws on the model of de Kooning's abstract paintings, especially in the image's uncanny descriptions of flesh, which range from white to brown, red, coral and pink. Reflecting on de Kooning's centennial exhibition in 2004, Saville says, 'de Kooning's painting *Door to the River* ... helped me understand that instead of painting graduated flat and opaque pigments around a form to create the illusion of mass, I could mix two or three base colours and run them together to create a multitude of tonality. This constructed form in a way that felt visually exciting. The paint seemed frozen in a moment of becoming' (fig.2).[16] Painting wet-on-wet allowed for nudging colours into each other, producing an image that is abundantly abstract while also affording it a convincing sense of weight, heft and physicality.

Saville's *Stare* heads are, as she puts it, about 'considering the anatomy of painting itself, not just the anatomy of the head'.[17] Yet if this consideration was licensed by de Kooning's model, it departed from it just as forcefully. Painted in the 1950s, de Kooning's women had enacted the fractious, contradictory meeting of the most forward-thinking art of his time with popular culture and the archaic force of Sumerian statues of women; in them, Marilyn Monroe transforms into Tell Asmar.[18] Saville's armature is not an archetype of womanhood but a photograph of a specific individual. And the work likewise shows painting meeting the era of digital reproducibility: Adobe Photoshop software entered Saville's process, allowing her to shift or 'swing' the colour to intensify contrast and bleed.[19] The *Stare* works recall their origin in medical photography, but further summon to mind surveillance – the

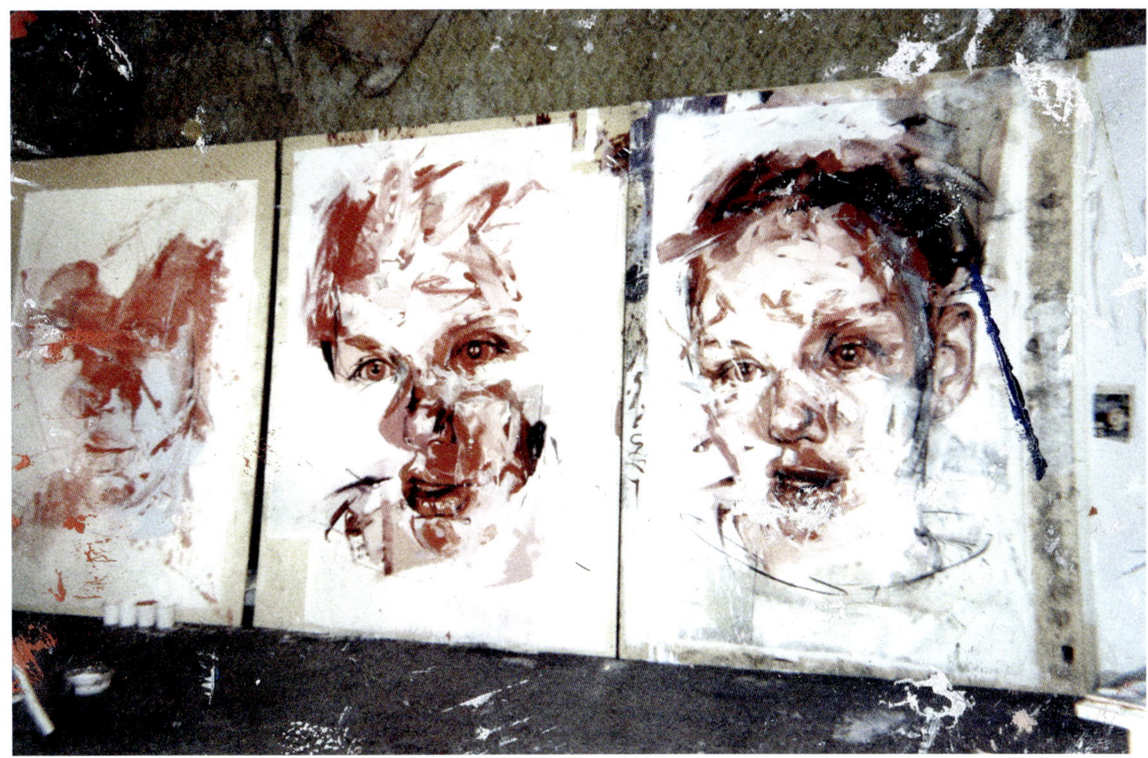

ID card, the mugshot – and the digital headshots that were coming to govern presentations of selfhood on social media in the first decade of the twenty-first century.

On the evidence of the *Stare* series, this was not a happy way of being. This self is pathological; it teeters uncomfortably on the border between life and death. In other words, the paintings register our own modernity, beyond anything de Kooning could have imagined. But although their times and conditions of possibility diverge, the two artists still have much in common. Both were activated by the image of women; both chafe at gendered assumptions and see portraying the female form as inseparable from the question of power. If his figures probe the nature of womanhood in uncomfortable ways, hers ask us to consider the complexities of female agency and beauty and question the constitution of femaleness itself. The *Stare* heads' armature, Saville reminds us, may or may not be a woman; the figure is androgynous.[20]

Ultimately, what Saville, whose portraits include male and gender-hybrid bodies,[21] derives from de Kooning is less about his attitude toward women, however defined, and more about his painting process. Through abstraction de Kooning suggested a path to painting something out of nothing; Saville paints a figure that is both something and nothing: a particular individual and mere scaffolding for painting's fundamentals. 'Women irritate me sometimes', de Kooning said.[22] The *Stare* works gave this irritation expanded resonance, playing it as fleshy inflammation and stimulus to action.

Research and editorial support by Julian Myers-Szupinska.

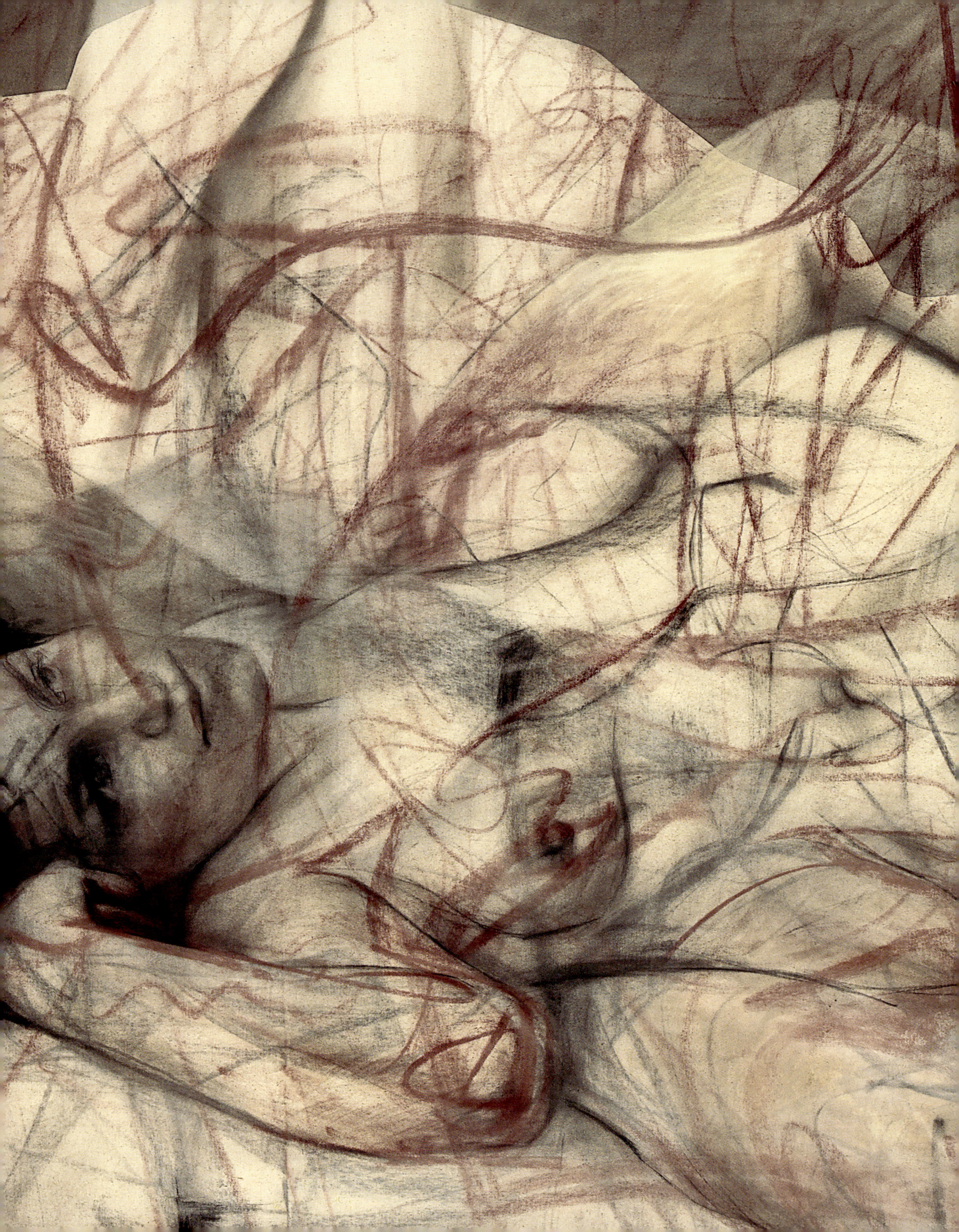

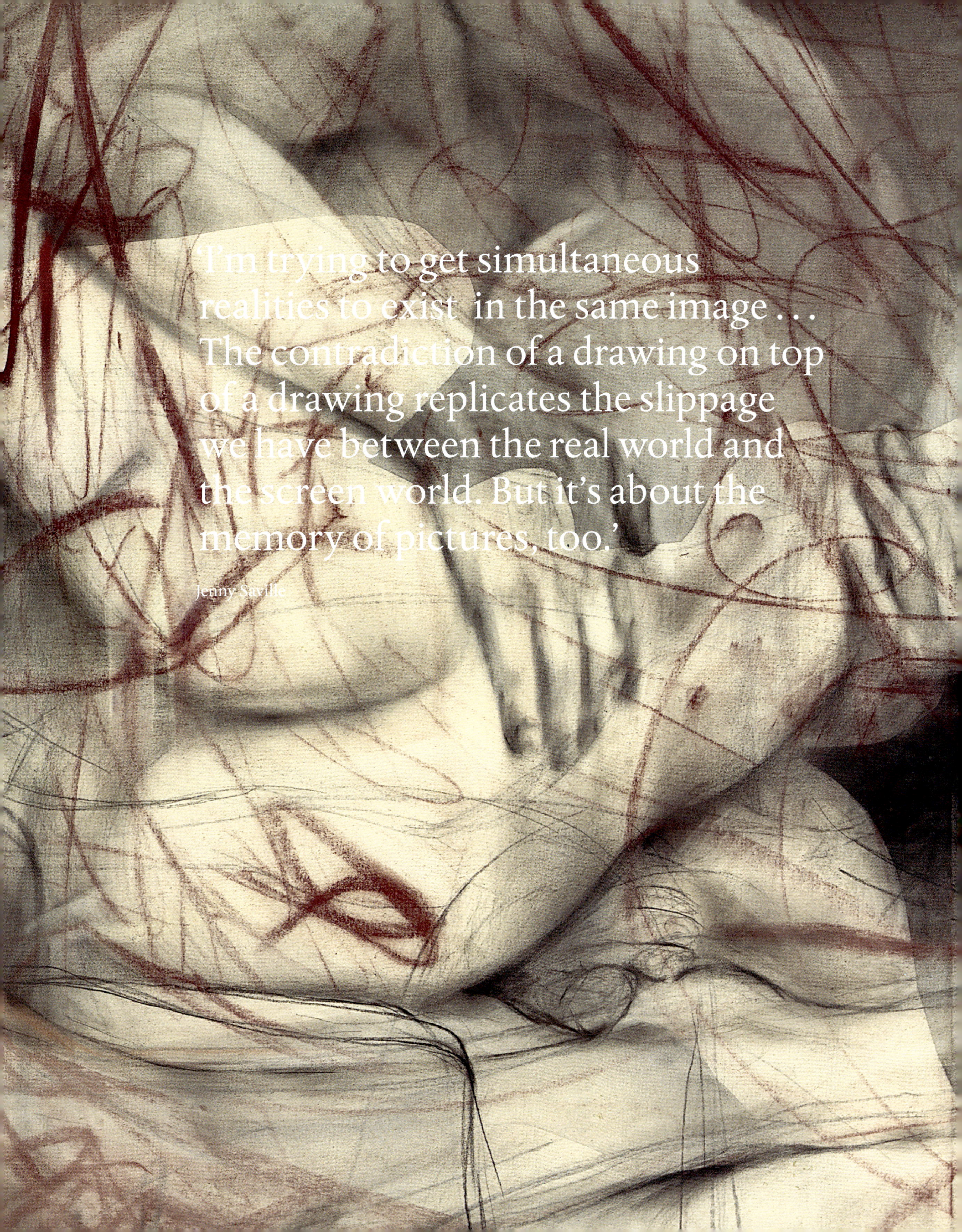

'I'm trying to get simultaneous realities to exist in the same image . . . The contradiction of a drawing on top of a drawing replicates the slippage we have between the real world and the screen world. But it's about the memory of pictures, too.'

Jenny Saville

23 *The Mothers* 2011

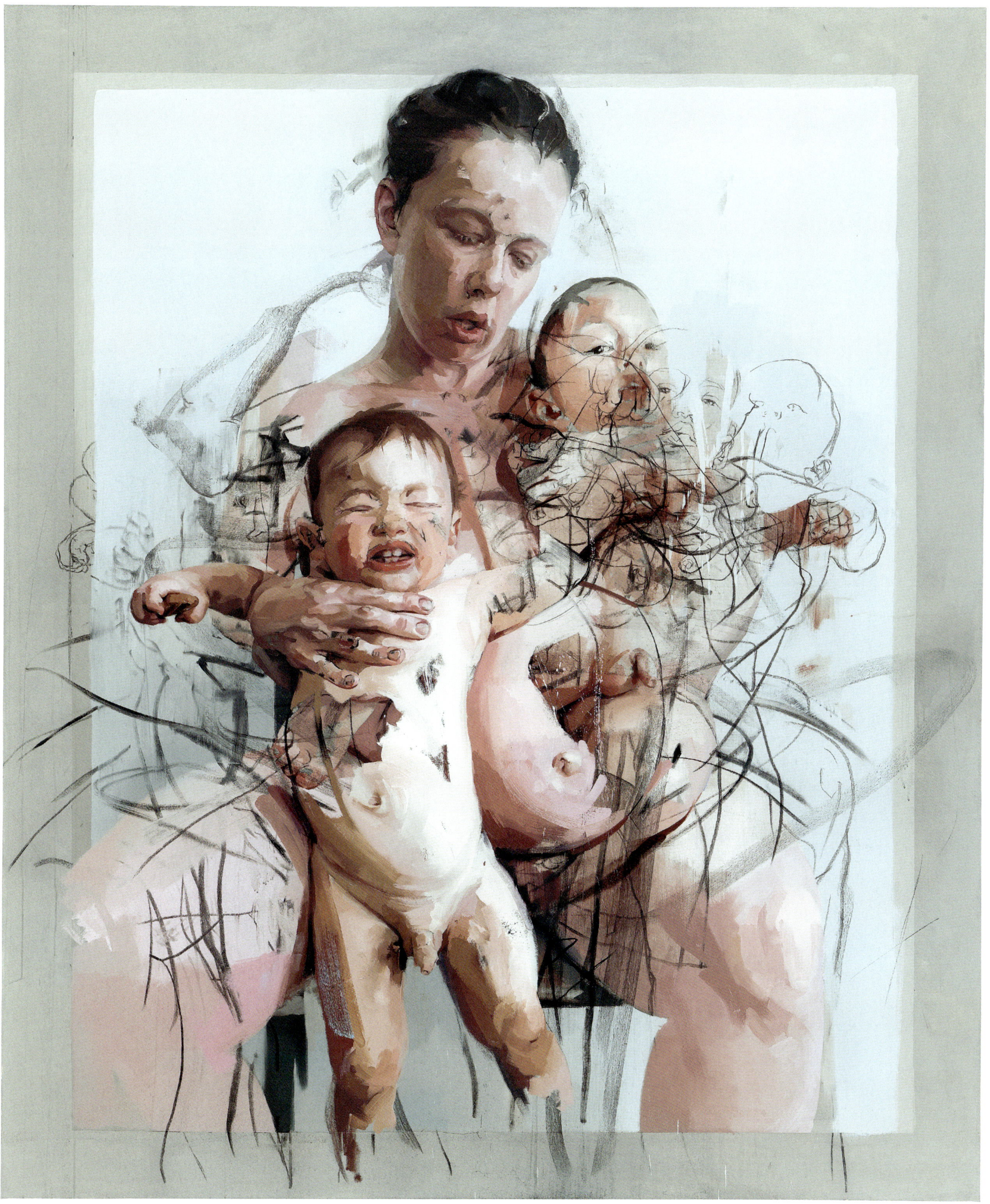

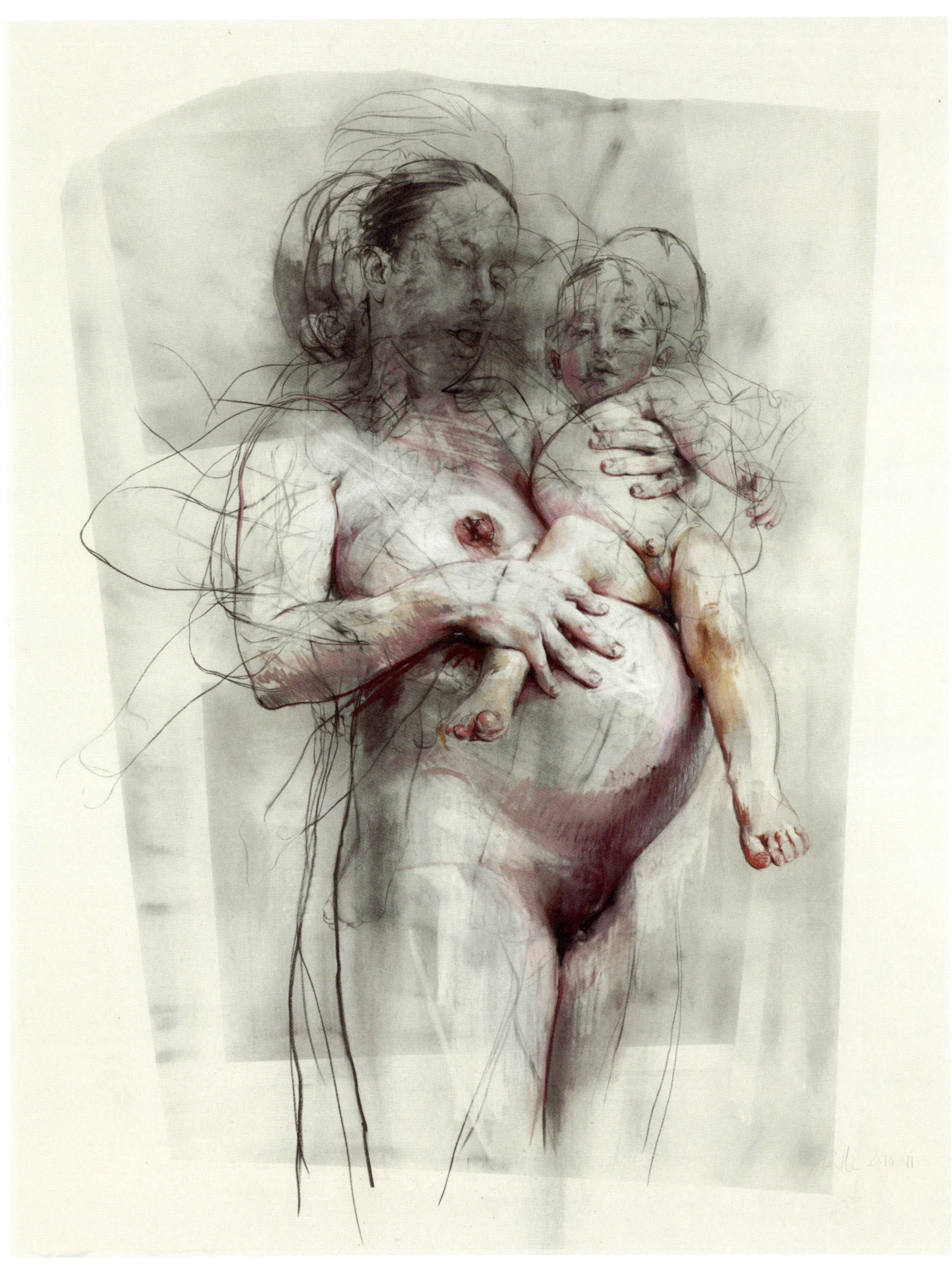

24 *Study for Pentimenti IV (after Michelangelo's* Virgin and Child*)* 2011

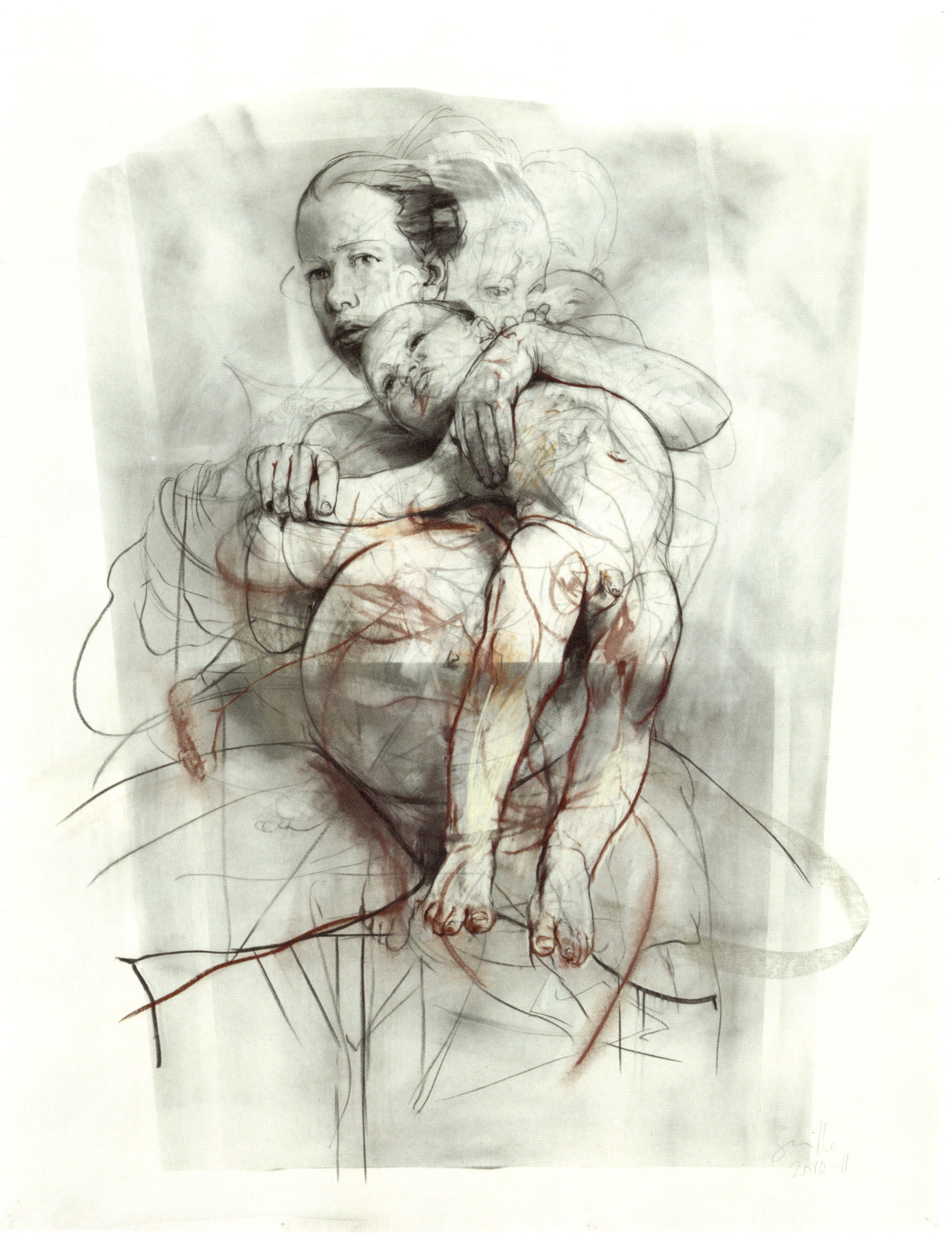

25 *Study for Pentimenti III (Sinopia)* 2011

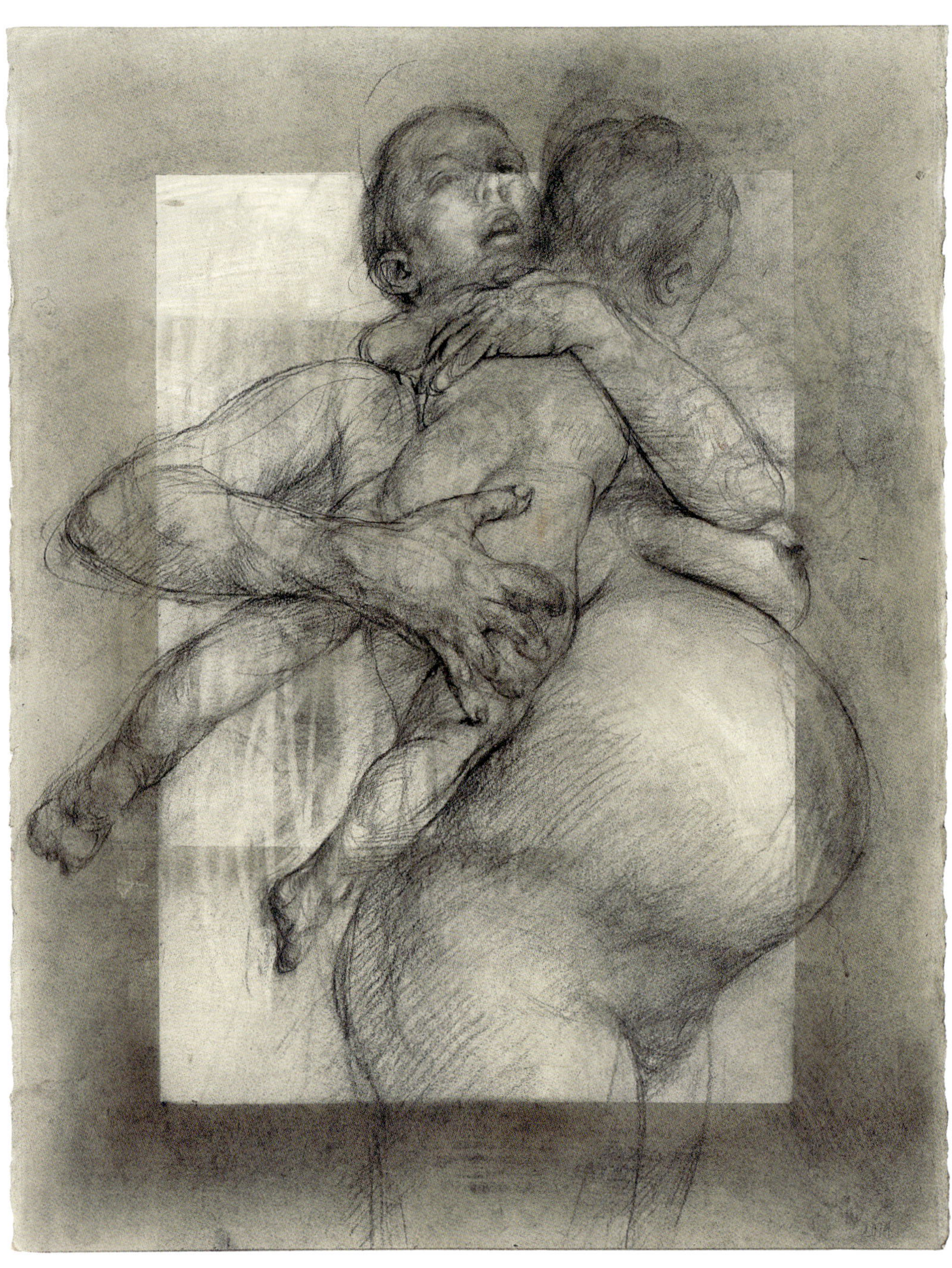

 Mother and Child Study VII 2019

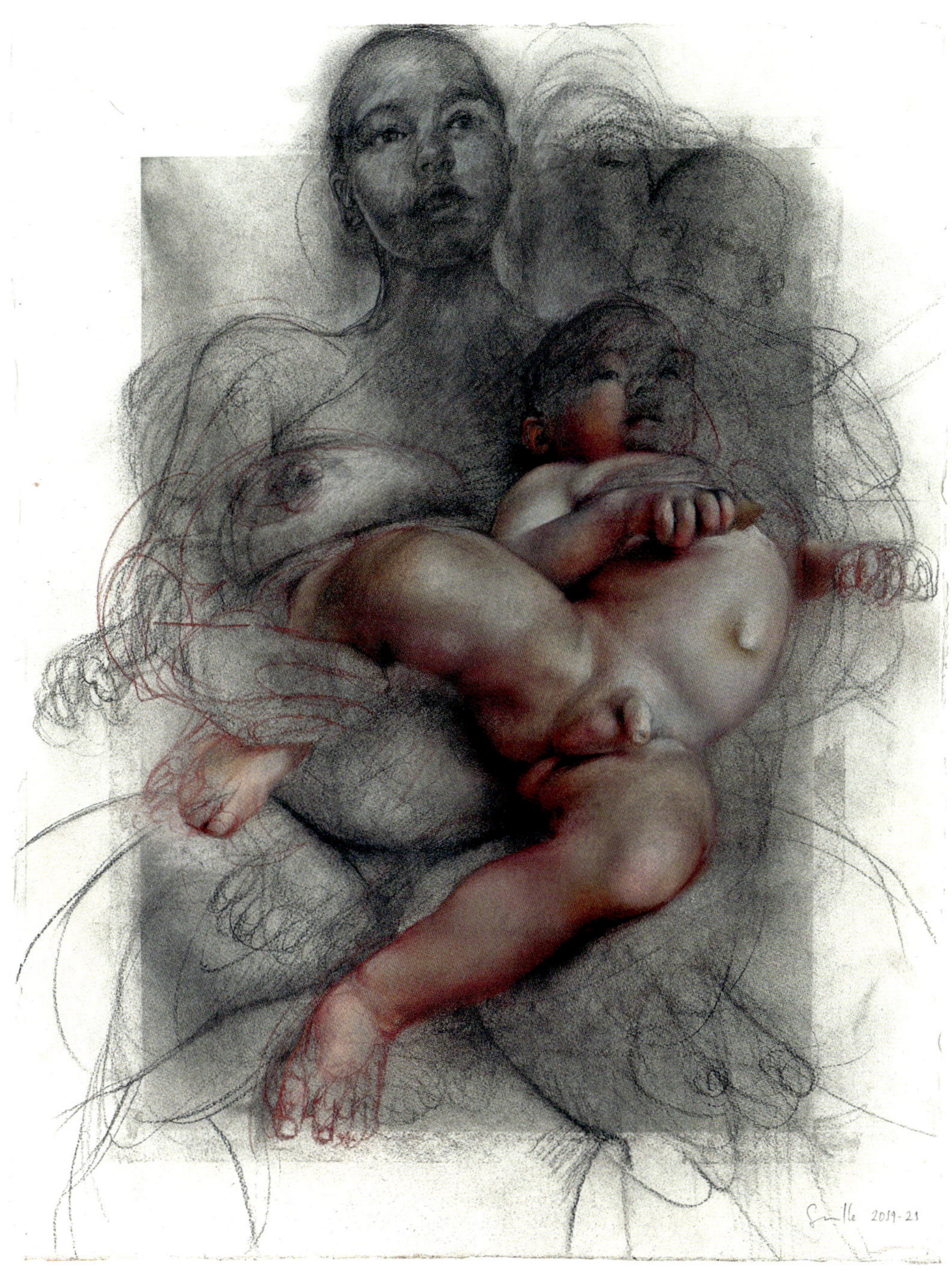

27 *Cartonetto Study* 2019–21

28 *Mother and Child Study II* 2009

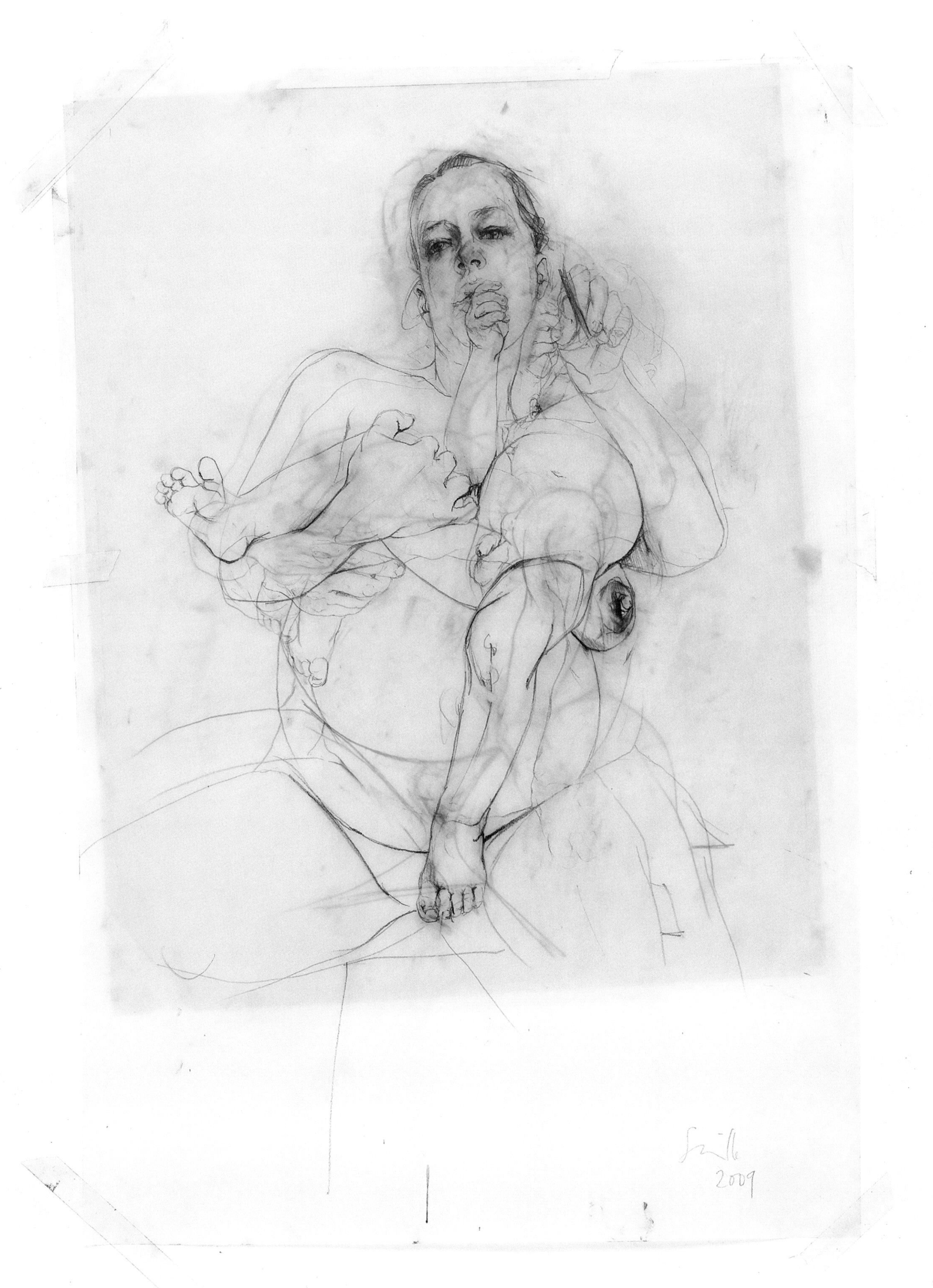

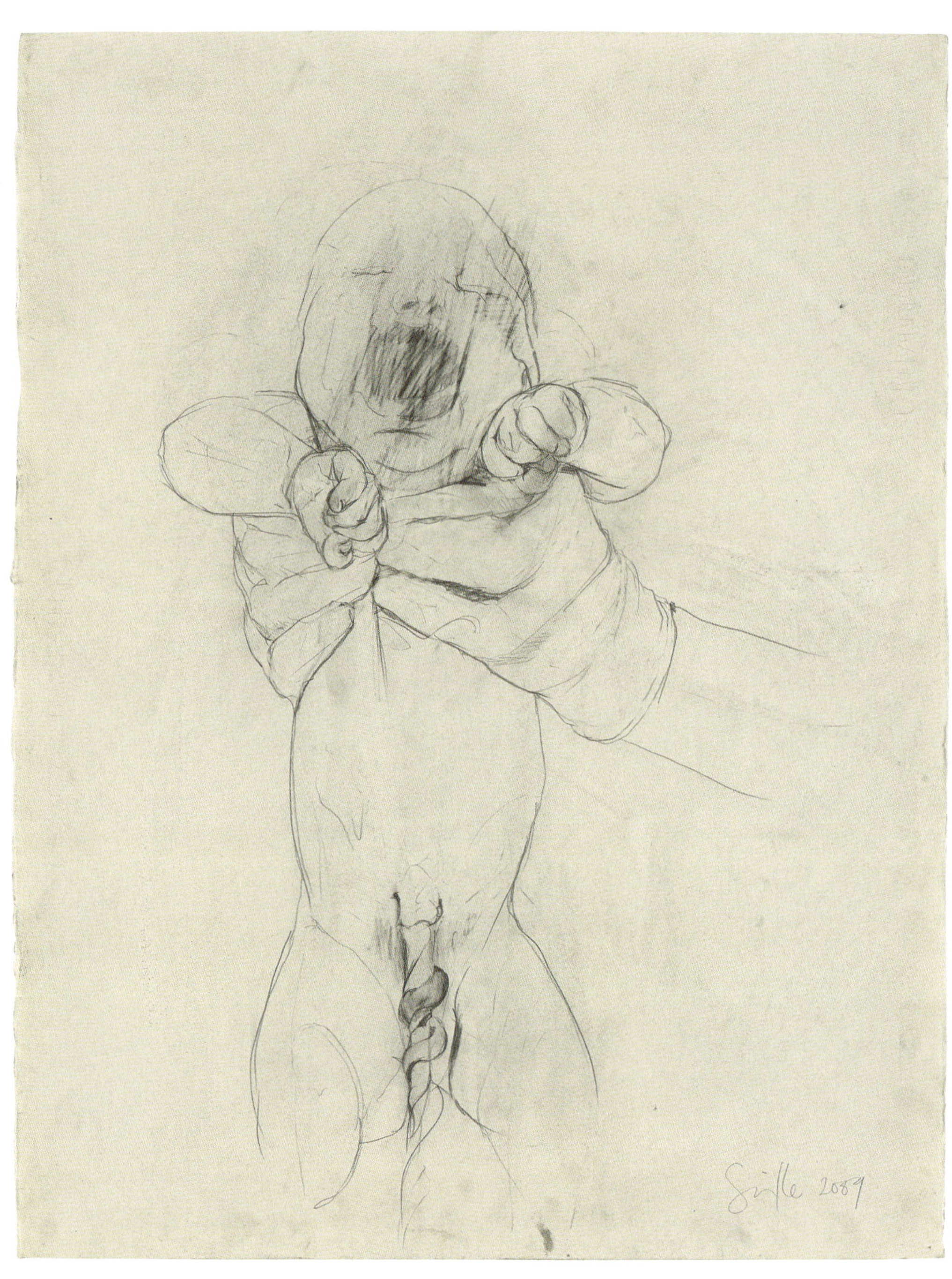

29 *Umbilical (Study)* 2009

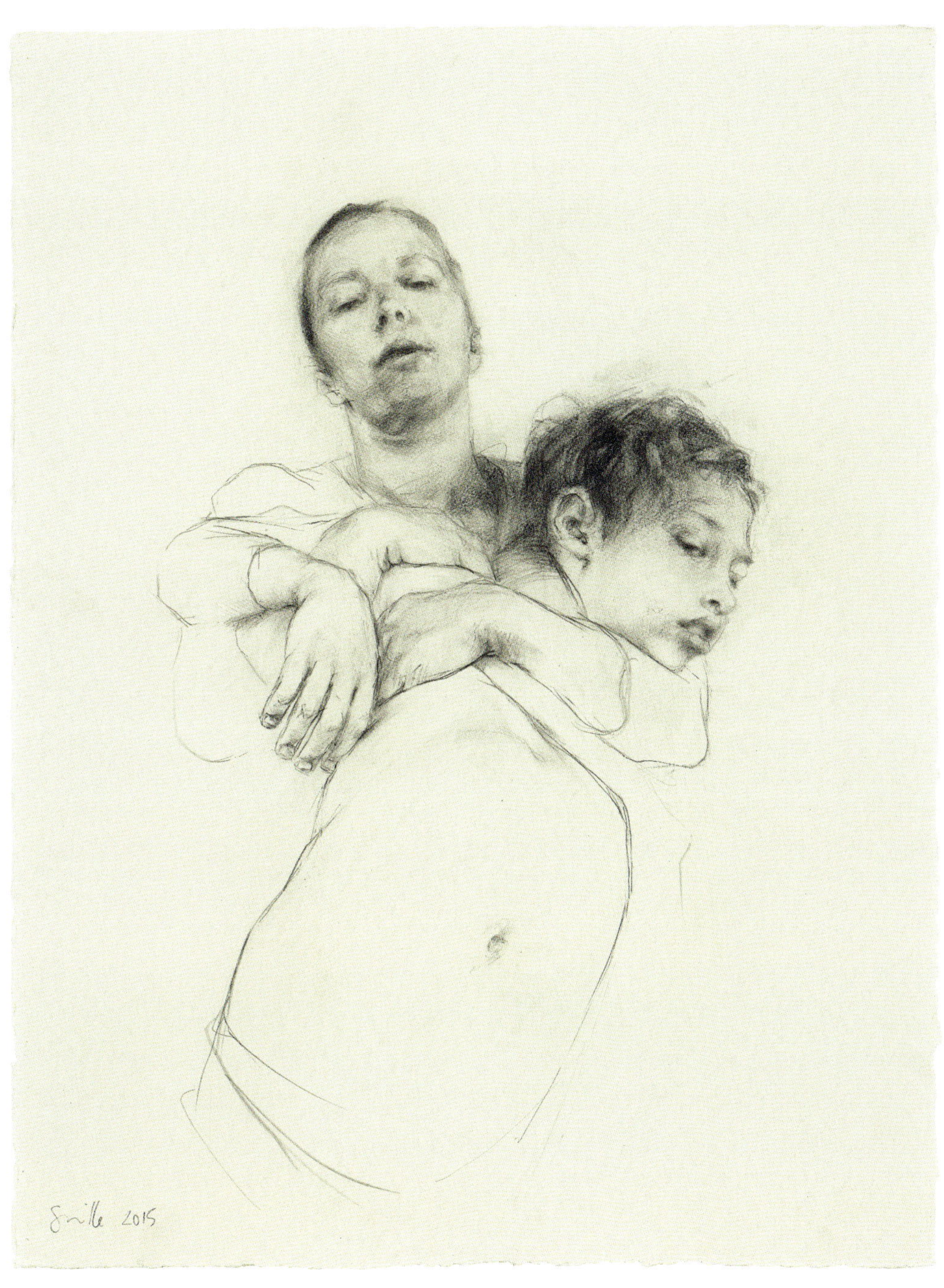

30 *Mother and Child (8) (Study)* 2015

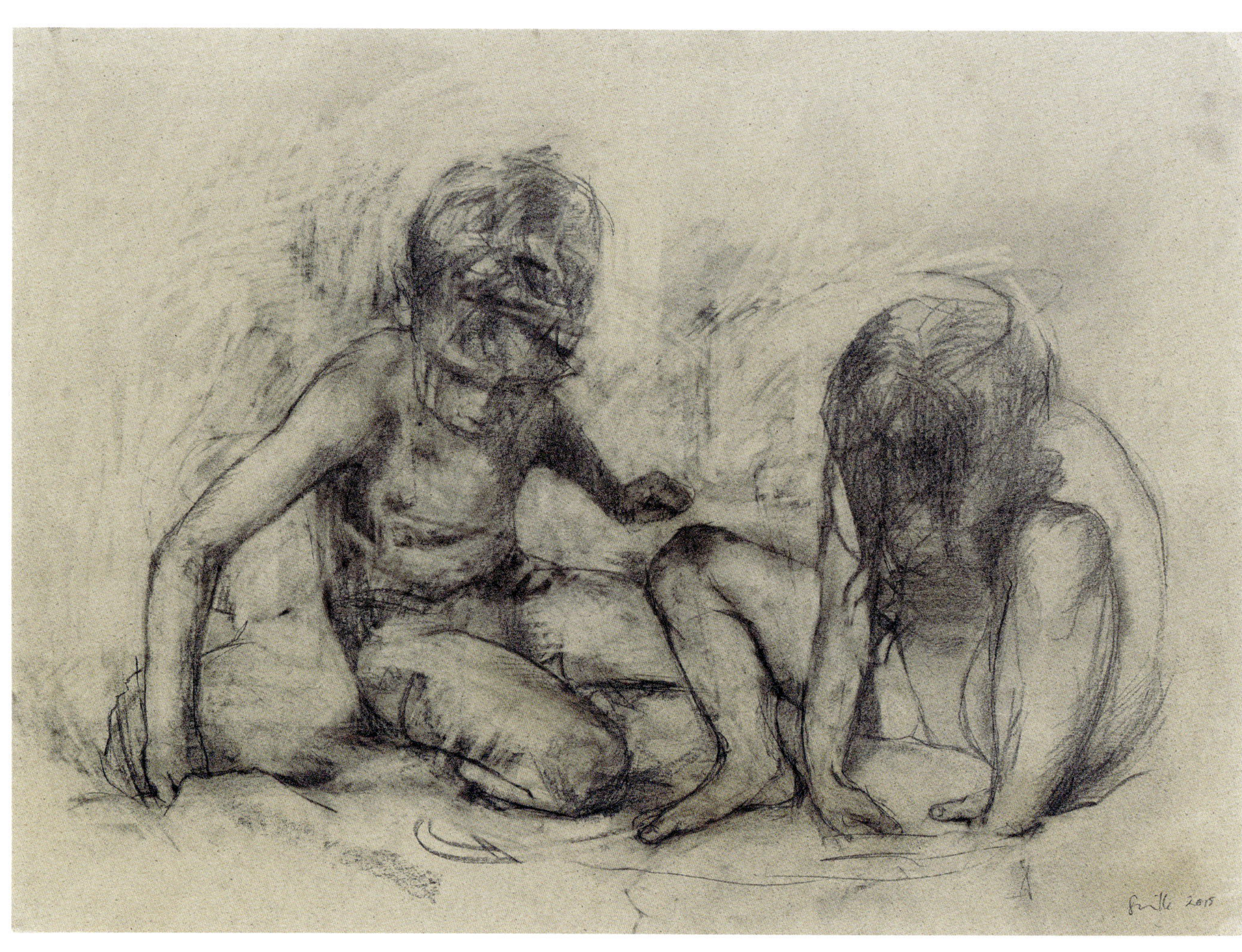

31 *Digging (Study) II* 2015

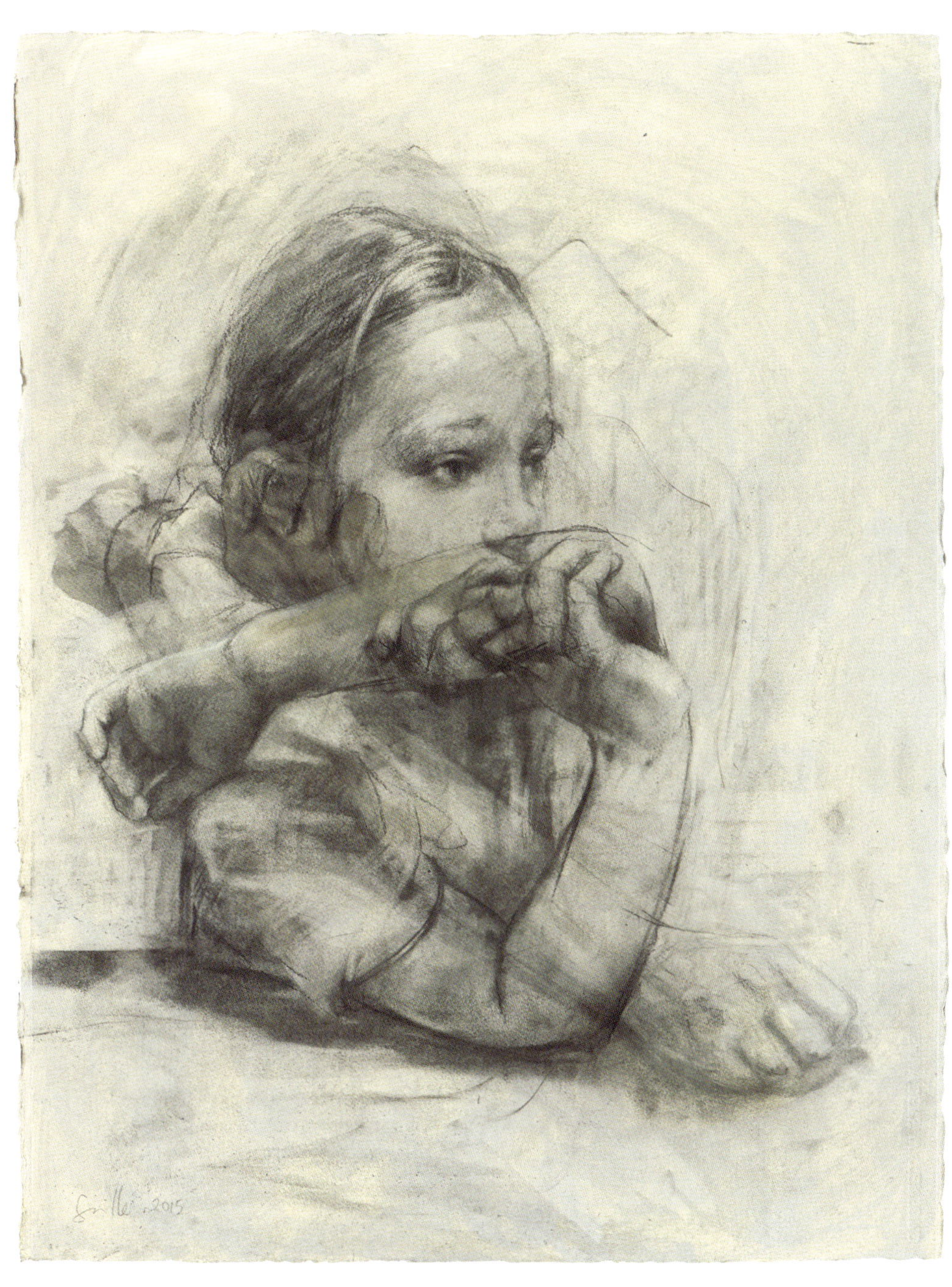

32 *Study of Arms II: A response to Titian's 'Study of a Young Woman', Uffizi, Florence* 2015

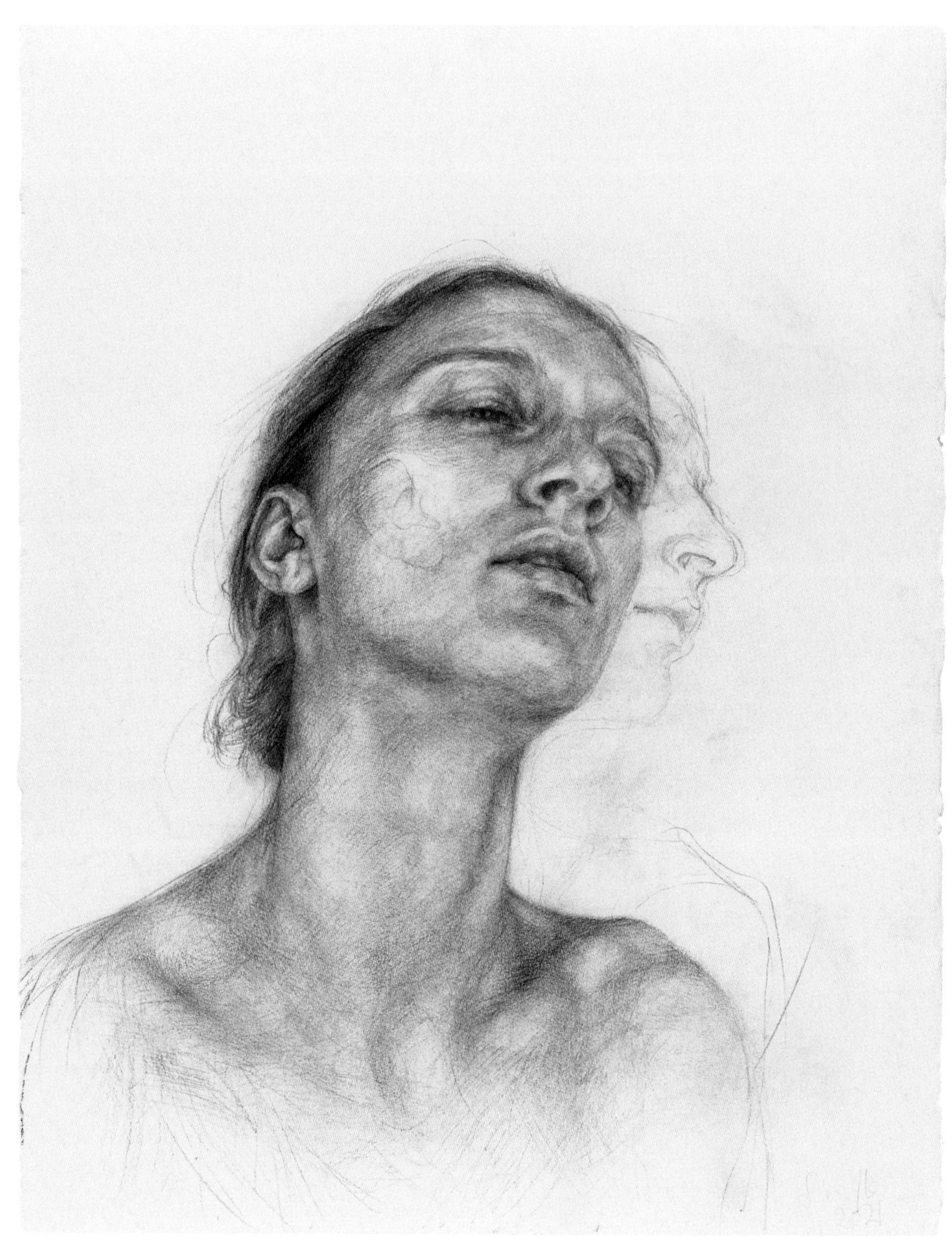

33 *Neck Study II* 2021

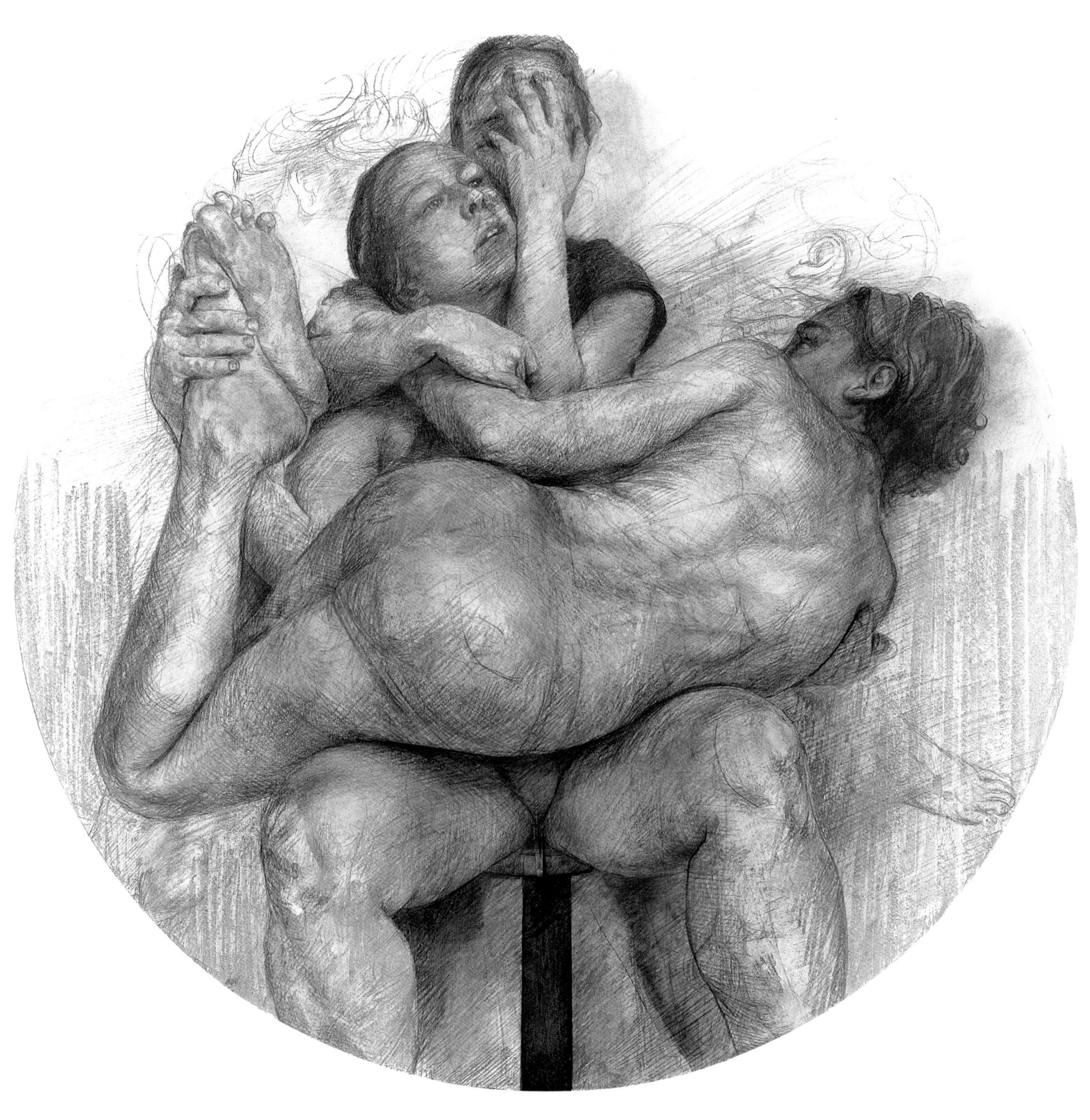

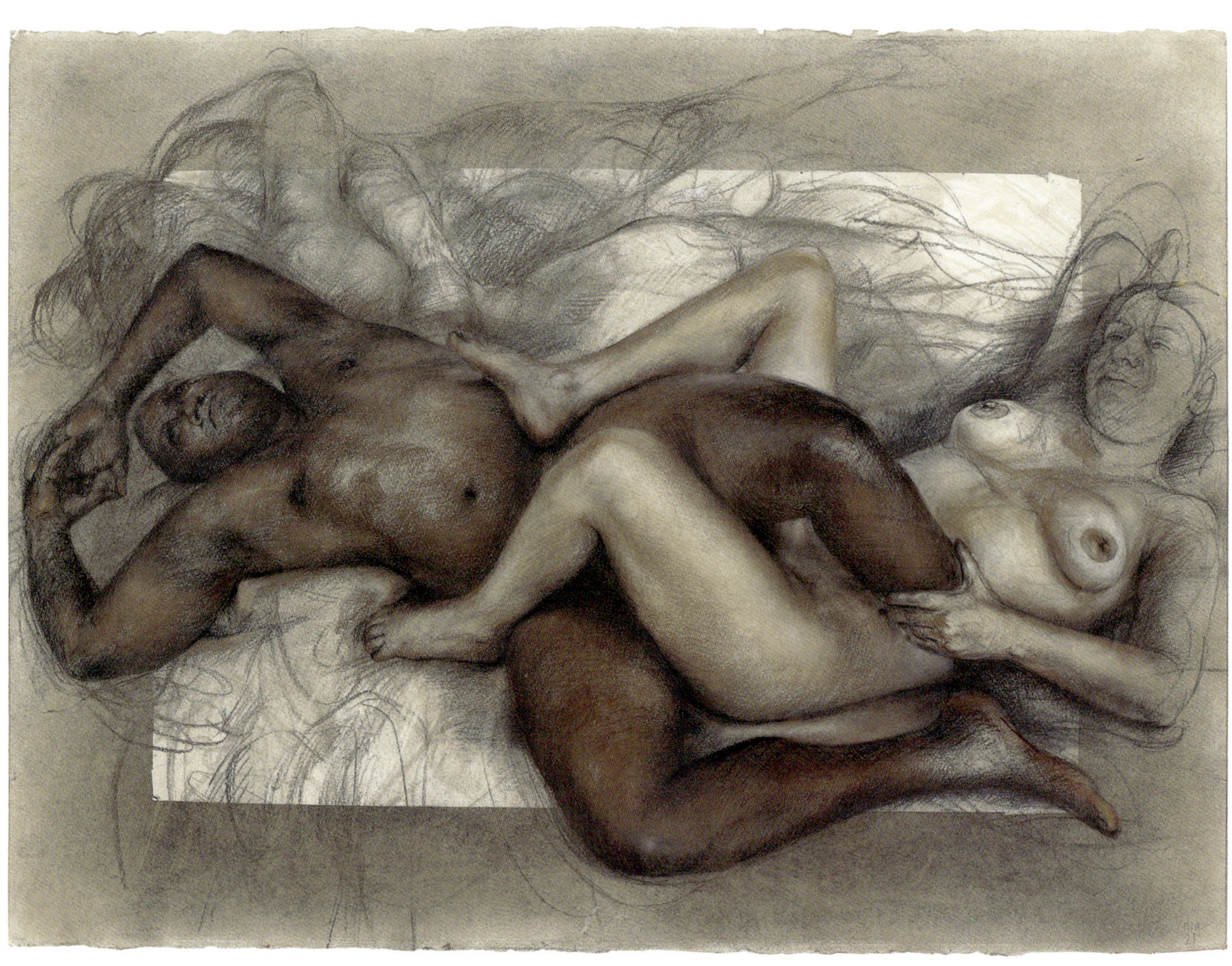

35 *Interlocking Figures Study* 2019–21

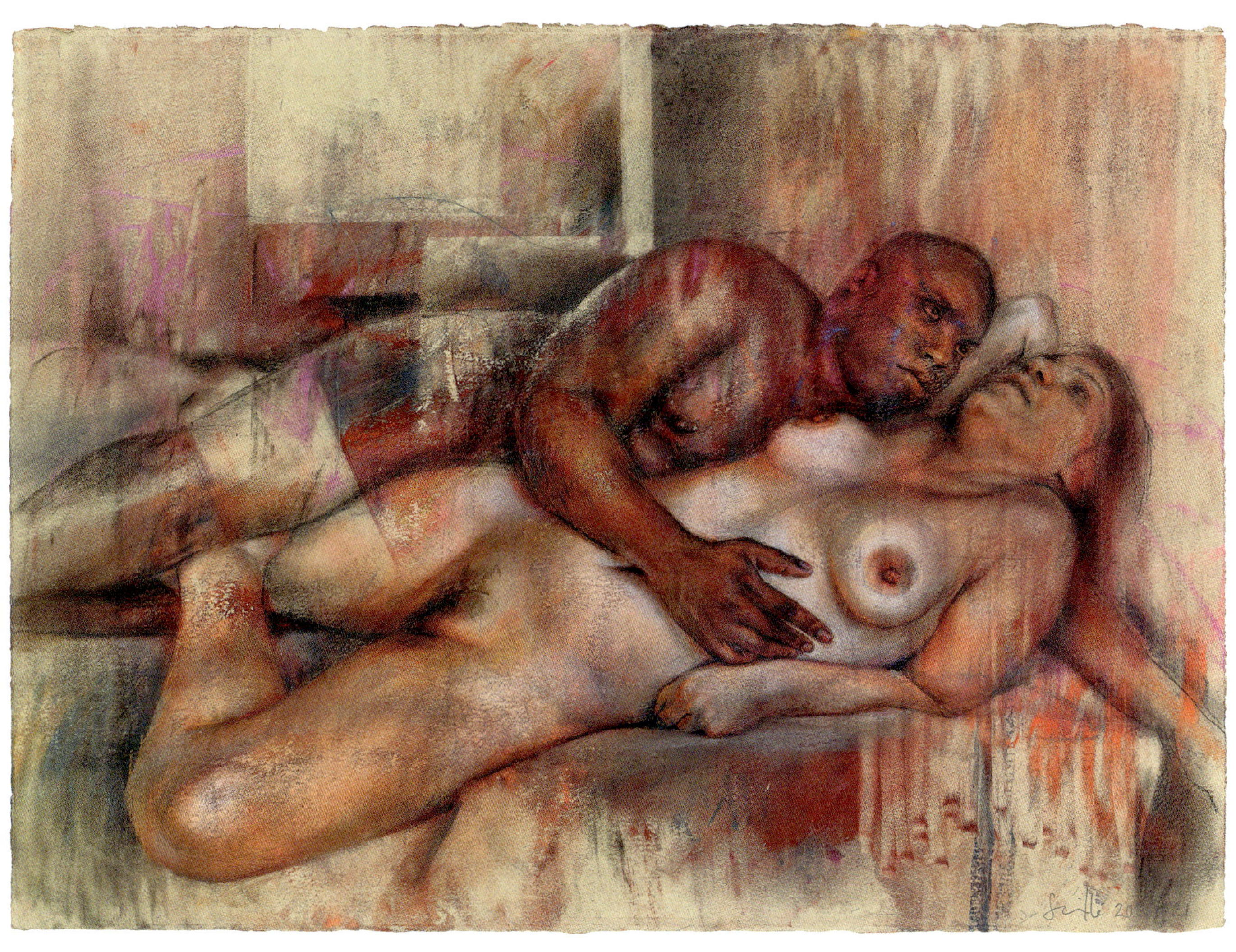

36 *Couples Study* 2016–21

37 *Figures on Box Lid Study* 2018

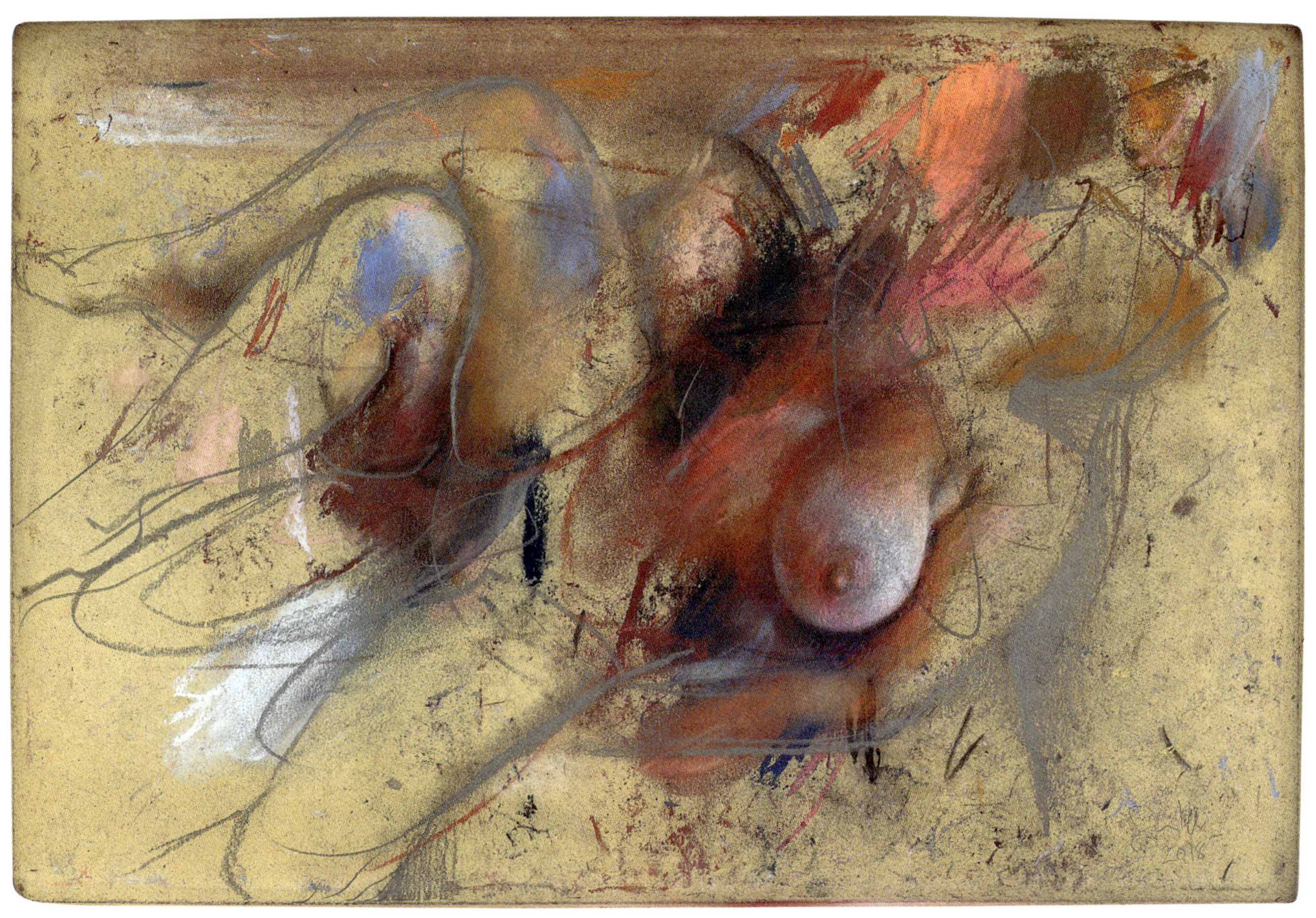

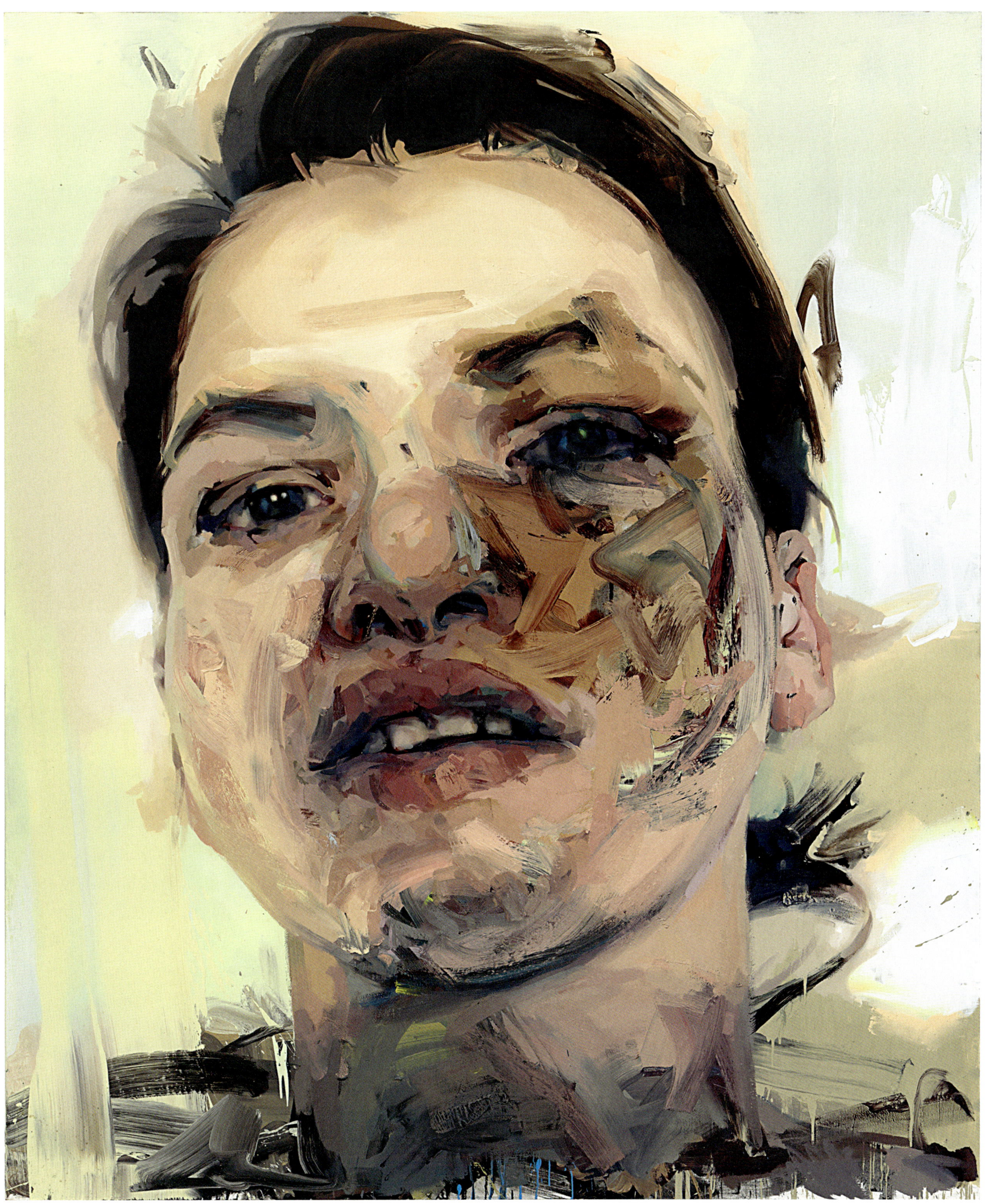

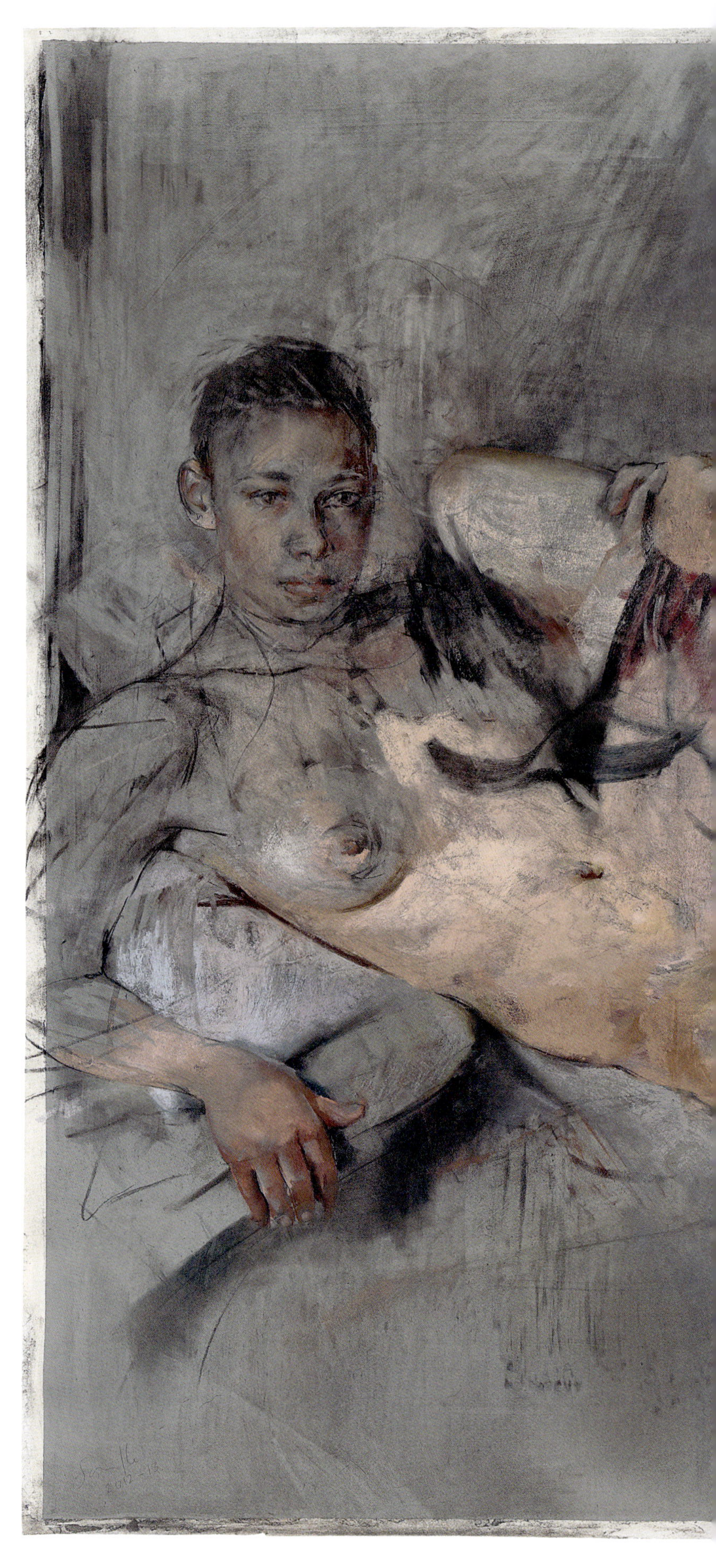

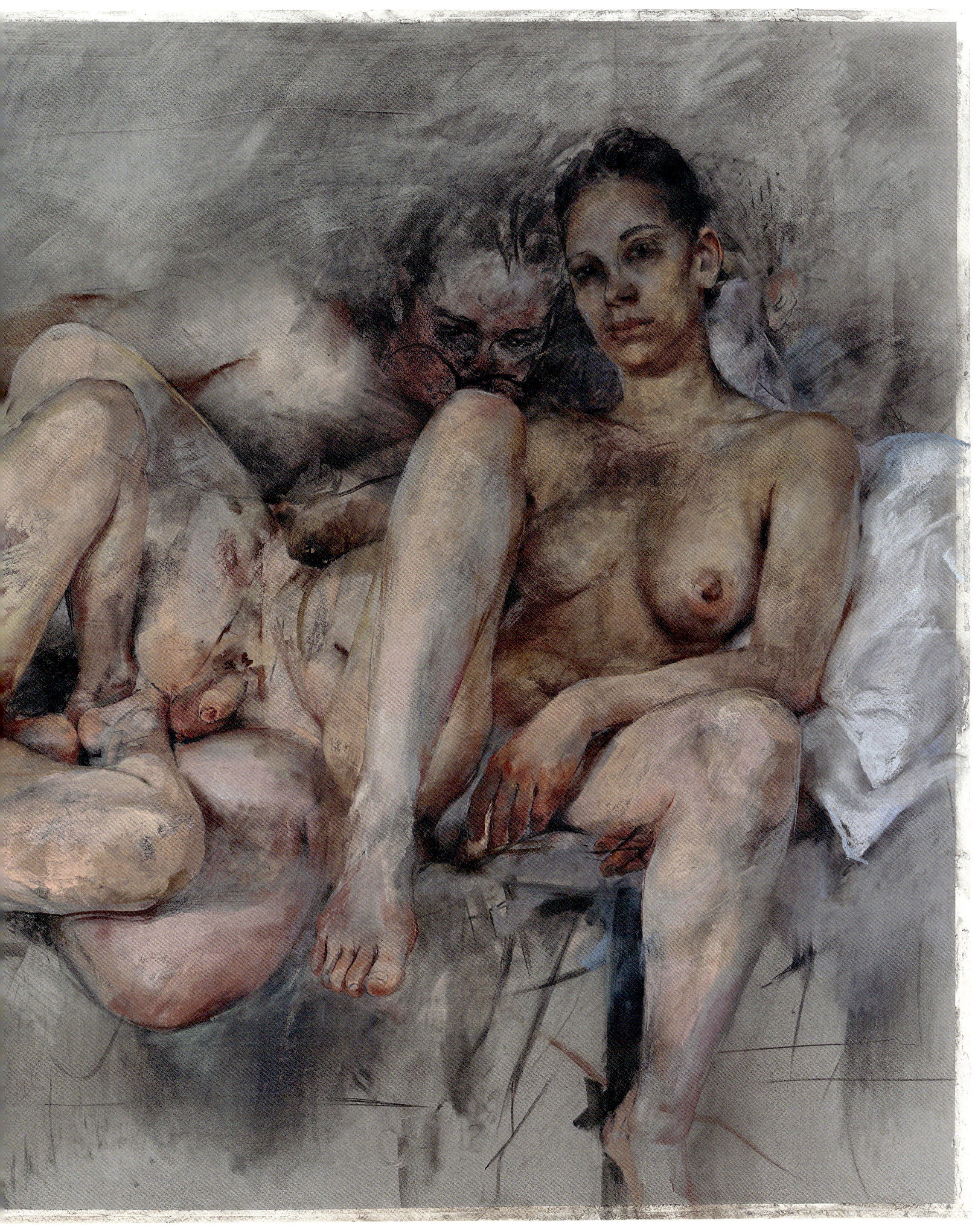

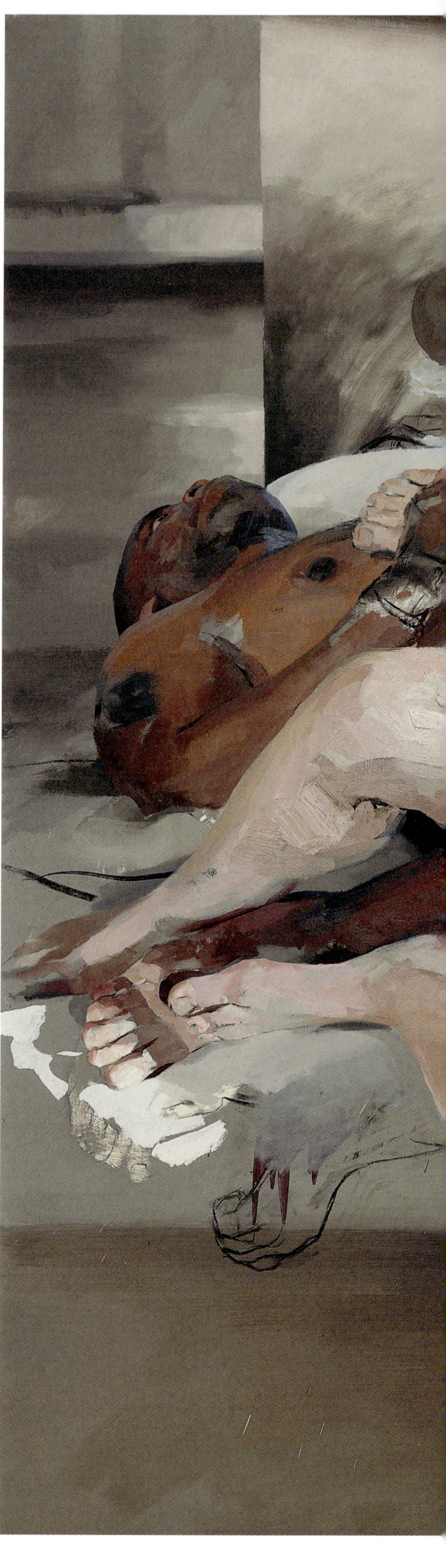

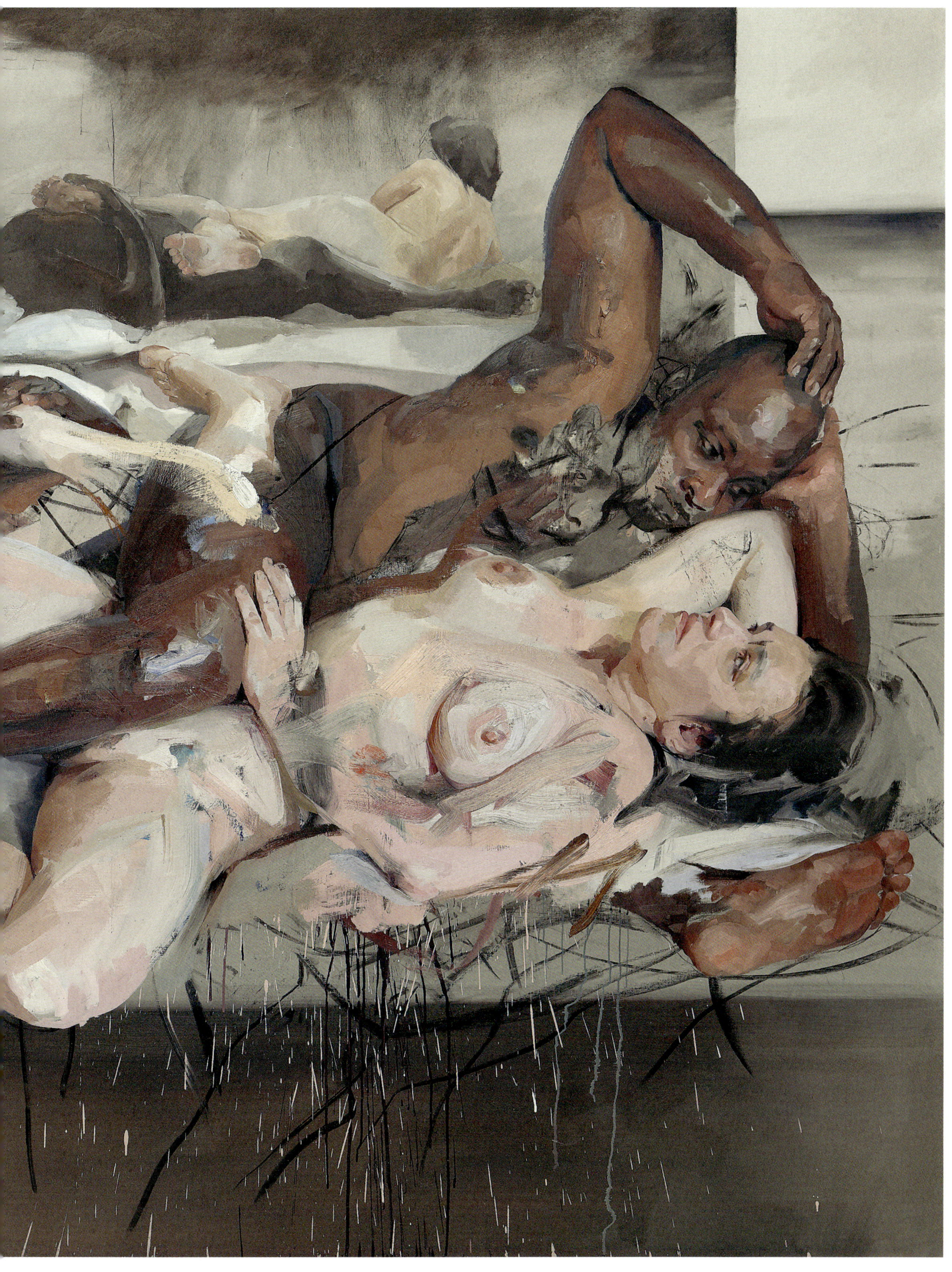

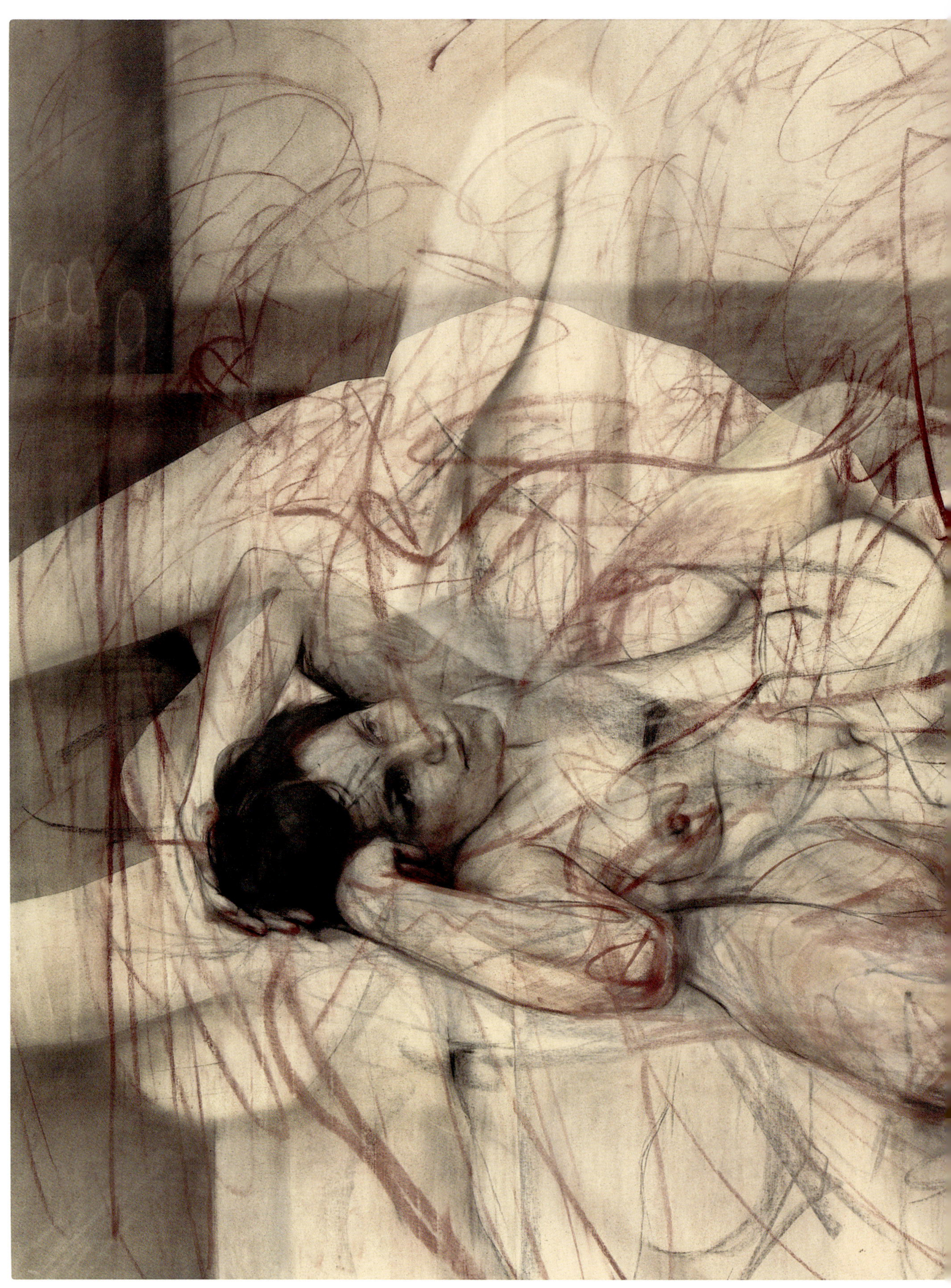

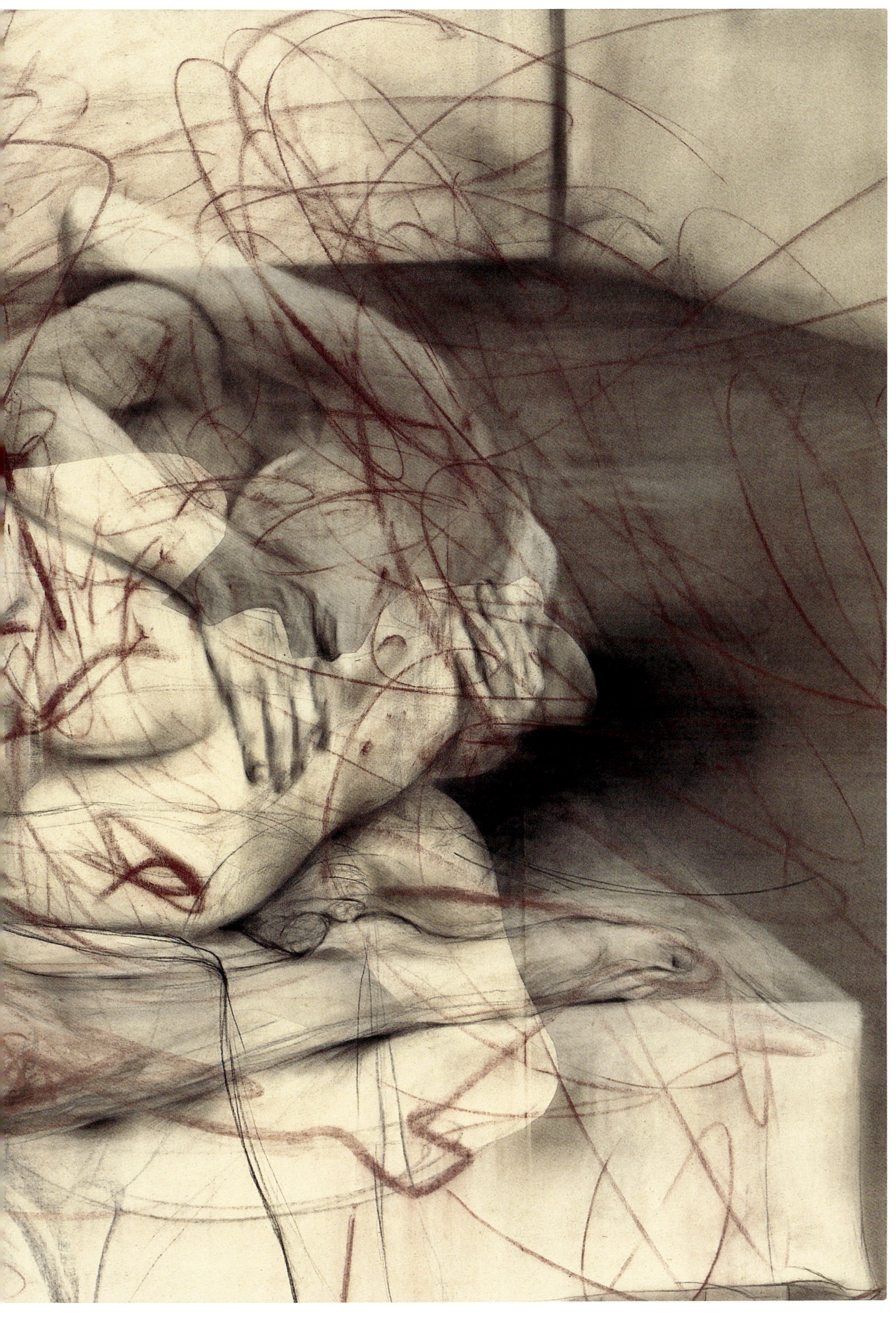

41 *One Out of Two (Symposium)* 2016

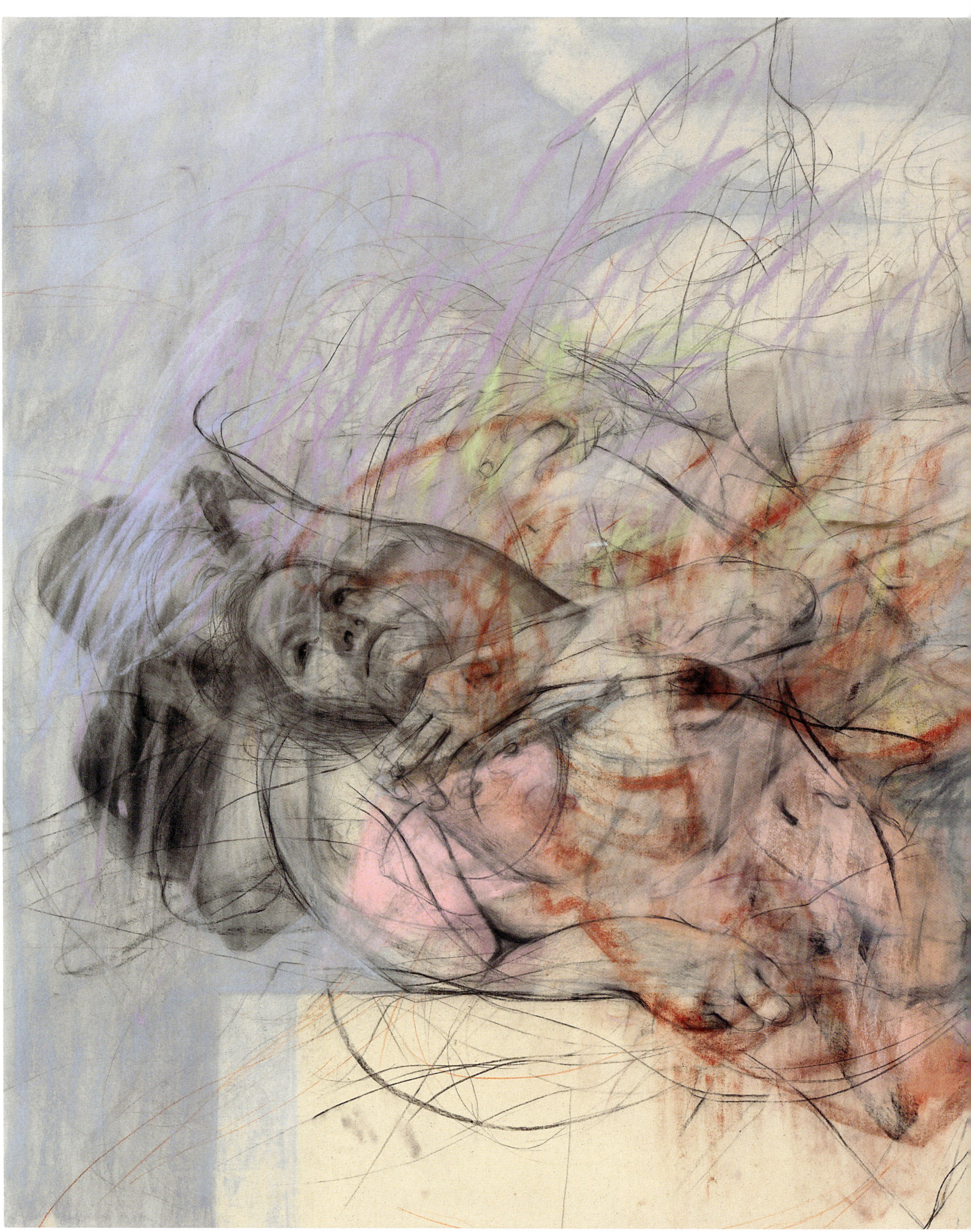

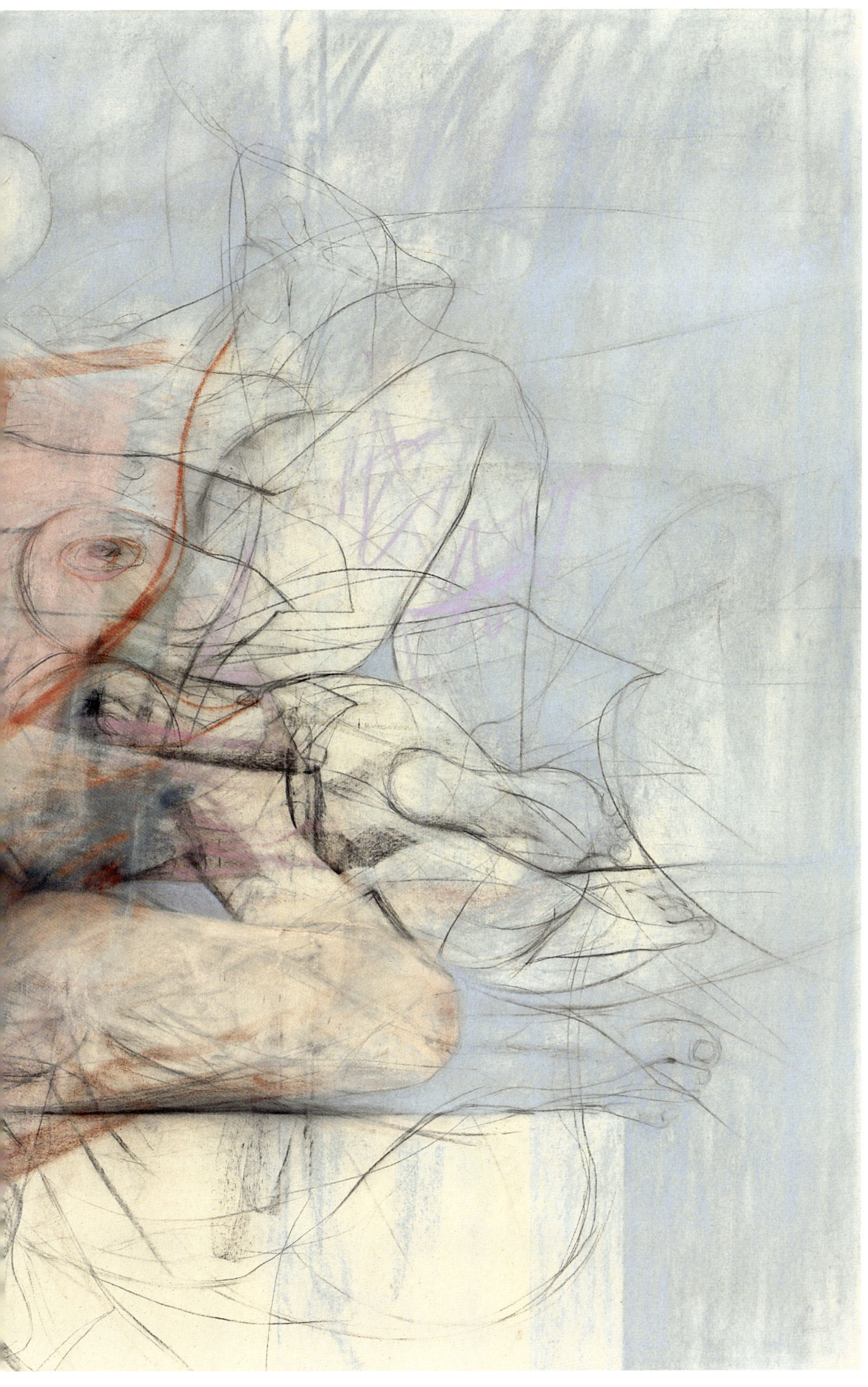

42 *Out of One, Two (Symposium)* 2016

43 *Pietà I* 2019–21

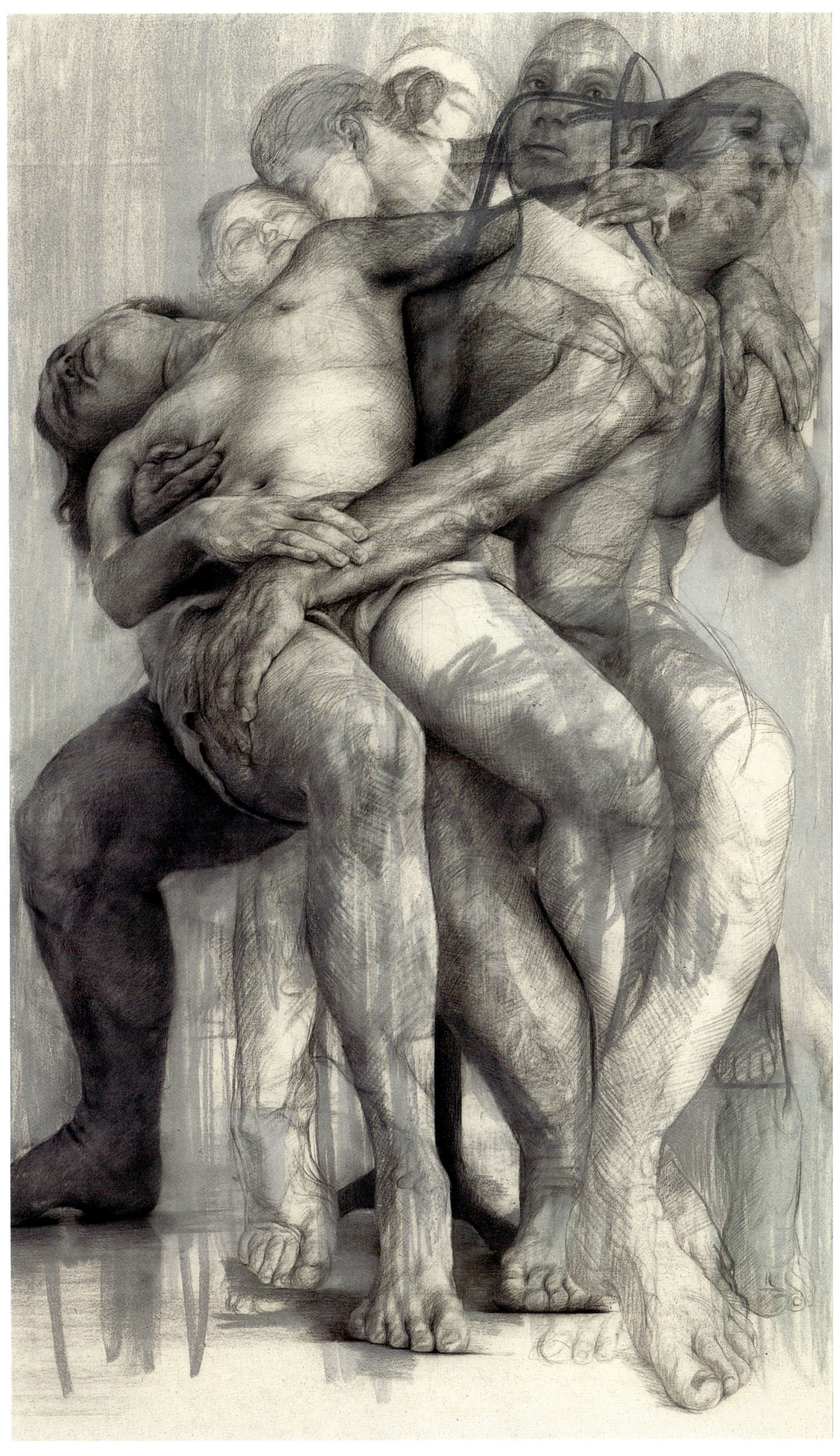

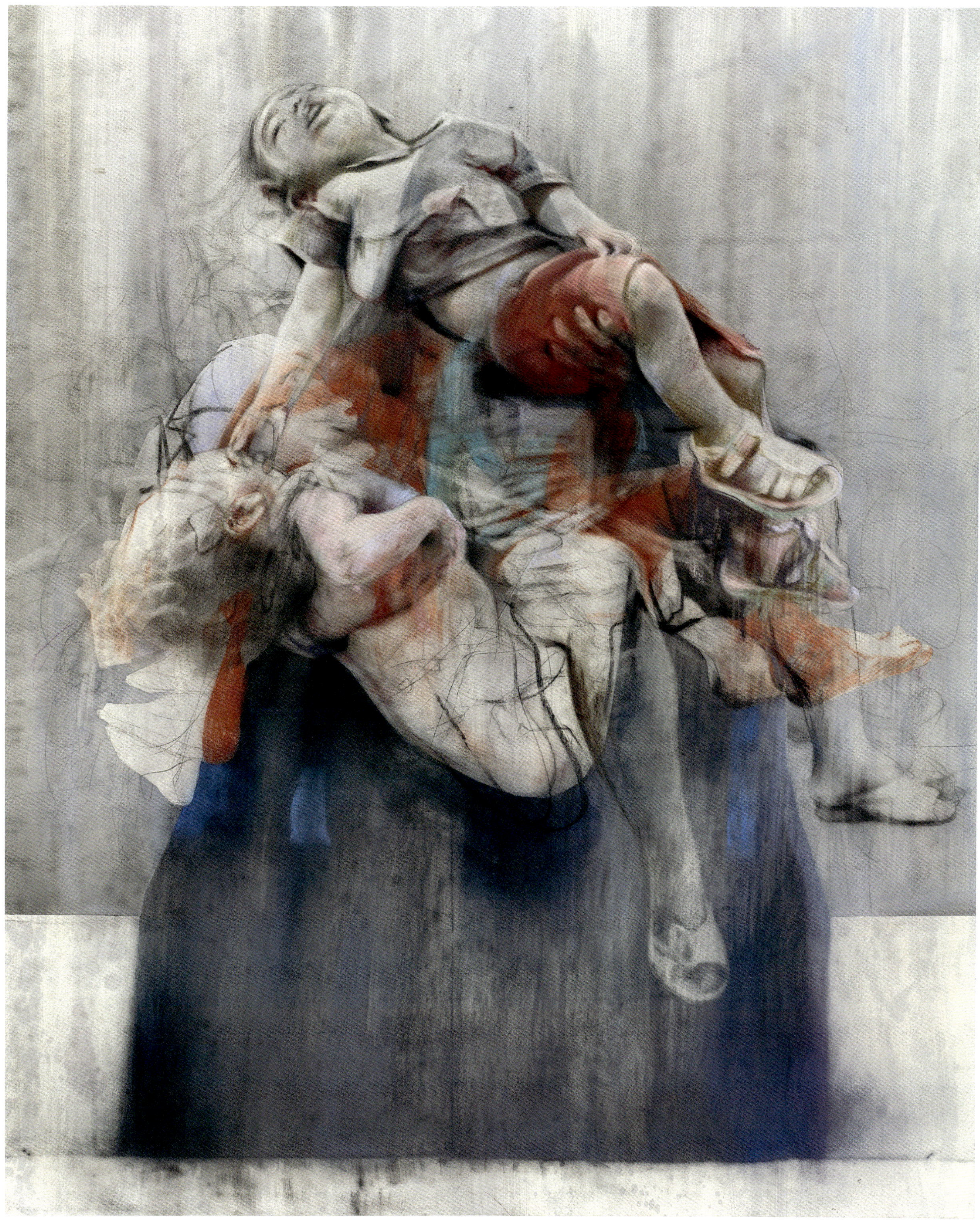

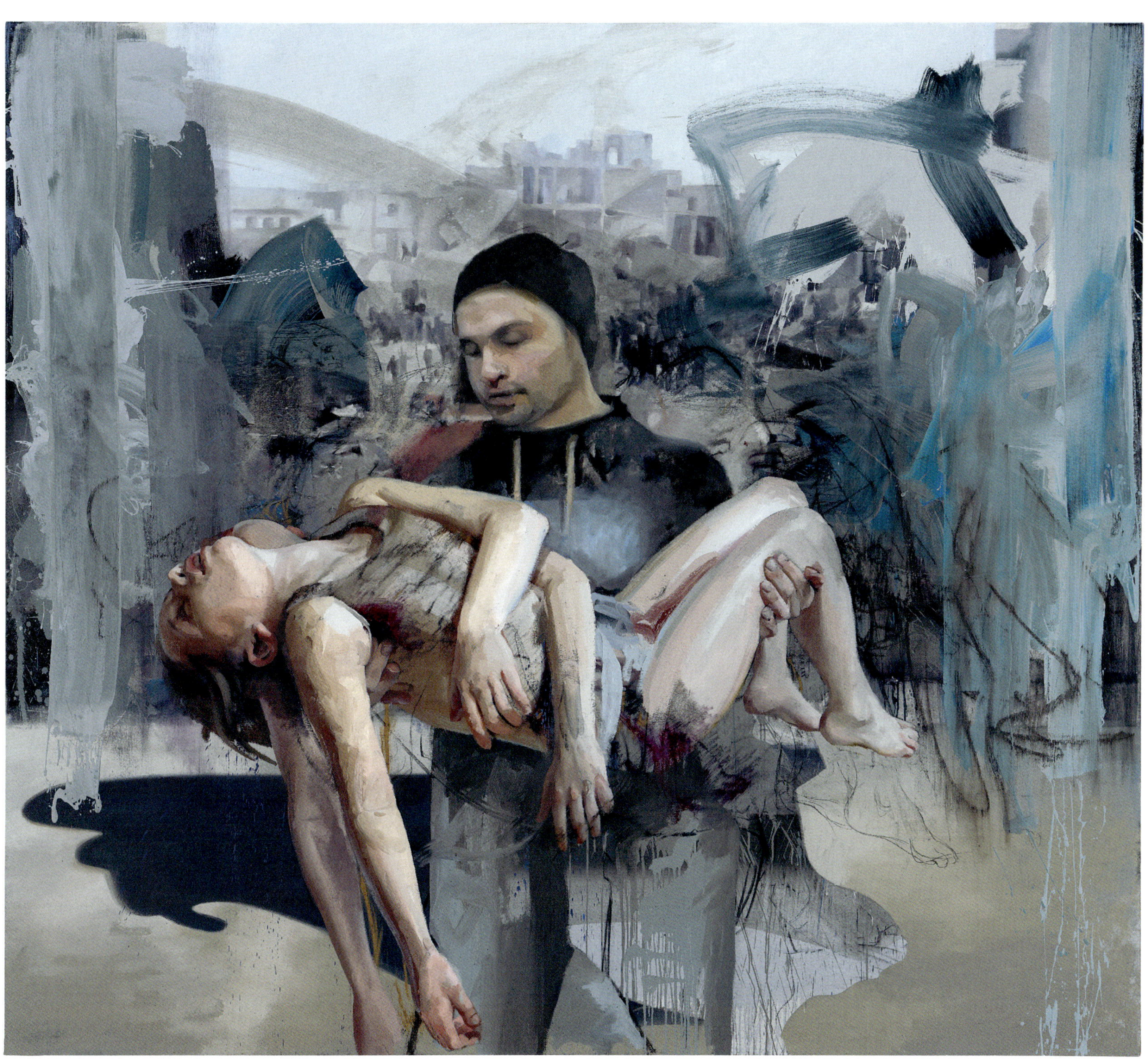

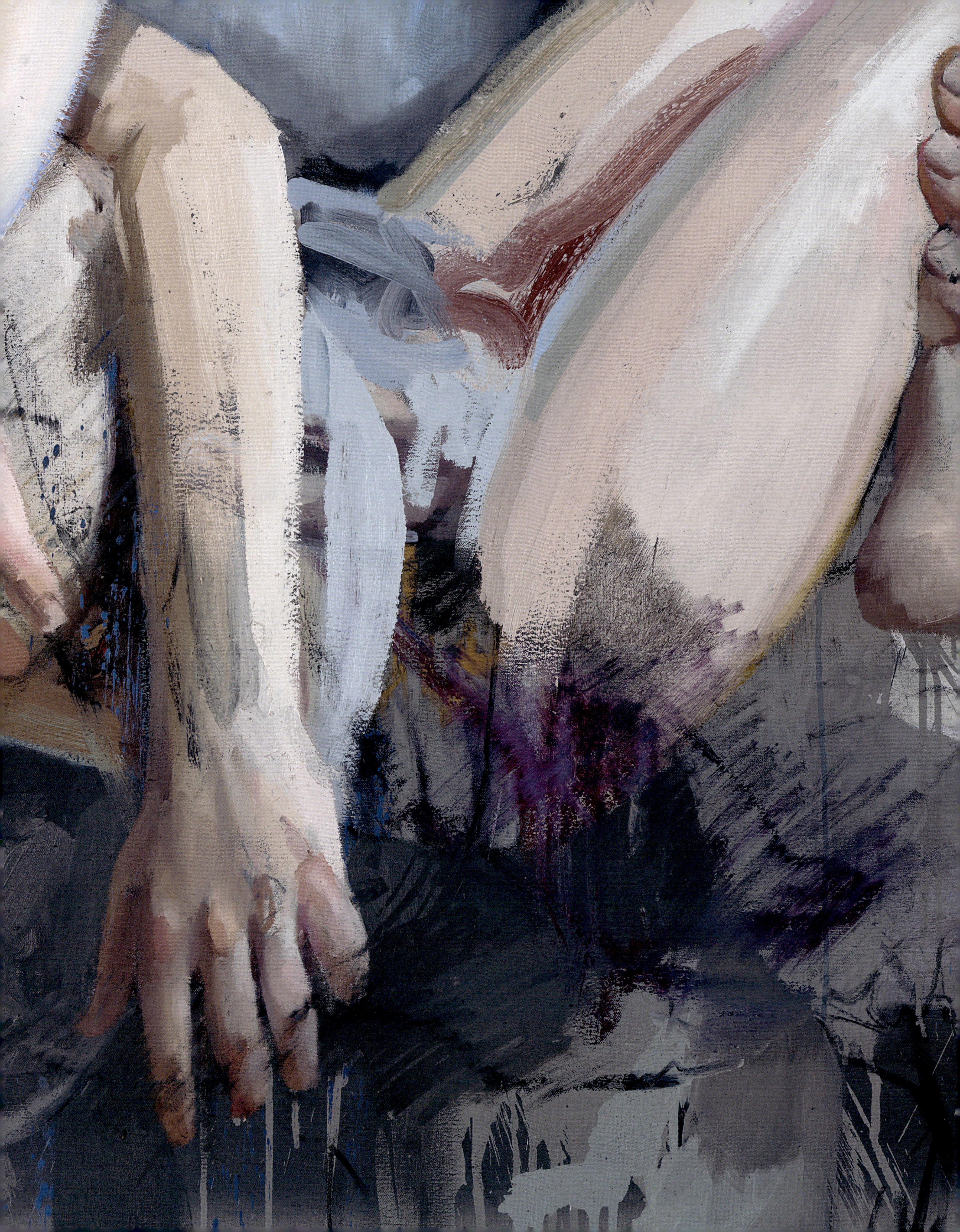

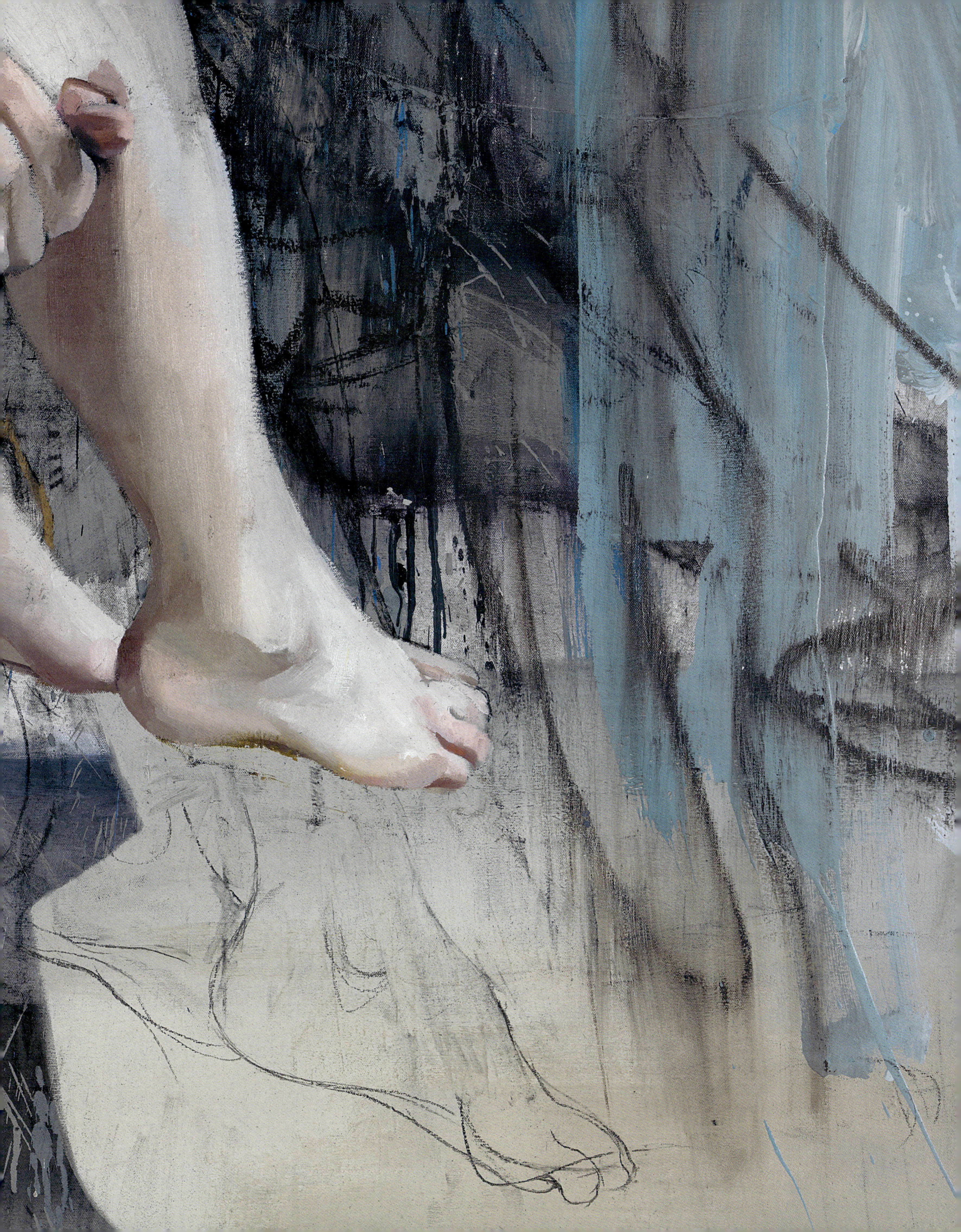

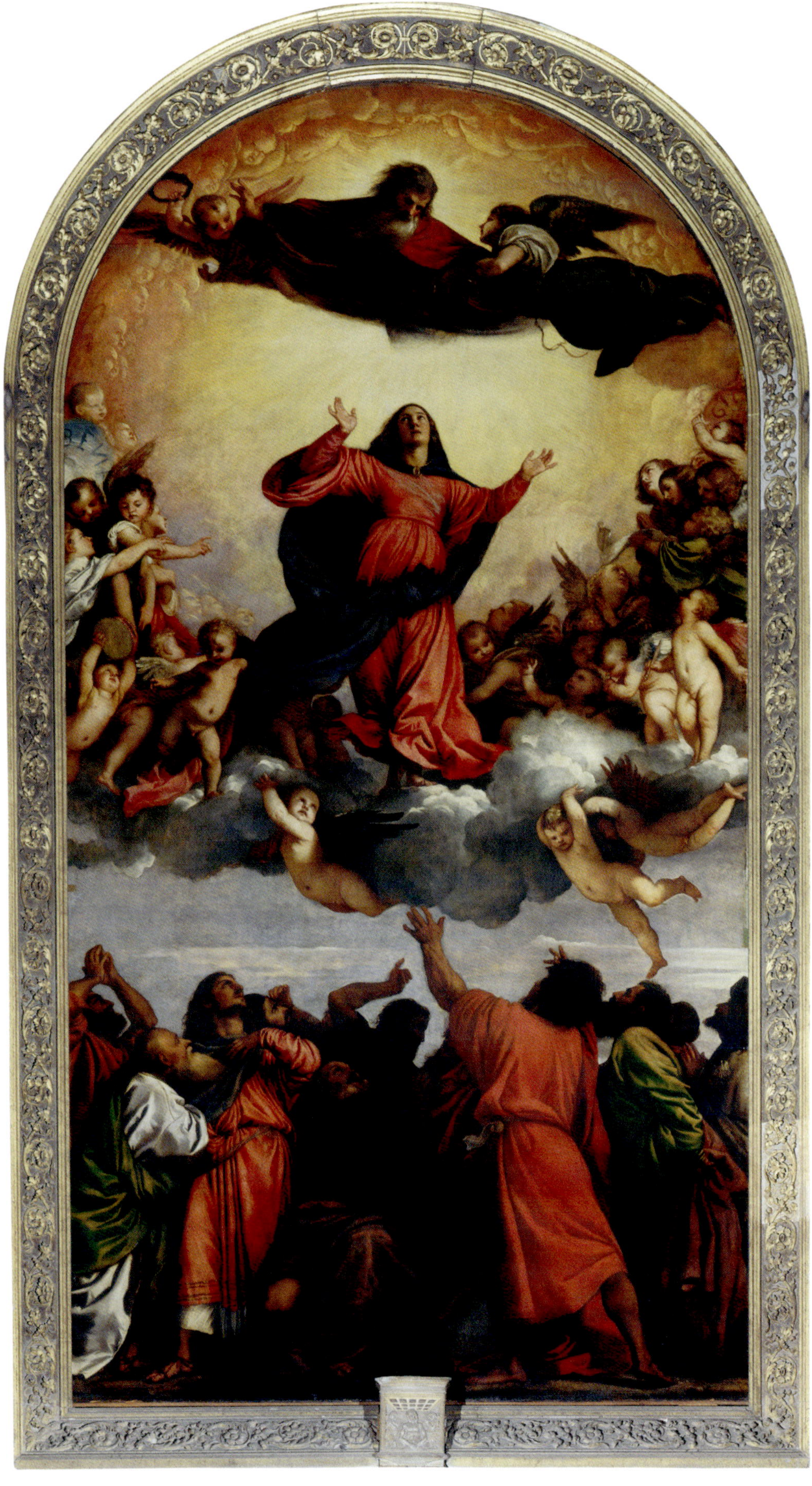

Fig.1
Titian (Tiziano Vecellio)
Assumption of the Virgin, 1516–18
Oil on panel
6900 × 3600 mm
Basilica di Santa Maria Gloriosa dei Frari, Venice

The Rainbow of the Flesh

Emanuele Coccia

Jenny Saville's work has often been compared to that of Francis Bacon and Lucian Freud, painters of flesh that is violently exposed and decomposed into impenetrable and resistant matter. Yet the obsession with which the artist returns to Titian's famous *Assumption of the Virgin* (fig.1), conserved in the basilica of Santa Maria Gloriosa dei Frari in Venice, should have rung an alarm bell in attempting to identify the work of an artist profoundly shaped by feminist academic culture with an experience of the flesh so thoroughly defined by a male gaze. Assumption, in Christian theology, is in fact the specular opposite of incarnation. Where the latter is the process through which a divinity assumes human form and enters into the vulnerable mortality of the human body, the former is instead the movement by which a human body – in Titian's case, Mary's – is called to the sky and takes on a celestial consistency, the same as that of the bodies of the resurrected. Impassive, subtle, spiritual, agile, and, above all, 'clear': resurrected bodies, in Christian theology, are literally made of light. It is this strange, paradoxical 'good news' (*euangelion* in Biblical Greek) that Saville took from Titian's hieroglyph, so as to generalise it in its most radical form: if resurrection is nothing but the transfiguration of bodies into light, then it is also the process that allows human flesh to become the same matter as the one out of which painting is made. Theology thus becomes an aesthetic manifesto: against Willem de Kooning's famous adage, 'Flesh was the reason why oil painting was invented',[1] Saville seems to suggest that *painting* is the sole reason why *flesh* was created.

All this becomes clear from taking into consideration Saville's most famous portraits. It is as though, in reality, these portraits were painted by recognising the traces of a human face in the imprint produced by a rainbow as it sets itself down on the earth or against a flat surface. The complexions of Saville's mythological subjects in *Teles* (2020–1), *Leucosia* (2021), *Odysseus I* (fig.2), *Odysseus II* (2021), and *Ligeia* (2020–1) are, first and foremost, pure iridescence. This is not just the result of a painterly choice; it's an analysis of anatomy. Flesh is always the reflection of light. It is light's iridescence. It would be difficult to find an attitude that is more distant from and radically opposed to the British tradition of which Freud and Bacon are an integral part. Flesh is not the cavern of some inaccessible interiority possessed by a subject that can barely express itself. It's pure surface. It's pure transmission. It is not a coincidence that the question of maternity returns so incessantly in Saville's painting. It is not a matter of simple biographical reflection. For centuries, we have studied, categorised, and represented bodies starting from the one-sided experience of flesh that belongs to male bodies. In doing so, we have, however, neglected the most important property of human flesh, of the matter of our experience: its transmissibility. What we call maternity, fundamentally, is nothing but this: the fact that some bodies, maternal ones, are capable of transmitting their own flesh to others, the experience and evidence that flesh does not belong to any one subject more than another, that it is the object and matter of exchange. Flesh is, literally, life in its capacity to circulate from one body to another, one place to another, one time to another. To be born means this: to make flesh circulate from one subject to another. There is nothing more superficial and nothing lighter than our flesh. This is the reason that painting must begin with maternity: only in this process does it reveal itself for what it is. Or rather: maternity is nothing but one of the forms through which flesh shows itself as made of painting, of reflections and colours.

This is what the identity between flesh and iridescence seems to affirm with geometric certainty. If we have still not fully understood what painting is, it is because we have not reflected on the rainbow, the place in which light reveals and transforms itself into a chromatic palette, showing itself to be the only great painter in the universe. Saville's work transforms the entire history of painting into a treatise on colour, to which every artist adds new chapters. To paint means to look for and to find the rainbow – the explosion of the colour palette – in the flesh of all things.

In this way, Saville's painting becomes atmospheric and meteorological. There is nothing more meteorological than a rainbow, nothing more unpredictable, freer, or more mysterious than our flesh. There is nothing more ephemeral than a rainbow: flesh is always ephemeral but not just because it is vulnerable. It is ephemeral like the reflection of the light of a sunset, and it is for this reason that it can exist only through painting.

Excerpt adapted from an essay first published in *Sirens: Jenny Saville at Casa Malaparte* (Gagosian, New York, 2022)

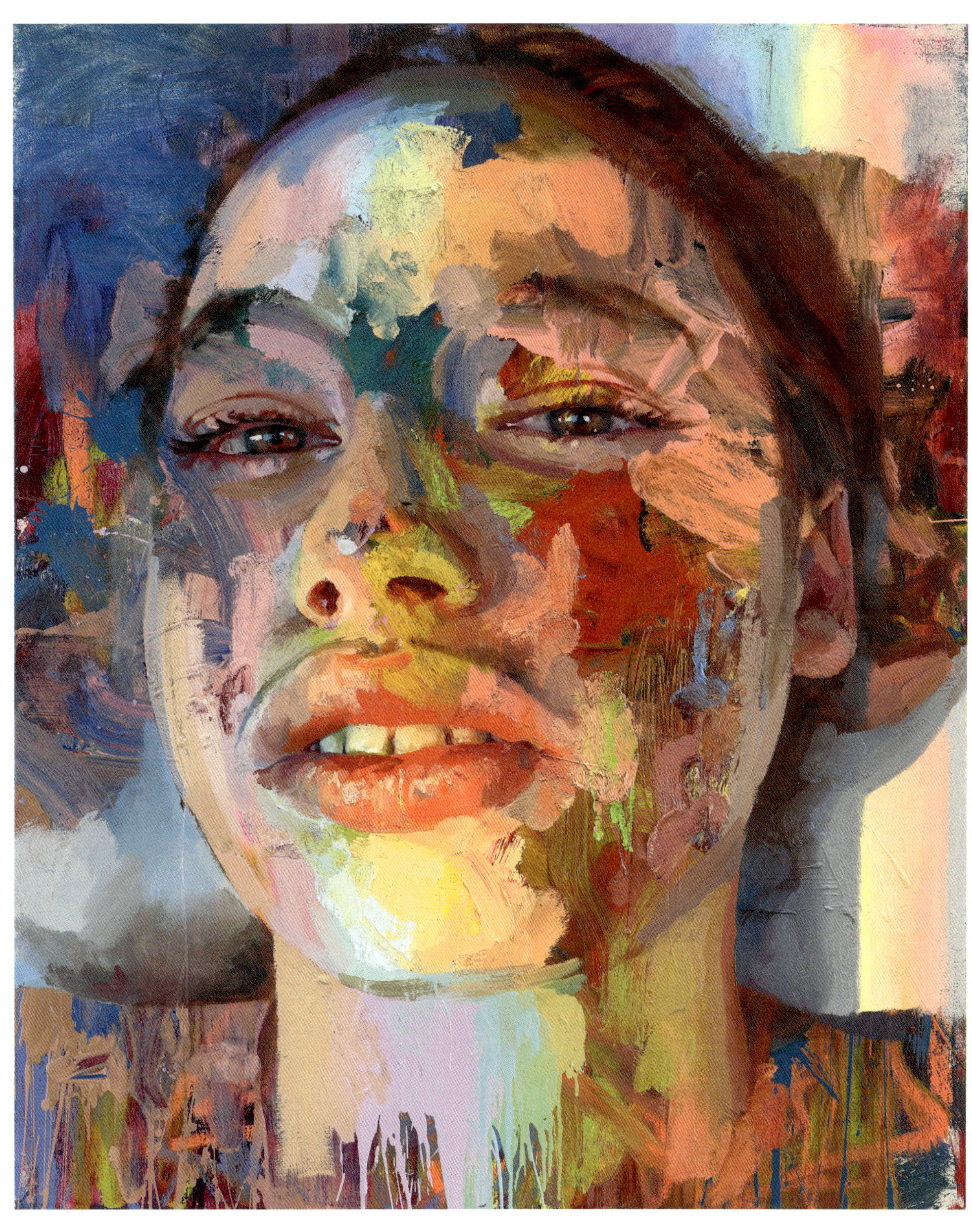

Fig.2
Jenny Saville
Odysseus I, 2020–1
Oil, oil stick and acrylic on canvas
1500 × 1200 mm
Forman Family Collection

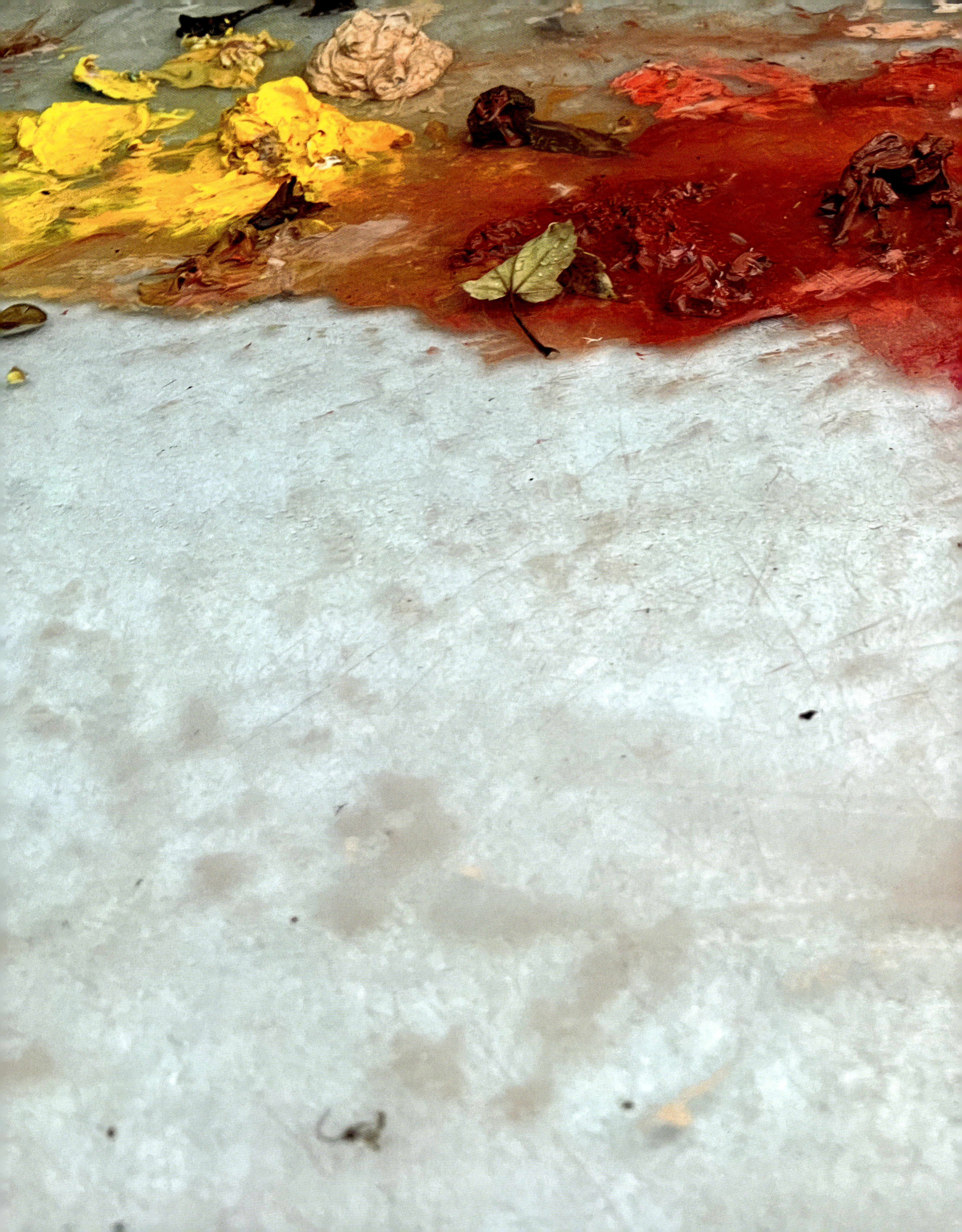

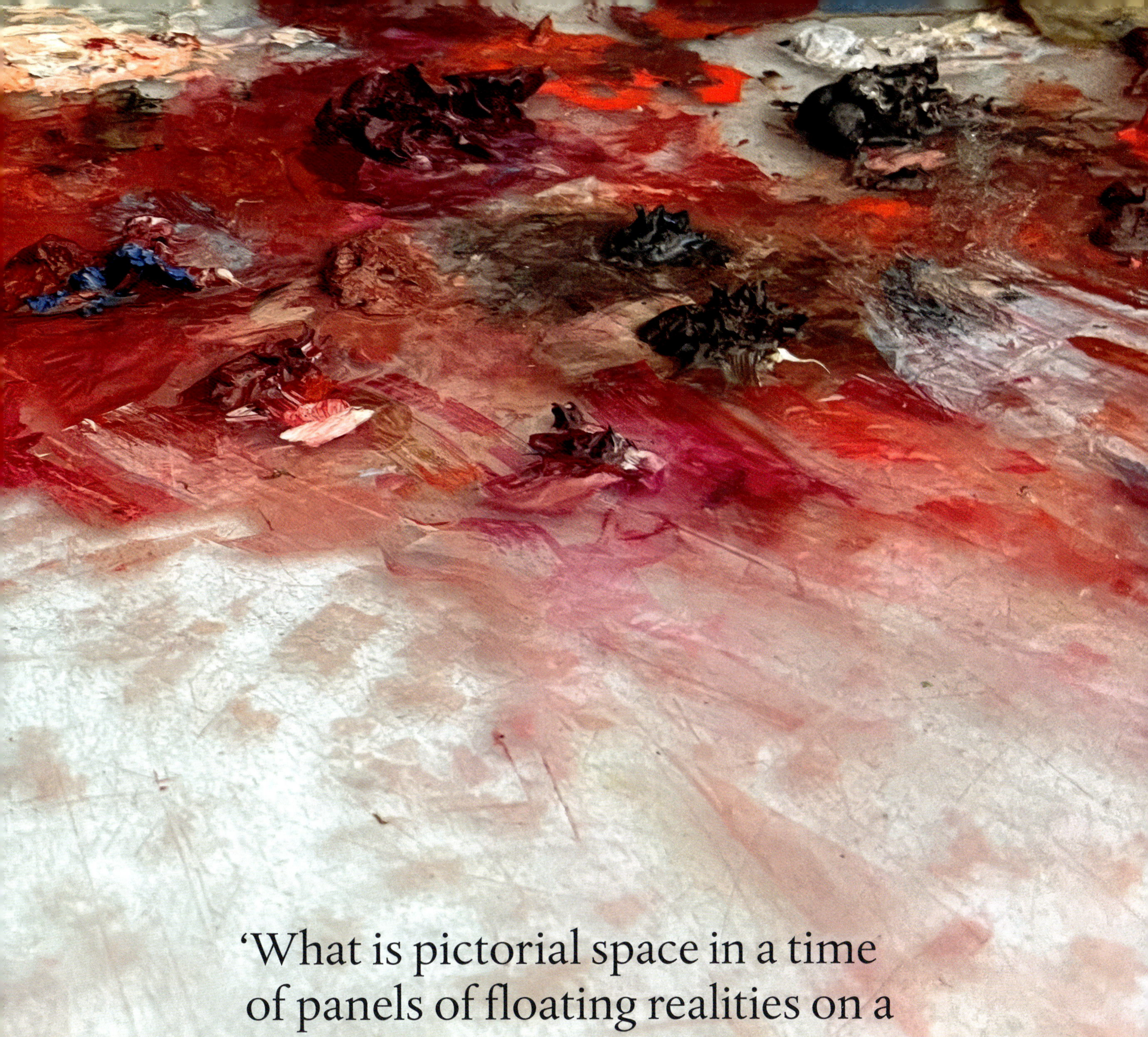

> ‘What is pictorial space in a time of panels of floating realities on a computer screen? . . . We are living in a profound moment . . . I want my painting to have the necessity of modern living.’
>
> Jenny Saville

46 *Self-Portrait (after Rembrandt)* 2019

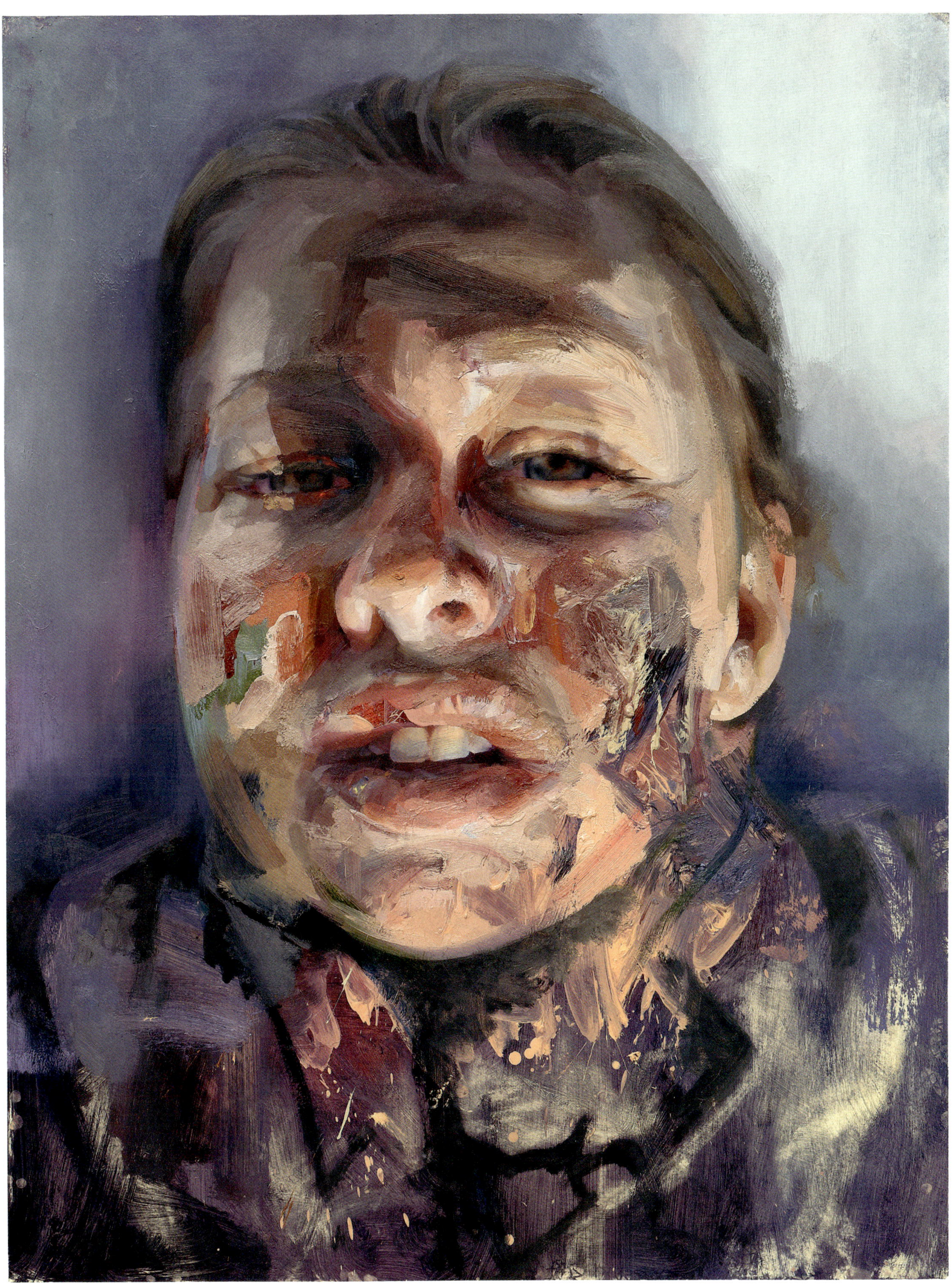

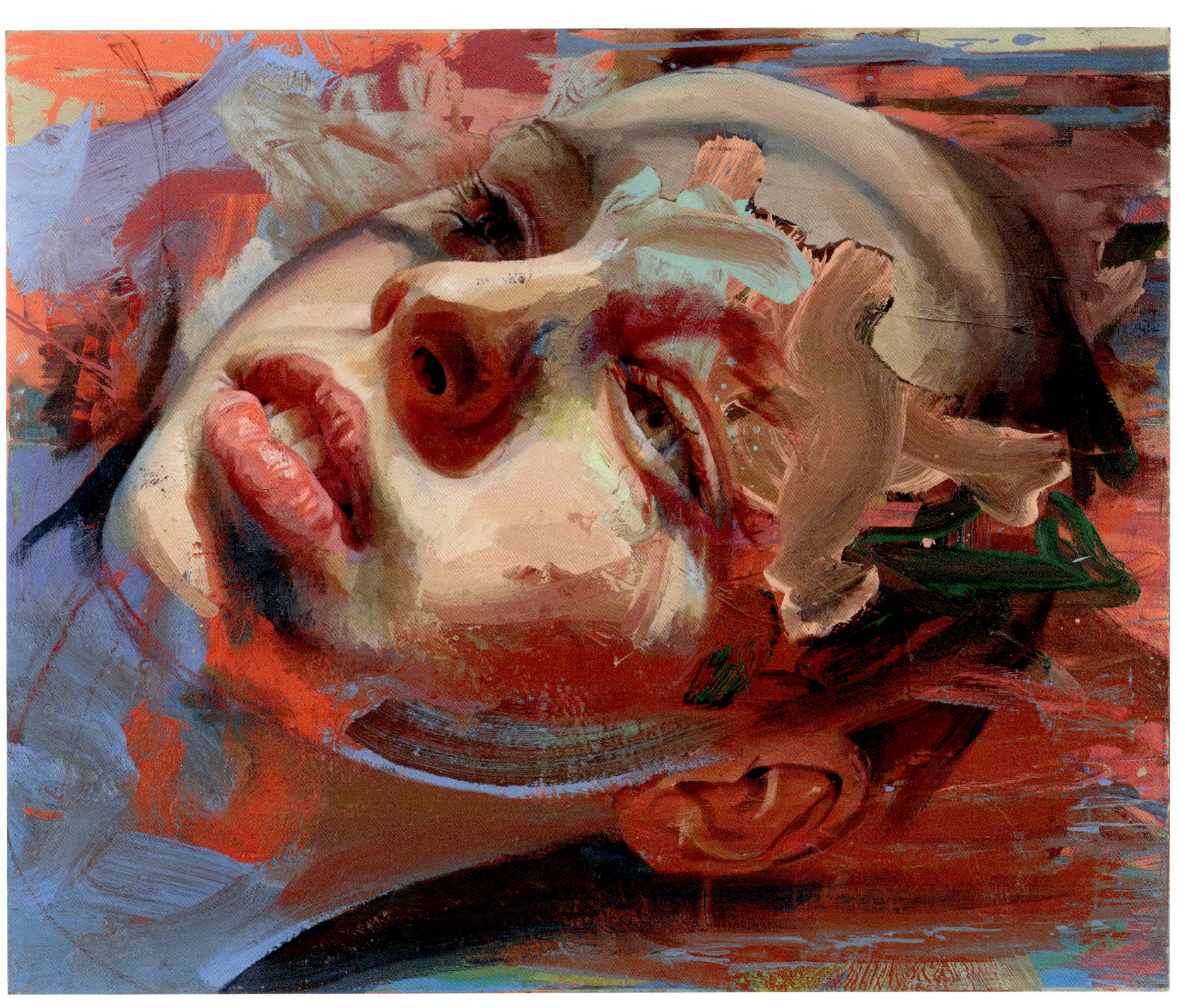

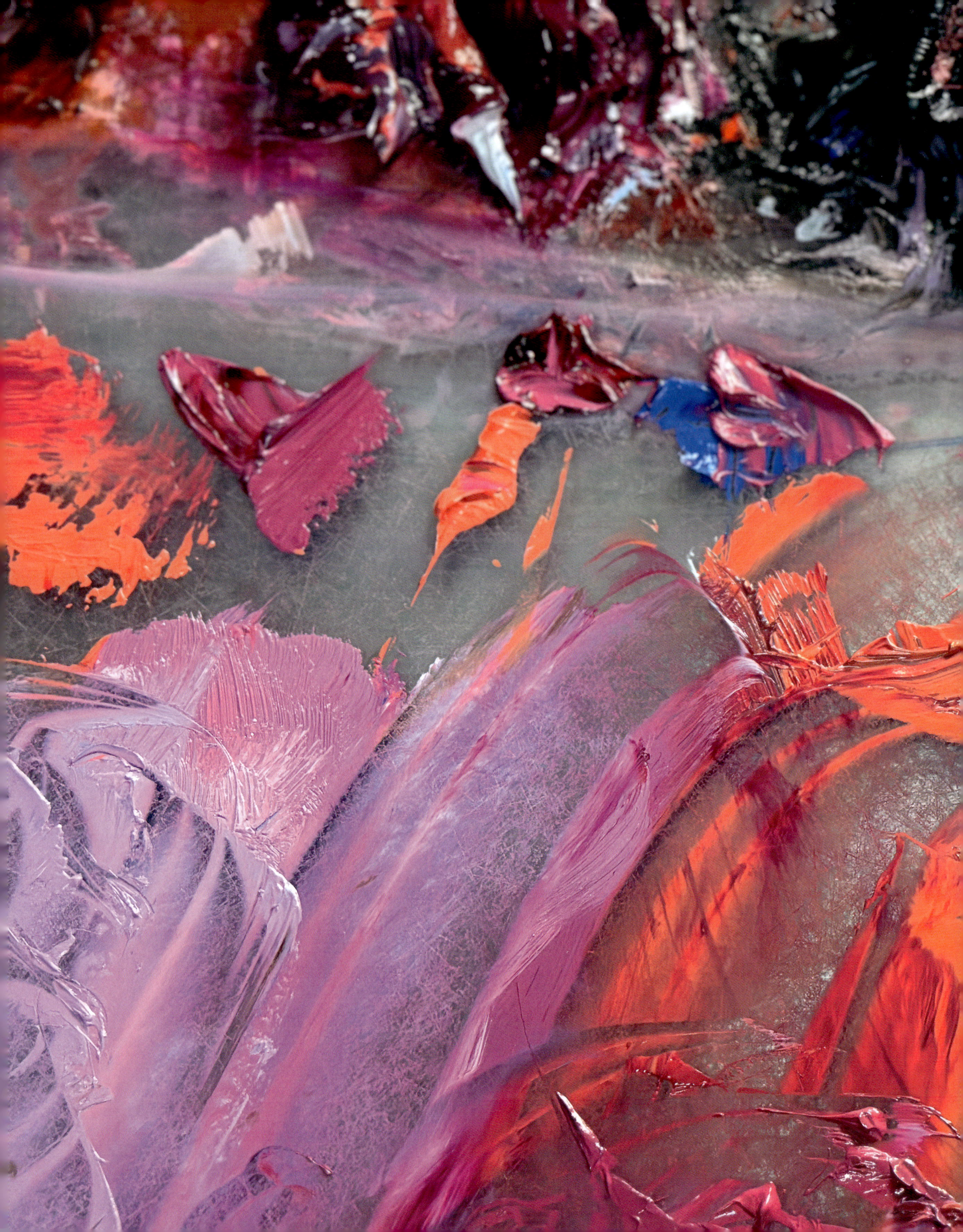

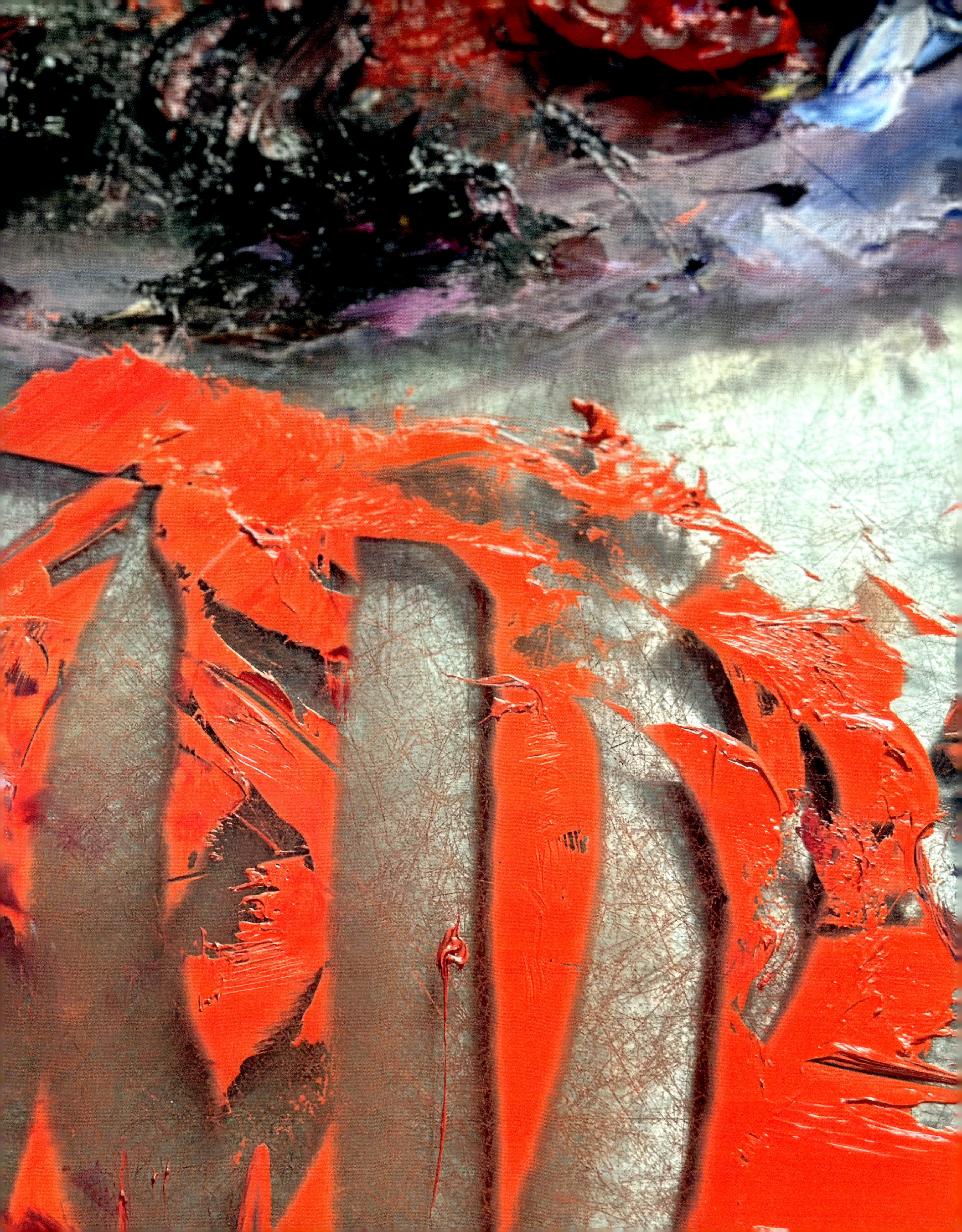

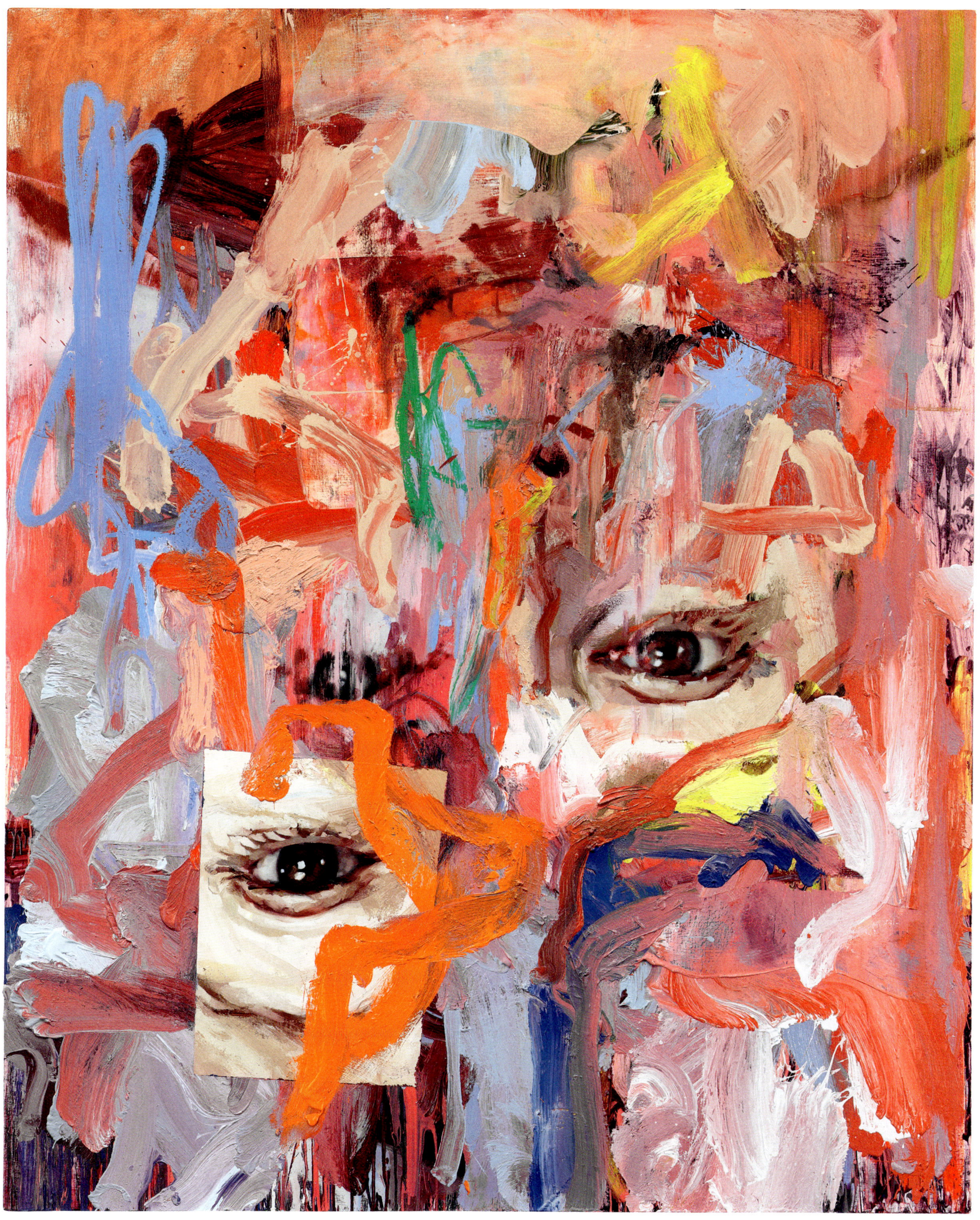

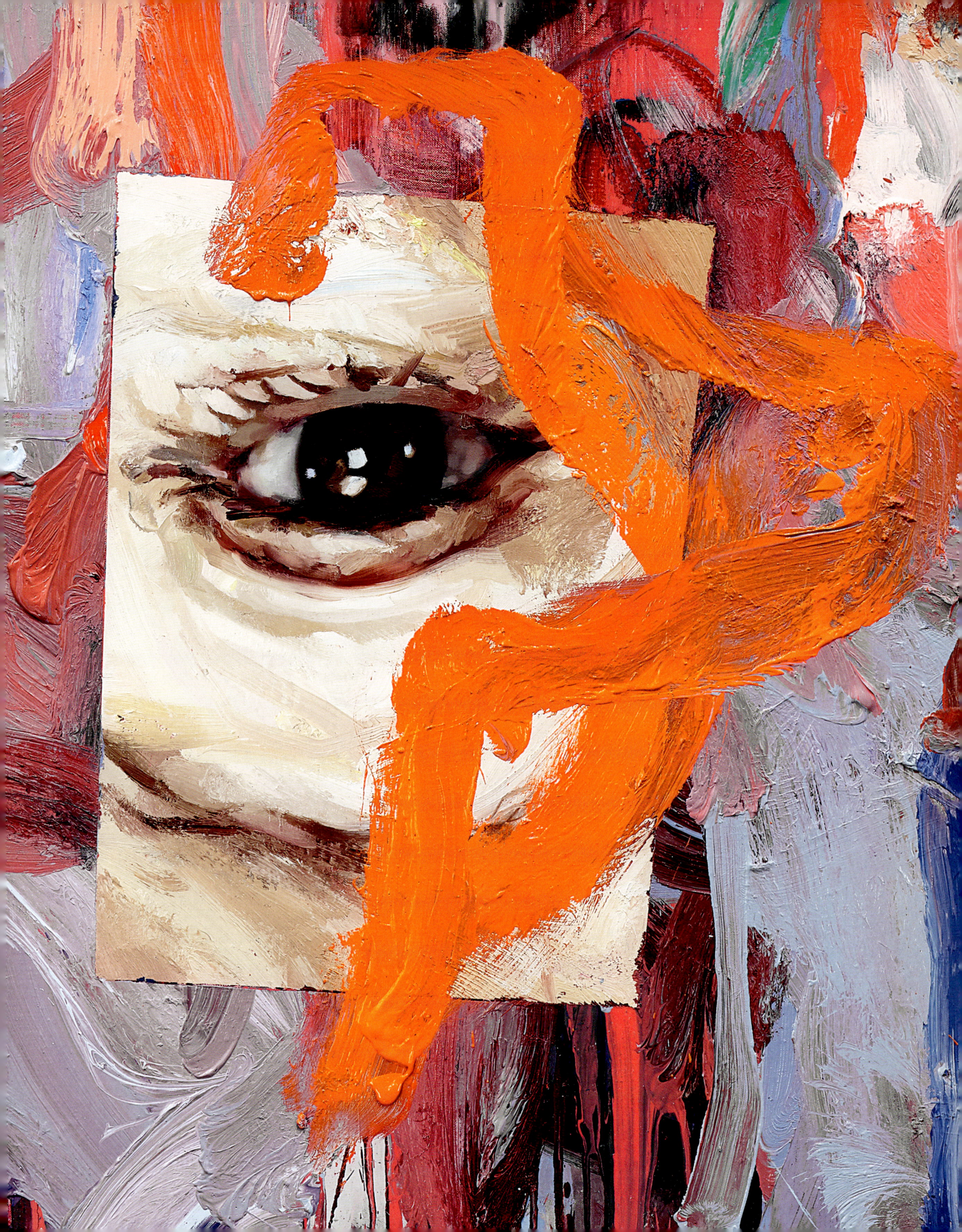

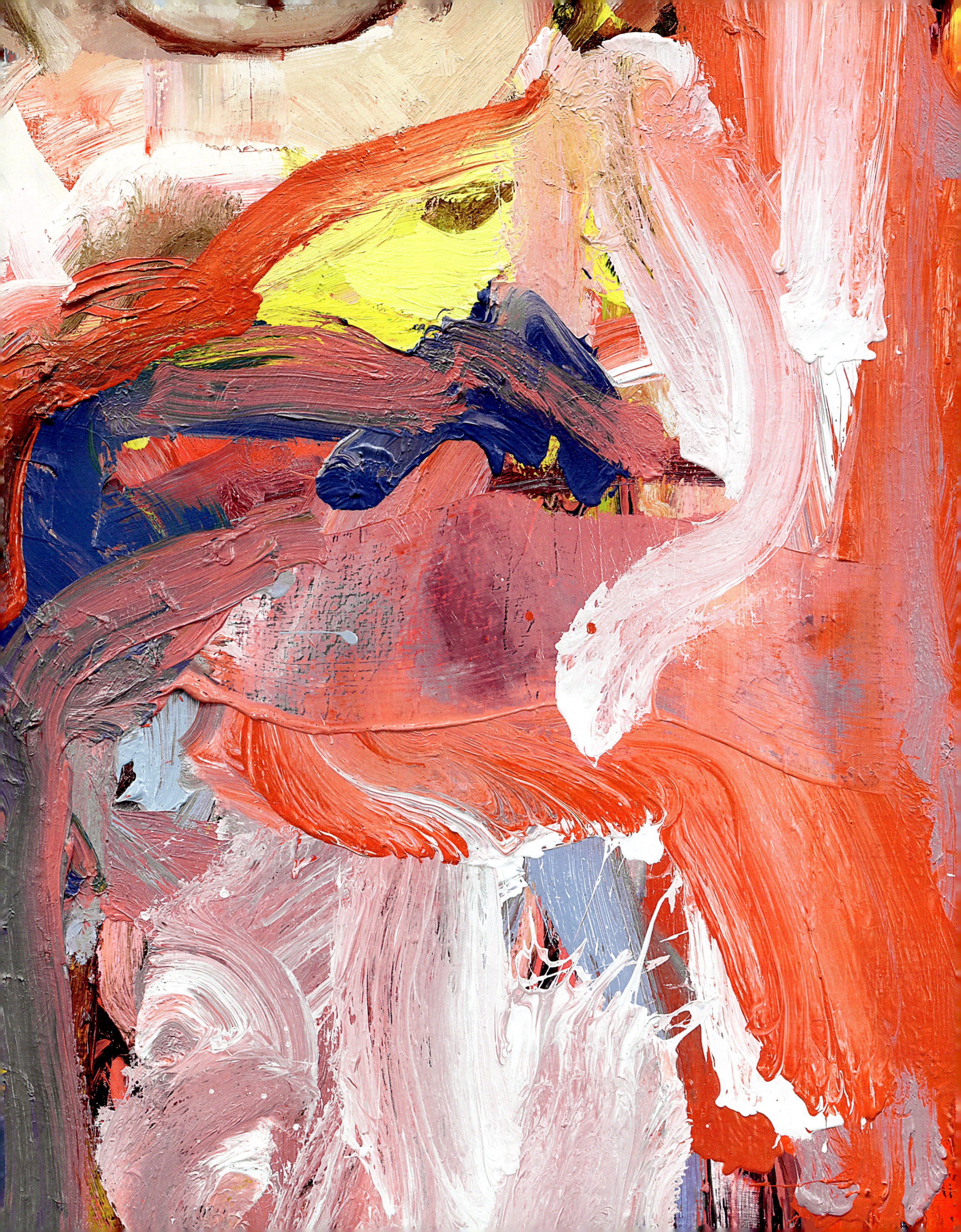

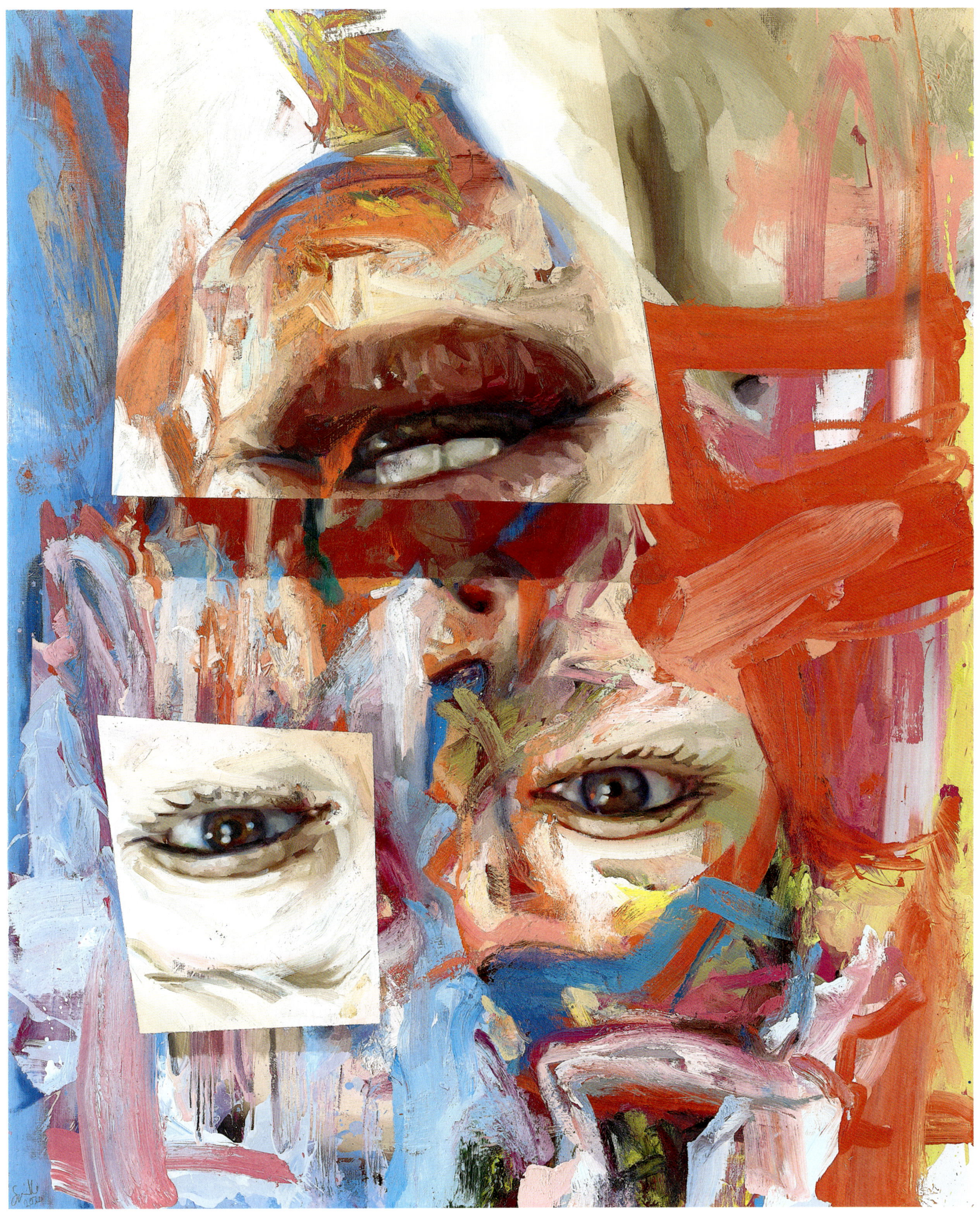

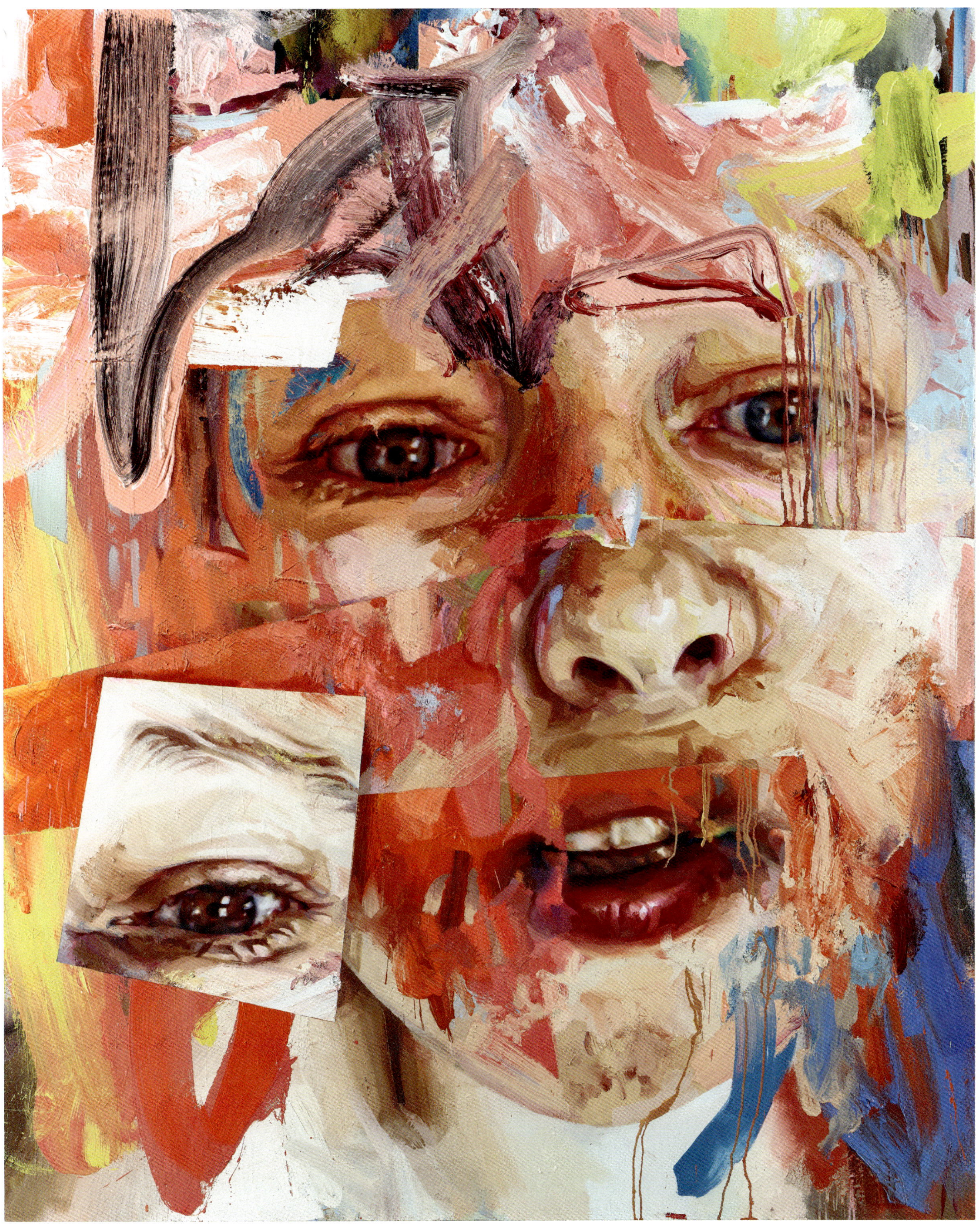

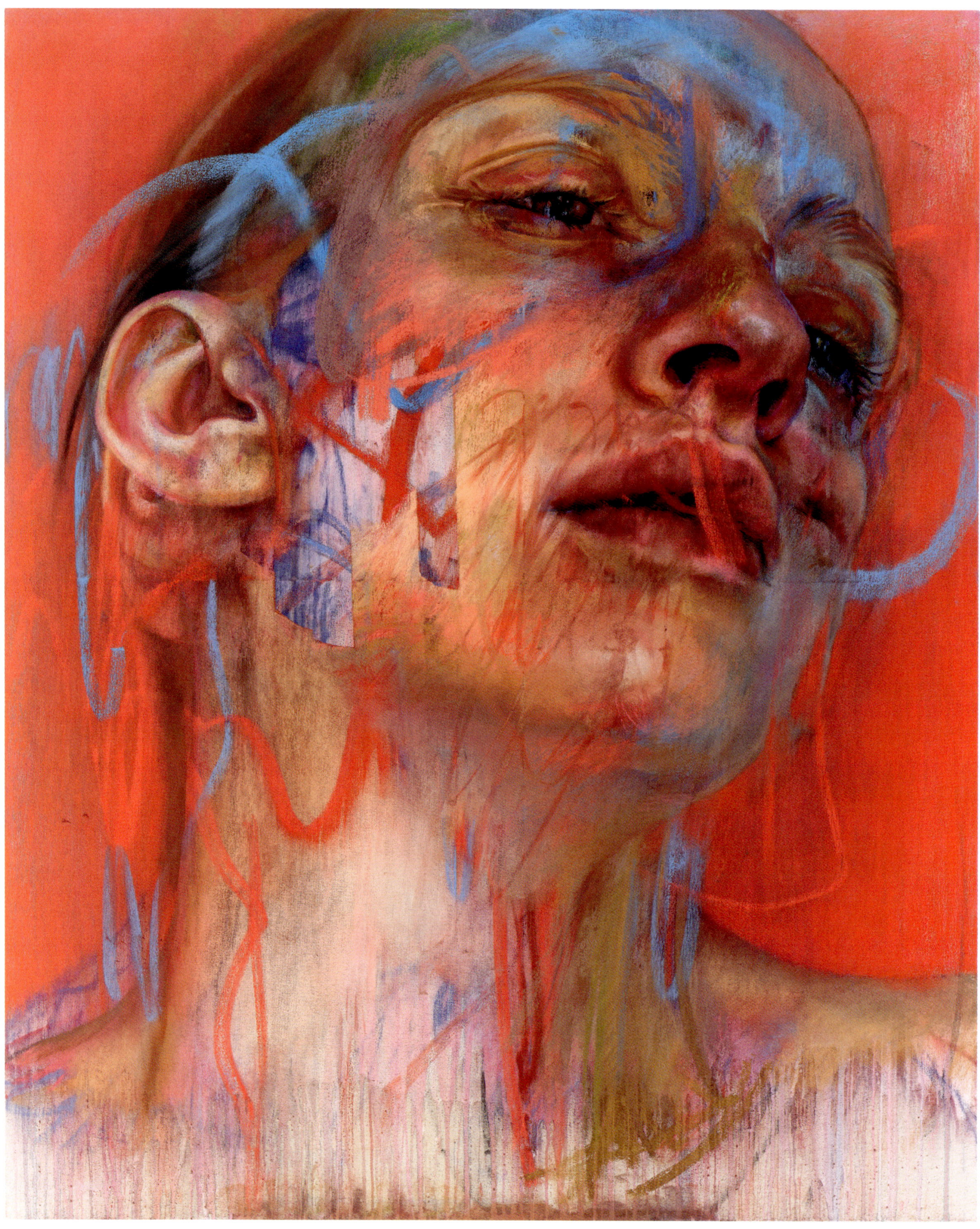

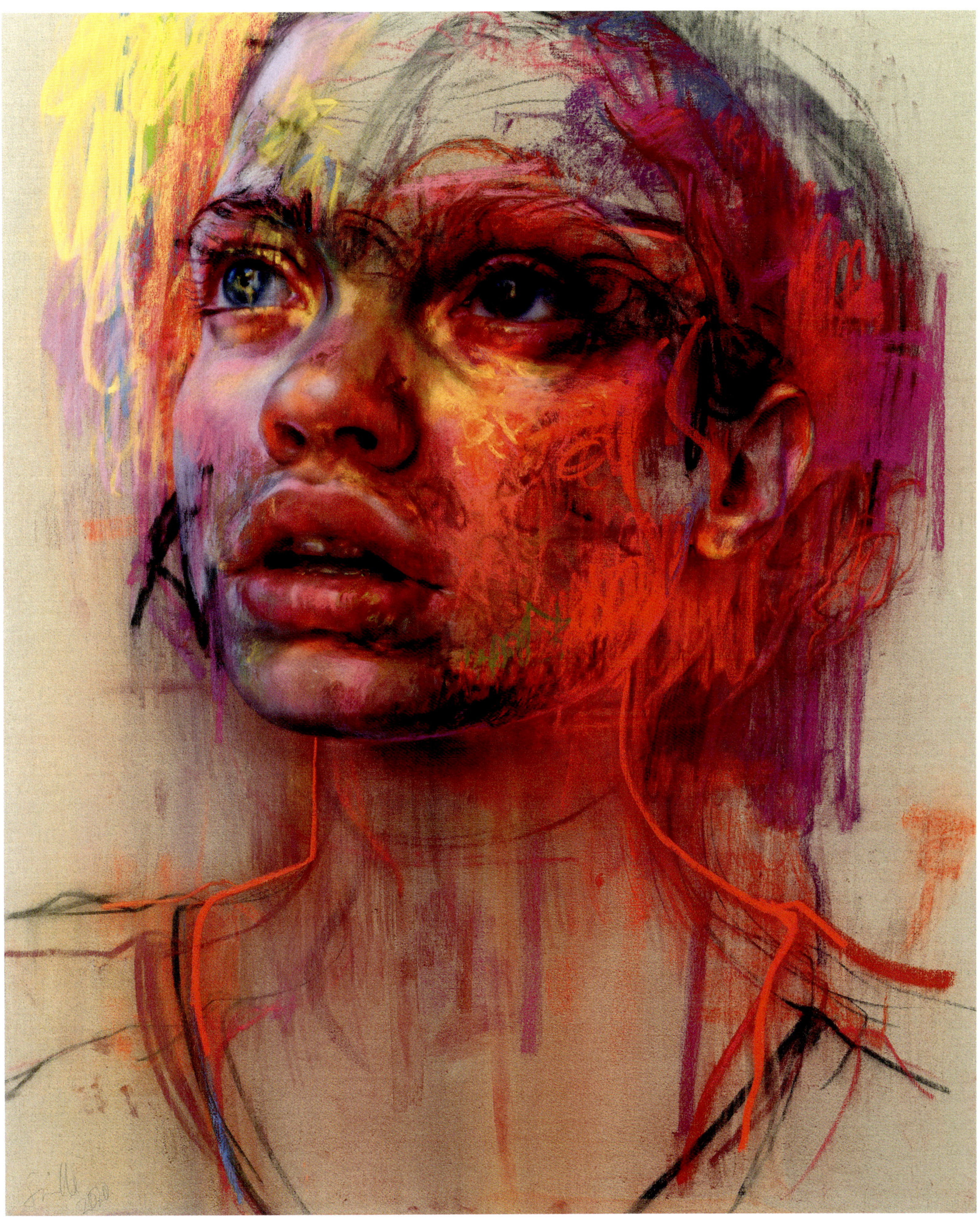

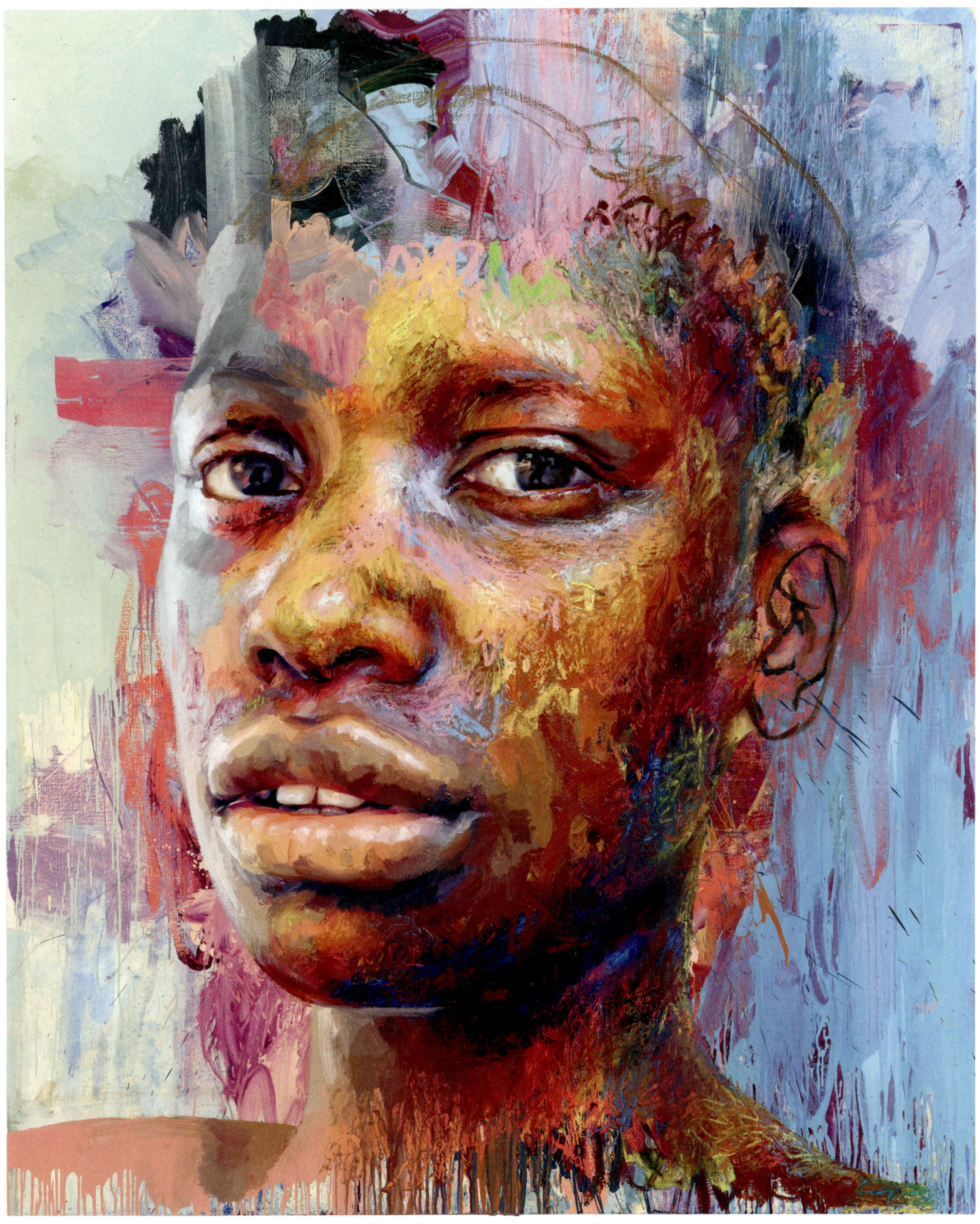

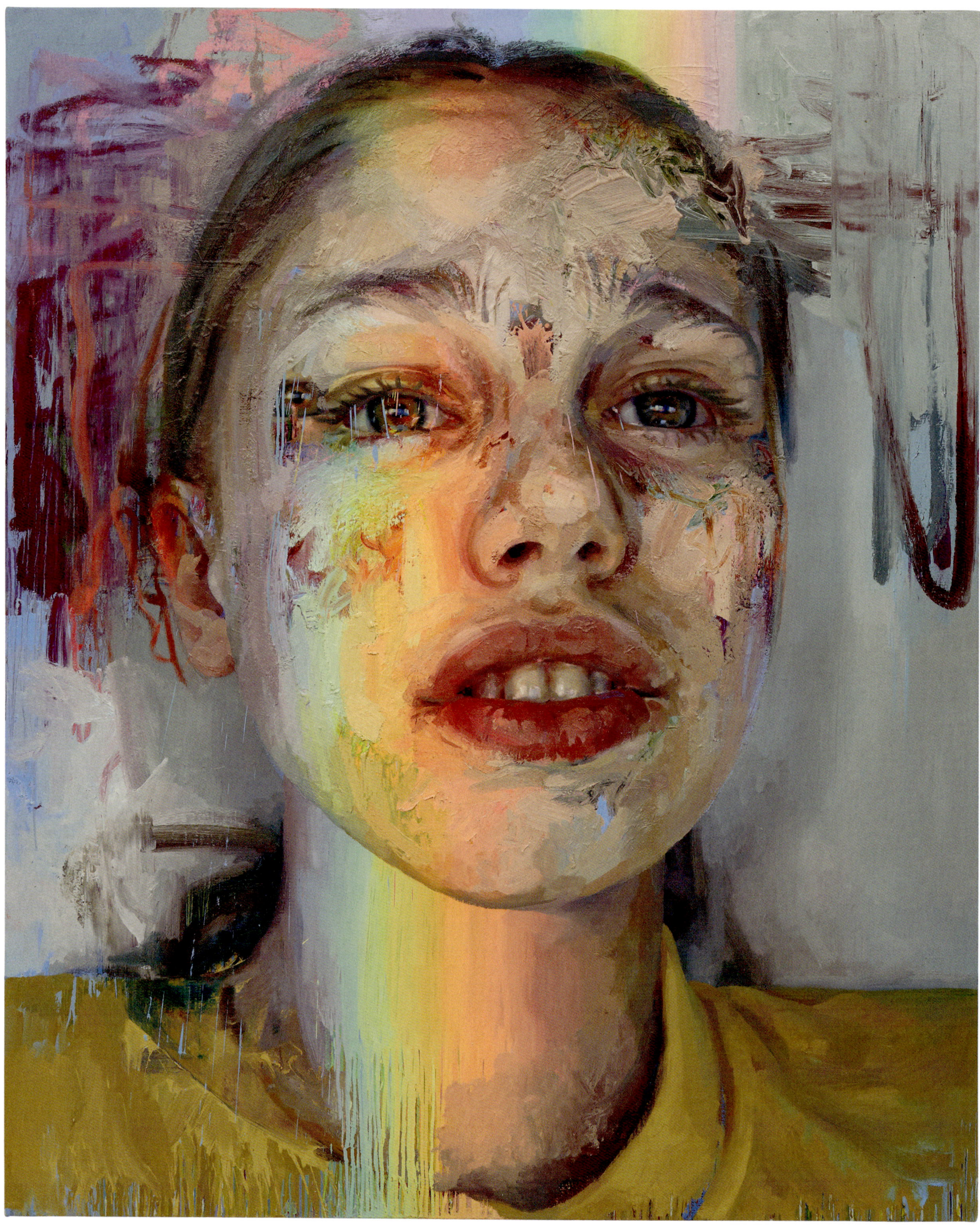

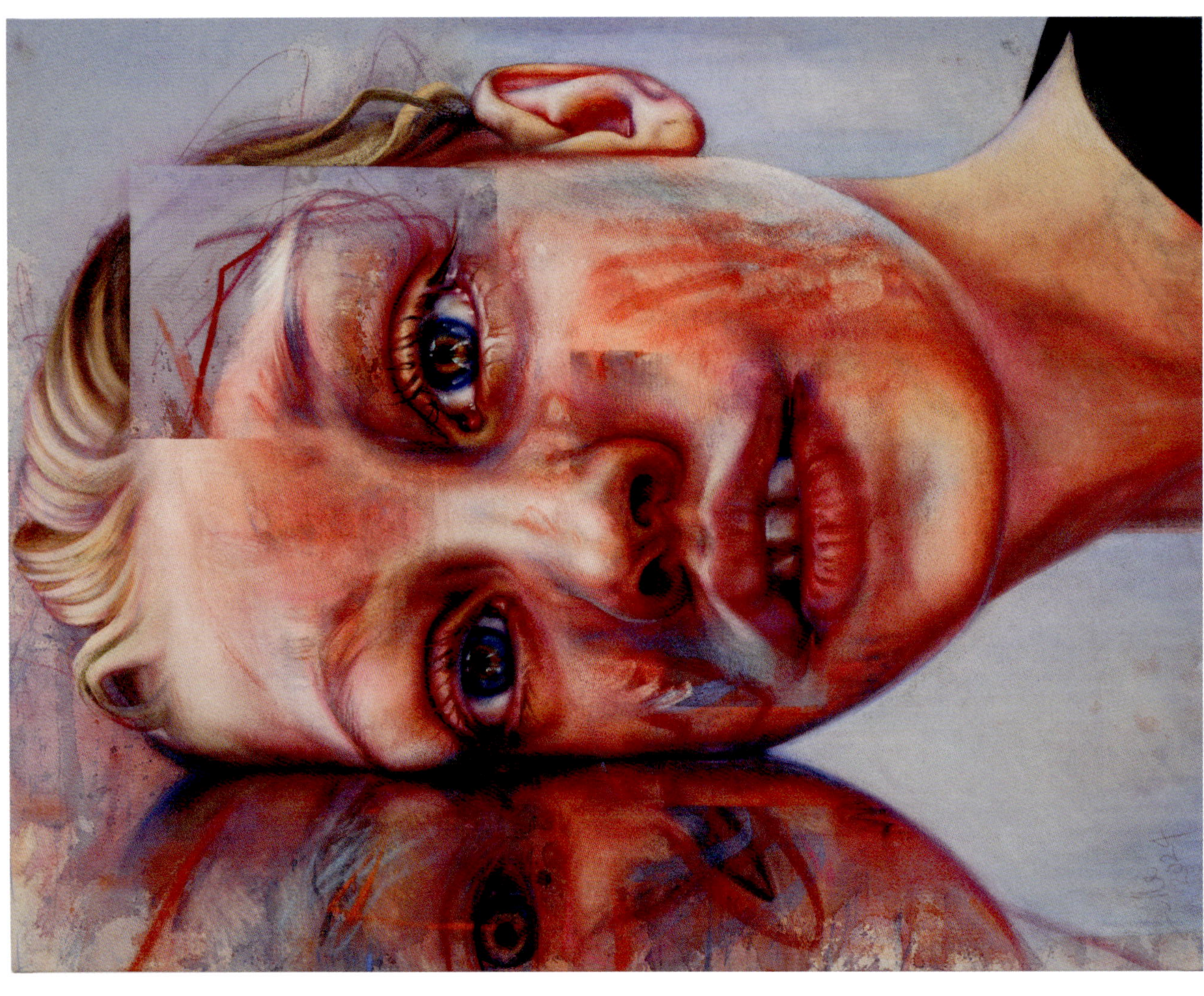

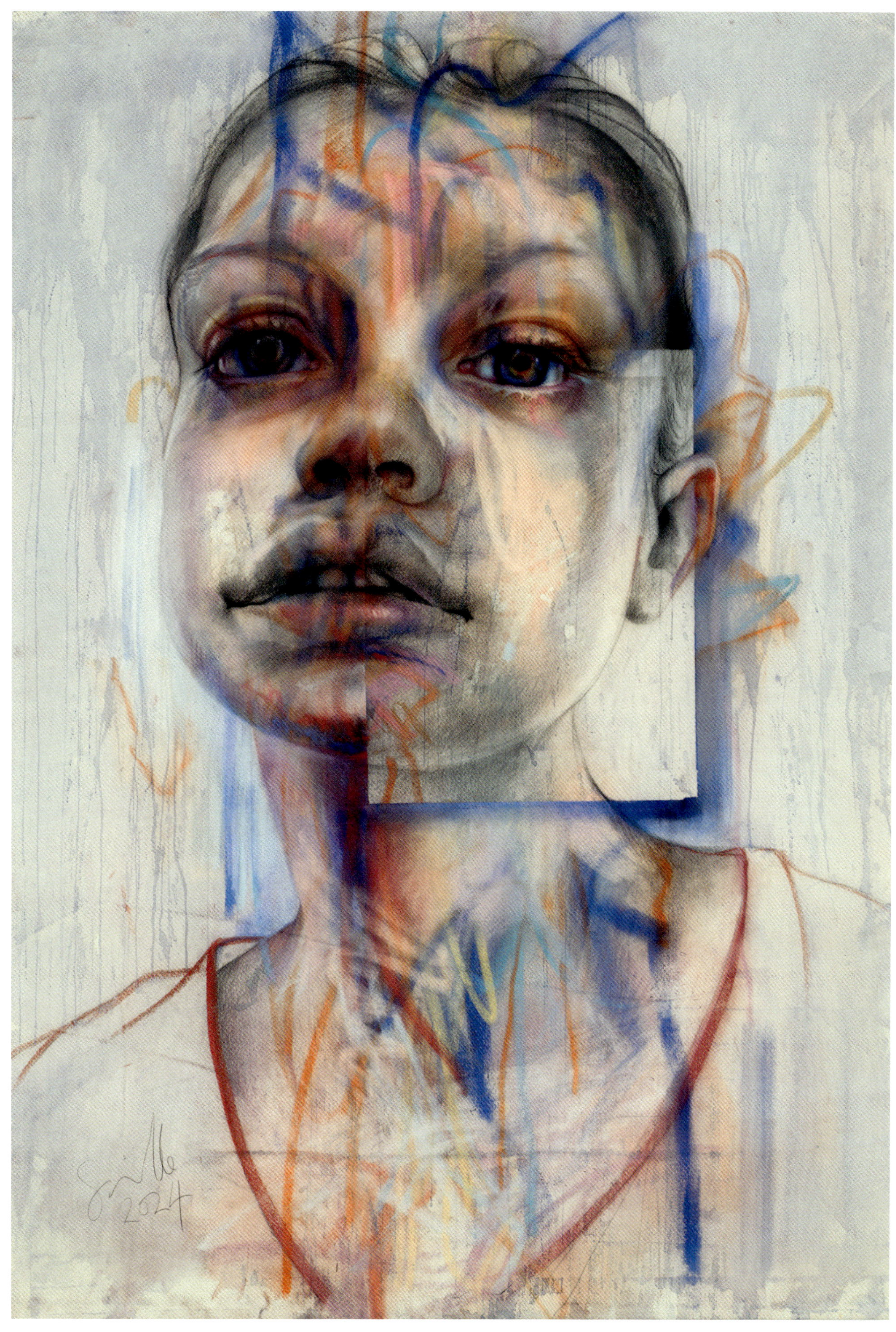
2024

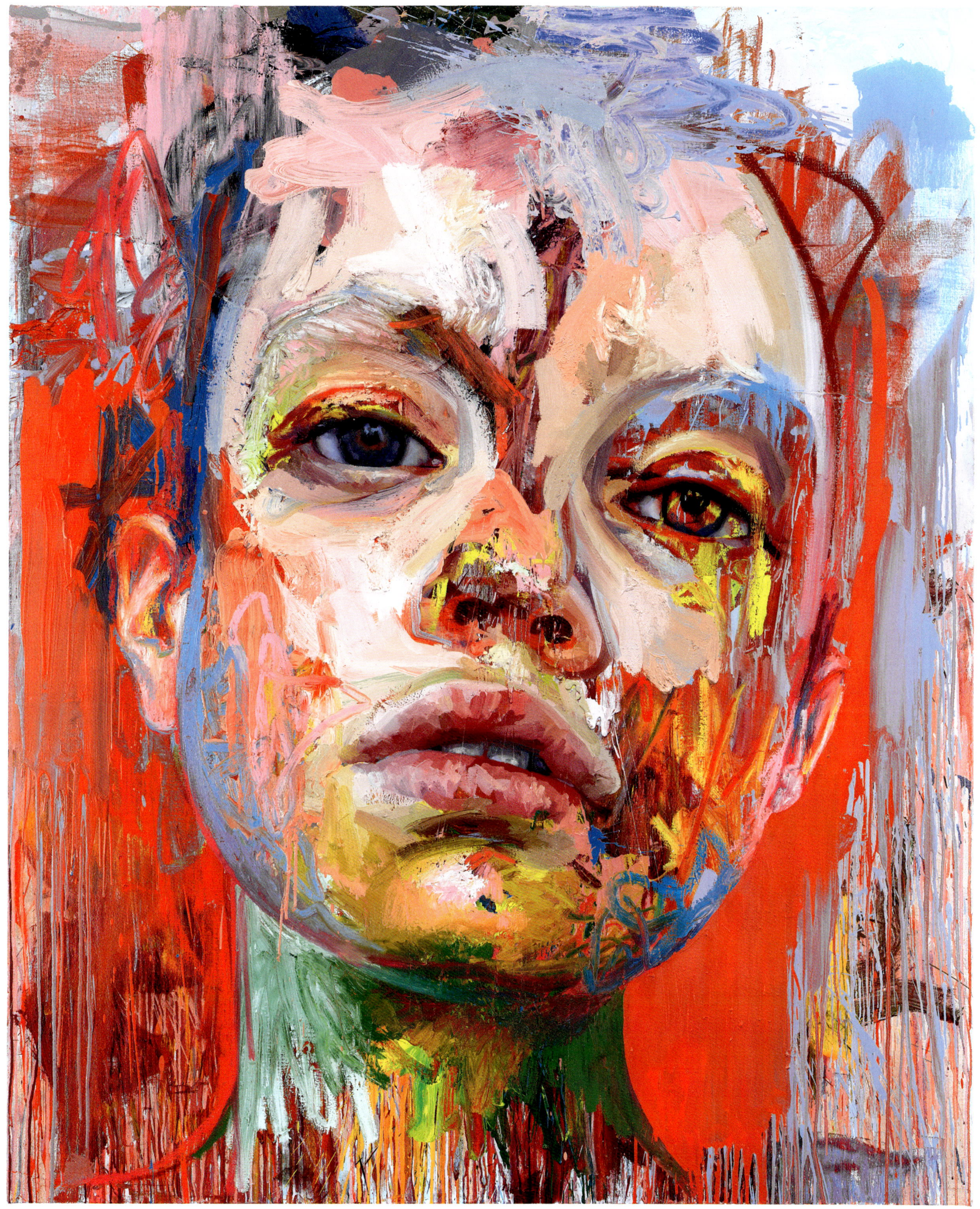

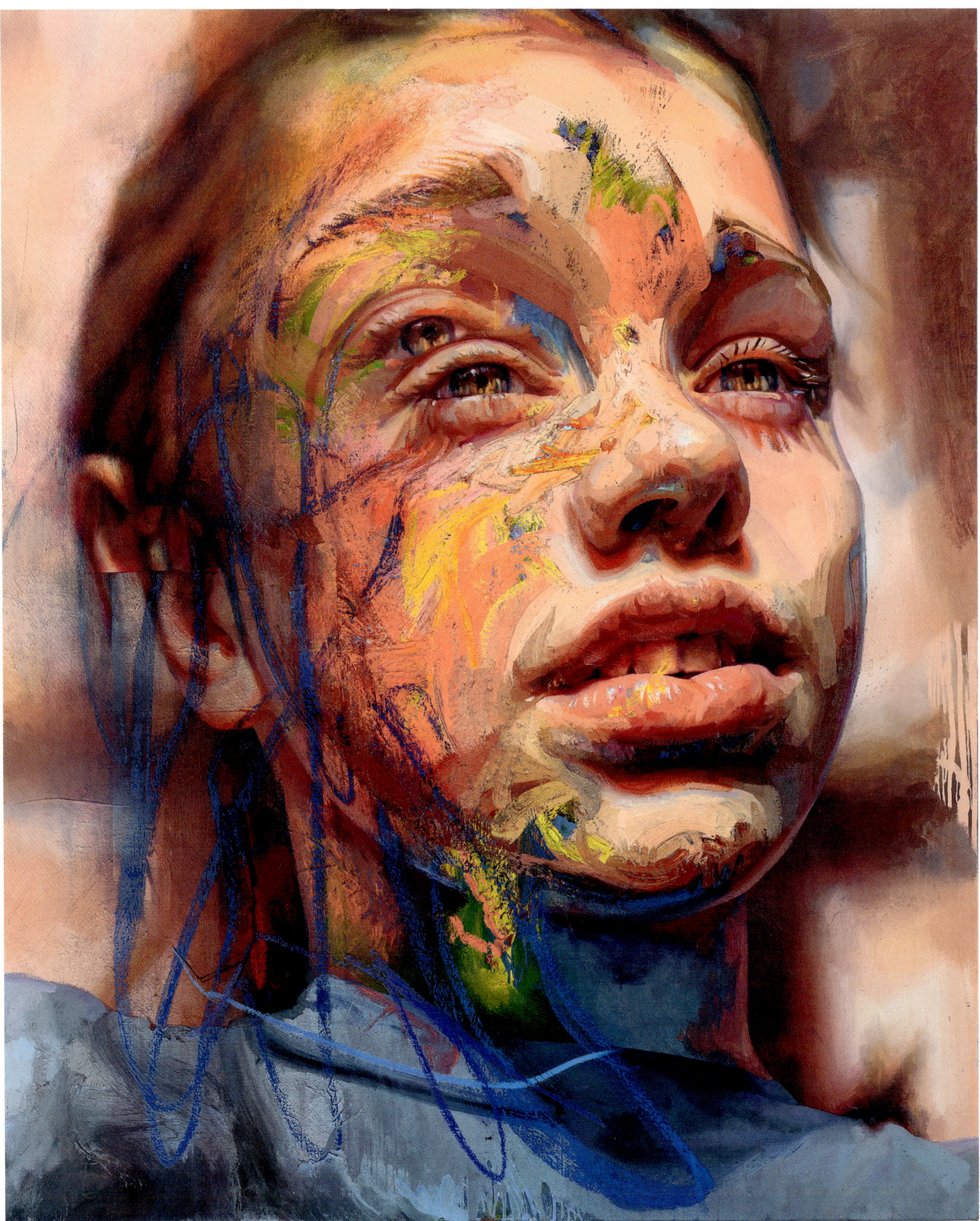

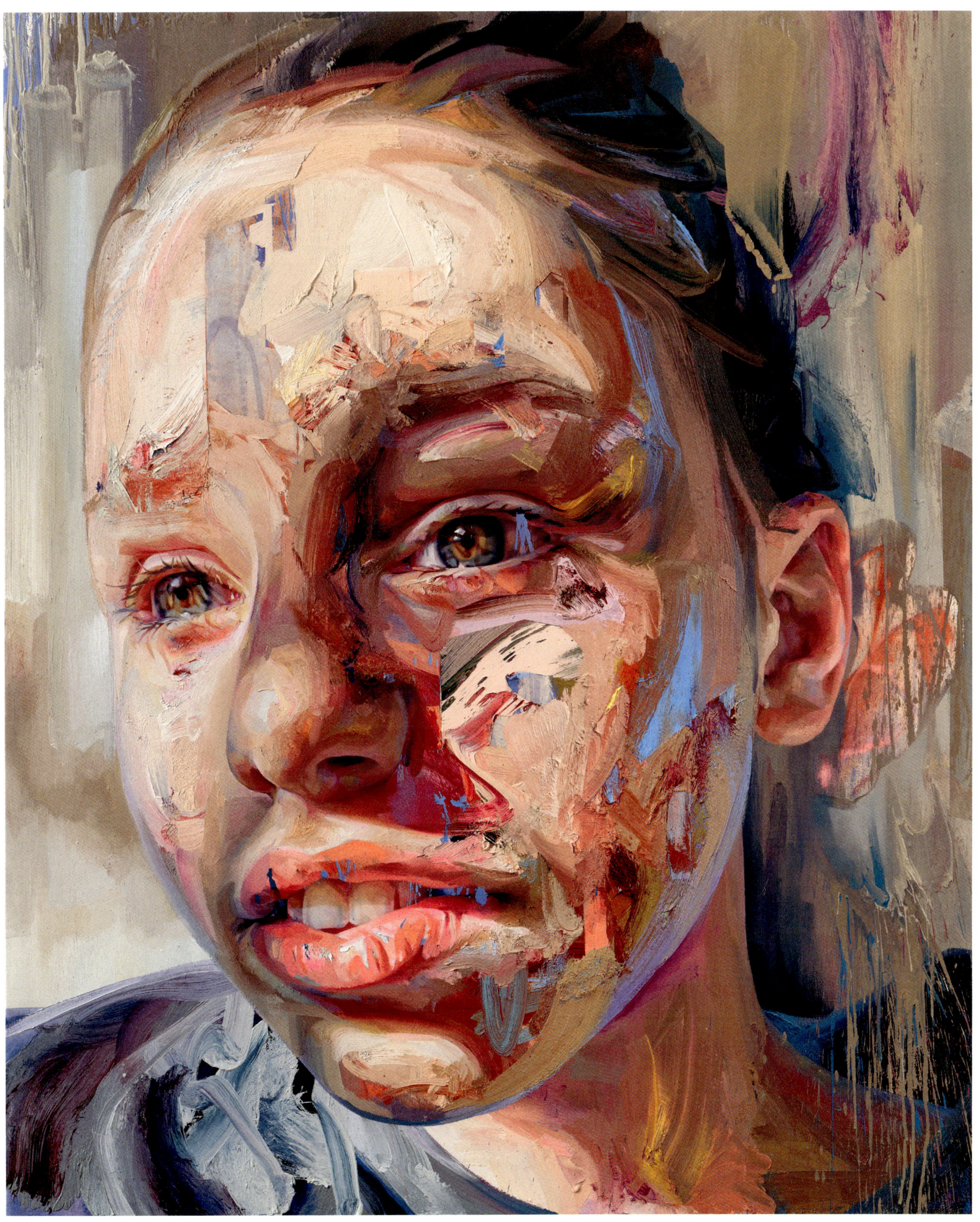

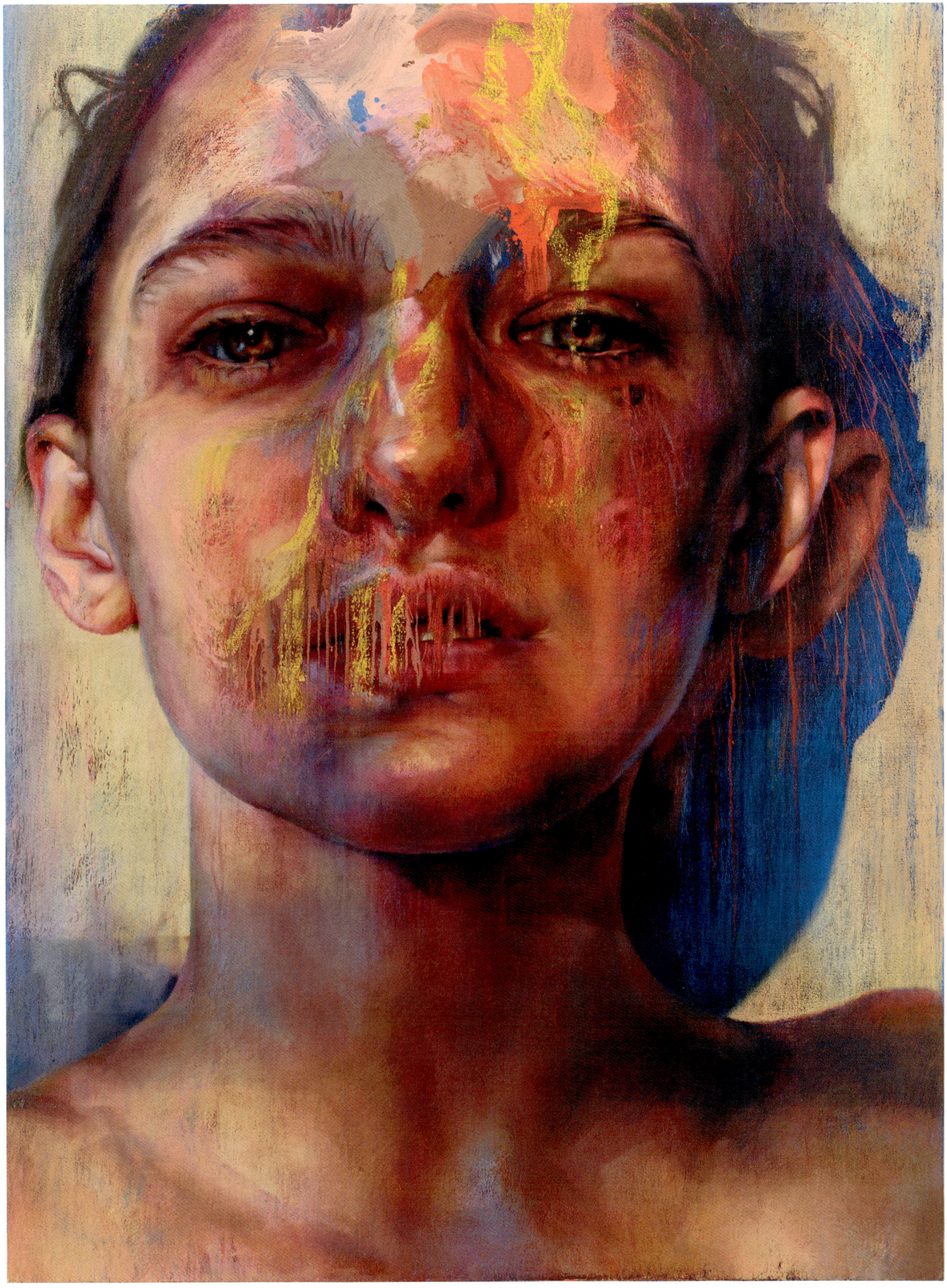

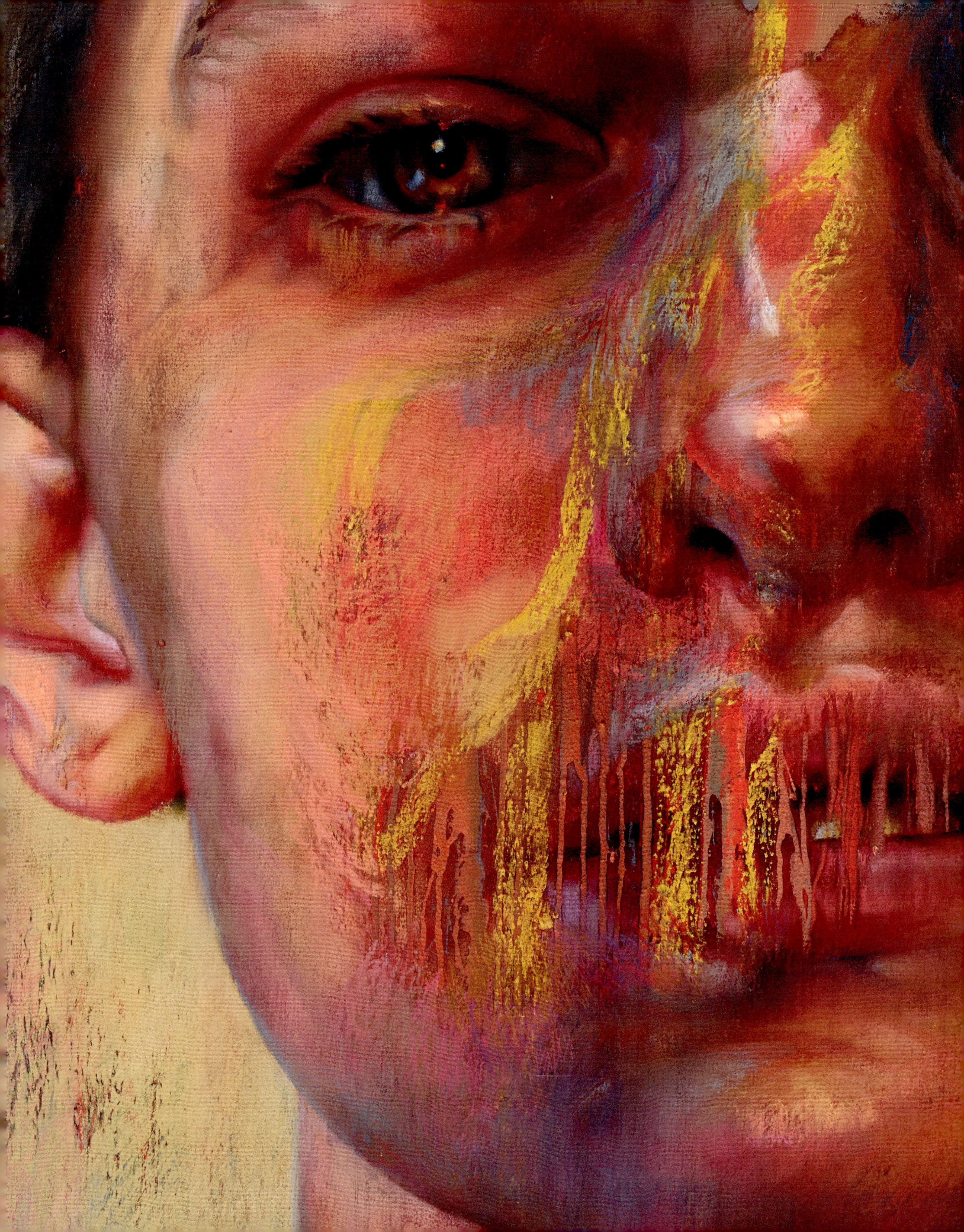

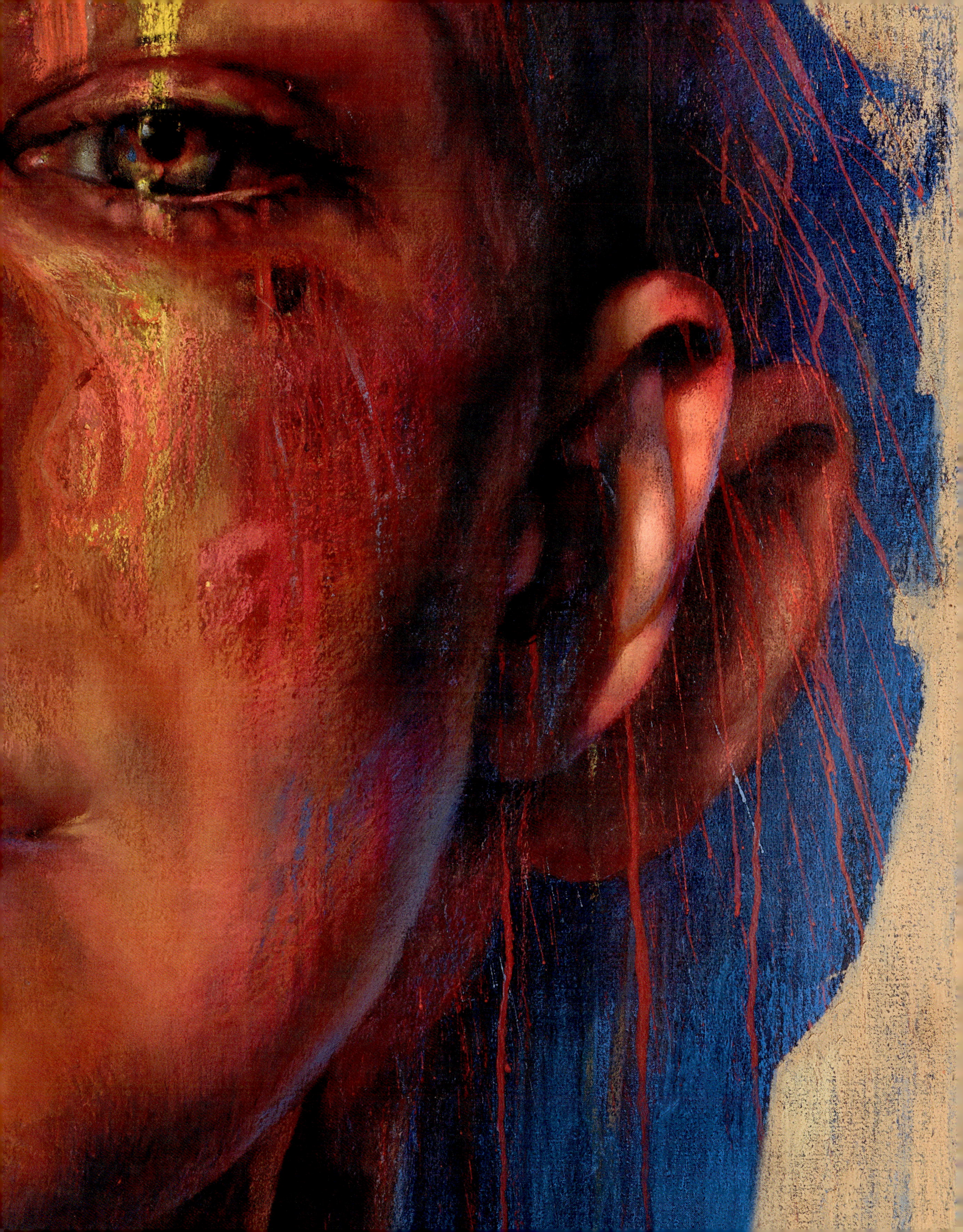

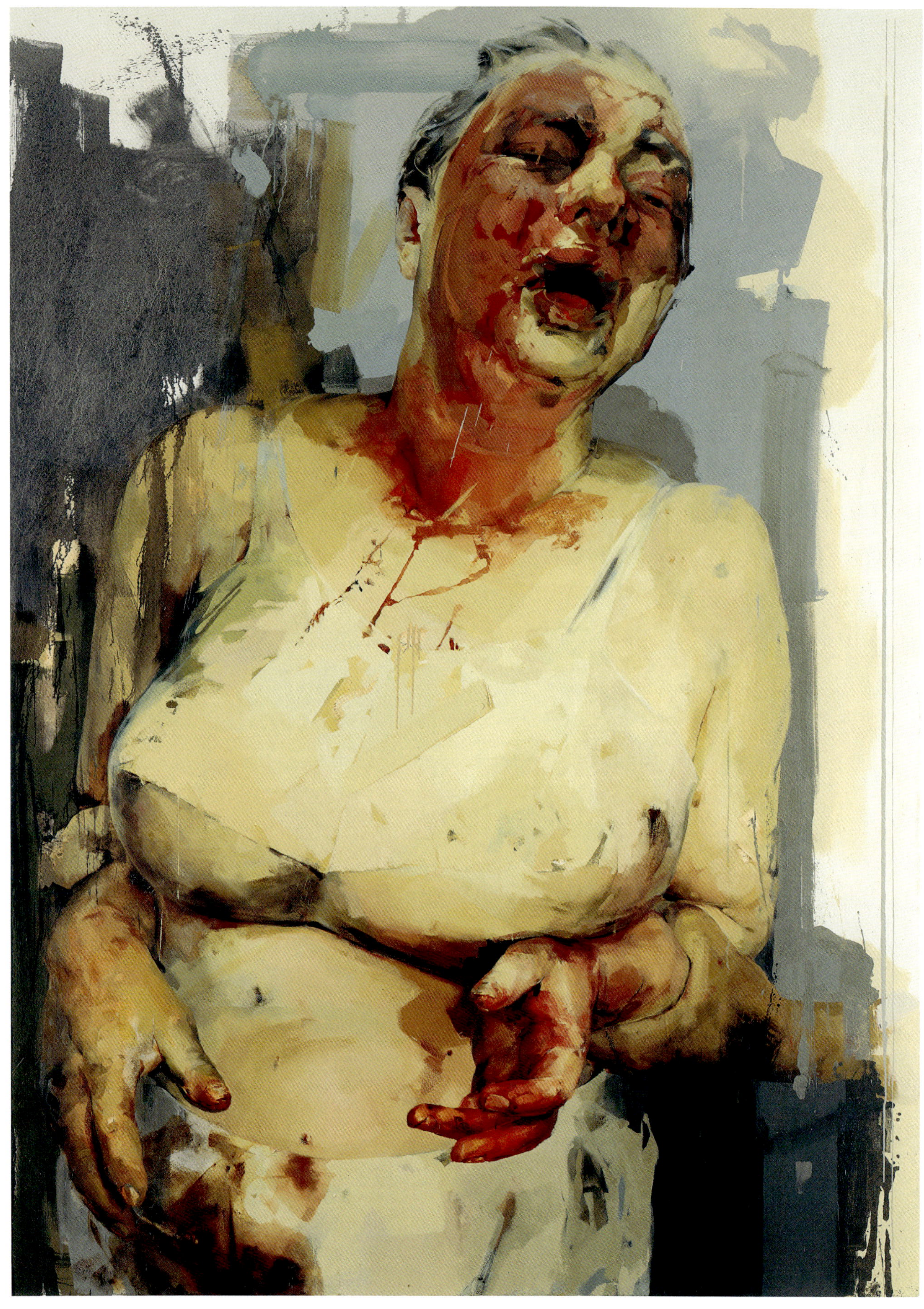

A Pathology of Paint

Nicholas Cullinan

Do you think about nostrils? Jenny Saville does. As she once explained to me: 'If I go to New York, I spend a day in the Met. The last time, I went round photographing nostrils; some artists paint great nostrils.'[1] More than this, she studies the anatomy of *why* this is so, explaining that Velázquez 'wins hands down' and that 'the reason is that Velázquez sees the nostril not necessarily as black. A lot of artists just do them dark, whereas he sees the light through the nostril. That's what makes his paintings so fleshy, they have such realism because he sees the light. Rembrandt puts bright red round noses as well, or ochre. So you can see, really feel, why certain artists are so good.'[2]

And that close looking is one of the many reasons why Saville is so good as an artist. Over a protean and constantly evolving body of work, encompassing painting, drawing and photography and spanning almost four decades, the body has always been the operative word for Saville, from pivotal early paintings such as *Propped* (cat.1) through to newer works, such as *Virtual* (cat.49), that experiment with the emerging and fragmented visual language of selfies, screens and digital portraiture as 'a play between the photographic and painterliness'.[3]

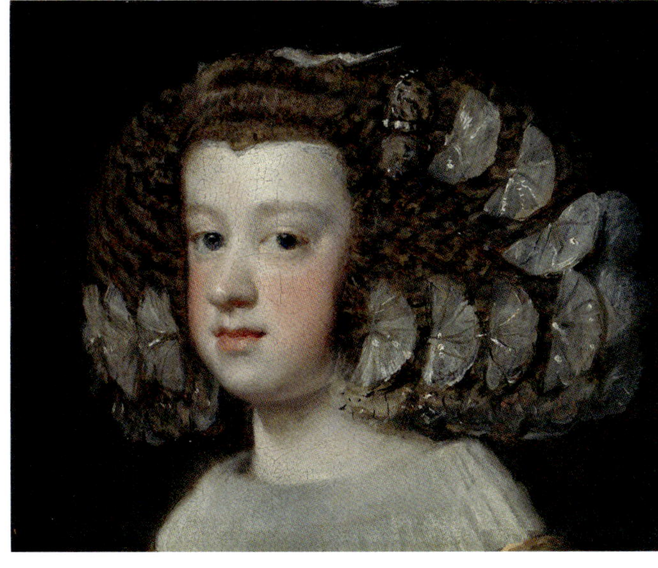

Fig.1
Jenny Saville
Pause, 2002–3
Oil on canvas
3048 × 2134 mm
Private Collection

Fig.2
Diego Rodríguez de Silva y Velázquez
María Teresa (1638–1683), Infanta of Spain, 1651–4
Oil on canvas
327 × 384 mm
The Metropolitan Museum of Art, New York

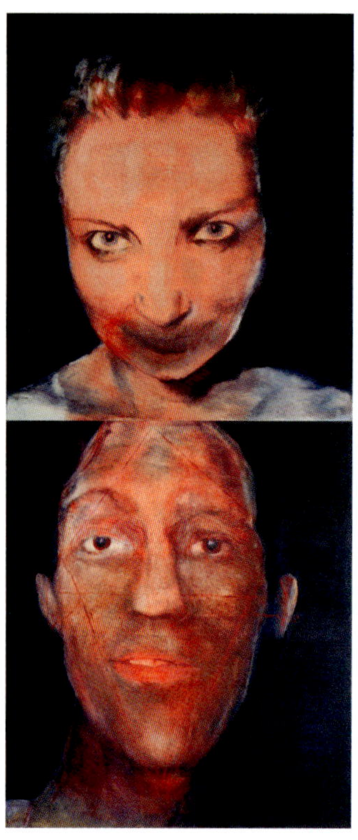

Fig.3
Marlene Dumas
The Occult Revival, 1984
Oil on canvas
2600 × 1100 mm overall,
2 parts, 1300 × 1100 mm each
Stedelijk Museum,
Amsterdam

Fig.4
Hilaire-Germain-Edgar Degas
La Coiffure, c.1986
Oil on canvas
1143 × 1467 mm
The National Gallery, London

As a young artist in the early 1990s, Saville quickly rose to prominence for paintings with lines inscribed upon voluptuous bodies, works proffering different ways to map and paint the human form, from the cartographic (*Plan*, cat.3) to the photographic (*Hybrid*, p.35). Beyond the body, her relationship to portraiture has always been complex – consider works such as *Fulcrum* (cat.6), its panoramic stacking of human bodies one atop another gesturing more toward an all-enveloping landscape than to any notion of a portrait.

In mapping out and dissecting a veritable anatomy of painting, Saville has cast her sharp and sometimes forensic gaze over an array of sources ranging from the museum to the morgue, from the old masters to contemporary concerns and conversations, from the ancient to the digital. Occasionally, Saville opts to zoom in, enlarging and translating a particular detail from a painting that was originally dainty and diminutive. This would explain how the large-scale painting *Stare* (cat.15) and its related works are indebted to the glassy gaze and fulsome, parted lips of Johannes Vermeer's *Girl with a Pearl Earring* (*c*.1665), in the Mauritshuis museum in The Hague. Rather than portraying a particular sitter, Vermeer's image is most probably a tronie – a generic depiction of a person's physiognomy, a common approach in seventeenth-century Dutch art and revisited recently by contemporary painters such as Marlene Dumas (see fig.3). Like these examples, the anonymous face (painted from a medical photograph) in Saville's *Stare* works has something depersonalised about it. We are invited to gaze at it over and over again, so that the image becomes defamiliarised to us as to the artist – we dissect its character and cartography, such as the scarlet birthmark plastered across it and rendered in expansively gestural and almost abstract brushstrokes, rather than sympathising with the sitter, whose skin and blood simply become an analogy for canvas and paint.

We should perhaps consider not just Saville's sources but also her technique for translating them, or, rather, how they are enmeshed. Drawing from an array of photographic reproductions of images ranging from old master paintings to medical photographs, which lie strewn about her as she paints, Saville then scales these source images up as she copies and adapts them to her own compositions on the canvas, using nothing more than her eyes and hand.

Often Saville combines disparate image sources to the most striking effects. *Pause* (fig.1), for example, with its hasty brushwork, apparently derives from a photograph of a bomb victim staggering, dazed, away from the blast with her clothes ripped off, but it is also in part indebted to Edgar Degas's *La Coiffure* (Combing the Hair), from about 1896 (fig.4), in the National Gallery, London. Saville seems to have been impressed by the overall sanguine palette of the Degas work, as shown by the ruddy face and left hand of the woman in *Pause*. In Saville's works, the injuries inflicted on the skin of the face are often also those

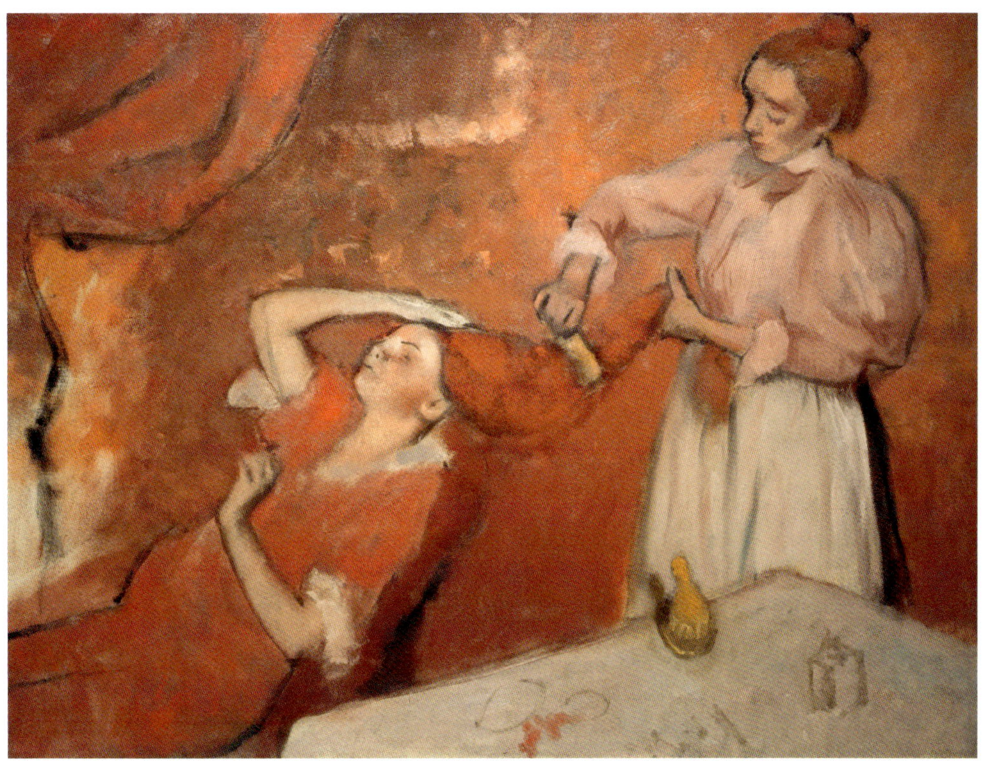

perpetrated against the canvas. Her uniquely visceral work constitutes a veritable pathology of paint.

Tenderness, rather than violence, is the motif for Saville's series of variations on Leonardo's mother-and-child compositions (cats 23–28; cat.30). Saville has observed that while producing these works, in the early 2010s, she was both painting flesh and making flesh,[4] a description that mirrors, from a uniquely female perspective, Willem de Kooning's observation that 'flesh was the reason why oil painting was invented'.[5] But here the emphasis seems less on a painterly rendering of flesh using impastoed oil paint, as with Saville's previous work, and more on contours that suggest and gesture toward a resolved composition only then to evaporate before our eyes. Saville's use of a supposedly outmoded material such as pastel is notable in itself, and posits her as the heir to eighteenth-century masters of that medium such as Rosalba Carriera – indeed, Saville has adopted pastel to increasingly striking effect over the last few years, in works such as *Prism* (cat.52). The anxious line captured in these nervous palimpsests traces and retraces just as the surface judders and fidgets, like the sitters depicted, in a manner that becomes almost Futurist in its ability to convey movement and simultaneity. The perspective is never fixed; rather, the contours squirm and wiggle as much as the figures switch position, resisting both fixity and our gaze. This restlessness is shared by Saville's overarching development, in which her hand and eye are always searching.

Notes

The Anatomy of a Painting

1. I quote some of Jenny Saville's published statements below. Attribution to her of facts or opinions not in quotation marks come from conversations or emails between us. In developing this text, I am indebted, as usual, to the review and suggestions of my first reader, Jeanne Collins.
2. Christopher Ricks, *Dylan's Visions of Sin* (Ecco, New York, 2004), pp.7–8.
3. David Cohen, 'Young Art Runs Free', *Times Saturday Review* (UK), 15 September 1992, p.11.
4. Denis Diderot, 'The Salon of 1763', in Jean Seznec and Jean Adhemar (eds), *Diderot Salons*, Vol. 1 (Oxford University Press, Oxford, 1957), pp.139–40. Quoted here from Pierre Rosenberg, *Chardin* (Royal Academy of Arts, London, and The Metropolitan Museum of Art, New York, 2000), cat.2. I discuss the history of the critical reception of this painting in 'Un tableau dégoûtant', in Laure Blanc-Benon and Nicolas Rialland (eds), *Jacqueline Lichtenstein, une voie en philosophie de l'art* (Sorbonne Université Presses, Paris), forthcoming.
5. Aristotle, *Poetics*, c.335 BC, 4:5–20.
6. Philip Conisbee, *Painting in Eighteenth-Century France* (Cornell University Press, Ithaca, NY, 1981), p.162.
7. Saville herself exhibited the work with a mirror in her thesis exhibition in Glasgow in 1992.
8. Luce Irigaray, *This Sex Which Is Not One*, 1977, Eng. trans. C. Porter and C. Burke (Cornell University Press, Ithaca, NY, 1985), p.205.
9. Saville, 'On de Kooning', interview with Kara Vander Weg, September 2013, in John Elderfield (ed.), *Willem de Kooning: Ten Paintings, 1983–1985* (Gagosian, New York, 2013), p.88. De Kooning had boasted, 'I get the paint right on the surface, nobody else can do that', to Emilie Kilgore, quoted by David Sylvester in Sylvester, Richard Shiff, and Marla Prather, *Willem de Kooning: Paintings* (National Gallery of Art, Washington, DC, 1994), p.16. Saville saw the exhibition this catalogue accompanied and thinks she may have read this statement in the catalogue.
10. Willem de Kooning, 'The Renaissance and Order', lecture delivered at Studio 35, New York, fall 1949, and published in *trans/formation* 1, no.2 (1951). Most recently reprinted in Sally Yard, *Willem de Kooning: Works, Writings, and Interviews* (Ediciones Polígrafa, Barcelona, 2007), pp.111–13; p.111 for the quotation. Also available online at https://www.dekooning.org/documentation/words/the-renaissance-and-order
Saville may not have read the entire essay but did know this often quoted statement, and the one I quote below.
11. Ibid., p.112.
12. Saville, quoted in Mark W. Scala, 'Fragmentation and Reconstitution: Painterly Figuration since 1980', in Scala (ed.), *Paint Made Flesh* (Frist Center for the Visual Arts, Nashville, TN, 2009), p.65. Saville's statement originally appeared in Charles Darwent, 'Big Really Does Mean Beautiful', *Independent*, April 17, 2000.
13. Eugène Delacroix, journal entry, 11 January 1857, in *The Journal of Eugène Delacroix*. trans. Walter Pach (Grove Press, New York, 1948), p.533.
14. Ibid, p.566. Journal entry, 25 January 1857.
15. Clement Greenberg, 'American-Type Painting', *Partisan Review* 22 (spring 1955). Repr. in *Clement Greenberg: The Collected Essays and Criticism*, Vol. 3, *Affirmations and Refusals 1950–1956*, ed. John O'Brian (The University of Chicago Press, Chicago and London, 1993), p.222.
16. The only comparable woman-on-man violence in the context of contemporary art that comes to mind is that of Valerie Solanas on 3 June 1968. Although she shot Andy Warhol with a pistol, Solanas was the founder and sole member of a feminist organisation that she called SCUM, the Society for Cutting Up Men.
17. Leo Steinberg, 'Month in Review', *Arts* 30, no.2, November 1955, p.46.
18. Ibid.
19. Clare Henry, 'Critic opts for the Young and the Old', *Herald* (Scotland), 11 September 1992, p.16. See also David Cohen, 'Young Art Runs Free', *Times Saturday Review* (UK), 5 September 1992, p.11.
20. Saville, in Simon Schama, 'Interview with Jenny Saville: New York, May 2005', in *Jenny Saville* (Rizzoli, New York, 2005), pp.124, 127. Beyond the scope of this essay but worthy of note is what Emily Braun calls 'how painting the figure was written out of the history of British modernist painting'. See her 'Skinning the Paint', in Scala (ed.), *Paint Made Flesh*, p.40, n.4. She cites the popular textbook by Hal Foster, Rosalind Krauss, Yve-Alain Bois and Benjamin Buchloch, *Art since 1900: Modernism, Antimodernism, Postmodernism*, 2 vols. (Thames and Hudson, New York, 2004): here, Francis Bacon gets one paragraph and one reproduction; Lucian Freud, Frank Auerbach and Leon Kossoff do not appear. Braun correctly observes (p.30) that it was only with the recognition of a new generation of figural painters, including Saville, that their predecessors began to receive their critical due – 'Yet the taint of "conservatism" still clings to their work'. That taint may well have encouraged the new generation of painters not to allow it to be applied to them. As late as 1996, though, the exhibition *L'Informe: Mode d'emploi*, at the Centre Pompidou, Paris (see note 41 below), included none of the four, nor, for that matter, de Kooning or any other figural painter.
21. Mary Richardson, quoted in Lynda Nead, 'The Damaged Venus', gives an excellent account of the incident. In Nead, *The Female Nude: Art, Obscenity and Sexuality* (Routledge, London and New York, 1992), pp.34–43; quotation at p.35.
22. Ibid., p.37.
23. On Jo Spence's work see ibid, pp.79–82.
24. See Thomas Harris, *The Silence of The Lambs* (St. Martin's Press, New York, 1988). The film, now readily available on home media, was issued by Strong Heart/Demme Productions/Orion Pictures on 30 January, 1991. The quotations in the text below come from a transcript of the film's dialogue.
25. Clarice's surname is not only the name of the gregarious bird but also a play on 'staring.'
26. Marcus Aurelius' most famous statement of the mind/body dualism was 'This Being of mine, whatever it really is, consists of a little flesh, a little breath, and the part that governs'. *Meditations*, AD 170–5, II, 2.
27. *The Genius of Venice 1500–1600* (Royal Academy of Arts, London, 1983–4). *The Flaying of Marsyas* was subsequently shown in *Titian: Prince of Painters* at the Palazzo Ducale, Venice, in 1990, and at the National Gallery of Art, Washington, DC, 1990–1; in *Le Siècle de Titien: L'âge d'or de la peinture à Venise*, Grand Palais, Paris, 1993; and in *Unfinished: Thoughts Left Visible*, Met Breuer, New York, 2016.
28. See Martin Gayford, 'A Conversation with Jenny Saville', in *Jenny Saville: Territories* (Gagosian, New York, 1999), p.30.
29. Elaine Scarry, *The Body in Pain: The Making and Unmaking of the World* (Oxford University Press, New York and Oxford, 1985). Saville has not read this book but has read Susan Sontag, *Regarding the Pain of Others* (Picador, New York, 2003), on photographic images of, mainly, the war wounded, which does not mention Scarry's book.
30. Ann Hollander, *Seeing through Clothes* (University of California Press, Berkeley, 1975), pp.85–6.
31. Scarry, *The Body in Pain*, p.282, within a discussion of other objects, pp.281–6.
32. Ibid., pp.307–8, with the coat as an example.
33. The portrayal of Buffalo Bill in both the book and the film was very reasonably criticised in and beyond the press as transphobic and homophobic in presenting transsexualism as a dangerous psychosis leading to criminal behaviour.
34. Saville in 'An interview with Jenny Saville, 20 September 2016', in Lauren Mahony, 'Chronology', *Jenny Saville* (Rizzoli and Gagosian, New York, 2018), p.368.

35. Saville in Gayford, 'A Conversation with Jenny Saville', p.30.
36. Saville in 'Jenny Saville in conversation with John Richardson', in *Jenny Saville: Continuum* (Gagosian, London, 2012), p.16.
37. Mahony, 'Chronology', p.164.
38. Julia Kristeva, *Powers of Horror: An Essay on Abjection*, trans. Leon. S. Roudiez (Columbia University Press, New York and London, 1982), p.4.
39. Irigaray, *This Sex Which Is Not One*, p.114.
40. This point is made differently by Braun in 'Skinning the Paint', p.38.
41. Robert Morris, 'Anti Form', *Artforum* 6, no.8 (April 1968). The development of this subject was the subject of the 1996 exhibition *L'Informe: Mode d'emploi*, at the Centre Pompidou, Paris, memorialised in Yves-Alain Bois and Rosalind Krauss (eds), *Formless: A User's Guide* (Zone Books, New York, 1997), which took its inspiration from Georges Bataille's writings. Krauss observes in the book's conclusion (p.237) that Bataille's term *'l'informe'* had largely been supplanted by Kristeva's 'abjection' because his texts were less widely known than Kristeva's *Powers of Horror*. However, Bataille's *Visions of Excess: Selected Writings, 1927–1939*, ed. and trans. Allan Stoekl (University of Minnesota Press, Minneapolis, 1985) appeared only three years after the English-language edition of *Powers of Horror*. The turn to Kristeva may well reflect the increasing interest in art made by women. Krauss discusses (pp.238–45) a Kristeva-influenced essay by Laura Mulvey, 'A Phantasmagoria of the Female Body: The World of Cindy Sherman', *New Left Review* no.188, July/August 1991, that had led to her own authorship of *Cindy Sherman* (Rizzoli, New York, 1993). Two years later, in 1995, the Centre Pompidou presented the ill-advised *Féminin-Masculin: Le Sexe d'art*, which occasioned an astonished review in *Artforum* ('French Lessons', *Artforum* 34, no.7, March 1996; a month before *L'Informe* opened), whose author, Elisabeth Lebovici, proved incapable of resisting amused mention of Angelica Pabst's catalogue essay *'Dans les régles de l'art'* (In the periods of art), on *'règles menstruelles'* in art.
42. *Documents 1929–1931*, 2 vols. (Éditions Jean-Michel Place, Paris, 1991).
43. Bataille's short text 'Abattoir' (Slaughterhouse) appeared as a 'dictionary entry' in *Documents*, 1929 no.6, pp.32–3 (pp.440–1 in the 1991 reprint). If she saw it, Saville would surely have been interested in his longer illustrated essay, 'Les Écarts de la Nature', in 1930 no.2, pp.79–82 (pp.106–10 in the 1991 reprint). Its modest title introduces a study of 'les monstres, les prodiges et les abominations' based on alarming eighteenth-century engravings.
44. Sean Tejaratchi (ed.), text by Katherine Dunn, *Death Scenes: A Homicide Detective's Scrapbook* (Port Townsend, WA: Feral House, 1996).
45. Janet Hobhouse, *The Bride Stripped Bare: The Artist and the Nude in the Twentieth Century* (Jonathan Cape, London, 1988); Gill Saunders, *The Nude: A New Perspective* (Harper & Row, New York, 1989); Marcia Pointon, *Naked Authority: The Body in Western Painting, 1830–1908* (Cambridge University Press, Cambridge, 1990); Nead, *The Female Nude*; Kathleen Adler and Pointon (eds), *The Body Imaged: The Human Form and Visual Culture since the Renaissance* (Cambridge University Press, Cambridge, 1993); Andrew Benjamin, ed., *The Body* (Journal of Philosophy and the Visual Arts, London, 1993).
Such books continue: as this text was being written, though I did not consult it, Lauren Elkin published *Art Monsters: Unruly Bodies in Feminist Art* (Farrar, Straus & Giroux, New York, 2023).
46. Mary Douglas, *Purity and Danger: An Analysis of Pollution and Taboo* (Routledge & Kegan Paul, London, 1966), p.121.
47. Kristeva, *Powers of Horror*, pp.2–4, 46–8, 69–76, 113–14, and passim.
48. The subtitle of Saville's 1994 triptych *Strategy* (p.66), although perhaps inspired by Rubens's *Three Graces* (1630–5) in the Prado, reinforces that impression. So does the row of 5 ½ figures, alternatively standing and hanging, that all but fills the surface of *Shift* (1996–97; p.35).
49. The latter imperative is made evident in *Odalisque* of 2012–14 (cat.40), an unusual painting in its inclusion of a background mirror purporting to reflect the far sides of the figures.
50. This subject is discussed, with a bibliography, in relationship to Saville's work in my 'Shored Fragments (For Jenny Saville)', in *Jenny Saville: Oxyrhynchus* (Gagosian, London, 2015), pp.7–28.
51. This statement of Saville's, and subsequent ones quoted without a citation, come from her interview with Alison McDonald, published as 'Jenny Saville: Oxyrhynchus', in *Gagosian* (September–October 2014), pp.19–23.
52. Saville did paint some figure compositions that form a singular scene, such as *Byzantium* of 2018, however improbable its components.
53. Brice Marden, quoted in John Yau, 'An Interview with Brice Marden', in Eva Keller and Regula Malin (eds), *Brice Marden: Drawings and Paintings, 1964–2002* (Scalo and Daros Services, Zurich, 2003), p.51.
54. Greenberg, 'After Abstract Expressionism', *Art International*, 25 October 1962. Reprinted. in *Clement Greenberg: The Collected Essays and Criticism*, Vol. 4. *Modernism with a Vengeance, 1957–1969*, ed. O'Brian (The University of Chicago Press, Chicago and London, 1993), p.127.
55. Edmund Burke's *Philosophical Enquiry into the Origins of Our Ideas of the Sublime and Beautiful* is readily available in online versions, as is Immanuel Kant's discussion of the sublime, which appears in Part 1, Book II, of his *Critique of Judgment*.
56. Burke, *A Philosophical Enquiry*, part I, section VII, 51.
57. Ibid., part II, section XVI, 116.
58. Jon Cook, Introduction, in *William Hazlitt: Selected Writings*, ed. Cook (Oxford University Press, Oxford, 1991), p.xix.
59. Michael Fried, *Realism, Writing, Disfiguration: On Thomas Eakins and Stephen Crane* (The University of Chicago Press, Chicago and London, 1987), p.69.
60. Krauss describes the term 'abject' as 'a kind of feminine sublime' in a discussion of Mulvey's work. See Bois and Krauss (eds), *Formless*, p.238.
61. Geoffrey Galt Harpham, *On the Grotesque: Strategies of Contradiction in Art and Literature* (Princeton University Press, Princeton, NJ, 1982), p.14.
62. Kristeva, *Powers of Horror*, p.4.
63. Harpham, *On the Grotesque*, pp.8–9.
64. Ibid, pp.8–11, quoting from Hugh Kenner, *A Homemade World: The American Modernist Writers* (William Morris and Co., New York, 1975), p.41.
65. Ibid., p.66.
66. Charles Baudelaire, 'On the Essence of Laughter', 1855, in *The Painter of Modern Life and Other Essays*, trans. and ed. Jonathan Mayne (Da Capo, New York, 1964), pp.156–7. Discussed in Harpham, *On the Grotesque*, p.70.
67. Baudelaire, 'On the Essence of Laughter', p.156.
68. Ruskin, *The Stones of Venice*, 1851–3, III.iii.67, discussed in Harpham, *On the Grotesque*, p.185.

The Hard-Won Image

1. The Newbery Medal is awarded to 'the most distinguished student completing the Diploma course' at Glasgow School of Art.
2. Willem de Kooning in John Elderfield, *de Kooning: a Retrospective*, (The Museum of Modern Art, New York, 2011), p.18.

On Jenny Saville and Willem de Kooning

1. Much of the information in this essay comes from conversations between Jenny Saville and the author at the artist's studio in Oxford, England, on 19 June 2023, and from email correspondence with the artist, 29 January–6 March 2024.
2. 'I was attracted to its power the moment I saw it. It felt ancient and modern simultaneously. It was a forceful woman, an icon with agency and movement. I hadn't seen anything like it before and knew it was important to me'. Saville, correspondence with the author, 6 March 2024.
3. 'In the flesh' is Saville's distinctive phrase. Saville, Sotheby's presentation

on Willem de Kooning, Sotheby's New York, 12 November 2022. With thanks to Cristina Colomar and Gagosian for access to the recording of the event. See also Saville's interview with Kara Vander Weg, 'Jenny Saville on Willem de Kooning', *Gagosian Quarterly*, 13 April 2018. Available online at https://gagosian.com/quarterly/2018/04/13/jenny-saville-willem-de-kooning
4. Saville, Sotheby's presentation.
5. De Kooning, interview with David Sylvester, 1960, in Sylvester, *Interviews with American Artists* (Yale University Press, New Haven, 2001), p.49.
6. De Kooning, quoted in Selden Rodman, 'Revolution in Paint: Willem de Kooning', *Conversations with Artists* (Capricorn Books, New York, 1961), p.102. Emphasis in original.
7. A notorious 1969 review argues that de Kooning, in the *Woman* series, 'flays [his subjects], beats them, stretches them on racks, draws and quarters them'. Emily Genauer, 'De Kooning's Complaint', *Newsday*, 8 March 1969.
8. Saville, Sotheby's presentation.
9. Ibid.
10. Ibid.
11. Saville in 'Jenny Saville on Willem de Kooning'.
12. Saville, correspondence with the author, 6 March 2024.
13. 'I decided that I would make the same painting over and over again. Portrait painting is seen to be imbued with the sitter. … If you take that away and forget the personality … I want to concentrate on the personality of the paint. I just need[ed] an armature'. Saville, Sotheby's presentation.
14. The series encompasses collages, drawings, digital prints and paintings, all based on transformations of the same root photograph. 'I used that *Stare* image all over the place. I wanted to get as fluid as possible with the image', Saville says. Correspondence with the author, 6 March 2024.
15. Saville: 'When I was in my twenties, a lot of the most exciting paintwork I was seeing was in abstract painters like de Kooning and [Cy] Twombly. Because abstraction traditionally dealt with the "fundamentals" of painting, painting itself was pushed to levels that it hadn't [been] through "representational" painting. Figurative painting dealt with the "fundamentals" of being human or being "represented", but I wanted the excitement in paint and the potential metaphors paint held to also work in a representational way. The tension between bringing these two worlds together I think is the crux of my work'. Correspondence with the author, 6 March 2024.
16. Saville, correspondence with the author, 3–14 February 2024.
17. Ibid.
18. Kaelen Wilson-Goldie connects de Kooning and Tell Asmar in her review of the exhibition *From Ancient to Modern: Archaeology and Aesthetics*, at New York University's Institute for the Study of the Ancient World in 2015. In *Artforum* 54, no.1 (September 2015), available online at https://www.artforum.com/events/from-ancient-to-modern-archaeology-and-aesthetics-213347
Griselda Pollock examines de Kooning's *Woman* series and Marilyn Monroe in her essay 'Massacred Women Do Not Make Me Laugh, Nor Do the Agonies of Marilyn Monroe's Body', in *Killing Men & Dying Women: Imagining Difference in 1950s New York Painting* (Manchester University Press, Manchester, 2022), pp.157–71.
19. 'I used Photoshop to shift the colours.' Saville, Sotheby's presentation. See also Simon Schama, 'Interview with Jenny Saville', in Richard Calvocoressi and Mark Stevens (eds), *Jenny Saville* (Rizzoli, New York, 2005), p.125: 'Learning how to use Photoshop helped enormously. I started swinging the colours on so they almost separated from the image'.
20. 'I had this tiny image of a woman, or I don't know the gender – it could be a boy or a woman – from a dermatological book, with a port wine stain'. Saville, Sotheby's presentation.
21. See, for example, Del LaGrace Volcano's essay 'On Being a Jenny Saville Painting', in *Jenny Saville: Territories*, ed. Mollie Dent-Brocklehurst (Gagosian, New York, 1999) and Jack Halberstam, 'Technotopias: Representing Transgender Bodies in Contemporary Art', in *In a Queer Time and Place: Transgender Bodies, Subcultural Lives* (New York University Press, New York, 2005), 111–12.
22. De Kooning, quoted in Selden Rodman, 'Revolution in Paint: Willem de Kooning', *Conversations with Artists* (Capricorn Books, New York, 1961), p.102.

The Rainbow of the Flesh

1. De Kooning said: 'Flesh was the reason why oil painting was invented. Never before in history had it taken such a place in painting. For the Egyptians, it was something that didn't last long enough; for the Greeks, it – and everything else – took on the texture of painted marble and plaster walls. But for the Renaissance artist, flesh was the stuff people were made of. It was because of man, and not in spite of him, that painting was considered an art.' Willem de Kooning, 'The Renaissance and Order' (1949), in Thomas B. Hess, *Willem de Kooning* (The Museum of Modern Art, New York, 1968), p.142. See also note 10 on p.186 of this publication.

A Pathology of Paint

1. Jenny Saville, in Nicholas Cullinan, 'Jenny Saville: Painting the Self', *Gagosian Quarterly*, Winter 2020, p.30. Available online at https://gagosian.com/quarterly/2020/12/01/interview-jenny-saville-painting-self
2. Ibid.
3. Ibid., p.28.
4. 'I was working on the Stare Head when I was pregnant with my son, and it was so profound to be making flesh in my body while I was trying to produce flesh on a canvas.' Saville in conversation with Simon Groom, 2018, quoted in 'Jenny Saville Now', Simon Groom, *Gagosian Quarterly*, Summer 2018.
5. Willem de Kooning, 'The Renaissance and Order' (1949). See also note 10 on p.186 of this publication.

Further Reading

Monographs and exhibition catalogues

Richard Calvacoressi and Mark Stephens (eds), *Jenny Saville* (Rizzoli and Gagosian, New York, 2018)

John Elderfield (ed.), *Jenny Saville: Oxyrynchus* (Rizzoli, New York, 2015)

Sergio Risaliti (ed.), *Jenny Saville* (Silvana Editoriale, Milan, 2018)

Jenny Saville: Elpis (Gagosian, New York, 2022)

Jenny Saville: Continuum (Gagosian, New York, 2012)

Jenny Saville (Rizzoli, New York, 2005)

Wider reading, essays and collections

Whitney Chadwick, *Women, Art, and Society* (Thames & Hudson, New York, 2021)

John Elderfield (ed.), *Willem de Kooning: Ten Paintings, 1983–1985* (Gagosian, New York, 2003)

Sarah Howgate, Sandy Nairne and Jo Higgins, *21st Century Portraits*, (National Portrait Gallery, London, 2013)

Luce Irigaray, *This Sex Which Is Not One*, 1977, English translation C. Porter and C. Burke (Cornell University Press, Ithaca, New York, 1985)

Charlotte Mullins (ed.), *Painting People: Figure Painting Today* (Distributed Art Publishers, New York, 2006)

Hilary Robinson, *Reading Art, Reading Irigaray: The Politics of Art by Women* (I.B. Tauris, London, 2006)

Shearer West, *Portraiture* (Oxford University Press, Oxford, 2004)

Interview

Jenny Saville and Roxane Gay, 'Fatness & Feminism', *Art in America*, 16 August 2021. Available online at https://www.artnews.com/art-in-america/interviews/fatness-feminism-representation-1234601645

List of Works

Works included in the exhibition tour at The Modern Art Museum of Fort Worth but not included in the exhibition at the National Portrait Gallery, London, are indicated with an asterisk (*). Works not on display are indicated with a double asterisk (**). Works on display at the National Portrait Gallery, London but not at The Modern Art Museum of Fort Worth are indicated with a triple asterisk (***). Dimensions given are unframed wherever possible and all are height × width.

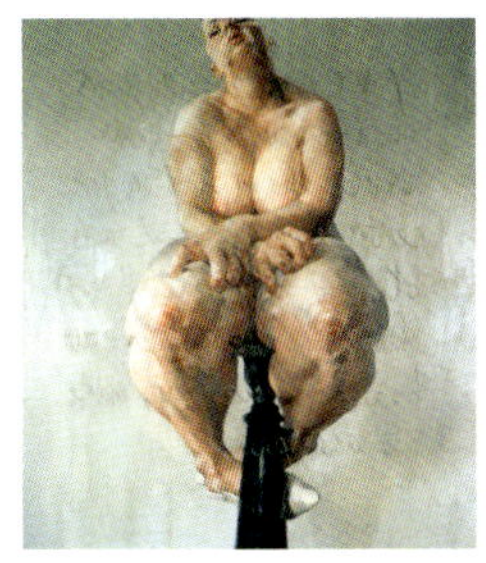

1
Propped, 1992
Oil on canvas
2134 × 1829 mm
Private Collection

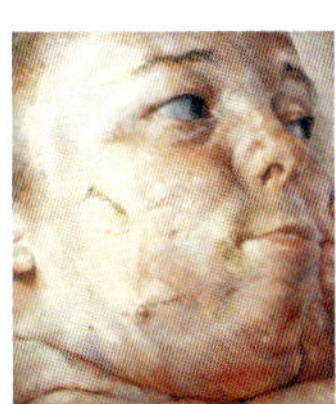

2
Interfacing, 1992
Oil on canvas
1220 × 1020 mm
Arora Collection

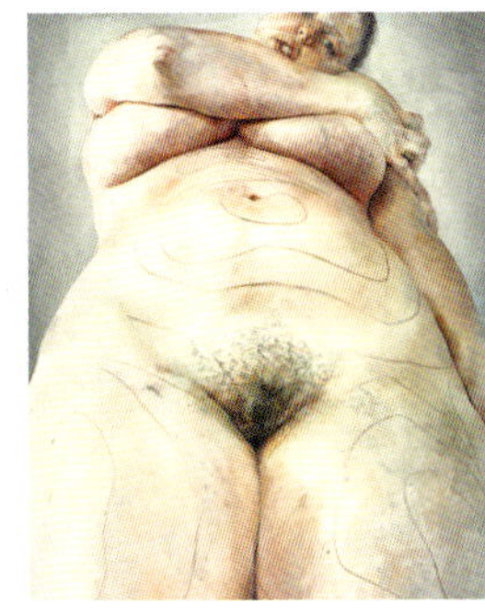

3
Plan, 1993
Oil on canvas
2740 × 2130 mm
Private Collection

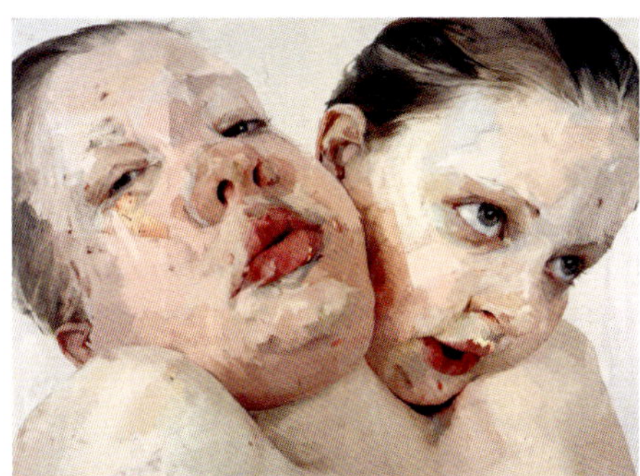

4
Hyphen, 1999
Oil on canvas
2743 × 3658 mm
Private Collection, Courtesy Gagosian

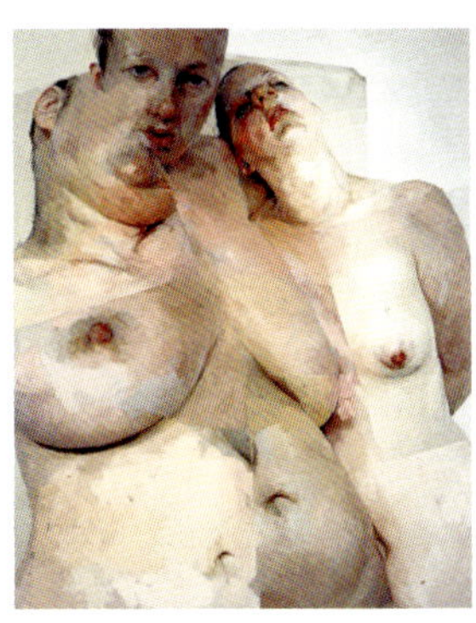

5
Ruben's Flap, 1998–9
Oil on canvas
3048 × 2438 mm
The George Economou Collection

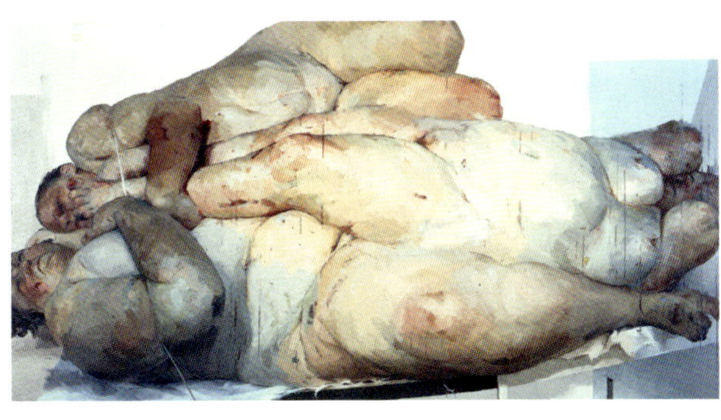

6
Fulcrum, 1998–9 *
Oil on canvas
2616 × 4877 mm
The Broad Art Foundation

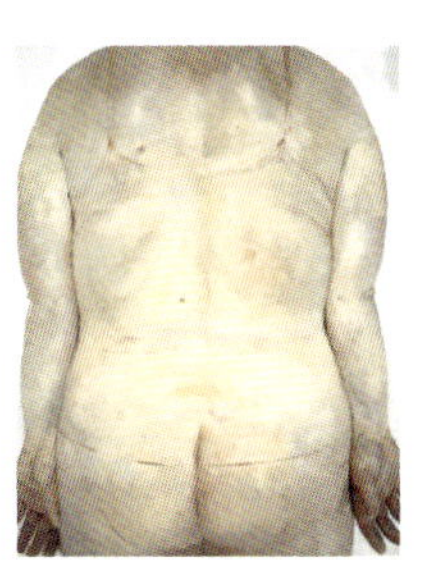

7
Trace, 1993
Oil on canvas
2130 × 1595 mm
Tate

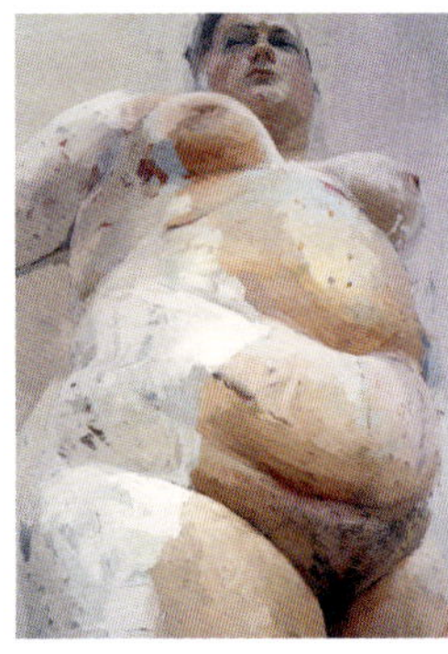

8
Hem, 1999 *
Oil on canvas
3048 × 2133 mm
San Francisco Museum of Modern Art

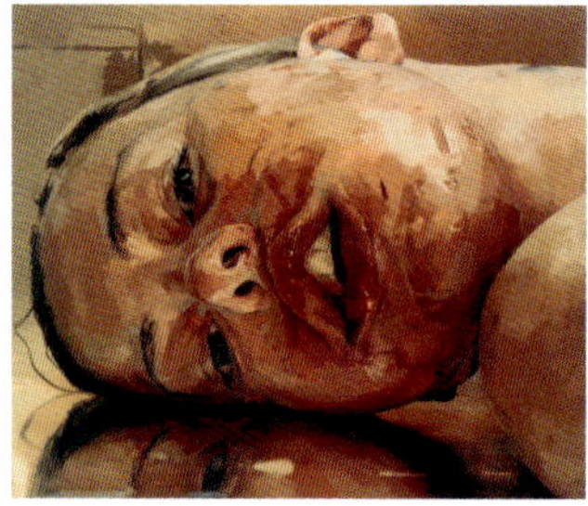

9
Reverse, 2002–3
Oil on canvas
2134 × 2438 mm
Private Collection, Courtesy Gagosian

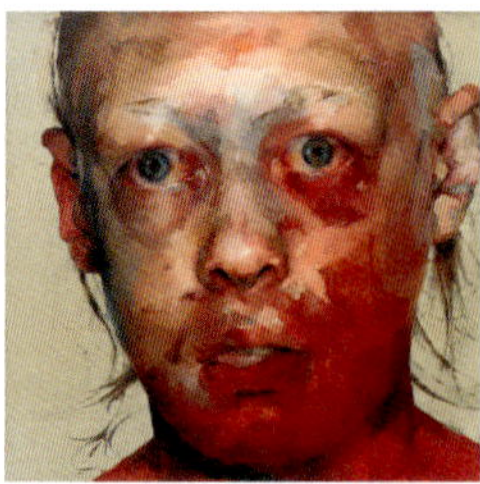

10
Figure 11.23, 1996–7
Oil on canvas
1525 × 1525 mm
ISelf Collection

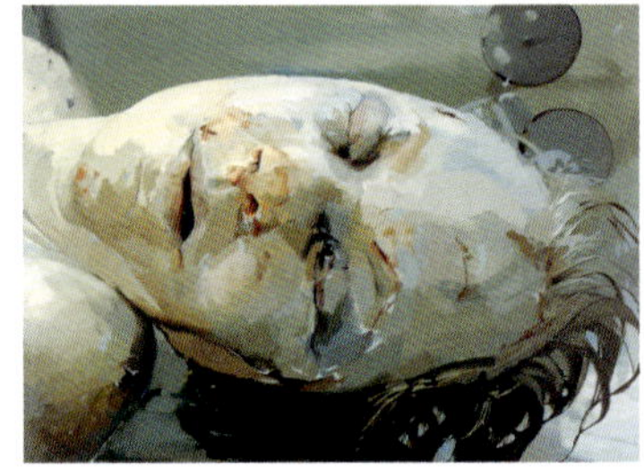

11
Still, 2003 *
Oil on canvas
2740 × 3660 mm
The Metropolitan Museum of Art, New York

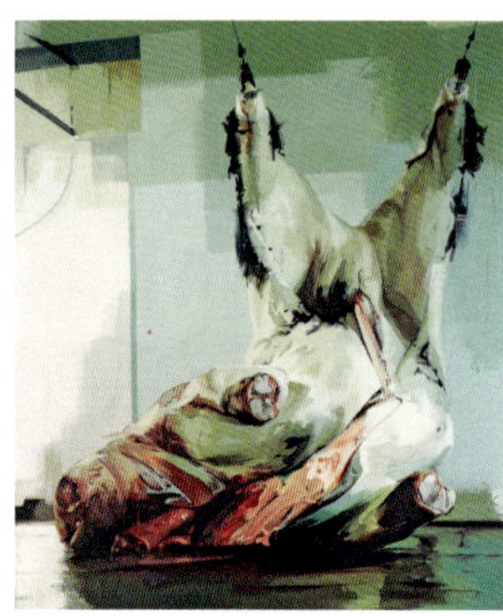

12
Torso II, 2004–5 **
Oil on canvas
3600 × 2940 mm
Private Collection

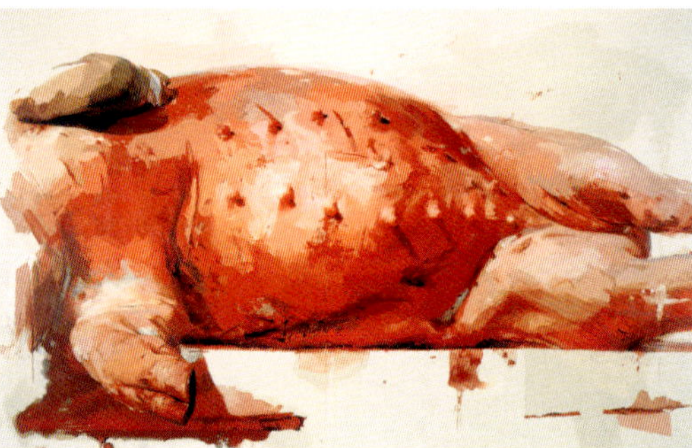

13
Suspension, 2002–3 *
Oil on canvas
2921 × 4521 mm
Private Collection, Courtesy Gagosian

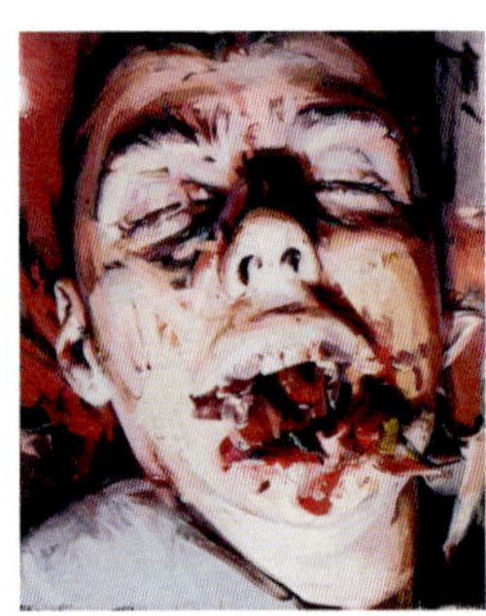

14
Witness, 2009
Oil on canvas
2700 × 2195 mm
The Museum of Fine Arts, Houston

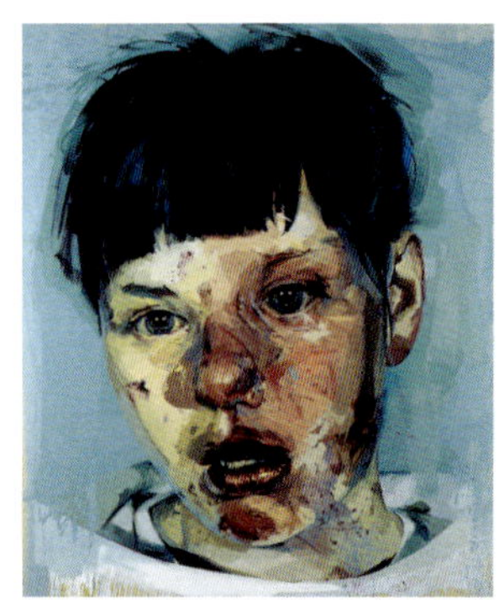

15
Stare, 2004–5
Oil on canvas
3050 × 2500 mm
The Broad Art Foundation, Los Angeles

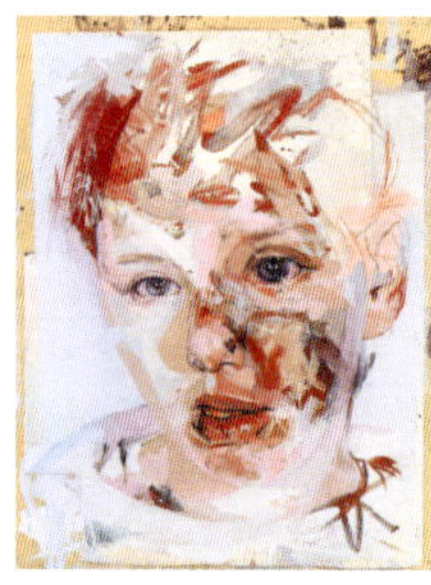

16
Red Stare Collage, 2007–9 *
Collage on board
2520 × 1873 mm
Seattle Art Museum

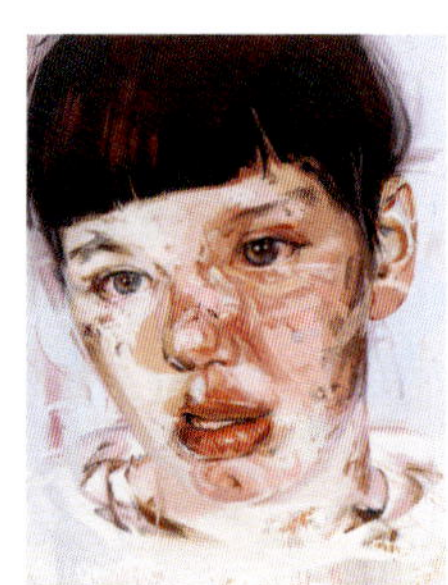

17
Red Stare Head IV, 2006–11
Oil on canvas
2520 × 1873 mm
Private Collection

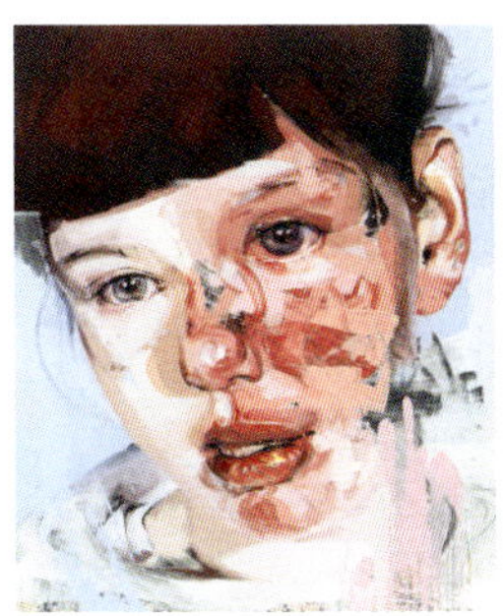

18
Red Stare Head I, 2007–11 *
Oil on canvas
2700 × 2200 mm
Private Collection, Aspen

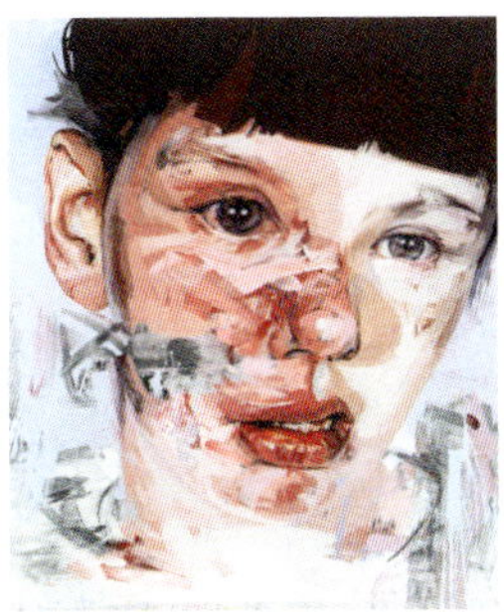

19
Red Stare Head II, 2007–11
Oil on canvas
2700 × 2200 mm
Private Collection

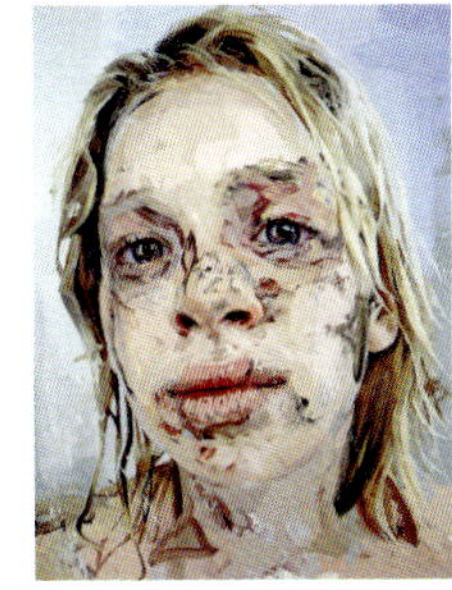

20
Bleach, 2008
Oil on canvas
2523 × 1873 mm
Collection of Lisa and
Steven Tananbaum

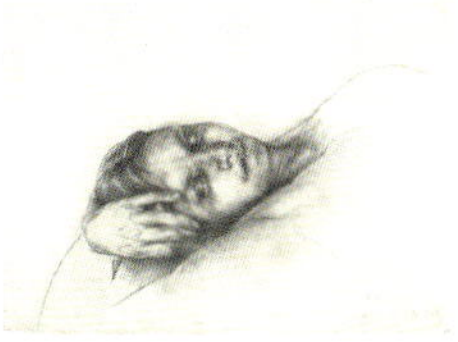

21
Rosetta Study, 2005
Pencil on paper
575 × 758 mm
Private Collection

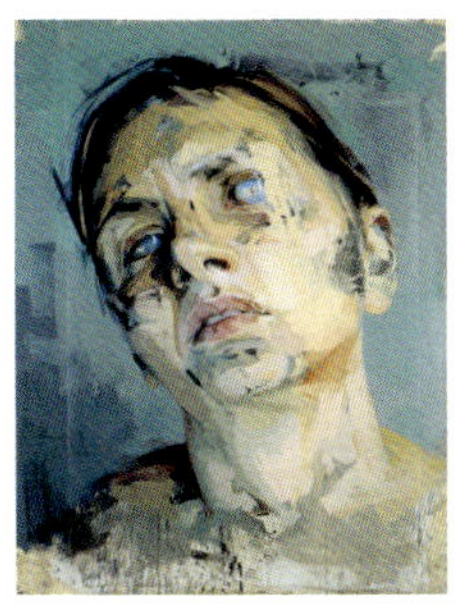

22
Rosetta II, 2005–6
Oil on paper, mounted on board
2520 × 1875 mm
Private Collection

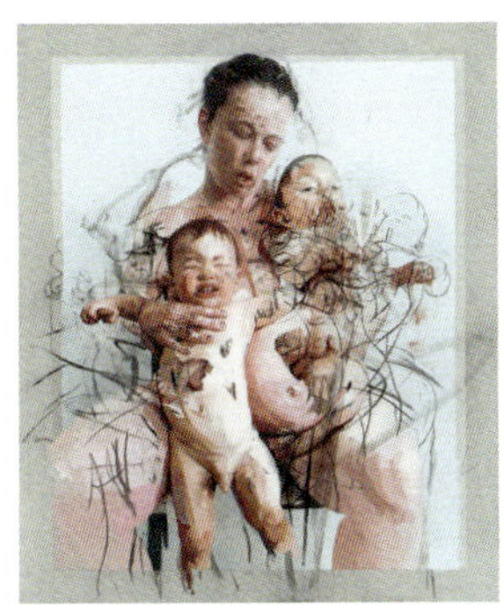

23
The Mothers, 2011
Oil and charcoal on canvas
2700 × 2200 mm
Collection of Lisa and
Steven Tananbaum

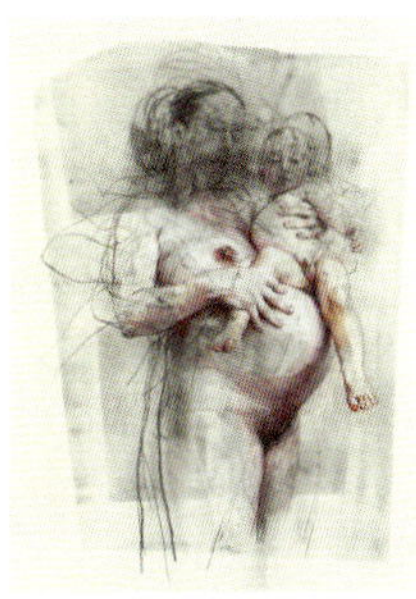

24
Study for Pentimenti IV (after Michelangelo's Virgin and Child), 2011
Charcoal and pastel on paper
1972 × 1475 mm
Casa Mer, Madrid

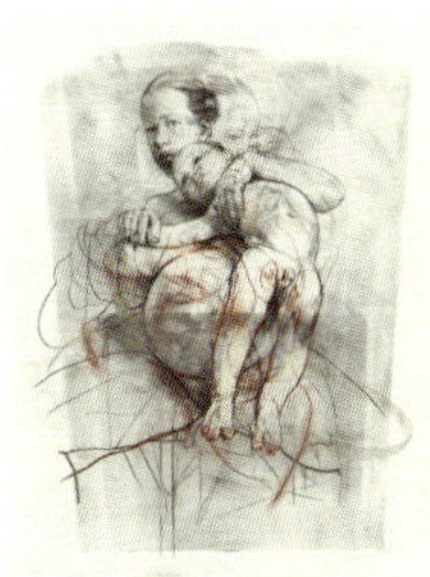

25
Study for Pentimenti III (Sinopia), 2011
Charcoal and pastel on paper
2000 × 1520 mm
Private Collection

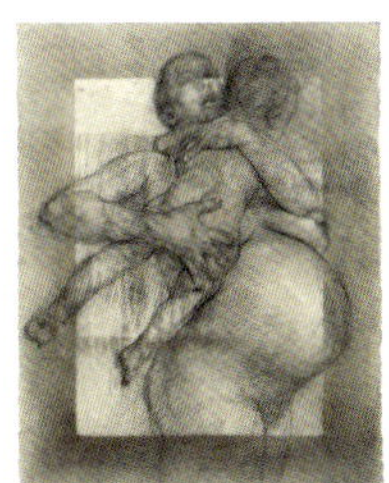

26
Mother and Child Study VII, 2019
Charcoal on paper
760 × 570 mm
Private Collection

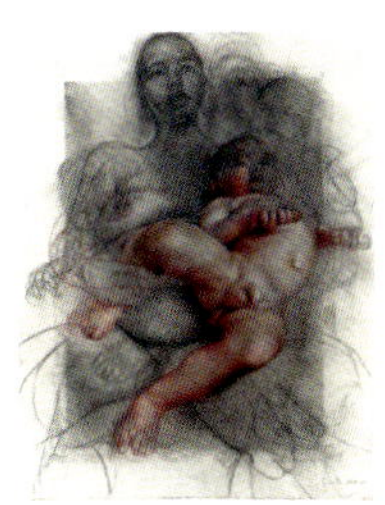

27
Cartonetto Study, 2019–21
Pencil and pastel on paper
760 × 570 mm
Private Collection

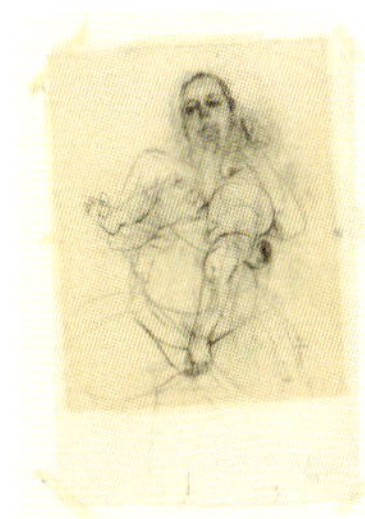

28
Mother and Child Study II, 2009
Pencil on vellum
1065 × 780 mm
Private Collection

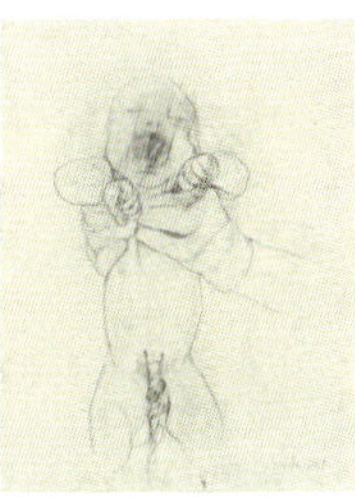

29
Umbilical (Study), 2009
Graphite on paper
760 × 570 mm
Private Collection

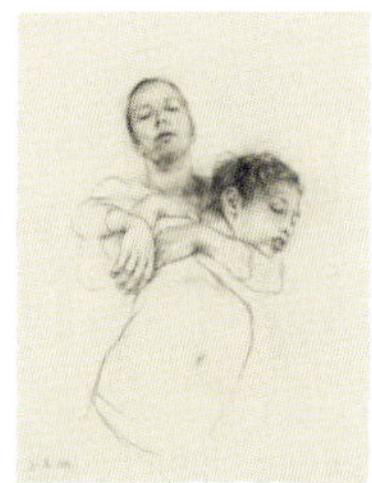

30
Mother and Child (8), (Study), 2015
Graphite on paper
760 × 570 mm
Private Collection

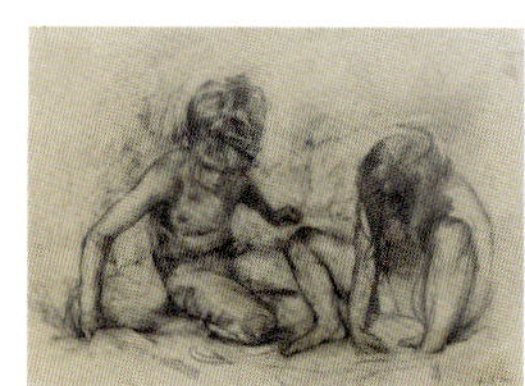

31
Digging (Study) II, 2015
Graphite on toned board
565 × 770 mm
Private Collection

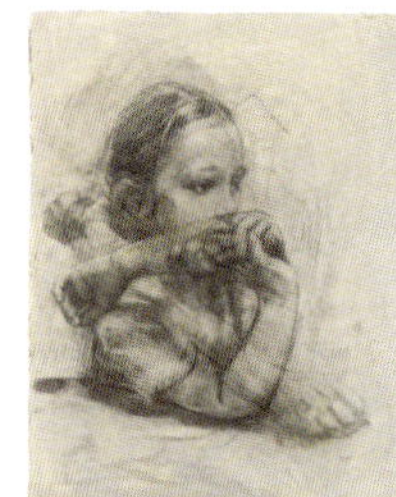

32
Study of Arms II: A response to Titian's 'Study of a Young Woman', Uffizi, Florence, 2015 ***
Charcoal and pastel on tinted acrylic ground on watercolour paper
765 × 567 mm
The Ashmolean Museum, University of Oxford

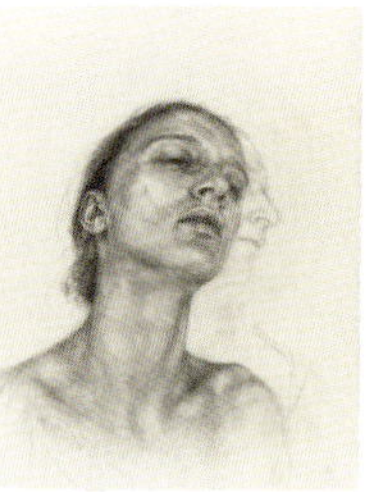

33
Neck Study II, 2021
Pencil on paper
760 × 570 mm
Private Collection

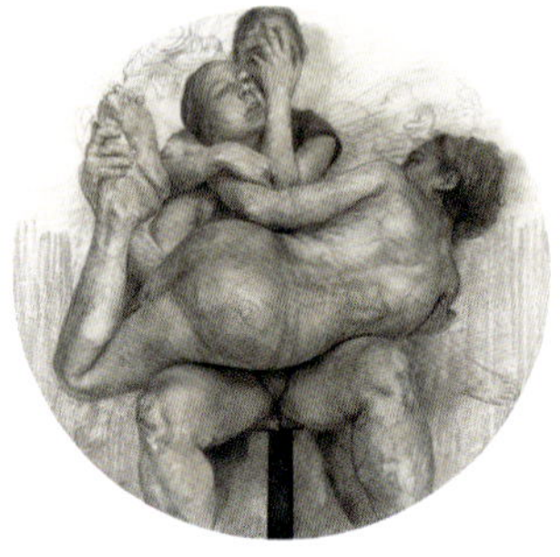

34
Arc, 2020–1
Charcoal and pastel on gesso panel
1200 mm (diameter)
Private Collection

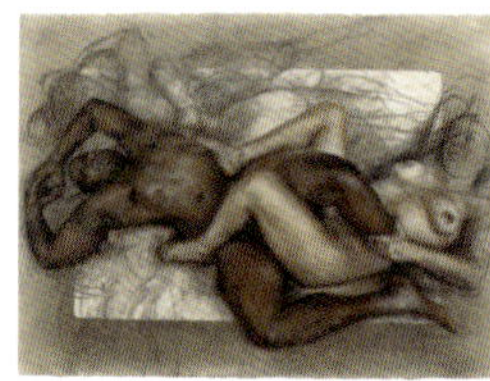

35
Interlocking Figures Study, 2019–21 ***
Charcoal and pastel on paper
570 × 760 mm
The Morgan Library and Museum, New York

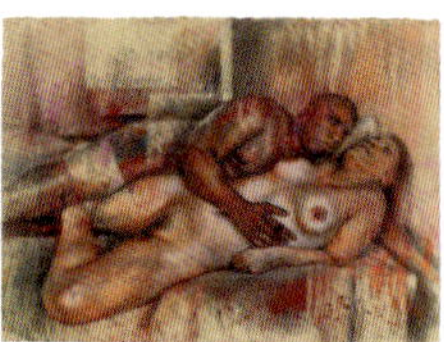

36
Couples Study, 2016–21
Charcoal and pastel on paper
570 × 764 mm
Private Collection

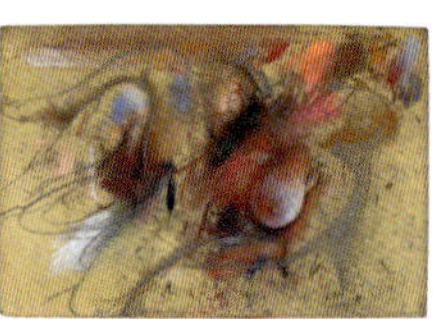

37
Figures on Box Lid Study, 2018
Pastel and pencil on cardboard
355 × 507 mm
Roman Family Collection

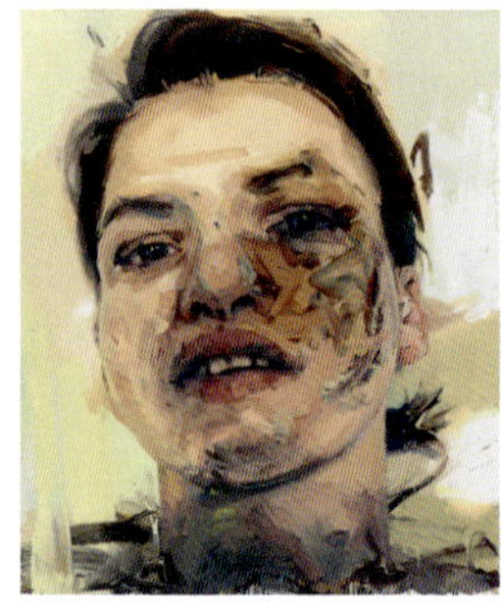

38
Shadow Head, 2007–13
Oil on canvas
2692 × 2197 mm
Collection Glenn and Amanda Fuhrman New York, Courtesy the FLAG Art Foundation

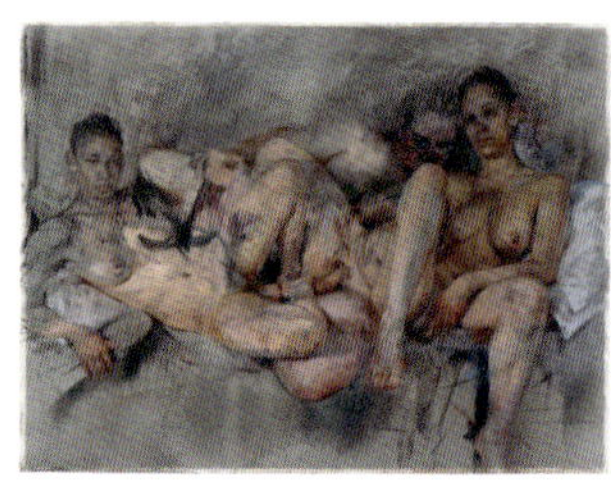

39
Compass, 2013
Charcoal and pastel on paper mounted on board
1530 × 2000 mm
Private Collection

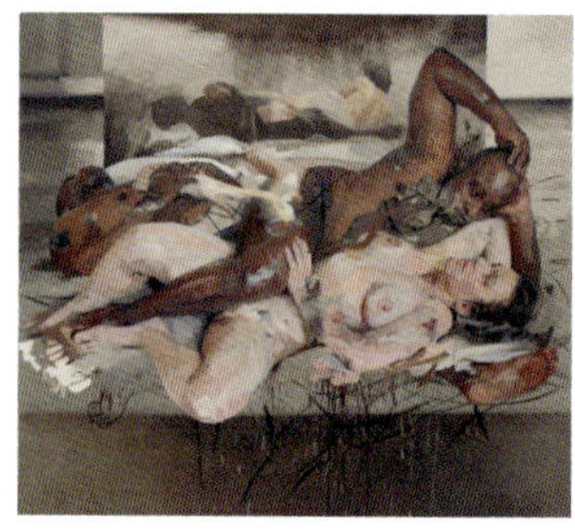

40
Odalisque, 2012–14
Oil and charcoal on canvas
2170 × 2365 mm
Craig Robins Collection, Miami

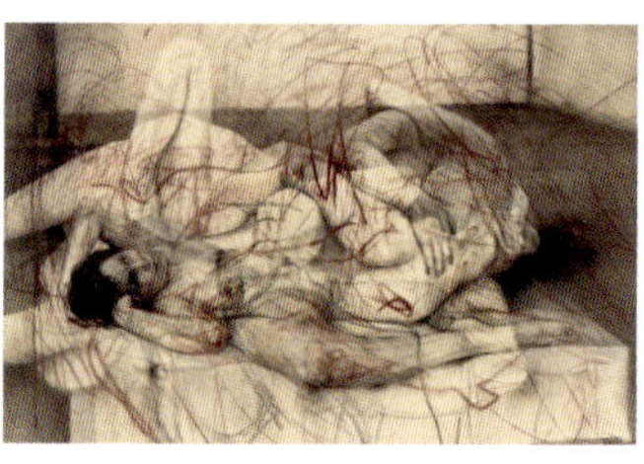

41
One Out of Two (Symposium), 2016
Charcoal and pastel on canvas
1520 × 2250 mm
Private Collection

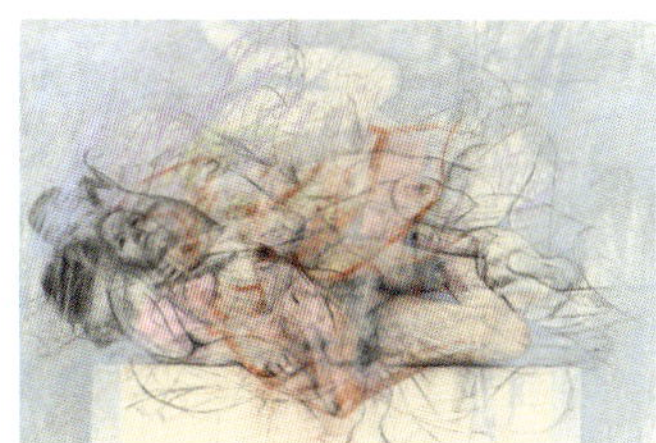

42
Out of One, Two (Symposium), 2016
Charcoal and pastel on canvas
1519 × 2250 mm
Private Collection

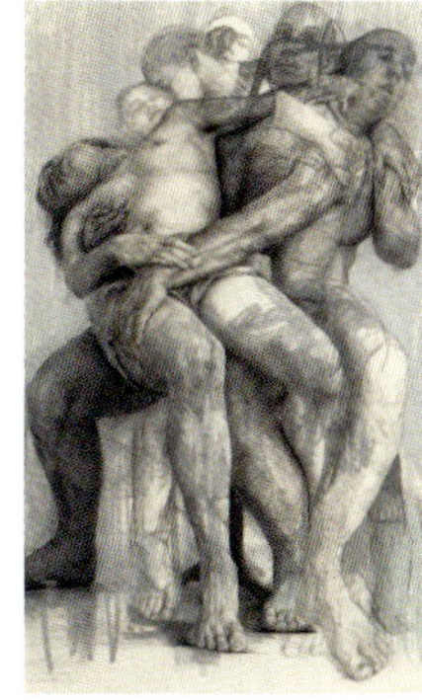

43
Pietà I, 2019–21
Charcoal and pastel
on canvas
2800 × 1600 mm
The George Economou
Collection

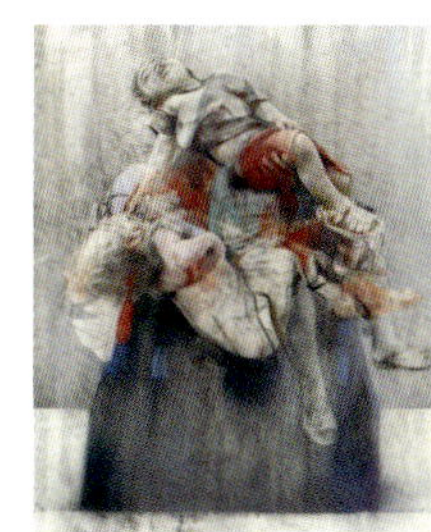

44
Aleppo, 2017–18
Pastel and charcoal on canvas
2000 × 1600 mm
National Galleries of Scotland,
Collection of the artist

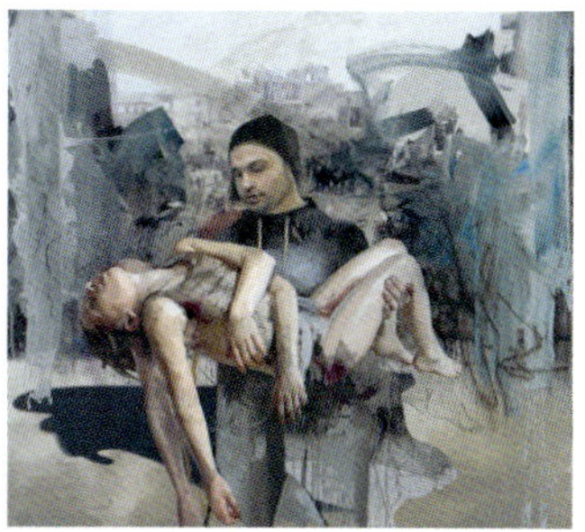

45
Blue Pieta, 2018 *
Oil on canvas
2502 × 2705 mm
The Broad Art Foundation

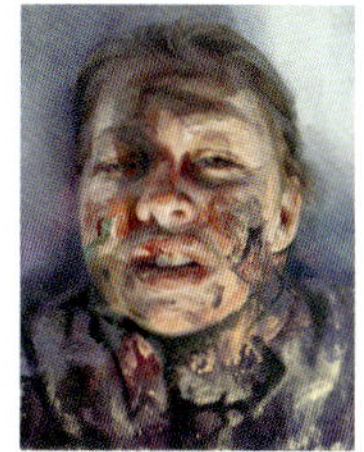

46
Self-Portrait
(after Rembrandt), 2019
Oil on paper
1375 × 1015 mm
Private Collection,
Courtesy Gagosian

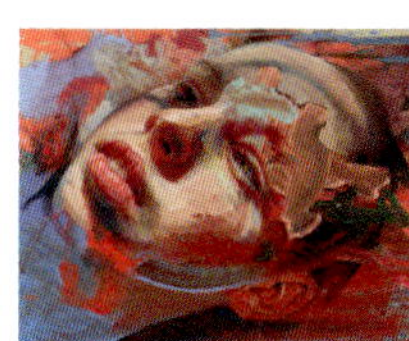

47
Drift, 2020–2
Oil and oil stick on canvas
1000 × 1200 mm
Private Collection,
Courtesy Gagosian

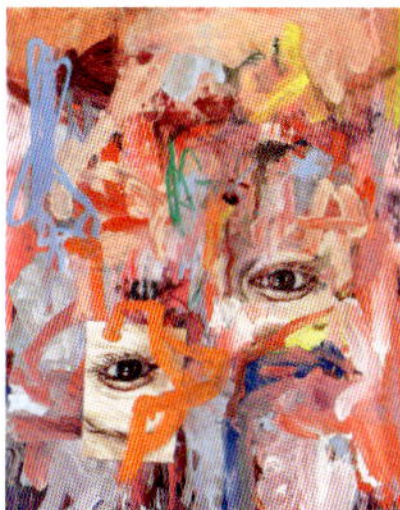

48
Cascade, 2020
Oil on linen
2000 × 1600 mm
Private Collection

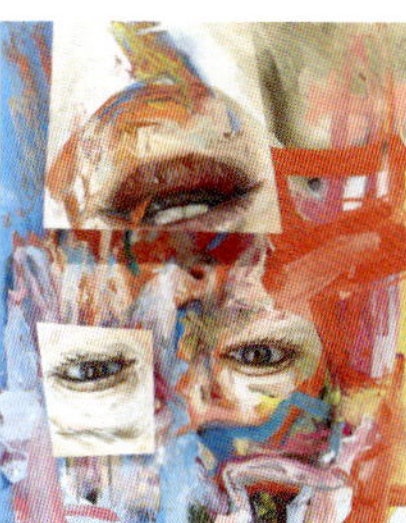

49
Virtual, 2020
Oil on canvas
2000 × 1600 mm
AMA Collection

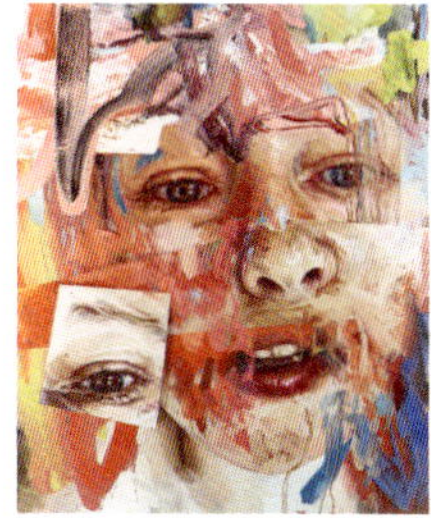

50
Stanza, 2020–2
Oil and oil stick on linen
2000 × 1600 mm
Private Collection

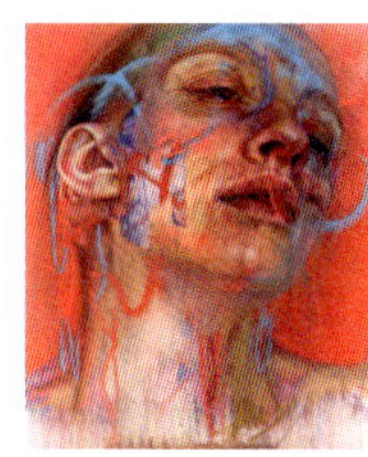

51
Latent, 2020–2
Acrylic and pastel on canvas
1500 × 1200 mm
The George Economou
Collection

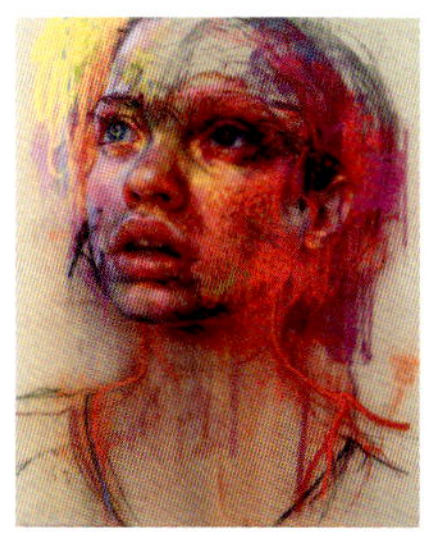

52
Prism, 2020
Pastel and charcoal on canvas
2000 × 1600 mm
Private Collection

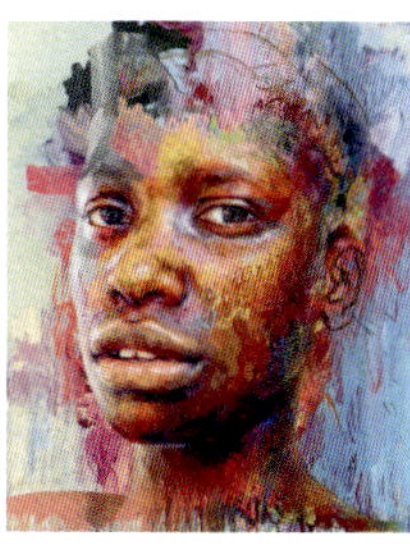

53
Chasah, 2020
Oil on linen
2000 × 1600 mm
Private Collection,
Courtesy Gagosian

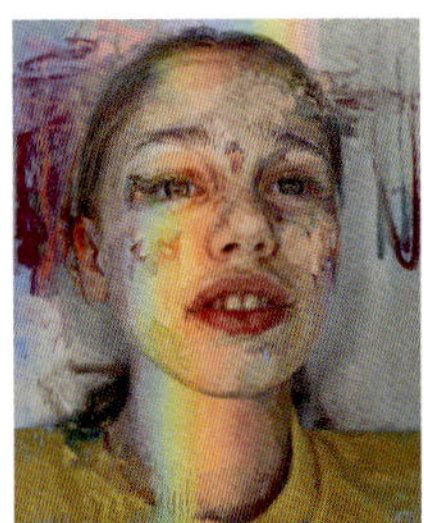

54
Messenger, 2020–1
Acrylic and oil on canvas
2000 × 1600 mm
Private Collection

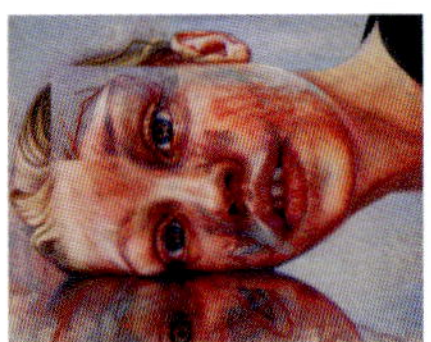

55
Tilt, 2024 *
Watercolour, charcoal and pastel on canvas
1200 × 1500 mm
LA Collection Privée

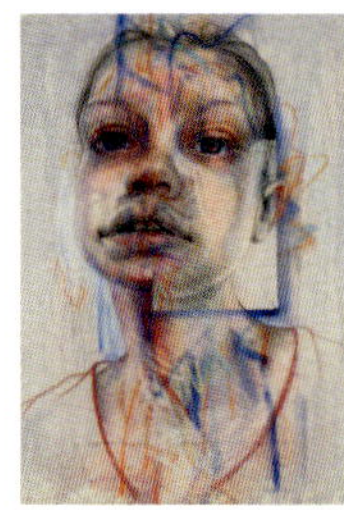

56
View I, 2024 *
Watercolour, pastel and charcoal on canvas
1800 × 1200 mm
Arora Collection

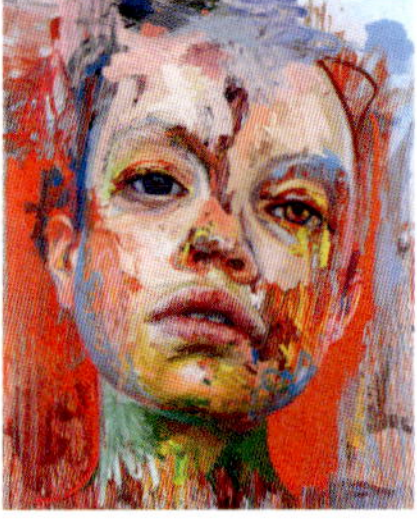

57
Rupture, 2020
Acrylic and oil on linen
2000 × 1600 mm
Private Collection

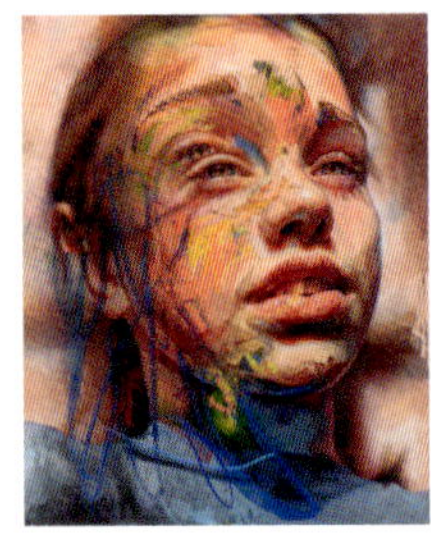

58
Oracle, 2019–23 *
Acrylic, oil and pastel on canvas
2000 × 1600 mm
Private Collection

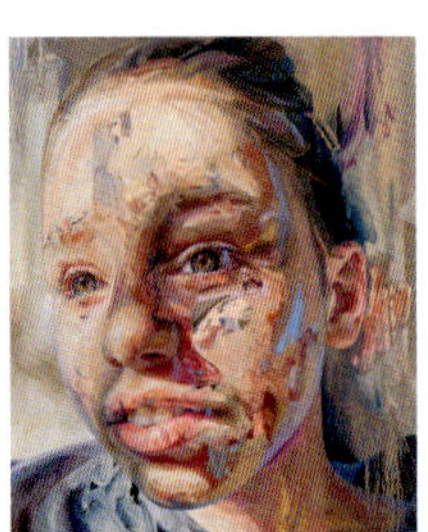

59
Melody, 2024 *
Oil and pastel on canvas
2000 × 1600 mm
Collection of Lisa and Steven Tananbaum

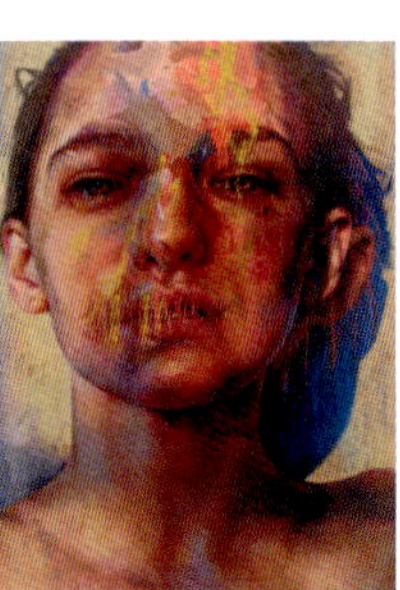

60
Eve, 2022–3
Oil, acrylic and pastel on linen
2200 × 1600 mm
Arora Collection

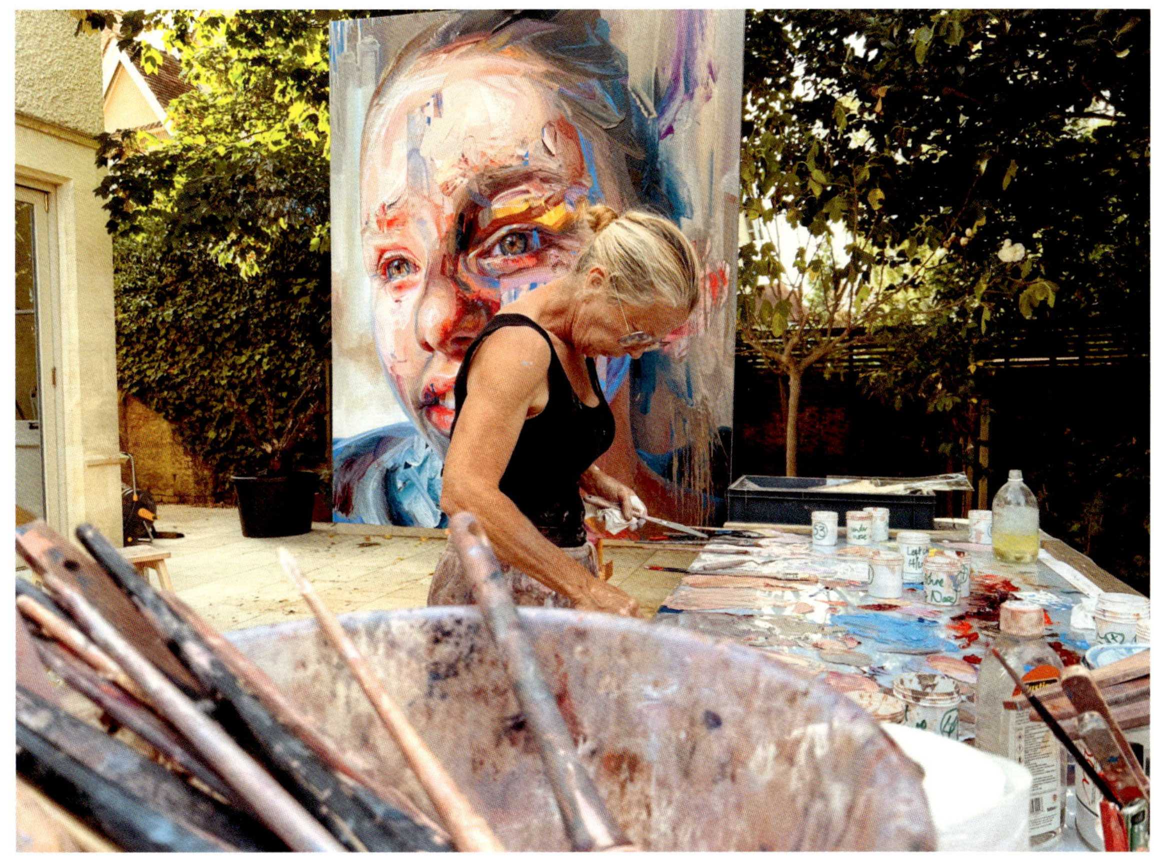

Illustrations

pp.1–8 and 200–8 Jenny Saville's Oxford studio, September 2023 by Sally Mann.

p.10 Jenny Saville at her degree show at the Glasgow School of Art, 1992 by Philip Sayer, for *The Times Saturday Review*.

Studio images by Jenny Saville: pp.14–15, 43, 54–5, 68–9, 84–5, 98, 146–7, 152–3.

p.32 Jenny Saville by an unknown photographer.

pp.44–5 Jenny Saville's studio, Wharf Road, London, *c.*1999 by Glen Luchford.

p.64 In-progress *Fulcrum* (1998–9), Wharf Road, London, *c.*1999 by Glen Luchford.

p.195 (above) Jenny Saville, 2024 by Arturo Saville.

Quotes

p.16 'Jenny Saville in conversation with John Richardson', in *Jenny Saville: Continuum* (Gagosian, London, 2012), p.16.

p.45 'In Conversation: Jenny Saville and Martin Gayford', Gagosian, London, June 2023. Available online at https://gagosian.com/quarterly/2023/06/22/video-in-conversation-jenny-saville-and-martin-gayford

p.69 'Jenny Saville: Painting the Self', *Gagosian Quarterly*, Winter 2020, p.30.

p.105 Rachel Cooke, 'Jenny Saville: "I want to be a painter of modern life, and modern bodies"', *The Guardian*, Saturday 9 June 2012.

p.147 'Jenny Saville', *Gagosian Premieres*, Episode 3, Tuesday 22 December 2020. Available online at https://gagosian.com/premieres/episodes/jenny-saville

Picture Credits

The National Portrait Gallery would like to thank the copyright holders for granting permission to reproduce works illustrated in this book. Every effort has been made to contact the holders of copyright material, and any omissions will be corrected in future editions if the publisher is notified in writing.

Unless otherwise stated, images are © Jenny Saville. All rights reserved, DACS 2025, Courtesy Gagosian.

pp.1–8 All images courtesy Sally Mann © Sally Mann. p.10 © Philip Sayer. p.12 National Portrait Gallery, London. © Jenny Saville. p.19 © Musée du Louvre, Dist. GrandPalaisRmn / Angèle Dequier. p.20 © The Lucian Freud Archive. All Rights Reserved 2025 / Bridgeman Images. p.21 Photograph by A.E. Smith © Chronicle via Alamy Stock Photo. p.22 © Jo Spence Memorial Archive, The Image Centre. Image courtesy of Victoria and Albert Museum, London. p.24 Kroměříž, Archidiocese Olomouc, Archiepiscopal Palace © Archdiocesan Museum Kroměříž p.27 (right) © Succession H. Matisse / DACS 2025. Digital image, The Museum of Modern Art, New York, 2025. p.29 © Willem de Kooning Revocable Trust / ARS, NY and DACS, London 2025. Digital image Carnegie Museum of Art, Pittsburgh, PA, 2025. Gift of G. David Thompson. © Photo Scala, Florence. p.30 © Jasper Johns / VAGA, New York / DACS, London 2025. Christie's Images, London, 2025 © Photo Scala, Florence. p.32 Courtesy of Gagosian. p.33 (left) © The Lucian Freud Archive. All Rights Reserved 2025 / Bridgeman Images. p.35 (centre) © The Estate of Francis Bacon. All rights reserved, DACS / Artimage 2025. Photo: Prudence Cuming Associates Ltd. p.36 (left) © Willem de Kooning Revocable Trust / ARS, NY and DACS, London 2025. Digital image, The Museum of Modern Art, New York, 2025 © Photo Scala, Florence. p.36 (centre) © Cy Twombly Foundation. Courtesy Gagosian. p.36 (right) © Willem de Kooning Revocable Trust / ARS, NY and DACS, London 2025. Digital image © The Museum of Modern Art, 2025 © Photo Scala, Florence. p.37 (left) Image from Yale University, Everett V. Meeks, B.A. 1901, Fund. p.37 (right) © Opera di Santa Maria del Fiore / A. Quattrone, 2025 © Photo Scala, Florence. p.38 (left) Photo © Isabella Stewart Gardner Museum / Bridgeman Images. p.38 (centre) © The Trustees of the British Museum. p.38 (right) © 2025 Casa Buonarroti. p.39 (left) © Succession Picasso / DACS, London 2025 / Bridgeman Images. p.39 (centre) © The Estate of Francis Bacon. All rights reserved, DACS / Artimage 2025. Photo: Prudence Cuming Associates Ltd. p.40 (left) Photo Tate Images. © The Estate of Alberto Giacometti (Fondation Giacometti, Paris and ADAGP, Paris), licensed in the UK by ACS and DACS, London 2025. p.40 (right) © Frank Auerbach, estate of the artist, courtesy Frankie Rossi Art Projects. p.41 (left) Staatliche Museen zu Berlin, Kupferstichkabinett / Jörg P. Anders. p.43 © Jenny Saville. p.44 © Glen Luchford. p.60 Presented by Larry Gagosian (Tate Americas Foundation), 2023. p.63 Gift of Vicki and Kent Logan. p.64 © Glen Luchford. p.68 © Jenny Saville. p.76 Gift of Martin and Toni Sosnoff, 2011. p.83 Gift of Martin Sosnoff, 2015. p.90 Gift of Jeffrey and Susan Brotman in honour of Chiyo Ishikawa. p.98 © Jenny Saville. p.101 © Willem de Kooning Revocable Trust / ARS, NY and DACS, London 2025. Digital Image © The Museum of Modern Art, 2025 © Photo Scala, Florence. p.102 © Willem de Kooning Revocable Trust / ARS, NY and DACS, London 2025. Purchase, with funds from the Friends of the Whitney Museum of American Art. Digital image © Whitney Museum of American Art, 2025 © Photo Scala, Florence. p.103 © Jenny Saville. p.117 Presented by the artist, Jenny Saville, 2016. p.142 Cameraphoto, 2025 © Photo Scala, Florence. p.183 The Metropolitan Museum of Art, New York. The Jules Bache Collection, 1949. p.184 © Marlene Dumas. Photo courtesy Collection Stedelijk Museum Amsterdam. p.185 © The National Gallery. Bought (Knapping Fund), 1937. p.195 © Arturo Saville. pp.200–8 All images courtesy Sally Mann © Sally Mann.

Lenders

AMA Collection
Arora Collection
The Ashmolean Museum, University of Oxford
The Broad Art Foundation, Los Angeles
Casa Mer, Madrid
Cingilli Collection
The George Economou Collection
Collection Glenn and Amanda Fuhrman, New York, courtesy the FLAG Art Foundation
Gagosian
ISelf Collection
LA Collection Privée
The Metropolitan Museum of Art, New York
The Morgan Library and Museum, New York
The Museum of Fine Arts, Houston
National Galleries of Scotland
Private Collections
Craig Robins Collection, Miami
Roman Family Collection
San Francisco Museum of Modern Art
Seattle Art Museum
Collection of Lisa and Steven Tananbaum
Tate

Director's Acknowledgements

I extend my deepest thanks and congratulations to all those within the National Portrait Gallery and outside it who have made *Jenny Saville: The Anatomy of Painting* possible. In addition to my thanks to Jenny Saville, Sarah Howgate, Gagosian and The Modern Art Museum of Fort Worth, we are indebted to the institutions and individuals who have loaned works to the exhibition, both in London and as it travels to Texas, as well as to all the exhibition's supporters.

I would like to acknowledge my colleagues Rosie Wilson, Director of Programmes, Partnerships and Collections; Anna Starling, Director of Commercial and Operations; Denise Vogelsang, Director of Audiences; Sarah Hilliam, Director of Development; Liz Smith, Director of Learning and Engagement, and the wider Gallery team including Stuart Ager, Poppy Andrews, Sophie Colley, Jessica Daley, Andrea Easey, Adriana Ferlauto, Andrew Horn, Jahnavi Inniss, Chloe Jamieson, Sarah Morris, Georgia Perkins, Anna Pharoah, Melanie Pilbrow, Abi Ponton, Skye Redman, Eleanor Shakeshaft, Jude Simmons, Ed Simpson, Eloise Stewart, Georgia Smith, Oliver Tratt, Pauline Velge, Rachel Whitehouse, Helen Whiteoak, and the entire Art Handling team.

I extend my gratitude to Emanuele Coccia, Nicholas Cullinan, John Elderfield, Roxane Gay and Andrea Karnes and for their thought-provoking contributions to this book, and to Sally Mann for her intimate photographs of Saville's studio.

My final thanks are to Kara Green, Senior Publishing Manager, and the Publications team, especially Katie Anderson, Picture Researcher; Zoe Bott, Commercial Sales and Marketing Assistant; Laura Cherry, Project Editor; Jemma Jacobs, Publishing Assistant and Priti Kothary, Production Manager, without whose dedication, creativity and expertise this publication would not have been possible.

Victoria Siddall
Director, National Portrait Gallery, London

Curator's Acknowledgements

My thanks above all go to Jenny Saville for her energy and collaborative spirit. *The Anatomy of Painting* has been a long time in the making, and all the time she has dedicated to the exhibition was time spent away from the studio. As well as being an extraordinary artist, Saville speaks engagingly about her practice and art historical influences, and I felt privileged to spend two days with her discussing this on a memorable trip to see her exhibition in Paris, which formed the basis of our conversation for this book.

At Gagosian I would like to thank Cristina Colomar, Stefan Ratibor, Harry Thorne and Jess Topping, who have worked tirelessly on the project. The exhibition tour to The Modern Art Museum of Fort Worth came about through reconnecting with the Museum's then-Director Marla Price in London. It has been a pleasure to work with Chief Curator Andrea Karnes and I am grateful for her insightful essay.

I have been struck by the warm response of lenders to this exhibition, agreeing to share their works for London and the tour. The ambition of the project could not have been realised without its incredibly generous supporters.

My thanks go to Nicholas Cullinan for inviting Jenny Saville to exhibit at the National Portrait Gallery, to our Interim Director Michael Elliott, and to Victoria Siddall for ably picking up the project with enthusiasm on her arrival.

I am indebted to many colleagues at the National Portrait Gallery, in particular Andrea Easey, Adriana Ferlauto, Andrew Horn, Sarah Morris and Eloise Stewart for their contributions to realising this exciting project. Support from the Curatorial team, especially Tanya Bentley, on other contemporary projects, has allowed me to work on the exhibition. I am particularly grateful to the Publications team for all their work bringing together this outstanding book, as well as to David Frankel, Rosalind Furness and Sara Harrison for their careful copy editing and proofreading. The book is a testament to the talent and sensitivity of its designer, Peter Willberg.

Finally, I would like to thank James, Thomas and Django for keeping the home fires burning and for allowing me to immerse myself in this fascinating work.

Sarah Howgate
Senior Curator of Contemporary Collections, National Portrait Gallery, London

First published to accompany
the exhibition *Jenny Saville: The Anatomy of Painting* at the

National Portrait Gallery, London
June 20 to September 7, 2025

The Modern Art Museum of
Fort Worth, Texas
October 12, 2025 to January 18, 2026

First published in the United States
of America in 2025 by
Rizzoli Electa, a Division of
Rizzoli International Publications, Inc.
49 West 27th Street
New York, NY 10001
rizzoliusa.com

Originally published in Great Britain by
National Portrait Gallery Publications
National Portrait Gallery
St Martin's Place
London WC2H 0HE

This exhibition has been made possible as a result of the Government Indemnity Scheme. The National Portrait Gallery, London, would like to thank HM Government for providing indemnity and the Department for Culture, Media and Sport and Arts Council England for arranging the indemnity.

Supported by

GAGOSIAN

Text pp. 17–31 by John Elderfield
Text pp. 65–7 by Roxane Gay
Text pp. 99–103 by Andrea Karnes
Text pp. 143–5 by Emanuele Coccia, adapted from an essay first published in *Sirens: Jenny Saville at Casa Malaparte* (Gagosian, New York, 2019). Original text translated from Italian by Dylan J. Montanari.
Text pp. 183–5 by Nicholas Cullinan

ISBN: 978-0-8478-7592-4
Library of Congress Control Number: 2025931883
2025 2026 2027 2028 / 10 9 8 7 6 5 4 3 2 1

For Rizzoli Electa
Publisher: Charles Miers
Associate Publisher:
Margaret Rennolds Chace
Editor: Klaus Kirschbaum
Assistant Editor: Emily Ligniti

For the National Portrait Gallery
Director of Commercial and Operations:
Anna Starling
Senior Publishing Manager: Kara Green
Project Editor: Laura Cherry
Picture Research: Katie Anderson
Production Manager: Priti Kothary
Publishing Assistant: Jemma Jacobs
Design: Peter Willberg
Copy editors: David Frankel,
Rosalind Furness
Proofreader: Sara Harrison

The authorized representative in the EU for product safety and compliance is Mondadori Libri S.p.A., via Gian Battista Vico 42, Milan, Italy, 20123
mondadori.it

Front cover: Jenny Saville, *Drift*, 2020–2 © Jenny Saville. All rights reserved, DACS 2025, Courtesy Gagosian

Back cover: Jenny Saville by Nigel Parry, 1995 © Nigel Parry, nigelparryphoto.com

Printed and bound in the UK
by Gomer Press
Origination by DL Imaging

Visit us online
Instagram.com/RizzoliBooks
Facebook.com/RizzoliNewYork
X: @Rizzoli_Books
Youtube.com/user/RizzoliNY

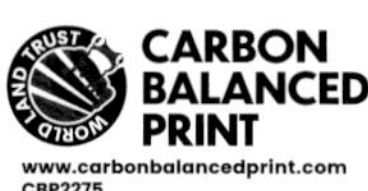

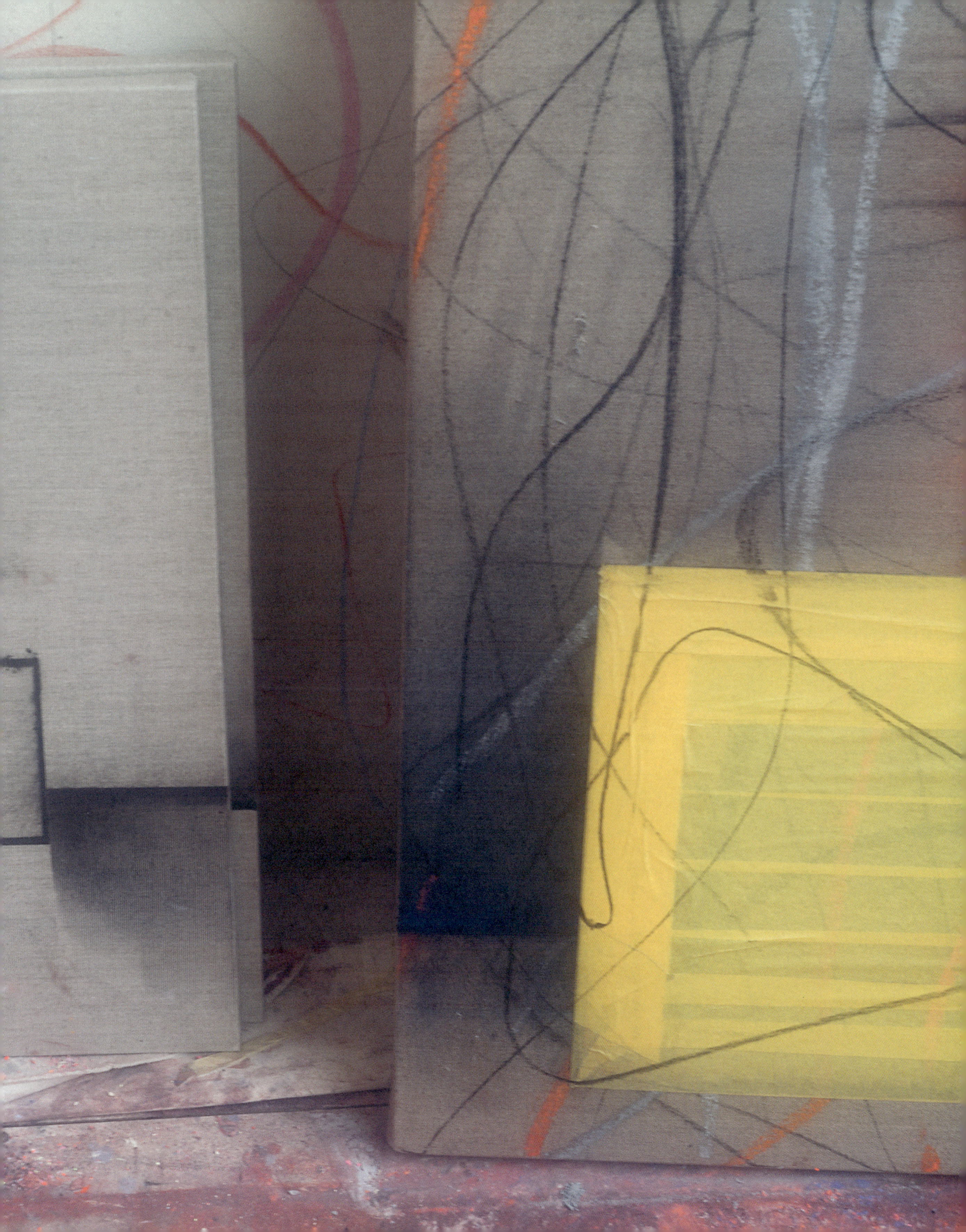

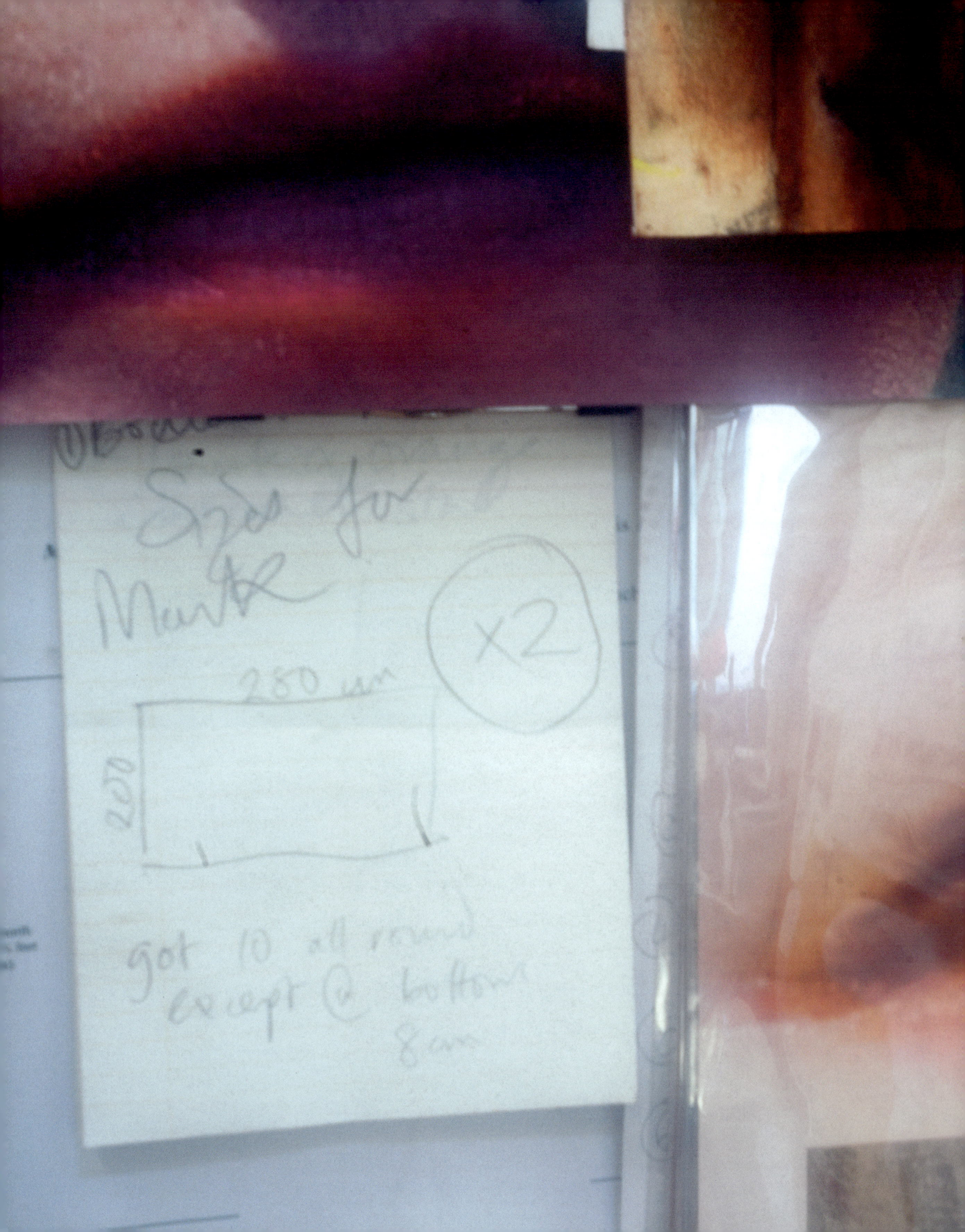
Mark
x2
280 cm
200
got 10 all around
except @ bottom
8 cm

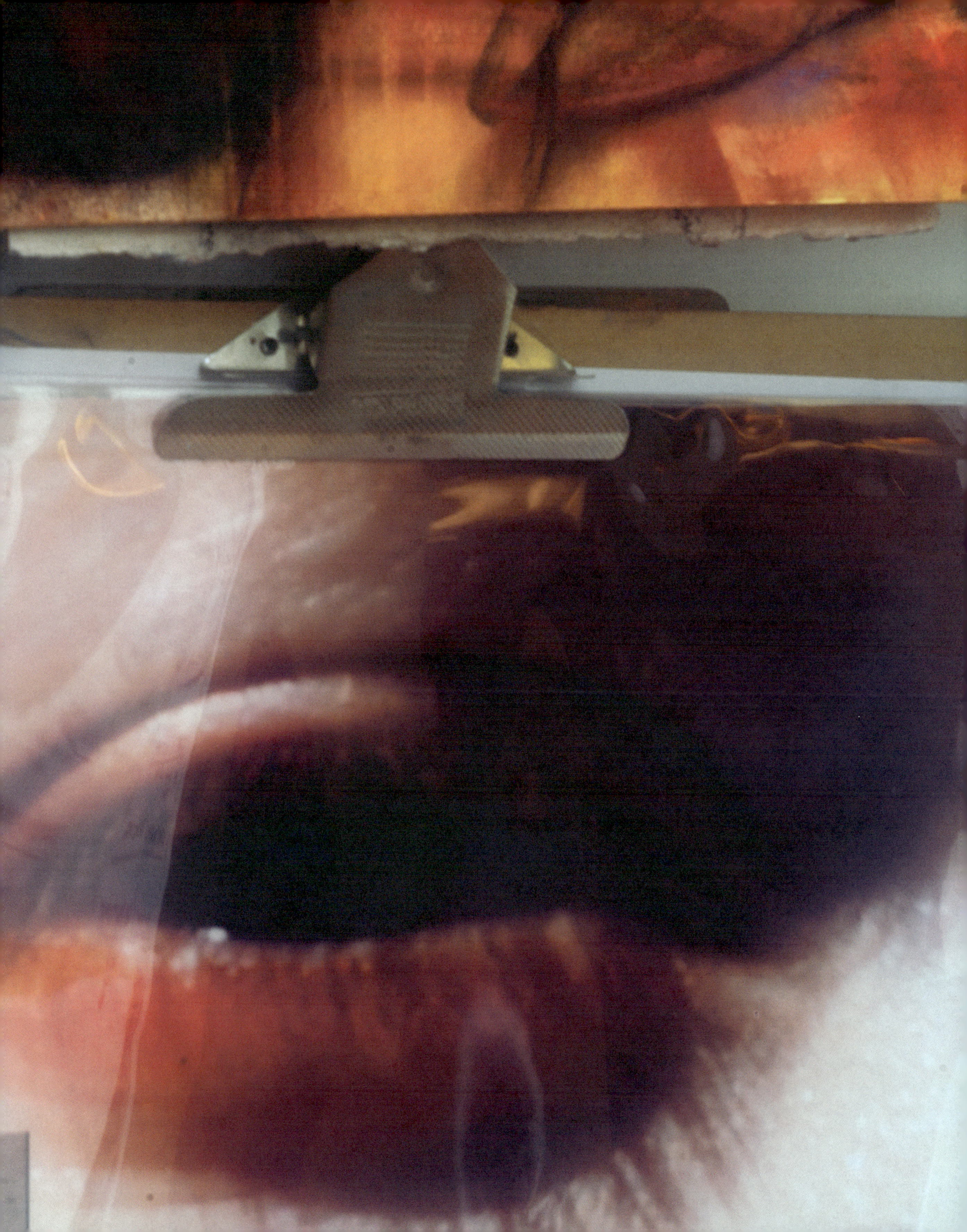

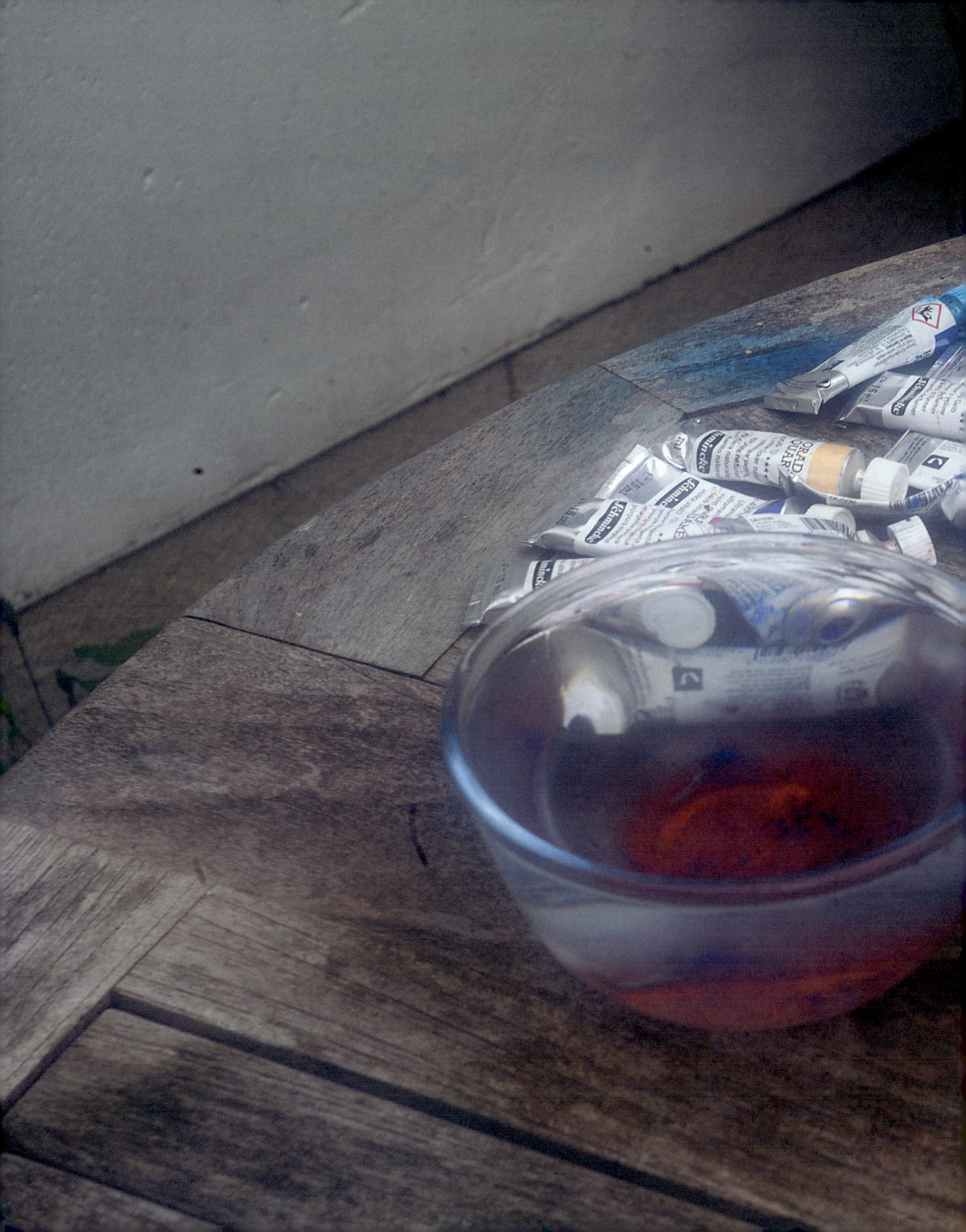
Schmincke
Schmincke
Schmincke

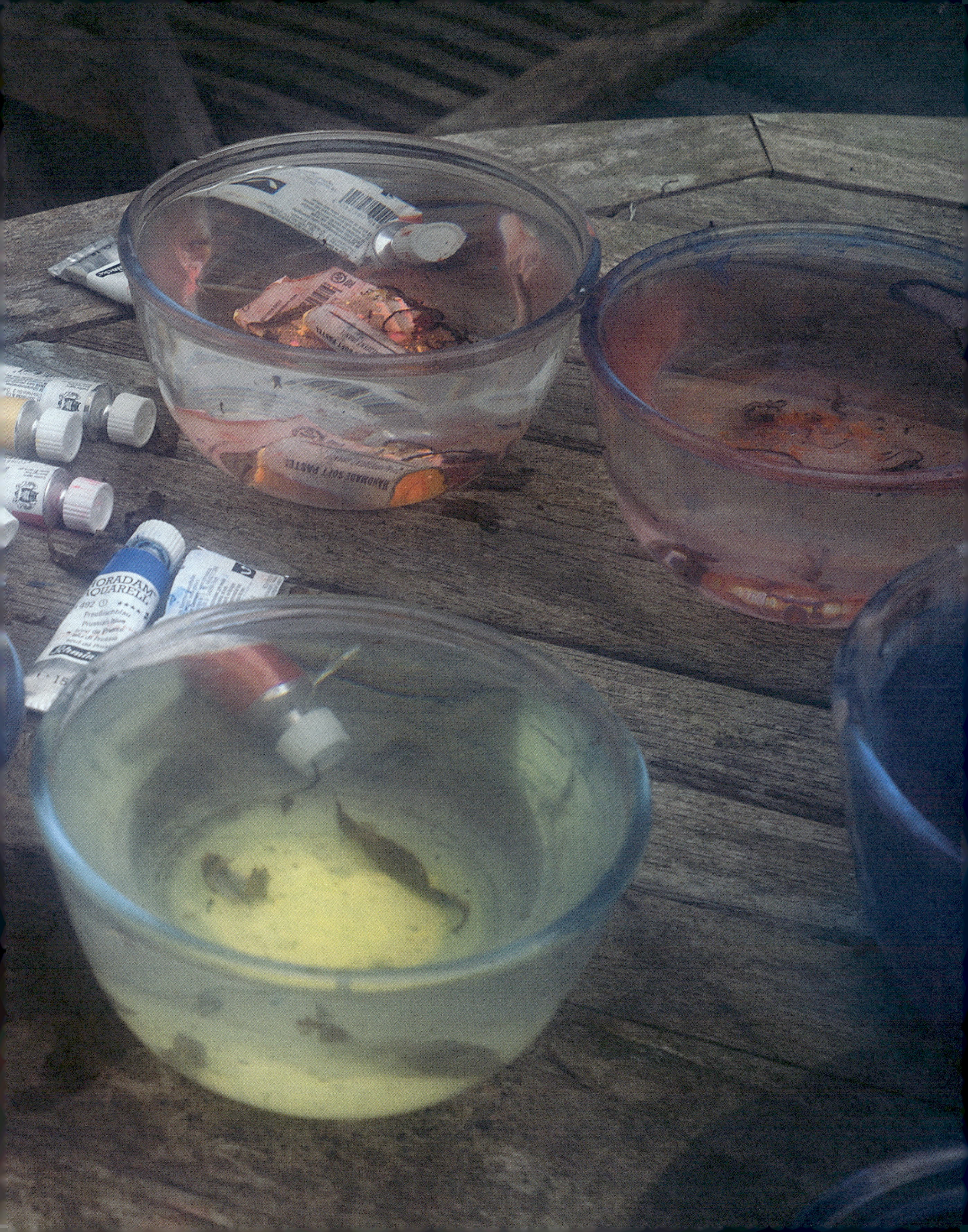
HANDMADE SOFT PASTEL

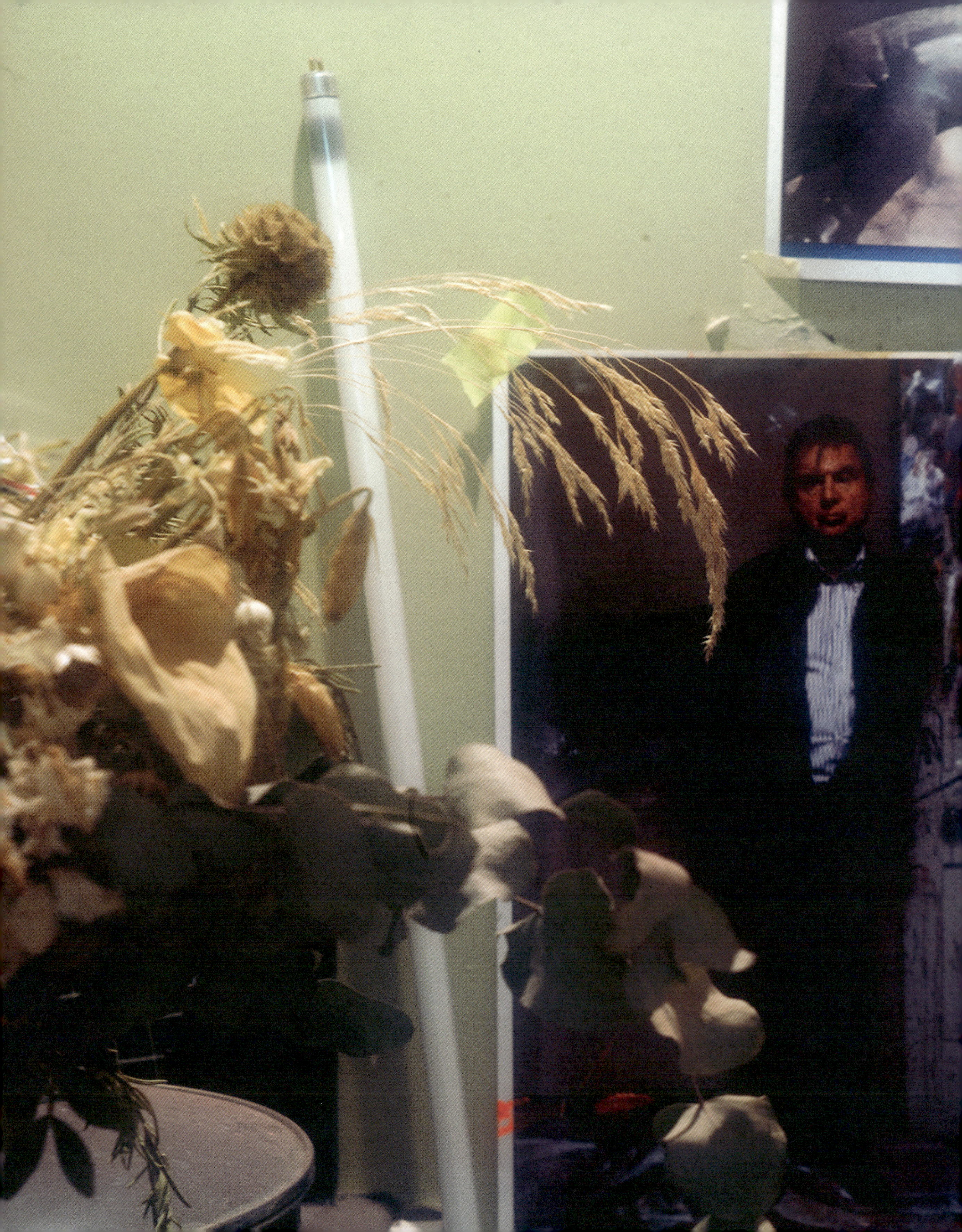

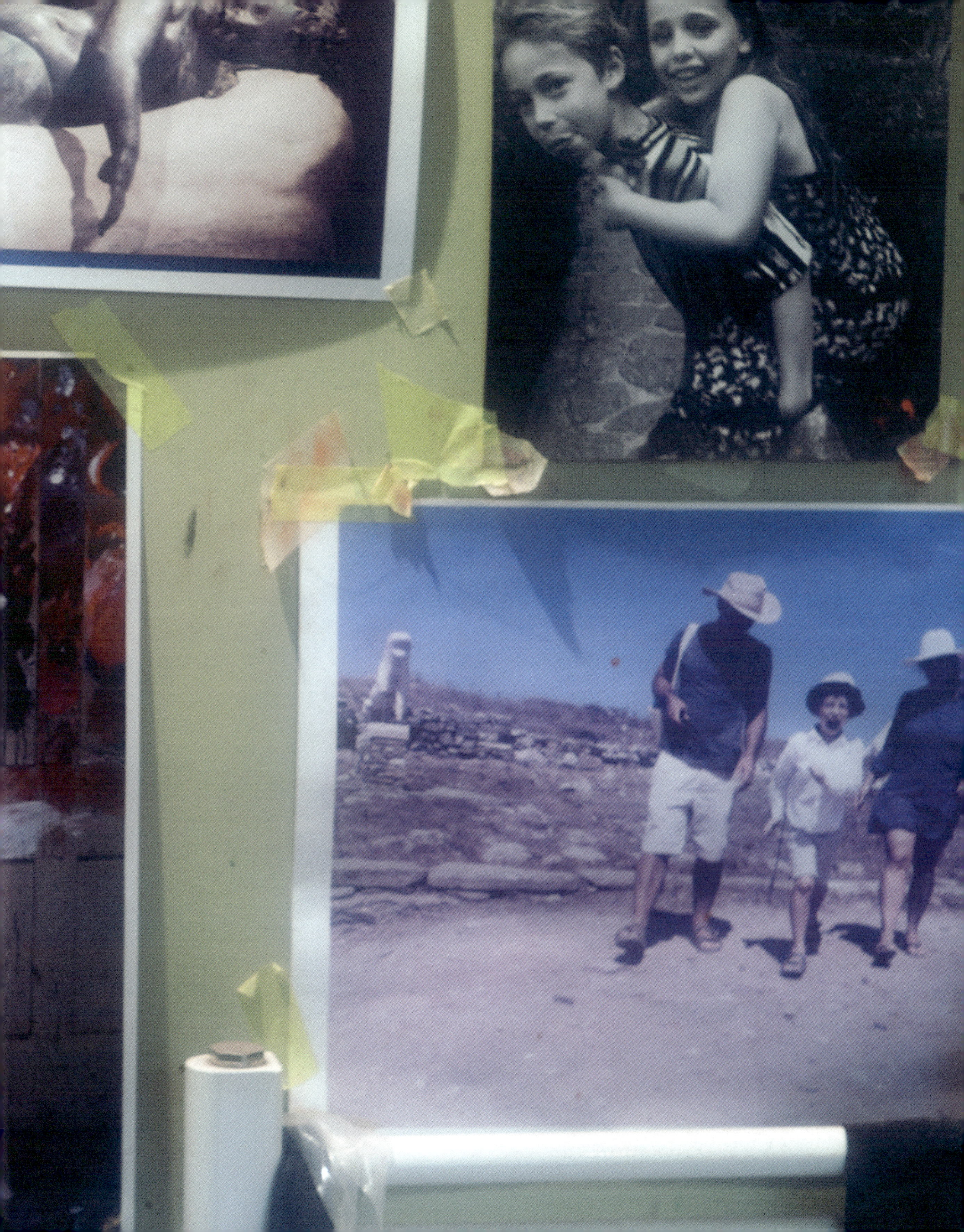

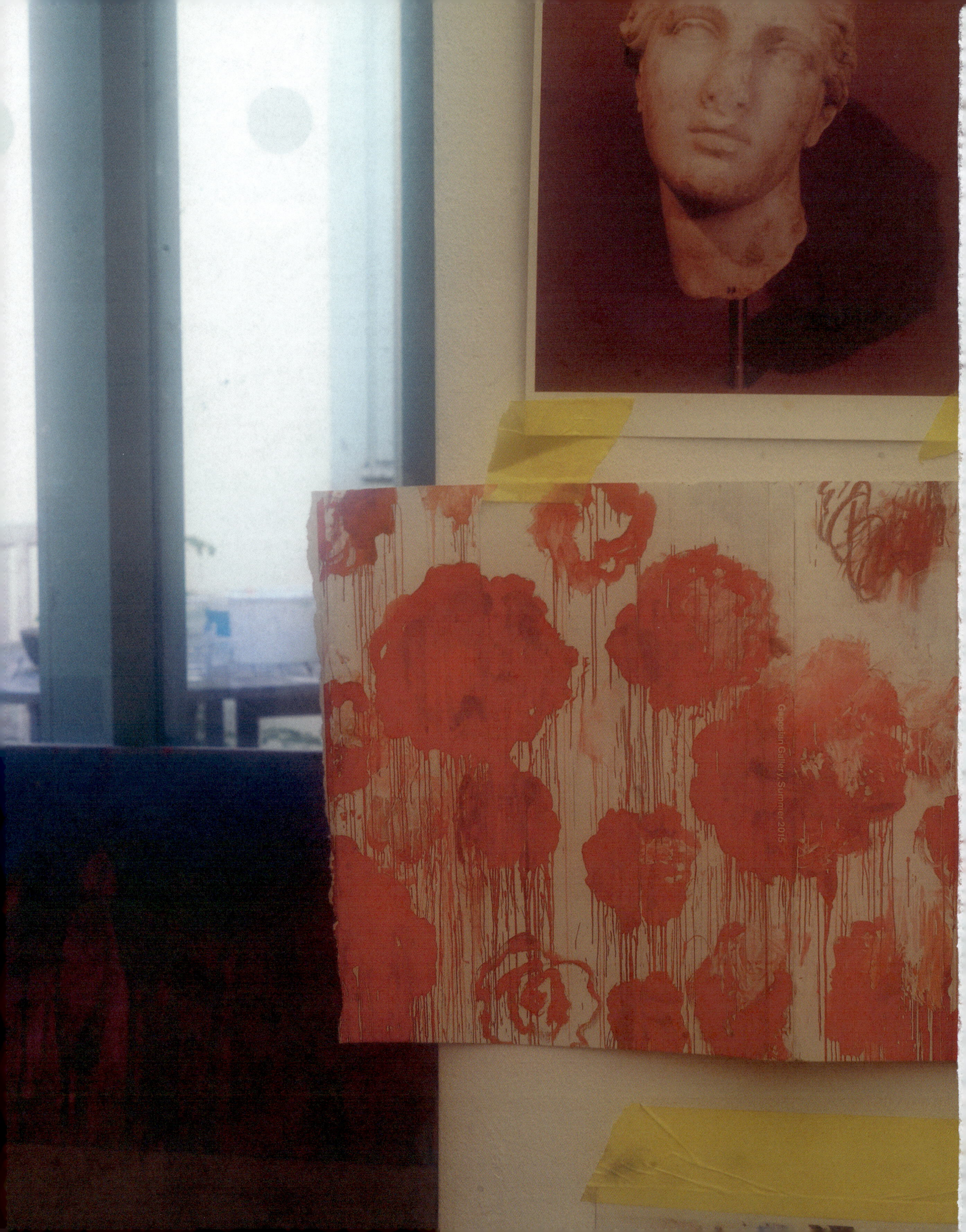
Gagosian Gallery, Summer 2015